Inga Jensen

Method	Description	Applications	Cost	Computer	Chapters

TIME SERIES FORECASTING MODELS

Method	Description	Applications	Cost	Computer	Chapters
Exponential Smoothing	Similar to moving averages but averages weighted exponentially, giving more weight to most recent data.	Short-range forecasts for operations, such as inventory, scheduling, control, pricing, and timing special promotions.	Low	Yes	8
Autoregressive models	Employed with economic variables in order to account for relationships between adjacent observations in a time series.	Short- and medium-range forecasting for economic data ordered in a time series: price, inventory, production, stocks, and sales.	Medium	Yes	7 & 9
Adaptive Filtering	Similar to moving averages and exponential smoothing, but uses the iterative method to determine "best" weights.	Short-range forecasting for earnings per share, stock prices, day-to-day demand, and inventory control.	Medium	Yes	8
Box and Jenkins Techniques	This approach does not assume any particular pattern in the historical data of the series to be forecast. It uses an iterative approach of identifying a possibly useful model from a general class of models.	Same as above	High	Yes	9

EDB 104

Business
Forecasting

JOHN E. HANKE AND ARTHUR G. REITSCH
Eastern Washington University

Business Forecasting

Allyn and Bacon, Inc.
Boston / London / Sydney / Toronto

Library of Congress Cataloging in Publication Data

Hanke, John E   1940–
  Business forecasting.

  Includes index.
  1. Business forecasting.   I. Reitsch, Arthur G., 1938–   joint
author. II. Title.
HB3730.H28   338.5′44   80-26859

ISBN 0-205-07139-2

Series Editor: Richard Carle

Printed in the United States of America.
10 9 8 7 6 5 4 3 2   85 84 83

Contents

Preface

The past decade has witnessed several important developments in the area of business forecasting. Both the theory and practice of forecasting have been advanced by the advent of the computer and the increasing complexity and competitiveness of the business environment. Firms of all sizes find it essential to predict variables that directly affect decision making and performance.

Unfortunately, few managers and business school students are familiar with the full range of existing forecasting techniques, and few have the knowledge required to select and apply the appropriate model in a specific situation. This book is designed to help correct this problem. It is written in an elementary, understandable way. Much of the learning in a subject such as forecasting comes from trial and error, and involves considerable experience. The text provides numerous examples and cases to show how and why each forecasting model works. The problems at the end of chapters are practical, real-life situations that have been tested on students over a five-year span. Computer output is provided and computer programs are available in the instructor's manual to supplement this practical approach.

Students should tackle actual business forecasting projects as a part of their educational efforts. Such projects require "hands on" experience in the art and science of forecasting. *Business Forecasting* is designed so that actual industrial and organizational projects can be used as a part of the learning process.

The book is organized into four parts. The first part lays the groundwork by discussing the nature of forecasting problems (Chapter 1) and by reviewing the statistical background needed to understand the forecasting techniques to be introduced in the remaining chapters (Chapter 2).

The second part of the book deals with how the forecaster can use the relationships that exist between variables. The linear relationship between two variables is investigated in the correlation chapter (Chapter 3). Linear relationships are used to forecast in the regression chapter (Chapter 4) and in the multiple regression chapter (Chapter 5).

The third part of the book analyzes the forecasting techniques employed when the data are time series values. Chapter 6 uses the decomposition method to forecast. Chapter 7 examines the various models that are used to solve problems involving autocorrelation.

The final chapters deal with several specific forecasting models. Chapter 8 looks at naive, exponential smoothing, autoregressive, and adaptive filtering models. Chapter 9 presents the Box–Jenkins methods, and Chapter 10 looks at simulation as a forecasting tool.

Those who find one or more of the forecasting models discussed in this book to be of particular relevance may want to use one of the specific computer programs developed by the authors. The programs are available upon request.

As all authors, we are indebted to many people who have contributed to the final product. We should especially like to thank Professors Susan Solomon, Yvonne Sloan, and Shik Chun Young of Eastern Washington University for their valuable chapter and case contributions. We would also like to thank James L. Starr, Acting Manager of the Stanford Graduate School of Business Computing Facility, for providing data and computer runs; and Marilyn Love, a former EWU student, for providing a time series analysis case. We are particularly grateful to our students who suffered through five years of early drafts, and without whom the book would have been finished much earlier. Finally, we thank the person who has read the book more than anyone should have to, our typist, Ruth Kembel.

Introduction to Forecasting

1

This book is concerned with the process of business forecasting. More specifically, it is concerned with making educated guesses as to what will happen at some future time. Forecasting is necessary so that persons and organizations can make plans for the future and make the decisions that must always be faced in an atmosphere of uncertainty.

Forecasting is often viewed as a dismal endeavor because so many forecasters have been wrong. Predictions as to future outcomes rarely are precisely on the mark; the forecaster can only endeavor to make the inevitable errors small rather than large.

Need for Forecasting

In view of inherent inaccuracies in the process, then, why is forecasting necessary? The answer is that all organizations operate in an atmosphere of uncertainty and that, in spite of this, decisions must be made that affect the future of the organization. Educated choices about the future are more valuable to organizations who must operate in a climate of uncertainty than are uneducated guesses. This book discusses various ways of making forecasts that rely on logic and a commonsensical methodology.

1

This is not to say that *intuitive forecasting* is bad. On the contrary, the "gut" feelings of persons who manage organizations are often the best forecasts available. This text discusses forecasting techniques that can be used to *supplement* the common sense and management ability of decision makers. A decision maker is better off understanding quantitative forecasting techniques and using them wisely than being forced to plan for the future in ignorance of available supplemental information.

Since the world in which organizations operate has always been changing, forecasts have always been necessary. However, recent years have brought about more rapid changes than have ever been known. New technology and new disciplines have sprung up overnight; government activity at all levels has intensified; competition in many areas has become more keen; international trade has stepped up in many industries; social-help and service agencies have been created and have grown. These factors have combined to create an organizational climate that is more complex, more fast-paced, and more competitive. Organizations that cannot react quickly to changing conditions and that cannot foresee the future with any degree of accuracy are doomed to extinction.

The electronic computer, along with the quantitative techniques it makes possible, have become more than a convenience for modern organizations; they have become essential. The complexities discussed above generate tremendous amounts of data and a tremendous need for extracting useful information from this data. More specifically, the modern tools of forecasting, along with the capabilities of the electronic computer, have become almost indispensable for organizations operating in the modern world.

Who needs forecasts? Almost every organization, large and small, private and public, uses forecasting either explicitly or implicitly. This is because almost every organization must plan to meet the conditions of the future for which it has imperfect knowledge. In addition, the need for forecasts cuts across all functional lines as well as across all types of organizations. Forecasts are needed in finance, marketing, personnel and production areas; in government and profit-making organizations; in small social clubs and in national political parties. Consider the following questions that suggest the need for some forecasting procedure:

- If we increase our advertising budget by 10%, how will sales be affected?
- What revenue might the state government expect over the next two-year period?
- How many units must we sell to recover our fixed investment in production equipment?
- What factors can we identify that will help explain the variability in monthly unit sales?
- What is a year-by-year prediction for the total loan balance of our bank over the next ten years?

• Will there be a recession? If so, when will it begin, how severe will it be, and when will it end?

Types of Forecasts

Faced with the need to make decisions in an atmosphere of uncertainty, what types of forecasts are available to organization managers? Forecasting procedures might first be classified as *long-term* or *short-term*. Long-term predictions are necessary to set the general course of an organization for the long run. As such, they become the particular focus of top management. Short-term forecasts are used to design immediate strategies and are used by mid-management and first-line management to meet the needs of the immediate future.

Forecasts might also be classified in terms of their position on a micro–macro continuum (a micro-forecast focuses on small details while a macro-forecast deals with large, summary values). For example, a plant manager might be interested in forecasting the number of workers needed for the next several months, while the Federal Government is forecasting the total number of people employed in the entire country. Again, different levels of management in an organization tend to focus on different levels of the micro–macro hierarchy. Top management would be interested in forecasting the sales of the entire company, for example, while individual salespersons would be much more interested in forecasting their own sales volume.

Forecasting procedures can also be classified according to whether they tend to be more quantitative or qualitative. At one extreme, a purely qualitative technique is one requiring no overt manipulation of data. Only the "judgment" of the forecaster is used. Even here, of course, the forecaster's "judgment" is actually a result of the mental manipulation of past historical data. At the other extreme, purely quantitative techniques need no input of judgment; they are mechanical procedures that produce quantitative results. Some quantitative procedures require a much more sophisticated manipulation of data than others, of course. This book emphasizes the quantitative forecasting techniques because a broader understanding of these very useful procedures is needed. However, we must emphasize again that judgment and common sense must be used along with the mechanical and data-manipulative procedures discussed here. Only in this way can intelligent forecasting take place.

Choosing a Forecasting Method

The above discussion suggests several factors to be considered in choosing a forecasting method. The level of detail must be considered: Are forecasts of specific details needed (a micro-forecast)? Or, is the future status of some over-all or summary factor needed (a macro-forecast)? Is the forecast needed for some point in the near future (a short-term forecast), or for a point in the distant future (a long-term forecast)? And, to what extent are qualitative (judgment) and quantitative (data manipulative) factors appropriate?

In addition to these considerations we must recognize that all forecasts are basically a projection of past data and experiences into an uncertain future. This recognition suggests the following basic steps in the forecasting process:

1. Data collection.
2. Data reduction or condensation.
3. Model building.
4. Model extrapolation (the actual forecast).

Step one above suggests the importance of getting the proper data and making sure they are correct. This is often the most challenging part of the entire forecasting process, and often the most difficult to monitor since subsequent steps can be performed on any data. Collection and quality control problems usually abound whenever it becomes necessary to obtain data in an organization.

Step two, data reduction, is often involved since it is possible to have too much data in the forecasting process as well as too little. Some data may not be relevant to the problem and may just cloud the issue. Other data may be appropriate but only in certain historical periods. For example, in forecasting the sales of small cars we may wish to use only car sales data since the oil embargo rather than data over the past fifty years.

Step three, model building, involves fitting the collected data into a forecasting model that is appropriate in terms of minimizing the forecasting error. Obviously, judgment is involved in this process. Since this book discusses numerous forecasting models and their applicability, it is our hope that the reader's ability to exercise good judgment in the choice and use of appropriate forecasting models will increase.

Once the appropriate data have been collected and possibly reduced, and an appropriate forecasting model has been chosen, the actual forecasting model extrapolation occurs (step four). Often the accuracy of the process is checked by forecasting for recent periods in which the actual historical values are known. The forecasting errors can then be observed, and a decision as to the appropriateness of the process can be made.

Managing the Forecasting Process

The points discussed in this chapter serve to underline our belief that some sort of management ability or common sense must be involved in the forecasting process. Of course, this ability may exist simultaneously with technical expertise in the same person, but it is essential that it be applied whenever quantitative techniques are employed. Unfortunately, it sometimes is not, especially when the aura of the computer is present. Again, quantitative techniques in the forecasting process must be regarded as what they really are; namely, tools to be used by the manager in arriving at better decisions. With this in mind several key questions should come to mind if management of the forecasting process is being properly conducted:

- Why is a forecast needed?
- Who will use the forecast and what are their specific requirements?
- What level of detail or aggregation is required and what is the proper time horizon?
- What data are available and will the data be sufficient to generate the needed forecast?
- What will the forecast cost?
- How accurate can we expect the forecast to be?
- Will the forecast be made in time to help the decision-making process?
- Does the forecaster clearly understand how the forecast will be used in the organization?
- Is a feedback process available to evaluate the forecast after it is made and adjust the forecasting process accordingly?

In the following chapters, various forecasting models and procedures are studied. First, a review of basic statistical concepts appears followed by a three-chapter discussion of regression analysis procedures. Forecasting time series data is then discussed in the next two chapters. Finally, more advanced forecasting techniques are discussed in Chapters 8, 9, and 10.

A Review of Basic Statistical Concepts

2

Before beginning our study of specific forecasting techniques, it is important to review those basic concepts that underlie all statistical investigations. These basic concepts may be briefly categorized as descriptive statistics, probability distributions, sampling distributions, estimation, hypothesis testing, and Chi-Square tests.

In most statistical procedures, we are involved in making inferences about all the items of interest, called the population, after conducting measurements on some of the items, called the sample. This procedure is called *statistical inference* and involves the necessity of clearly identifying the two groups of items we are dealing with, i.e., the population and the sample. Throughout the rest of this chapter, and, indeed, the rest of this text, these two groups should be kept clearly in mind.

Descriptive Statistics

The purpose of descriptive statistical procedures is briefly describing a large collection of measurements with a few key summary values. The most common way of doing this is by averaging the values. In statistics the most common way of averaging is by using the *mean*, which involves adding all values and dividing by the number of them. Since both the population and the sample taken from it possess a mean, we may identify two formulae for computing means. The appropriate formula depends on whether the values collected constitute all the values of interest (the population) or a partial collection of them (a sample).

Population values are usually identified using Greek letters, and the symbol chosen for the population mean is the Greek letter μ ("mu"). The formula for the population mean is

$$\mu = \frac{\Sigma(X)}{N} \qquad \text{(2-1)}$$

where: $\Sigma(X)$ represents the sum of all the values of the population.
N represents the population size.

The symbol for the sample mean is $\bar{X}$ ("X-bar"), and is found as

$$\bar{X} = \frac{\Sigma(X)}{n} \qquad \text{(2-2)}$$

where: $\Sigma(X)$ represents* the sum of all the values of the sample,
n represents the sample size.

In addition to measuring the central tendency of a group of values by computing the mean, we are often interested in the extent to which the values are dispersed around the mean. For this purpose the *standard deviation* of either group can be computed. The standard deviation can be thought of as the typical difference between the group values and their mean. Following are the formulae for the standard deviations of the population (σ) and the sample (s)

$$\sigma = \sqrt{\frac{\Sigma(X - \mu)^2}{N}} \qquad \text{(2-3)}$$

$$s = \sqrt{\frac{\Sigma(X - \bar{X})^2}{n - 1}} \qquad \text{(2-4)}$$

where the numerators represent the squared differences between the measured items and their mean.

Finally, many statistical procedures make use of the population or sample *variance*. The variance of a collection of measurements is the

---

*Throughout this text a simplified summation notation is used. The notation $\Sigma(X)$ means to sum all the X values. Some texts use a more formal and complete notation such as

$$\sum_{i=1}^{n} X_i$$

which means the same thing but becomes rather messy and difficult to follow when many terms are involved.

same as standard deviation except that the square-root is not taken. Thus, the population variance (σ^2) and the sample variance (s^2) can be computed as

$$\sigma^2 = \frac{\Sigma(X - \mu)^2}{N} \tag{2-5}$$

$$s^2 = \frac{\Sigma(X - \bar{X})^2}{n - 1} \tag{2-6}$$

For example, consider the following collection of people's ages, where the items are considered to be a sample from the population rather than the population itself:

$$23,\ 38,\ 42,\ 25,\ 60,\ 55,\ 50,\ 42,\ 32,\ 35$$

For this sample

$$\bar{X} = \frac{\Sigma(X)}{n} = \frac{402}{10} = 40.2$$

TABLE 2.1   *Calculation of s.*
$$\bar{X} = 40.2$$

X	$X - \bar{X}$	$(X - \bar{X})^2$
23	−17.2	295.84
38	−2.2	4.84
42	1.8	3.24
25	−15.2	231.04
60	19.8	392.04
55	14.8	219.04
50	9.8	96.04
42	1.8	3.24
32	−8.2	67.24
35	−5.2	27.04
		$\Sigma = 1339.60$

$$s^2 = \frac{1339.6}{10 - 1} = 148.84$$

$$s = \sqrt{148.84} = 12.2$$

Thus, the sample mean is 40.2 years, the sample variance is 148.84, and the sample standard deviation is 12.2 years, as shown in Table 2.1. Had the original collection of values been identified as a population rather than a sample, the calculations would have been the same except that the denominator used in calculating variance and standard deviation would have been 10 (N) instead of 9 ($n - 1$). The term ($n - 1$) is known as the *degrees of freedom.*

We use the term degrees of freedom to indicate the number of items of information that are free of each other in the sense that they cannot be deduced from each other. For example, a person can make two predictions about the outcome of a coin flip: (1) heads will be visible or (2) tails will not be visible. If we flip the coin and heads appears, the person has not made two correct predictions since the outcomes are not independent. If the coin turns up heads, then, of course, tails will not be visible. The key concept is independence.

In the example presented in Table 2.1, the ages of ten people constitute a sample with ten degrees of freedom. We could have included anyone's age in the sample, and, therefore, each of the ages is free to vary. When we calculate the mean, all ten ages are used to account for a total mean age equal to 40.2 years.

The computation of the sample standard deviation differs. When we calculate the sample standard deviation, an estimate of the population mean is used (the sample mean $\bar{X}$). A bias is introduced because the $\Sigma(X - \bar{X})^2$ for a given distribution is a minimum value. If we were to subtract any value other than 40.2 from every item in our distribution, square these differences, and sum them, the total sum of squares would be larger than 1339.6. By using the sample mean as an estimate of the population mean in our computation, we will usually obtain a standard deviation that is smaller than the population standard deviation. However, we can correct for this bias by dividing the $\Sigma(X - \bar{X})^2$ by the appropriate degrees of freedom. Since we used the sample mean as an estimate of the population mean in our computation of the sample standard deviation, only nine of the ages are free to vary. If nine of the ages are known, the tenth can be accounted for because the $\Sigma(X - \bar{X})$ must sum to zero. Only nine ages are required for us to account for the totality of information. When a sample statistic is used as an estimate of a population parameter in a computation, one degree of freedom is lost.

In summary, in a statistical investigation there are usually two groups of values, the population and the sample, each of which has the characteristics shown in Table 2.2.

TABLE 2.2 *Population and Sample Characteristics.*

Characteristic	Population	Sample
Mean	μ	$\bar{X}$
Variance	σ^2	s^2
Standard Deviation	σ	s

Probability Distributions

A *random variable* is the name given to a quantity that is capable of taking on different values in an experiment, the exact outcome being a chance or random event. If only certain specified values are possible, the random variable is called a *discrete variable*. Examples include the number of rooms in a house, the number of people arriving at a supermarket checkout stand in an hour, and the number of defective units in a batch of electronic parts. If any value of the random variable is possible within some range, it is called a *continuous variable*. Examples of this type of variable are the weights of people, the length of a manufactured part, and the time between car arrivals at a toll bridge.

If we are dealing with a discrete random variable, its *probability distribution* lists all possible values that the variable can take on, along with the probability of each. For instance, the number of no-sales days for a salesperson during a month might be described by the probability distribution shown in Table 2.3. These values are based on the salesperson's past experience. The values in the X column list all possible values (no-sales days) that are possible, while the $P(X)$ column lists the corresponding probabilities. Notice that since all possible values of X are listed, the probabilities sum to 1.00, or 100%. This is true for all probability distributions.

TABLE 2.3 *Probability Distribution.*

X	$P(X)$
1	.10
2	.20
3	.25
4	.15
5	.30

The *expected value* of a random variable is the average value that the variable takes on over many trials. The expected value for a discrete probability distribution can be found by multiplying each possible X value by its probability, and summing these products. Formula (2–7) illustrates this principle.

$$E(X) = \Sigma[X \cdot P(X)] \tag{2-7}$$

For the probability distribution given above, the expected value is found as follows:

$$E(X) = (1)(.10) + (2)(.20) + (3)(.25)$$
$$+ (4)(.15) + (5)(.30)$$
$$= 0.10 + 0.40 + 0.75 + 0.60 + 1.50$$
$$E(X) = 3.35$$

Thus, if we were to observe the salesperson for a very large number of months and record the number of no-sales days, the average would be 3.35.

For a continuous distribution the probability of obtaining a specific value is zero. For instance, the probability of anyone weighing 150 pounds is zero since this would mean that their weight is exactly 150.000000 . . . no matter how accurate a scale is used. We deal with continuous distributions by finding the probability that a value will fall in some interval when randomly drawn from the distribution. We might compute the probability that a person's weight would fall in the interval 140 pounds to 150 pounds, for instance.

Some theoretical distributions occur over and over again in statistics; for this reason they are usually examined in introductory texts. One of these is the *binomial distribution*. The requirements for a binomial experiment are as follows:

1. There are n identical trials, each of which results in one of two possible outcomes.
2. The probability of each outcome remains fixed from trial to trial.
3. The trials are independent.

We are interested in finding the probability of X successful occurrences in the n trials, where a successful occurrence is arbitrarily defined to be one of the two possible outcomes. The various values of X along with their probabilities form the binomial distribution. These probabilities can be found from the following binomial formula:

$$P(X) = C_x^n \pi^x (1 - \pi)^{n-X} \text{ for } X = 0, 1, 2 \ldots n \qquad (2\text{-}8)$$

where: C_x^n is the number of combinations of n things taken X at a time.
π is the probability of success on each trial.
X is the particular number of successes we are interested in.
n is the number of trials.

An easier way of finding binomial probabilities is to refer to a binomial distribution table such as found in the Appendix. The probabilities are grouped by blocks representing n, and have columns headed by p and rows indicated by x. For example, suppose we randomly draw eight items from a production line that is known to produce defective parts 5% of the time. What is the probability of getting exactly zero defectives? The answer, from the binomial table in the Appendix, is .6634 (here, $n = 8$, $\pi = .05$, $X = 0$).

A second distribution of interest is the *Poisson distribution*, a theoretical distribution that closely approximates the arrivals of items per unit space or time. The Poisson distribution is frequently used to approximate the distribution of arrivals of cars at a toll bridge, arrivals of factory workers at a tool crib, "arrivals" of defects in a length of rope or cable, and arrivals of customers at the checkout counter at a supermarket. In each of these cases the distribution of arrivals can be approximated by the Poisson distribution if a single parameter is known, that is, the mean number of arrivals per unit time or space. For example, suppose the mean number of arrivals of cars at a toll bridge is 2.6 cars per minute. If this value is taken to the Poisson table in the Appendix, we see that the probability is .2176 that exactly 3 cars will arrive in any particular minute. Or, suppose that there are an average of 3.1 defects per hundred feet of wire cable produced by a machine. The table tells us that in any hundred foot length of cable there is then a .0450 chance of zero defects. Following is the formula for the Poisson distribution. Notice that if the mean (μ) is specified, then probabilities of different X values can be found.

$$P(X) = e^{-\mu} \frac{\mu^X}{X!} \qquad \text{for } X = 0, 1, 2 \ldots \qquad (2\text{-}9)$$

where: μ = mean number of arrivals per unit time or space.
   e = a mathematical constant approximately equal to 2.71828.

A third distribution of interest, because many populations can be approximated by it, is the *normal distribution*. It is specified by knowing its two parameters, the mean and standard deviation. A normal curve is

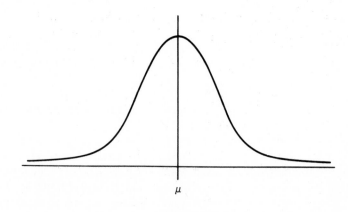

μ

FIGURE 2–1   *Normal Distribution.*

symmetrical and bell shaped as shown in Fig. 2–1.

Probabilities of values drawn from a normal distribution falling into various intervals can be found by first converting all intervals to standard units called *Z-scores*. The Z-score of any *X* value is the number of standard deviations from the central value of the curve (μ) to that value. Thus, the formula for *Z* is

$$Z = \frac{X - \mu}{\sigma} \qquad\qquad \textbf{(2-10)}$$

where: *X* is the particular value of interest.
              μ is the mean.
              σ is the standard deviation.

After the Z-score has been computed, the normal curve table can be consulted to find the area under the curve between the center of the curve (μ) and the value of interest (X). For example, suppose a population of part weights made by a certain machine is normally distributed with mean 10 pounds and standard deviation 2 pounds. What is the probability that a part drawn at random from the machine falls between 9 and 12 pounds? The normal curve with the appropriate area shaded is demonstrated in Fig. 2–2.

Since normal curve tables are designed to give areas from the center of the curve to some point, we must find two separate areas, one on each side of the mean, and add these areas together. This will produce the probability of a value falling in this interval. The two Z-scores are

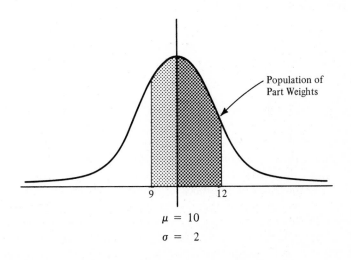

FIGURE 2–2 *Normal Curve Area.*

$$Z_1 = \frac{9 - 10}{2} = -\frac{1}{2} = -0.5$$

$$Z_2 = \frac{12 - 10}{2} = \frac{2}{2} = 1.0$$

The negative sign on the first Z-score is disregarded since it simply indicates that the X value of interest (9) is less than the mean of the curve (10). These two Z-scores can be taken to the normal curve table in the Appendix to produce the two areas, which are then added together:

$$Z_1 = -0.5 \rightarrow 0.1915$$

$$Z_2 = 1.0 \rightarrow \underline{0.3413}$$

$$0.5328$$

We conclude that the chances are about 53% that a part randomly drawn from this population of parts will weigh between 9 and 12 pounds.

Finally, the *t distribution* is frequently used in statistical tests when small sample sizes are used and where it can be assumed that the populations being investigated are normally distributed. The Appendix shows values taken from the *t* distribution. Notice that only one value need be specified before referring to the table, namely, the degrees of freedom (abbreviated *df*). Once the degrees of freedom are known, the *t* values can be found that exclude certain percentages of the curve. For example, if the *t* distribution of interest has 14 degrees of freedom, then a *t* value of 2.145 on each side of the curve center will include 95% of the curve and exclude 5% of it. An example using the *t* distribution will be presented later in this chapter.

Sampling Distributions

In most statistical applications we find ourselves taking a random sample from the population under investigation, computing a statistic from the sample data, and drawing conclusions about the population on the basis of this sample. A *sampling distribution* is the distribution of all possible values of the sample statistic that could be obtained from the population. For instance, we might take a random sample of 100 persons from a population and weigh them, then compute their mean weight. We can think of this sample mean, $\bar{X}$, as having been drawn from the distribution of all possible $\bar{X}$s of sample size 100 that could be taken from the population. Similarly, each sample statistic that can be computed from sample data can be considered as having been drawn from some sampling distribution.

The *Central Limit Theorem* states that as the sample size becomes larger the sampling distribution of $\bar{X}$ tends toward the normal distribution, and that the mean of this normal distribution is μ, the population mean, and the standard deviation is $\sigma/\sqrt{n}$. This sampling distribution will tend toward normality regardless of the shape of the population distribution from which the sampled items were drawn. Figure 2–3 demonstrates how such a sampling distribution might appear.

The Central Limit Theorem is of particular importance in statistics since it allows us to compute the probability of various sample results through our knowledge of normal curve probabilities. For example, what is the probability that the mean of a random sample of 100 weights drawn from a population will be within 2 pounds of the true population weight if the standard deviation of the population is estimated to be 15 pounds? Figure 2–4 illustrates the appropriate sampling distribution.

Chances are about 82% that the sample mean will be within 2 pounds of the true mean, reflecting the sample size of 100 and the estimated variability of the population, $\sigma = 15$. As we shall see, this ability to calculate probabilities of sample results will enable us to arrive at useful results in estimating and hypothesis testing.

Estimation

A *point estimate* of a population parameter is a single value calculated from the sample data that estimates the unknown population value. Table

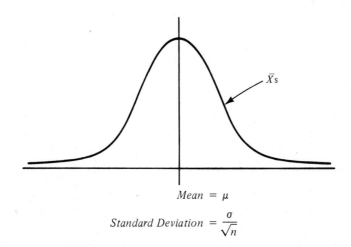

$$\text{Mean} = \mu$$

$$\text{Standard Deviation} = \frac{\sigma}{\sqrt{n}}$$

FIGURE 2–3 *Sampling Distribution of $\bar{X}$.*

15

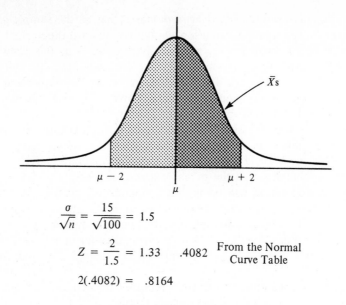

$$\frac{\sigma}{\sqrt{n}} = \frac{15}{\sqrt{100}} = 1.5$$

$$Z = \frac{2}{1.5} = 1.33 \quad .4082 \quad \text{From the Normal Curve Table}$$

$$2(.4082) = .8164$$

FIGURE 2–4 *Sampling Distribution Area.*

2.4 contains a list of various population parameters and the sample statistics that provide point estimates of them.

An *interval estimate* or *confidence interval* is an interval within which the population parameter of interest probably lies. It is found by forming an interval around the point estimate, and is computed using either the normal distribution or *t* distribution. For example, suppose we wish to form an interval estimate for the population mean. The sample size is 400, the sample mean (the point estimate) is 105 pounds, and the sample standard deviation (an estimate of σ) is 10 pounds. Within what interval is it 95% likely that μ lies? The interval can be found by forming an interval around $\bar{X}$ using 1.96 standard deviations from the $\bar{X}$ sampling distribution (1.96 standard deviations on each side of the mean of any

TABLE 2.4 *Population and Sample Values.*

Population Parameter	Sample Statistic (Estimate)	
Mean (μ)	$\bar{X}$,	the Sample Mean
Standard Deviation (σ)	s,	the Sample Standard Deviation
Variance (σ²)	s^2,	the Sample Variance
Percentage (π)	p,	the Sample Percentage

normal curve will include approximately 95% of the values). The calculations are

$$\bar{X} \pm Z \frac{\sigma}{\sqrt{n}} \qquad \text{(2-11)}$$

$$105 \pm 1.96 \frac{10}{\sqrt{400}}$$

$$105 \pm 1.96\,(0.5)$$

$$105 \pm 0.98$$

$$104.02 \text{ to } 105.98$$

Thus, it is 95% likely that the sample mean was chosen from the sampling distribution in such a way that the true mean is somewhere in the interval 104.02 to 105.98.

Likewise, confidence intervals can be formed around point estimates of the population percentage using the following formula:

$$P \pm Z \sqrt{\frac{\pi(1 - \pi)}{n}} \qquad \text{(2-12)}$$

In practice, we usually estimate π, the population percentage, with p, the sample percentage, in computing the standard deviation of the sampling distribution. For example, a 99% confidence interval for the true percentage, π, of the population that is familiar with our product can be formed around the point estimate, $p = 0.23$, with $n = 150$.

$$0.23 \pm 2.58 \sqrt{\frac{(0.23)(0.77)}{150}}$$

$$0.23 \pm 2.58\,(0.034)$$

$$0.23 \pm 0.088$$

$$0.142 \text{ to } 0.318$$

In this example the point estimate of π is .23. Given the sample size of 150, it is 99% likely that the sample was drawn in such a way that the true value of π is somewhere in the interval, .142 to .318.

Hypothesis Testing

In many statistical situations we are interested in testing some claim about the population rather than estimating one of its parameters. This procedure is called *hypothesis testing*, and involves the following steps:

1. State the hypothesis being tested (called the null hypothesis, symbol H_0) and state the alternative hypothesis (the one accepted if H_0 is rejected, symbol H_1).
2. Collect a random sample of items from the population and compute the appropriate sample statistic.
3. Assume the null hypothesis is true and consult the sampling distribution from which the sample statistic is drawn under this assumption.
4. Compute the probability that such a sample statistic could be drawn from the sampling distribution.
5. If this probability is high, do not reject the null hypothesis; if this probability is low, the null hypothesis can be rejected with low chance of error.

When the above procedure is followed, two types of errors can occur, as shown in Table 2.5.

TABLE 2.5 *Results of Hypothesis Test.*

		Do Not Reject H_0	Reject H_0
State of Nature	H_0 True	Correct Decision	Type I Error Probability: α
	H_0 False	Type II Error Probability: β	Correct Decision

Hopefully, the correct decision concerning the null hypothesis will be reached after examining sample evidence, but there is always a possibility of rejecting a true H_0 and failing to reject a false H_0. The probabilities of these events are known as *alpha* (α) and *beta* (β), respectively. Alpha is also known as the *significance level* of the test.

As an example of a simple hypothesis test, suppose we wish to test the hypothesis that the average weight of parts produced by a certain machine is still 50 pounds, the average weight of the parts in past years. A random sample of 100 parts is taken. It is assumed that the standard deviation of part weights is 5 pounds regardless of the mean weight since this value has remained constant in past studies of parts. If we assume the null hypothesis is true (the null hypothesis states that the mean part weight is 50 pounds), the appropriate sampling distribution is the normal distribution. The test is demonstrated in Fig. 2–5.

If the null hypothesis is true, the sample statistic, $\bar{X}$, will be between points *a* and *b* with a 95% chance. Therefore, there is a 5% chance that it will not. Points *a* and *b* can be found by using the normal curve table, which indicates that $z = 1.96$.

$$50 \pm 1.96 \,(0.5)$$

$$50 \pm 0.98$$

$$a = 49.02 \qquad b = 50.98$$

We can now form the *decision rule* for this test as follows:

1. Take a random sample of 100 items from the population under investigation and compute the sample mean weight.
2. If this sample mean weight is between 49.02 pounds and 50.98 pounds, do not reject the null hypothesis. If it is outside this interval, reject the null hypothesis.

In stating the decision rule in this way, the probability of rejecting the null hypothesis when it is true, that is, committing a Type I error, is 5% ($\alpha = 0.05$). This can be seen on the curve in Fig. 2–5 that shows an area of 0.025 on each end of the sampling distribution.

Table 2.6 summarizes six hypothesis tests that are commonly used in various statistical studies. In each of these tests the indicated sample statistic is computed, the appropriate sampling distribution is consulted

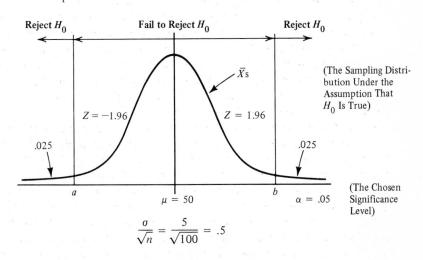

H_0: $\mu = 50$ pounds (the Null Hypothesis)

H_1: $\mu \neq 50$ pounds (the Alternative Hypothesis)

FIGURE 2–5 *Hypothesis Test.*

19

TABLE 2.6 *Summary of Hypothesis Tests.*

H_0	Sample Statistic	Sampling Distribution	Parameters of Sampling Distribution
$\mu = 50$*	$\bar{X}$	Normal	μ and $\dfrac{\sigma}{\sqrt{n}}$
$\pi = .30$*	P	Normal	π and $\sqrt{\dfrac{\pi\,(1-\pi)}{n}}$
$\mu_1 - \mu_2 = 0$	$\bar{X}_1 - \bar{X}_2$	Normal	$\mu_1 - \mu_2$ and $\sqrt{\dfrac{\sigma_1^2}{n_1} + \dfrac{\sigma_2^2}{n_2}}$
$\pi_1 - \pi_2 = 0$	$P_1 - P_2$	Normal	$\pi_1 - \pi_2$ and $\sqrt{\pi(1-\pi)\left(\dfrac{1}{n_1} + \dfrac{1}{n_2}\right)}$
$\sigma^2 = 100$*	$\dfrac{(n-1)(s^2)}{\sigma^2}$	Chi-Square	$df = n - 1$
$\sigma_1^2 = \sigma_2^2$	$\dfrac{s_1^2}{s_2^2}$ $\left(\begin{array}{c}\text{large}\\\text{over}\\\text{small}\end{array}\right)$	F	$df_n = n_1 - 1$ $df_d = n_2 - 1$

*Example Values

after assuming the null hypothesis is true, a decision rule is formed that specifies the range within which the statistic will most likely be, and a decision to reject or not reject the null hypothesis is reached.

The first hypothesis test in Table 2.6 is illustrated in Fig. 2–5. Figures 2–6 through 2–10 are examples to illustrate the use of the remaining hypothesis tests summarized in Table 2.6.

Example. 1. For several years, 30% of the population has had a favorable impression of our product. Recent events lead us to suspect that this percentage may have dropped. In order to test the hypothesis that the percentage is still 30%, we randomly select 50 persons and find that 27% of them have a favorable impression of our product. On the basis of the evidence in Fig. 2–6, what should we conclude?

Decision Rule. If $p < .17$, reject H_0.

Conclusion. Since $p = .27$ do not reject H_0. Based on the sample evidence we fail to reject the hypothesis that the population percentage is .30 at the 2% level of significance. There is not enough sample evidence to say that the percentage of people favoring our product has decreased.

20

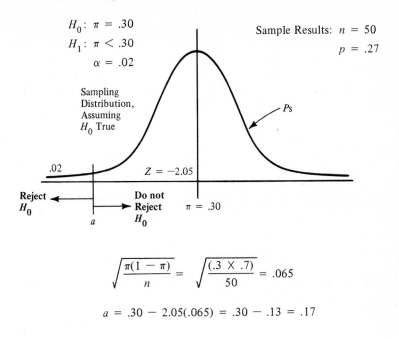

$$\sqrt{\frac{\pi(1-\pi)}{n}} = \sqrt{\frac{(.3 \times .7)}{50}} = .065$$

$$a = .30 - 2.05(.065) = .30 - .13 = .17$$

FIGURE 2–6   *Hypothesis Test.*

Example 2.   Can we conclude that two cable manufacturing machines produce cables of different average lengths? The sample evidence appears in Fig. 2–7.

Decision Rule.   If $\bar{X}_1 - \bar{X}_2$ is within .31 of 0, do not reject H_0.

Conclusion.   Since $\bar{X}_1 - \bar{X}_2 = 5$ feet, reject H_0. Based on the sample evidence, we reject the hypothesis that the two population means are equal at the 5% level of significance. It appears that the average lengths of cables produced by the two machines are different.

Example 3.   We wish to determine if the percentages of students that work part time at two universities are the same, or if the percentage is higher at University 1. Based on the sample evidence in Fig. 2–8, what is our conclusion?

Decision Rule.   If $p_1 - p_2 > .144$, reject H_0.

Conclusion.   Since $p_1 - p_2 = .05$, do not reject H_0. Based on the sample evidence we cannot reject the hypothesis that the population percentages are equal at the 5% level of significance. The evidence does not support the notion that a higher percentage of students work part time at University 1 than University 2.

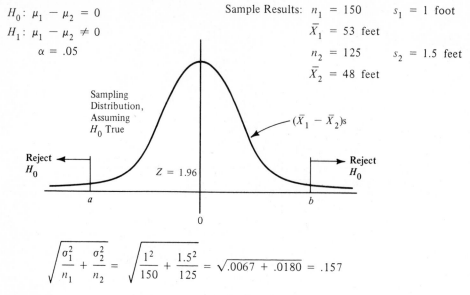

$H_0: \mu_1 - \mu_2 = 0$

$H_1: \mu_1 - \mu_2 \neq 0$

$\alpha = .05$

Sample Results: $n_1 = 150$ $s_1 = 1$ foot

$\bar{X}_1 = 53$ feet

$n_2 = 125$ $s_2 = 1.5$ feet

$\bar{X}_2 = 48$ feet

Sampling Distribution, Assuming H_0 True

$(\bar{X}_1 - \bar{X}_2)$s

Reject H_0

$Z = 1.96$

Reject H_0

a

b

0

$$\sqrt{\frac{\sigma_1^2}{n_1} + \frac{\sigma_2^2}{n_2}} = \sqrt{\frac{1^2}{150} + \frac{1.5^2}{125}} = \sqrt{.0067 + .0180} = .157$$

NOTE: Since the population variances are unknown, we use sample estimates.

a and b: $0 \pm 1.96(.157) = 0 \pm .31$

FIGURE 2–7 *Hypothesis Test.*

Example 4. We suspect that the variability in fill volume of an automatic bottle filling machine has increased because the variance of number of ounces per bottle was 135 in a random sample of 24 bottles. In previous measurements the variance has always been around 100. Can we conclude that the fill process has deteriorated? The sample evidence appears in Fig. 2–9.

Decision Rule. If $[(n-1)s^2]/\sigma^2 > 41.638$, reject H_0.

Conclusion. Since $[(n-1)s^2]/\sigma^2 = [(23)(135)]/100 = 31.05$, do not reject H_0. The sample evidence does not support a rejection of the hypothesis that the population variance is 100 at the 1% level of significance. More evidence is needed before we can conclude that the variability of fill volume has increased.

Example 5. On the basis of random samples taken from two branch banks, we have concluded that the mean account level, measured in thousands of dollars, is the same at each bank. But, what about variability? On the basis of the evidence in Fig. 2–10, could we conclude that the variances of the two banks are different?

Decision Rule. If $[s^2 \text{ (large)}]/[s^2 \text{ (small)}] > 2.04$, reject H_0.

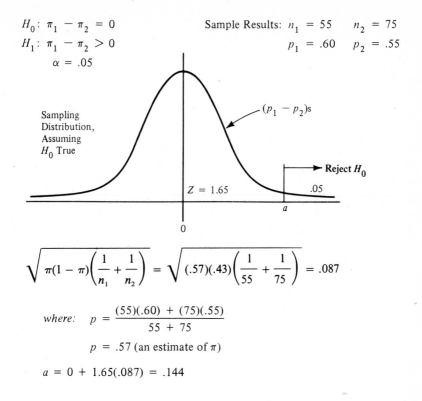

$$H_0: \pi_1 - \pi_2 = 0 \qquad \text{Sample Results: } n_1 = 55 \qquad n_2 = 75$$
$$H_1: \pi_1 - \pi_2 > 0 \qquad p_1 = .60 \qquad p_2 = .55$$
$$\alpha = .05$$

Sampling
Distribution,
Assuming
H_0 True

$(p_1 - p_2)s$

Reject H_0

$Z = 1.65$ .05

a

0

$$\sqrt{\pi(1-\pi)\left(\frac{1}{n_1} + \frac{1}{n_2}\right)} = \sqrt{(.57)(.43)\left(\frac{1}{55} + \frac{1}{75}\right)} = .087$$

where: $p = \dfrac{(55)(.60) + (75)(.55)}{55 + 75}$

$p = .57$ (an estimate of π)

$a = 0 + 1.65(.087) = .144$

FIGURE 2–8 *Hypothesis Test.*

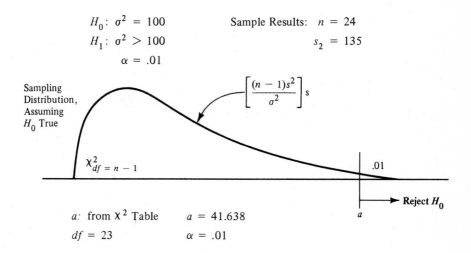

$$H_0: \sigma^2 = 100 \qquad \text{Sample Results: } n = 24$$
$$H_1: \sigma^2 > 100 \qquad s_2 = 135$$
$$\alpha = .01$$

Sampling
Distribution,
Assuming
H_0 True

$\left[\dfrac{(n-1)s^2}{\sigma^2}\right]s$

$\chi^2_{df = n-1}$ .01

Reject H_0

a

$a:$ from χ^2 Table $\qquad a = 41.638$

$df = 23 \qquad \alpha = .01$

FIGURE 2–9 *Hypothesis Test.*

Conclusion. Since $[s^2 \text{ (large)}] / [s^2 \text{ (small)}] = 325/130 = 2.5$, reject H_0. Based on the sample evidence we reject the hypothesis that the two population variances are equal at the 10% level of significance. One of the banks apparently has account balances that vary more widely than the other.

Example 6. As a final example, let us consider a hypothesis test where the sample size is small and for which the t distribution is the appropriate sampling distribution. Suppose it is desired to test the hypothesis that the mean score of students on a national examination is 500, against the alternative hypothesis that it is less than 500. A random sample of 15 students is taken from the population, which produces a sample mean of 475. The standard deviation of the population is estimated by the standard deviation of the 15 sampled items, which is 35.

The t distribution is the appropriate sampling distribution when n is small (as a rule-of-thumb, under 30), σ is unknown (and is being estimated by s), and the population can be assumed to be approximately normally distributed. The test statistic is $(\bar{X} - \mu)/(s/\sqrt{n})$. The test is demonstrated in Fig. 2–11, assuming a significance level of .05.

Decision Rule. If $(\bar{X} - \mu)/(s/\sqrt{n}) < -1.761$, reject H_0.

Conclusion. Since $(\bar{X} - \mu)/(s/\sqrt{n}) = -2.77$, reject H_0. The sample evidence supports rejection of the hypothesis that the population mean is 500 at the 5% level of significance. We conclude that the mean score of students on the national examination has decreased.

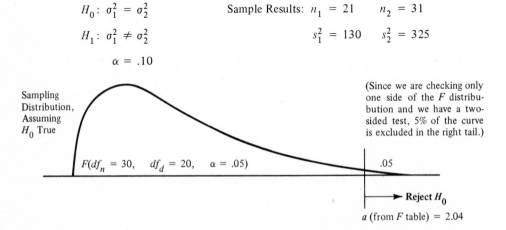

FIGURE 2–10 *Hypothesis Test.*

Chi-Square Tests

In statistical hypothesis testing a null hypothesis is developed that makes a statement about the condition of all things in the population. For instance, it may be hypothesized that the mean length of all parts produced by a machine is exactly five feet. Or, it may be stated that the true percentage of all persons who will vote in the next election is exactly 80%. Another hypothesis frequently of interest is one that states the true percentages in two different populations are equal. This hypothesis is stated

$$H_0: \pi_1 = \pi_2$$

We now consider more than two populations. Each population possesses some percentage, and it is hypothesized that all these percentages are equal. This null hypothesis is stated in the form

$$H_0: \pi_1 = \pi_2 = \pi_3 = \ldots \pi_K$$

for the K populations under consideration.

As in all hypothesis tests, we collect sample evidence from each of the populations under investigation, compute a sample statistic from these data, and compare this statistic to some tabulated value to see whether or not the null hypothesis may be rejected.

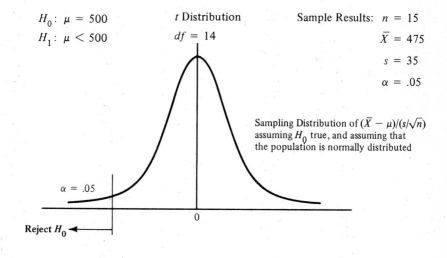

$H_0: \mu = 500$ t Distribution   Sample Results: $n = 15$

$H_1: \mu < 500$ $df = 14$ $\bar{X} = 475$

$s = 35$

$\alpha = .05$

Sampling Distribution of $(\bar{X} - \mu)/(s/\sqrt{n})$ assuming H_0 true, and assuming that the population is normally distributed

$\alpha = .05$

0

Reject H_0

t (from t Table with $\dfrac{\bar{X} - \mu}{s/\sqrt{n}} = \dfrac{475 - 500}{35/\sqrt{15}} = -2.77$

$\alpha = .05$ and $df = n - 1 = 14)$

$= 1.761$

Conclusion.   Since $2.77 > 1.761$, reject H_0.

Figure 2–11   *Hypothesis Test.*

25

In Table 2.7, data have been collected for 250 people as to their income level (high, medium, or low) and their favorite type of advertisement (each person is shown four TV advertisements and asked to choose their favorite).

TABLE 2.7 *Contingency Table.*

		1	2	3	4
	High	25	20	15	10
Income Level	*Medium*	20	20	20	25
	Low	15	25	25	30

Favorite Advertisement

Notice that the data for this test consist of frequency counts or tallies rather than measurements in some sort of units. Each cell contains the number of persons observed to fall in that particular cross-classification.

The null hypothesis to be tested states that the percentage of high, medium, and low income persons in the population preferring each advertisement is exactly the same. This may be stated as

For Ad. No. 1: $H_0: \pi_H = \pi_m = \pi_L$

For Ad. No. 2: $H_0: \pi_H = \pi_m = \pi_L$

For Ad. No. 3: $H_0: \pi_H = \pi_m = \pi_L$

For Ad. No. 4: $H_0: \pi_H = \pi_m = \pi_L$

Although these statements accurately indicate the test being made, they are rather lengthy. We might just as well say that the null hypothesis states that the two methods of classifying people are independent. That is, the classification by income and the classification by advertisement preference are not related to each other. This is equivalent to the four null hypotheses stated above. The null hypothesis can now be stated:

H_0: independence of classification exists in the population with regard to income level and advertising preference.

This statement says that knowledge of a person's income level in no way helps determine which advertisement a person will favor. Rejection of the null statement indicates that there *is* a relationship between a person's income level and a person's advertisement preference. The data in Table 2.7 constitute the sample evidence that will enable us to either reject or not reject this null hypothesis.

Incidentally, this hypothesis test is known by several names. It is sometimes called a *Chi-Square Test* because the Chi-Square distribution is the correct one to consult after the sample statistic has been computed. It is sometimes known as the *Independence of Classification Test* because that is an equivalent way of stating the null hypotheses. Finally, it is also known as the *Contingency Table Test* because the data table (Table 2.7) is called a contingency table.

Table 2.7 shows the *observed frequencies* that resulted from a cross-classification of 250 people by income level and advertisement preference. We now compute the frequencies that we would *expect* to find in each cell of the contingency table if the null hypothesis were true. These expected frequencies may or may not be identical to the observed frequencies. First, we total each of the rows and columns of the contingency table as shown in Table 2.8.

TABLE 2.8 *Contingency Table.*

Favorite Advertisement

		1	2	3	4		
	High	25	20	15	10	70	70/250 = 28%
Income Level	Medium	20	20	20	25	85	85/250 = 34%
	Low	15	25	25	30	95	95/250 = 38%
		60	65	60	65	250	

Next, we note that 70 out of 250 people, or 28%, are in the high income level. Therefore, if we select a random number of people from the total of 250, we would expect that 28% of them are high income people. Suppose we consider the 60 people who preferred advertisement one. Under the null hypothesis these people constitute a random sample of all persons since income level has nothing to do with advertisement preference. Hence, 28% of these people should be in the high income category. Twenty-eight percent of 60 is 16.8, and that is the number of people we would expect to find in the first cell of the contingency table.

Likewise, we would expect 28% of the people preferring advertisement two to be high income people, and so on. In the second row of the table we would expect 34% of each column total to be medium income persons (85/250 = 34%). Thus, for each cell of the contingency table we can compute the number of persons we would expect to find under the assumption that the null hypothesis is true. If these expected frequencies

27

TABLE 2.9   *Contingency Table.*

Favorite Advertisement

Income Level						Total
	High	25 [16.8]	20 [18.2]	15 [16.8]	10 [18.2]	70
	Medium	20 [20.4]	20 [22.1]	20 [20.4]	25 [22.1]	85
	Low	15 [22.8]	25 [24.7]	25 [22.8]	30 [24.7]	95
		60	65	60	65	250

are placed in the corner of each cell, the table appears as shown in Table 2.9.*

We now reason as follows. If the null hypothesis is really true, the expected frequencies computed under the assumption that it is true should be fairly close to the actual observed frequencies. They need not be exactly the same in each cell since we took a random sample of persons and must allow for chance error. Yet, the two values should not be too far apart. The next task is to compute a statistic that reflects the differences between these two values in each cell, and that follows a known distribution if the null hypothesis is true. Such a statistic is called a Chi-Square statistic and is computed as follows:

$$\chi^2 = \sum_{\substack{all \\ cells}} \frac{(f_0 - f_e)^2}{f_e} \qquad (2\text{-}13)$$

where f_0 = observed frequency.
where f_e = expected frequency.

The statistic is computed as shown in Table 2.10, beginning with the cell in the upper left-hand corner of Table 2.9 and moving across rows.

Thus, the statistic computed from the sample evidence in the contingency table is equal to 12.68. Notice that this statistic would have been larger if the observed frequencies had differed from the expected frequencies by larger amounts in each cell; whereas small differences in each cell would indicate that the two classification methods are independent.

---

*Statisticians recommend that expected frequencies should be equal to or greater than five in order to achieve reasonable results.

TABLE 2.10 χ^2 *Calculations.*

f_0	f_e	$(f_0 - f_e)$	$(f_0 - f_e)^2$	$(f_0 - f_e)^2/f_e$
25	16.8	8.2	67.24	4.00
20	18.2	1.8	3.24	0.18
15	16.8	−1.8	3.24	0.19
10	18.2	−8.2	67.24	3.69
20	20.4	−0.4	0.16	0.01
20	22.1	−2.1	4.41	0.20
20	20.4	−0.4	0.16	0.01
25	22.1	2.9	8.41	0.38
15	22.8	−7.8	60.84	2.67
25	24.7	0.3	0.09	0.00
25	22.8	2.2	4.84	0.21
30	24.7	5.3	28.09	1.14
				$\chi^2 = 12.68$

This hypothesis test thus becomes a one-tail test to the right since a rejection will occur with a large statistic and will not occur with a small statistic.

In order to determine the cut-off point for rejection, we consult the Chi-Square table. This table tabulates various values of the Chi-Square distribution for different degrees of freedom. For this test the number of degrees of freedom is equal to the number of rows minus one, times the number of columns minus one,

$$df = (r - 1)(c - 1) \tag{2-14}$$

$$df = (3 - 1)(4 - 1) = 2 \times 3 = 6$$

This method of computing degrees of freedom is intuitively appealing if we consider the original contingency table as shown in Table 2.11. Of the twelve cells in Table 2.11, how many are free to vary, given that the row and column totals must be maintained? The answer is six, since if six key values are specified, the remainder can be computed by knowing the row and column totals. For instance, if the six values represented by Xs in Table 2.11 are known, the remaining six values can be computed.

TABLE 2.11 *Abbreviated Contingency Table.*

		\multicolumn{4}{c}{Favorite Advertisement}	
		1	2	3	4	
Income Level	High	X	X	X		70
	Medium	X	X	X		85
	Low					95
		60	65	60	65	250

Thus, there are $(r - 1)(c - 1)$ degrees of freedom in this table or any other contingency table.

For six degrees of freedom the Chi-Square tabulated values are

$$\chi^2_{.05} = 12.592$$

$$\chi^2_{.02} = 15.033$$

$$\chi^2_{.01} = 16.812$$

Since the computed value for this test is 12.68, we may reject the null hypothesis at the 5% significance level, but not at the 2% significance level. If we are willing to take a 5% chance of rejecting a true null hypothesis, we may thus reject the notion that income level and advertisement preference are independent of each other.

Based on the sample evidence collected, we believe that one's preference for TV advertisements *does* depend on one's income level (at the 5% significance level). This has important implications for our firm if we are attempting to design an advertising campaign for the particular type of product we wish to sell. Specifically, by referring to Table 2.9, we can see that high income people tend to prefer advertisement one and that low income people tend to prefer advertisement four.

The Chi-Square test of independence measures the extent to which sample information *fits* a theoretical data tabulation. The theoretical data tabulation used in the above example is formulated on the assumption that a person's income in no way affects a person's advertisement preference. In general, the Chi-Square distribution test can be used to determine whether any collection of sample data fits some theoretical distribution.

For example, suppose it is hypothesized that people have no brand preference regarding the four brands of milk they may purchase at the supermarket. If this hypothesis is true, then in a sample of n buyers exactly one-fourth of them should choose each brand. If a sample of 100 buyers is randomly chosen, 25 of them should have purchased each of the four brands. Suppose the random sample is actually taken and reveals the information shown in Table 2.12.

TABLE 2.12   *Brand Preference.*

	A	B	C	D	Total
Number Buying	20	35	18	27	100

One-fourth of the buyers obviously did not choose each brand; however, we have examined only a small sample of buyers, not all buyers. The question becomes, "Is there enough sample evidence to reject the null hypothesis?'' The hypothesis under test is:

H_0: The population from which this sample was drawn is uniformly distributed.

Under this hypothesis an equal number of persons in the population prefer each brand. The sample evidence may or may not be strong enough to reject this notion. It is not apparent from the evidence whether preference exists for one brand or another in the population, or whether the differences observed in the sample are due to random error.

Suppose the actual observations are arrayed with the frequencies we would expect if the null hypothesis were true, as shown in Table 2.13.

The Chi-Square statistic can now be computed as shown in Table 2.14 by treating each column or category as a ''cell'' in a contingency table, using formula (2–13).

TABLE 2.13 *Brand Preference.*

	A	B	C	D	Total
Actual (observed)	20	35	18	27	100
Theoretical (expected)	25	25	25	25	100

TABLE 2.14 χ^2 *Calculations.*

f_0	f_e	$f_0 - f_e$	$(f_0 - f_e)^2$	$(f_0 - f_e)^2/f_e$
20	25	−5	25	1.00
35	25	10	100	4.00
18	25	−7	49	1.96
27	25	2	4	.16
				$7.12 = \chi^2$

To obtain a tabulated value from the Chi-Square table, it is necessary to know the number of degrees of freedom. In this particular test one degree of freedom is lost since the expected frequencies must total 100, the number of original data points. Thus, $df = k - 1 = 4 - 1 = 3$. From the Chi-Square table,

$$\chi^2_{.05} = 7.815$$
$$\chi^2_{.02} = 9.837 \qquad \text{for } df = 3$$
$$\chi^2_{.01} = 11.345$$

31

Since the computed Chi-Square value is smaller than any of the tabulated values, even at the .05 significance level, it is not possible to reject the null hypothesis. As usual in statistical tests this does not prove that the null hypothesis is true, it merely states that there is not enough sample evidence to reject it. As another example of a goodness-of-fit test, consider the data in Table 2.15.

TABLE 2.15   *Account Errors.*

Number of Errors	Number of Accounts Having These Errors
0	60
1	72
2	43
3	18
4	5
5 or more	2
	$n = 200$

These data reveal the number of errors in a random sample of 200 accounts taken from a firm's accounting records. The firm wishes to run a simulation of the accounting process and wants to use the Poisson distribution to describe the incidence of error. On the basis of the collected data, does this seem reasonable?

If we regard the data in Table 2.15 as the observed frequencies, we can then compute the expected frequencies under the assumption that the data were drawn from a population that is Poisson distributed. A goodness-of-fit χ^2 value can then be computed using Eq. (2–13), and a conclusion can be reached. First, the mean number of errors can be computed as shown in Table 2.16.

TABLE 2.16   *Mean Account Error Calculation.*

Number of Errors	Probability	Errors $\times$ Probability
0	60/200	0.00
1	72/200	0.36
2	43/200	0.43
3	18/200	0.27
4	5/200	0.10
5 or more	2/200	0.05
		Total = 1.21

Thus, the mean or expected value of the distribution is approximately 1.2. We can now enter the Poisson table (in the Appendix) and find the probabilities of different numbers of errors for a Poisson Distribution whose mean we estimate to be 1.2. These probabilities can then be multiplied by 200 (the number of sample observations) to get the expected frequencies of each cell. The χ^2 value can then be computed using Eq. (2–13). The calculations are shown in Table 2.17, where the last two categories are combined due to fewer than five expected observations in the five and over category.

TABLE 2.17 *Computation of χ^2 Value.*

Number of Errors	Probability (for $\mu = 1.2$)	Pr. × 200 f_e	f_o	$\frac{(f_o - f_e)^2}{f_e}$
0	0.3012	60.24	60	0.001
1	0.3614	72.28	72	0.001
2	0.2169	43.38	43	0.003
3	0.0867	17.34	18	0.025
4 or more	0.0338	6.76	7	0.009
				$\chi^2 = 0.039$

The χ^2 value of Table 2.17 is very small, indicating an almost perfect fit between the observed frequencies in each cell and the frequencies we would expect to see if the sample were drawn from a Poisson distribution. Thus, we expect that the null hypothesis of a Poisson population will not be rejected. The appropriate degrees of freedom are $K - 2$, where K is the number of categories. Two degrees of freedom are lost because the cells must total 200 and because one population parameter is being estimated with sample data (μ); therefore,

$$df = k - 2 = 3 \quad \text{for} \quad \begin{array}{ll} \alpha = 0.01 & \chi^2 = 11.3 \\ \alpha = 0.05 & \chi^2 = 7.8 \end{array}$$

Since the computed χ^2 value (.039) is less than the χ^2 tabulated value for either the .05 or .01 significance level, we cannot reject the hypothesis that the sample data were drawn from a Poisson Distribution. The firm is justified in using the Poisson Distribution to simulate the incidence of error in its accounting process.

In summary, observed distributions can be compared to theoretical distributions by use of the goodness-of-fit test. The distribution of expected frequencies from the theoretical population must be computed and compared with the sample values. If large differences exist across categories, a large Chi-Square value will be computed, and the hypothesis regarding the population will be rejected. If the actual frequencies are quite close to

33

the expected values across categories, a small Chi-Square value will be computed, and the hypothesis regarding the distribution of the population cannot be rejected.

PROBLEMS

*1. Do the same percentage of students work full time at University A and University B? The sample evidence is

$$N_A = 100 \qquad N_B = 125$$

$$P_A = .25 \qquad P_B = .28$$

*2. If no more than 5% of the electronics parts in a boxcar are defective, we wish to accept the entire shipment. In order to decide on acceptance, we randomly sample 100 parts and find that 7 of them are defective. Should the shipment be accepted?

*3. A teacher claims that a new method of teaching mathematics will raise the average standard mathematics score of sixth-grade students. The average test score is now 75 with a standard deviation of 10. A random sample of 30 students will be taught with the new method next fall.

1. State the null and alternative hypotheses.
2. Sketch the appropriate sampling distribution.
3. State the decision rule for the test (assume some significance level).

*4. Over the past several years the standard deviation of steel beam lengths has been 2 inches. The shop foreman claims that the production process has deteriorated and that the length variability of beams has increased. Can this claim be substantiated by the following evidence?

$$n = 30$$

$$s = 2.6 \text{ in.}$$

5.
$$H_0: \ \mu = 5 \text{ lbs} \qquad n = 10$$

$$H_1: \ \mu \neq 5 \text{ lbs} \qquad \bar{X} = 6.5 \text{ lbs}$$

$$\text{Reject } H_0? \qquad s = 1.5 \text{ lbs}$$

*6. Two manufacturers wish to sell us machines that package frozen food. We run both machines for a period of time, weigh the resulting packages, and conclude that the average weight in ounces of packages produced by the machines is equal. Since they both cost about the same in terms of initial cost and maintenance, we decide to buy the machine with the lowest package weight variability. After measuring the variability of the two machine sample packages, it is obvious that one has a smaller sample variance than the other.

---

*Problems marked with an asterisk are solved in the Answer Section at the end of the text.

Yet, is the difference large enough to permit us to reach a conclusion about the machines? The evidence is

$$n_1 = 12 \qquad n_2 = 22$$
$$s_1^2 = 4 \qquad s_2^2 = 8$$

*7. A salesman claims that his company can deliver light bulbs that have a higher average lifetime than the ones we currently use. We sample some of his bulbs to find out their average lifetime, and do the same for our current brand of bulbs. Should we buy from the new supplier after observing the following sample results?

	Old	New
	$\bar{X} = 200$ h	$\bar{X} = 210$ h
	$s = 20$ h	$s = 15$ h
	$n = 35$	$n = 18$

8. Consider the population of 200 family sizes presented in Table 2.18. Ten years ago the average family size was 2.9. Randomly select a sample of 30 sizes and test the hypothesis that the average family size has not changed in the last ten years. (*Hint:* Make sure your sample is *randomly* drawn from the population. Consult your instructor if you do not know how to do this).

*9. An accountant is investigating the stocks and bonds sales records of 180 new recruits. She is particularly interested in determining whether or not a relationship exists between sales volume and educational background. An investigation reveals the following data:

	Less than $500,000 Sales	$500,000 or more Sales	Totals
College Graduate	30	60	90
Not a College Graduate	60	30	90
Totals	90	90	180

Does a relationship exist between education and sales?

10. A random sample of voters in a recent election reveals the following:

	Democrat	Republican	Independent	Other
Male	153	161	23	5
Female	174	110	62	13

Do these sample data support the notion that men and women have different voting preferences?

TABLE 2.18   *Population of Family Sizes.*

(1) 3	(35) 1	(69) 2	(102) 1	(135) 5	(168) 6
(2) 2	(36) 2	(70) 4	(103) 2	(136) 2	(169) 3
(3) 7	(37) 4	(71) 3	(104) 5	(137) 1	(170) 2
(4) 3	(38) 1	(72) 7	(105) 3	(138) 4	(171) 3
(5) 4	(39) 4	(73) 2	(106) 2	(139) 2	(172) 4
(6) 2	(40) 2	(74) 6	(107) 1	(140) 4	(173) 2
(7) 3	(41) 1	(75) 2	(108) 2	(141) 1	(174) 2
(8) 1	(42) 3	(76) 7	(109) 2	(141) 2	(175) 1
(9) 5	(43) 5	(77) 3	(110) 1	(143) 4	(176) 5
(10) 3	(44) 2	(78) 6	(111) 4	(144) 1	(177) 3
(11) 2	(45) 1	(79) 4	(112) 1	(145) 2	(178) 2
(12) 3	(46) 4	(80) 2	(113) 1	(146) 2	(179) 4
(13) 4	(47) 3	(81) 3	(114) 2	(147) 5	(180) 3
(14) 1	(48) 5	(82) 5	(115) 2	(148) 3	(181) 5
(15) 2	(49) 2	(83) 2	(116) 1	(149) 1	(182) 3
(16) 2	(50) 4	(84) 1	(117) 4	(150) 2	(183) 1
(17) 4	(51) 1	(85) 3	(118) 2	(151) 6	(184) 2
(18) 4	(52) 6	(86) 3	(119) 1	(152) 2	(185) 4
(19) 3	(53) 2	(87) 2	(120) 3	(153) 5	(186) 3
(20) 2	(54) 5	(88) 4	(121) 5	(154) 1	(187) 2
(21) 1	(55) 4	(89) 1	(122) 1	(155) 2	(188) 5
(22) 5	(56) 1	(90) 2	(123) 2	(156) 1	(189) 3
(23) 2	(57) 2	(91) 3	(124) 3	(157) 4	(190) 4
(24) 1	(58) 1	(92) 3	(125) 4	(158) 2	(191) 3
(25) 4	(59) 5	(93) 2	(126) 3	(159) 2	(192) 2
(26) 3	(60) 2	(94) 4	(127) 2	(160) 7	(193) 3
(27) 2	(61) 7	(95) 1	(128) 1	(161) 4	(194) 2
(28) 3	(62) 1	(96) 2	(129) 6	(162) 2	(195) 5
(29) 6	(63) 2	(97) 4	(130) 1	(163) 1	(196) 3
(30) 1	(64) 6	(98) 3	(131) 2	(164) 7	(197) 3
(31) 2	(65) 4	(99) 2	(132) 5	(165) 2	(198) 2
(32) 4	(66) 1	(100) 6	(133) 2	(166) 7	(199) 5
(33) 3	(67) 2	(101) 4	(134) 1	(167) 4	(200) 1
(34) 2	(68) 1				

11. Test the following situation for independence of classification at the .02 significance level:

		Number of Stores Experiencing		
		Sales Increase	Stable Sales	Sales Loss
Type of	TV	15	14	6
Advertisement	Radio	7	20	2
Used by	Newspaper	10	15	1
Store				

*12. In a survey at a supermarket the following numbers of people were observed purchasing four brands of coffee:

Coffee				
A	B	C	D	E
74	53	81	70	82

Do these data support the notion that the population of coffee buyers prefer each of the five brands equally. Use $\alpha = .05$. (*Hint:* Could the data have been drawn from a uniform distribution?)

13. A computer program that is supposed to generate random numbers is tested. Specifically, the program is supposed to generate random numbers between zero and one. To test the program, ten-thousand numbers are generated with the following results:

Interval	Number Observed
0.0 to 0.1	950
0.1 to 0.2	1069
0.2 to 0.3	992
0.3 to 0.4	966
0.4 to 0.5	980
0.5 to 0.6	1051
0.6 to 0.7	1012
0.7 to 0.8	952
0.8 to 0.9	960
0.9 to 1.0	1068

Do these data support the notion of a random generator?

BIBLIOGRAPHY

HAMBURG, M., *Basic Statistics*, New York: Harcourt, Brace, Jovanovich, Inc., 1974.

HOEL, P., *Elementary Statistics*, Fourth Edition, New York: John Wiley and Sons, Inc., 1976.

LAPIN, L., *Statistics for Modern Business Decisions*, Second Edition, New York: Harcourt, Brace, Jovanovich, Inc., 1978.

LEVIN, R., *Statistics for Management*, Englewood Cliffs: Prentice-Hall, Inc., 1978.

MCALLISTER, H., *Elements of Business and Economic Statistics: Learning by Objectives*, New York: John Wiley and Sons, Inc., 1975.

RICHARDS, L. E. AND LACAVA, J. J., *Business Statistics: Why and When*, New York: McGraw-Hill, 1978.

Correlation

3

Our study of the relationship of variables begins with the simplest case, that of the relationship existing between two variables. Suppose two measurements have been taken on each of several objects. We wish to determine whether one of these measurable quantities, called *Y*, tends to move either up or down as the other quantity, called *X*, rises. For instance, suppose both age and income have been measured for several individuals as shown in Table 3.1.

TABLE 3.1   *Income and Age Measurements.*

Person Number	Y (Income)	X (Age)
1	$ 7800	22
2	8500	23
3	10,000	26
4	15,000	27
5	16,400	35

It appears that *Y* and *X* have a definite relationship. As *X* rises, *Y* tends to rise also. By observing this sample of five persons, it is tempting to conclude that the older a person becomes the more money that person makes. Of course, it is dangerous to reach conclusions on the basis of an inadequate sample size, a subject pursued later on. Yet, based on the observations ($n = 5$), a definite relationship appears to exist between Y and X.

These five data points can be plotted on a two-dimensional scale, with values of X along the horizontal axis and values of Y along the vertical axis. Such a plot is called a *scatter diagram* and appears in Fig. 3–1.

The scatter diagram helps to illustrate what intuition suggested when the raw data were first observed, namely, the appearance of a relationship between Y and X. This is called a *positive* relationship because as X increases, so does Y.

In other situations involving two variables, different scatter diagram patterns might emerge. Consider the plots in Fig. 3–2.

Diagram (a) of Fig. 3–2 suggests what is called a *perfect positive linear* relationship. As X increases, Y increases also, and in a perfectly predictable way. That is, the X and Y data points appear to lie on a straight line. Diagram (b) suggests a perfect *negative linear relationship*. As X increases, Y decreases in a perfectly predictable way.

Figures 3–2(c) and (d) illustrate *imperfect positive* and *negative linear* relationships. As X increases in these scatter diagrams, Y increases (c) or decreases (d), but not in a perfectly predictable way. Y might be slightly higher or lower than "expected." That is, the $X–Y$ points do not lie on a straight line.

Scatter diagrams in Figs. 3–2(a) through (d) illustrate what are called *linear relationships*. The $X–Y$ relationship, be it perfect or imperfect, can

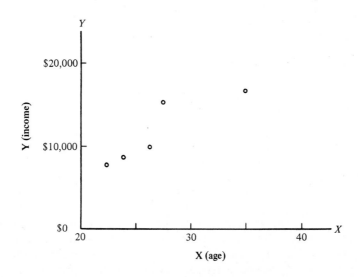

FIGURE 3–1   *X–Y Data Plot.*

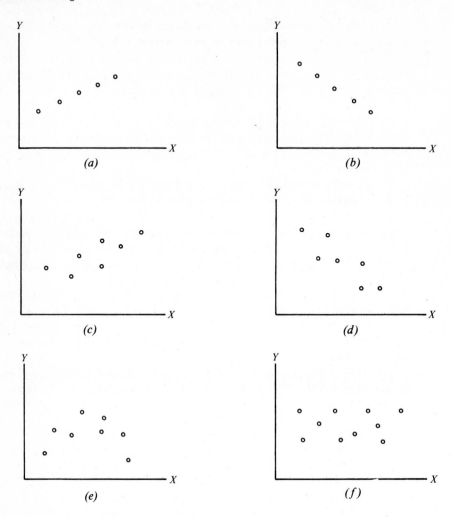

FIGURE 3–2 *X–Y Data Plots.*

be summarized by a straight line. In comparison, a *curved* relationship appears in Diagram (e).

Finally, Diagram (f) of Fig. 3–2 suggests that no relationship of any kind exists between variables X and Y. As X increases, Y does not appear either to increase or decrease in any noticeable fashion. On the basis of the sample evidence that appears in Diagram (f), we might conclude that in the world containing *all* the X–Y data points, there exists no relationship, linear or otherwise, between variables X and Y.

Consider the two scatter diagrams in Fig. 3–3.

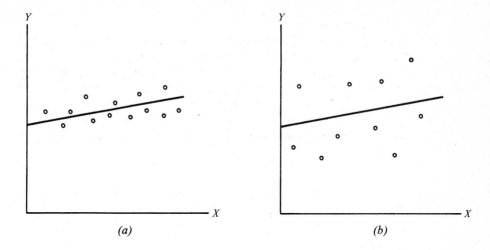

FIGURE 3-3   *X-Y Data Plots.*

Both scatter diagrams suggest imperfect positive linear relationships between *Y* and *X*. The difference is that this relationship appears quite strong in Fig. 3-3(a) because the data points are all quite close to the straight line that passes through them. In Fig. 3-3(b), a weaker relationship is suggested. The data points are farther away from the straight line that passes through them, suggesting that *X* and *Y* are less linearly related. Later in this chapter we shall see how to measure the strength of the relationship that exists between two variables.

As the two scatter diagrams in Fig. 3-3 suggest, it is often desirable to summarize the relationship between two variables by fitting a straight line through the data points. We will learn how to do this later, but let us say for the moment that we can fit a straight line to the points in a scatter diagram so that we have a "good" fit. The question now suggested is, "How rapidly does this straight line rise or fall?"

Answering this question requires the calculation of the slope of the line. The slope of any straight line is defined as the change in the *Y* associated with a change in *X*. Line slope is demonstrated in Fig. 3-4.

In Fig. 3-4(a) the change in *Y* between the two data points is one, while the change in *X* is two. Therefore, the slope of the line is one-half. In Fig. 3-4(b) the line has a negative slope. As *X* increases by one, *Y* *decreases* by 1.2. Therefore, the slope is –1.2.

To summarize, in investigating a relationship between two variables, we are first interested in knowing whether the relationship is linear (straight-line) or curved. If it is linear, we wish to know whether the relationship is positive or negative and how sharply the line that fits the data points rises or falls. Finally, we wish to know the *degree* of the

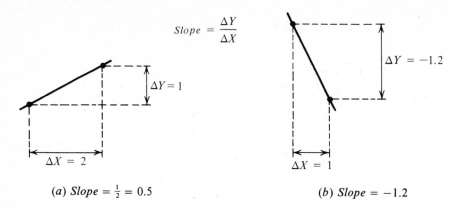

$$Slope = \frac{\Delta Y}{\Delta X}$$

$\Delta Y = 1$

$\Delta X = 2$

$\Delta Y = -1.2$

$\Delta X = 1$

(a) *Slope* = $\frac{1}{2}$ = 0.5   (b) *Slope* = −1.2

FIGURE 3–4   *Line Slopes.*

relationship; that is, how close the data points are to the line that best fits them.

Correlation Coefficient

We next turn to this latter consideration. We wish to have a means of measuring the amount of linear relationship that exists between the two variables of interest. To use the correct terminology, we wish to measure the *correlation* that exists between the two variables. One frequently used measurement of this relationship is the *coefficient of correlation.* Two variables with a perfect negative relationship have a correlation coefficient equal to negative one. At the other extreme, two variables with a perfect positive relationship have a correlation coefficient equal to positive one. Thus, the correlation coefficient varies between negative and positive one (−1 to +1) depending on the amount of correlation between the two variables being measured.

Scatter Diagram (a) on Fig. 3–2 illustrates a situation that would produce a correlation coefficient of +1. Scatter Diagram (b) has a correlation coefficient of −1. Diagrams (e) and (f) plot two variables that are not linearly related. The correlation coefficients for these relationships are equal to zero; that is, no linear relationships are present.

Next, it is important to distinguish between two groups of data points with which we are often concerned. In the *population* containing all the X–Y data points of interest, there is a correlation coefficient whose symbol is ρ, the Greek letter rho. If a random *sample* of these X–Y data points is drawn, the correlation coefficient for this sample data is called *r*. A summary of important points about ρ and *r* is given in Table 3.2.

TABLE 3.2   *Population and Sample Correlation.*

Population	Sample
Correlation coefficient: ρ	Correlation coefficient: *r*
$-1 \leq \rho \leq 1$	$-1 \leq r \leq 1$
ρ = −1 (perfect negative correlation)	*r* = −1 (perfect negative correlation)
ρ = 0 (no correlation)	*r* = 0 (no correlation)
ρ = 1 (perfect positive correlation)	*r* = 1 (perfect positive correlation)

Let us now consider a specific set of *X-Y* values, and assume that these points constitute the entire population of such data points. Suppose, for example, that in the data array of Table 3.3 *X* represents the number of sales training courses taken, and *Y* represents the number of no-sales days per month for the five salespeople on our staff.

TABLE 3.3   *Correlation Between Courses and No-Sales Days.*

Salesperson	No-Sales Days	Courses
1	3	7
2	4	6
3	5	5
4	6	4
5	7	3

A perfect negative relationship is apparent because as *X* moves in one direction (down), *Y* moves precisely in the other direction (up). Thus, for this population of data points we expect ρ to equal −1.

Frequently, *X* and *Y* are measured in different units such as pounds and dollars, sales units and sales dollars, unemployment rate and GNP dollars, etc. In spite of these differing methods of measuring *X* and *Y*, we may still be very interested in measuring the extent to which *X* and *Y* relate. This can be done by first converting the sample data measurements to standard units.

We do this by replacing the actual *X-Y* measurements by their *Z* scores. The *Z* score for each *Y* and *X* observation is computed to be the number of standard deviations from the observation to the mean of all observations. The means and standard deviations of Y and X can be found as

$$\mu_y = \frac{\Sigma Y}{N} = \frac{3 + 4 + 5 + 6 + 7}{5} = 5$$

$$\mu_x = \frac{\Sigma X}{N} = \frac{7 + 6 + 5 + 4 + 3}{5} = 5$$

$$\sigma_y = \sqrt{\frac{\Sigma (Y - \mu_y)^2}{N}} = \sqrt{\frac{4 + 1 + 0 + 1 + 4}{5}} = 1.4$$

$$\sigma_x = \sqrt{\frac{\Sigma (X - \mu_y)^2}{N}} = \sqrt{\frac{4 + 1 + 0 + 1 + 4}{5}} = 1.4$$

Now, the Z score for each observation can be found by determining the number of standard deviations from each observation to the mean.

$$Z_y = \frac{Y - \mu_y}{\sigma_y} \quad \text{for each } Y$$

and

$$Z_x = \frac{X - \mu_x}{\sigma_x} \quad \text{for each } X$$

When this is done, Table 3.4 shows how the original data observations appear.

TABLE 3.4   *Z-Score Computations for Courses Related to No-Sales Days.*

Salesperson	Z_y	Z_x	$Z_y \cdot Z_x$	
1	−1.4	1.4	−1.96	
2	−0.7	0.7	−0.49	
3	0	0	0	$\rho = \dfrac{-4.9}{5} = -.98 \cong -1.00$
4	0.7	−0.7	−0.49	
5	1.4	−1.4	−1.96	$\rho = -1.00$
			−4.9	

The third column shows the product of the two Z scores for each of the five observations. These cross-products are of interest because the mean of these values is the correlation coefficient.

We can thus define the correlation coefficient as follows: *The correlation coefficient is the mean cross-product of Z scores for two variables.* In our example the mean cross-product was found by adding these cross-products and dividing by the population size, five. The result is not precisely negative 1 since the computations were rounded. Without this rounding the correlation coefficient would be exactly equal to negative 1 since the original data pairs were perfectly negatively related. Thus, it appears that as the number of training courses taken increases, the number of no-sales days per month decreases.

Now let us consider the *X-Y* data pairs in Table 3.5 where the number of no-sales days per month is related to itself. In this case a perfect positive correlation exists.

TABLE 3.5   *No-Sales Days Related to Itself.*

Observation	Y No-Sales Days	X No-Sales Days	
1	3	3	
2	4	4	$\mu_y = 5 \qquad \sigma_y = 1.4$
3	5	5	$\mu_x = 5 \qquad \sigma_x = 1.4$
4	6	6	
5	7	7	

The mean and standard deviation of each variable were found as in the previous example. The data points converted to *Z* scores are shown in Table 3.6.

TABLE 3.6   *Z-Score Computations For No-Sales Days Related to Itself.*

Observation	Z_y	Z_x	$Z_y \cdot Z_x$	
1	−1.4	−1.4	1.96	
2	−0.7	−0.7	0.49	$\rho = \dfrac{4.9}{5} = .98 \cong 1$
3	0	0	0	$\rho = 1$
4	0.7	0.7	0.49	
5	1.4	1.4	1.96	
			4.9	

Again, the calculated value of ρ is not precisely 1 because of rounding errors.

The calculation of the correlation coefficient ρ using the cross-product of Z scores will always produce the correct value, but most cases have an easier way to perform the computations. The following formula is equivalent to finding ρ by calculating the mean cross-product of the Z scores.

$$\rho = \frac{\Sigma Z_y \cdot Z_x}{N} = \frac{N \Sigma XY - (\Sigma X)(\Sigma Y)}{\sqrt{N \Sigma X^2 - (\Sigma X)^2} \sqrt{N \Sigma Y^2 - (\Sigma Y)^2}} \quad (3\text{-}1)$$

$$\left(\begin{array}{c} \text{see the Appendix} \\ \text{for a proof of this} \\ \text{relationship} \end{array} \right)$$

To calculate ρ using this formula, a table of values is necessary. For the example introduced in Table 3.3, the computations are illustrated in Table 3.7.

TABLE 3.7 *Computational Approach to the Correlation of Courses and No-Sales Days.*

	Y	X	Y^2	X^2	XY
	3	7	9	49	21
	4	6	16	36	24
	5	5	25	25	25
	6	4	36	16	24
	7	3	49	9	21
Sums:	25	25	135	135	115

All the values needed to solve Eq. (3-1) are now calculated. The substitution and computations are

$$\rho = \frac{(5)(115) - (25)(25)}{\sqrt{(5)(135) - 25^2} \sqrt{(5)(135) - 25^2}} = \frac{575 - 625}{\sqrt{50} \sqrt{50}}$$

$$= \frac{-50}{\sqrt{50^2}} = \frac{-50}{50} = -1$$

$$\rho = -1$$

In similar fashion it can be shown that the correlation coefficient for the second example is positive 1.

Of course, most X-Y data sets will yield a correlation coefficient between these two extremes. In examining a collection of data points, we must use our judgment in deciding when the value for ρ becomes large enough to consider the two variables highly linearly correlated. In most cases involving a collection of X-Y population points, however, Eq.

(3–1) can be used to find the correlation coefficient, which measures the extent to which the two measured variables move together in a linear fashion.

It is usually the case that a sample of data points has been randomly drawn from the population under investigation. In this case Eq. (3–1) is used after replacing N, the population size, by n, the sample size. The formula for the sample correlation coefficient thus becomes

$$r = \frac{n \Sigma XY - (\Sigma X)(\Sigma Y)}{\sqrt{n \Sigma X^2 - (\Sigma X)^2} \sqrt{n \Sigma Y^2 - (\Sigma Y)^2}} \qquad (3\text{--}2)$$

The formula in Eq. (3–2) can be used to find the sample correlation coefficient for the X–Y data pairs presented in Table 3.1. If we are studying the relationship between age and income, it might be of interest to know the value of r for this data. The required values appear in Table 3.8.

TABLE 3.8   *Computations For the Correlation of Age and Income.*

	Y	X	Y^2	X^2	XY
	7800	22	60,840,000	484	171,600
	8500	23	72,250,000	529	195,500
	10,000	26	100,000,000	676	260,000
	15,000	27	225,000,000	729	405,000
	16,400	35	268,960,000	1225	574,000
Sums:	57,700	133	727,050,000	3,643	1,606,100

$$r = \frac{(5)(1,606,100) - (133)(57,700)}{\sqrt{(5)(3643) - (133)^2} \sqrt{(5)(727,050,000) - (57,700)^2}}$$

$$r = \frac{8,030,500 - 7,674,100}{(22.93)(17,491.71)} = \frac{356,400}{401,084.91}$$

$$r = .89$$

Thus, we see that the sample correlation coefficient confirms what was observed in Table 3.1 and Fig. 3–1. The value for r is positive, suggesting a positive linear relationship between age and income. Also, on a scale of 0 to 1, the value of r is fairly high (.89). This suggests a strong linear relationship rather than a weak one. The remaining question is whether or not the combination of sample size and correlation coefficient is strong enough to make meaningful statements about the population from which the data values were drawn.

Before proceeding to this question, we must make two important points in our discussion of correlation. First, it must always be kept in mind that we are measuring *correlation,* not *causation.* It may be perfectly valid to say that two variables are correlated on the basis of a high correlation coefficient. It may or may not be valid to say that one variable is *causing* the movement of the other. For instance, it may be true that the sales volume of a country store in a lightly populated area is highly correlated with the average stock market price in New York City. It might be concluded after examining a large sample of these two variables that such a high correlation exists. It is probably not true that one of these variables is causing the movement of the other. In fact, the movements of both these variables are probably caused by a third factor, the general state of the economy. The error of assuming causation on the basis of correlation is frequently made by politicians, advertisers, and others.

Second, note that the correlation coefficient is measuring a *linear* relationship between two variables. In the case where the correlation coefficient is low, we conclude that the two variables are not closely related in a non-horizontal linear way. It may be that they are closely related in a non-linear or curved fashion. Thus, a low correlation coefficient does not mean that the two variables are not related, only that a linear or straight-line relationship does not appear to exist.

Hypothesis Testing

Now, we should consider the usual problem of wishing to learn about the population of all values after examining only a few of the values, the sample. For example, suppose we wish to determine whether a high correlation exists between Y, the income of people in our company, and X, the years of company service. It would be useful to know the value of ρ, the correlation coefficient between X and Y for all company employees. It may be costly to obtain X–Y measurements on all employees, so a random sample of 25 employees is selected. The correlation coefficient between X and Y in this sample is .74. In other words, the sample evidence is

$$n = 25$$

$$r = .74$$

The value .74 becomes an estimate of ρ, the true but unknown population correlation coefficient. Yet, we may be uneasy about concluding that a correlation exists among *all* employees after examining only 25 of them. Specifically, the following question is formulated: Is the sample evidence enough to reject the hypothesis,

$$H_0: \rho = 0 \tag{3-3}$$

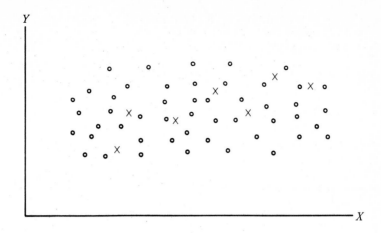

FIGURE 3–5 *Population and Sample Data Points.*

This null hypothesis states that *no* correlation exists between income and years of service among all company employees. The apparent correlation revealed in the sample has come about by chance. How could such a thing happen? Consider the data plot in Fig. 3–5, which represents the population of *X–Y* data points.

The dots represent the population values and suggest that no correlation exists. That is, as *X* values increase, *Y* values seem to be distributed randomly rather than tending upward or downward. The seven *X*s represent a possible random sample of seven data points drawn from this population. Notice that they tend to suggest a positive linear correlation between *X* and *Y*. In fact, the sample correlation coefficient would be positive, not zero. This has come about by chance even though in this population, $\rho = 0$.

The null hypothesis [Eq. (3–3)] could be true following the line of reasoning suggested by Fig. 3–5. The question, again, is, "Has enough sample evidence been collected to reject this null hypothesis?" The sample evidence consists of $n = 25$ and $r = .74$.

In order to test hypothesis (3–3), it is necessary to identify the appropriate sampling distribution. As indicated in Fig. 3–6, the *t* distribution is the sampling distribution for this test where the test statistic is $(r - \rho)/S_r$ and S_r is computed as:*

$$S_r = \sqrt{\frac{1 - r^2}{n - 2}} \qquad (3\text{--}4)$$

---

*Two degrees of freedom are lost because two population parameters (μ_x and μ_y) are estimated using sample values ($\bar{X}$ and $\bar{Y}$).

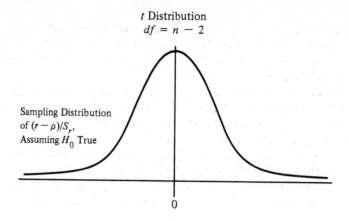

FIGURE 3–6   *t Distribution.*

In order to test the null hypothesis of Eq. (3–3), it is necessary to assume that it is true, calculate a *t* value, and see whether it appears likely to have come from such a distribution. If so, the null hypothesis cannot be rejected. If an unusually high or low value results, it can. The test proceeds as shown in Fig. 3–7.

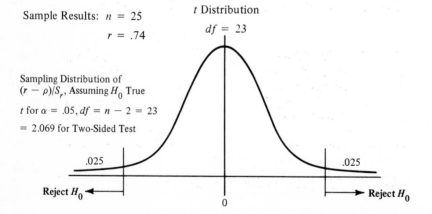

FIGURE 3–7   *Hypothesis Test for Years of Service and Income.*

Decision Rule: If $(r - \rho)/S_r$ is between -2.069 and 2.069, fail to reject H_0.

Conclusion: Since $(r - \rho)/S_r = (0.74 - 0)/0.14 = 5.29$, reject H_0. The sample data support a rejection of the hypothesis that the population correlation coefficient is zero at the 5% significance level.

Since the computed value of t exceeds the tabulated value from the t table, we can reject the null hypothesis with small chance of error. Our rejection is based on a fairly large value of the sample correlation coefficient ($r = .74$) and a fair sample size ($n = 25$). It is apparent from Eq. (3–4) that as r and n increase, the value of t becomes larger, thus making it more likely that the null hypothesis can be rejected. In our example we conclude that in the population of all X–Y data points there exists a linear relationship between the two variables, income and years of service.

Returning to our original example of income and age shown in Table 3.1, let us test the hypothesis

$$H_0: \quad \rho = 0$$

The test proceeds as shown in Fig. 3–8.

Decision Rule: If $(r - \rho)/S_r$ is between -5.841 and 5.841 fail to reject H_0.

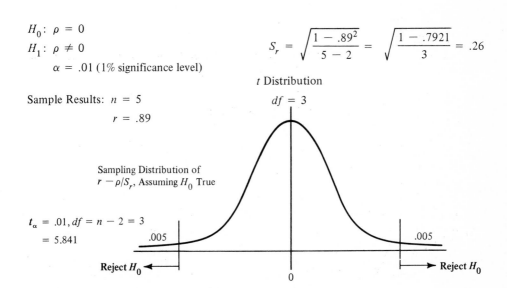

$H_0: \rho = 0$
$H_1: \rho \neq 0$
$\alpha = .01$ (1% significance level)

Sample Results: $n = 5$
$\qquad\qquad r = .89$

Sampling Distribution of
$r - \rho/S_r$, Assuming H_0 True

$t_\alpha = .01, df = n - 2 = 3$
$\quad = 5.841$

$$S_r = \sqrt{\frac{1 - .89^2}{5 - 2}} = \sqrt{\frac{1 - .7921}{3}} = .26$$

t Distribution
$df = 3$

.005   .005

Reject H_0 ←   → Reject H_0

0

FIGURE 3–8   *Hypothesis Test for Age and Income.*

Conclusion: Since $(r - \rho)/S_r = (0.89 - 0)/0.26 = 3.42$, do not reject H_0. The sample data does not support a rejection of the hypothesis that the population correlation coefficient is zero at the 1% significance level.

On the basis of the sample evidence, the hypothesis that the population correlation coefficient is zero cannot be rejected at the 1% significance level. Since the sample size is small, the high correlation coefficient will not permit a rejection of the null hypothesis at the 1% significance level.

Autocorrelation

A special situation arises when we are interested in measuring the extent to which a variable measured over time is correlated with itself when lagged one or more periods. This type of self-correlation is called *autocorrelation,* and can be illustrated by the data in Table 3.9.

TABLE 3.9   *Autocorrelated Data.*

		Original Data (Y)	Y Lagged One Period (X_2)	Y Lagged Two Periods (X_3)
19xx	January	123		
	February	130	123	
	March	125	130	123
	April	138	125	130
	May	145	138	125
	June	142	145	138
	July	141	142	145
	August	146	141	142
	September	147	146	141
	October	157	147	146
	November	150	157	147
	December	160	150	157

As Table 3.9 indicates, variables X_2 and X_3 are actually the Y values that have been "lagged" by one and two periods, respectively. We can now compute the correlation coefficient between Y and X_2. Likewise, the correlation coefficient between Y and X_3 can be computed. These r values will indicate the extent to which the original data measurements are correlated with themselves lagged one and two periods.

These correlation coefficients are computed using Eq. (3–2) and produce the following r values.

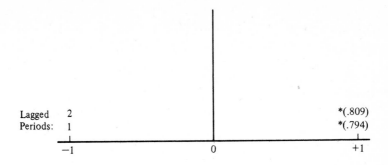

FIGURE 3-9 *Autocorrelation Coefficients.*

$$r\,(Y \text{ and } X_2) = .794$$

$$r\,(Y \text{ and } X_3) = .809$$

Thus, it is apparent that autocorrelation exists in the time series data lagged both one and two periods, and that these two correlations are approximately equal. In a later chapter the subject of autocorrelation will be treated in more depth.

The correlations found above are sometimes displayed on a graph, as shown in Fig. 3-9.

On the left vertical scale of Fig. 3-9 the number of lagged periods is indicated, while the correlation coefficients appear on the right. These coefficients are then plotted against the -1 to +1 range of the horizontal axis.

PROBLEMS

1. Suppose $n = 500$, $r = -.98$. Explain why the following statement is incorrect, "Movement of X is causing Y to move in the opposite direction." Correctly interpret the sample results above.

2. In a correlation problem, does $r = \rho$? Why? Explain the difference between r and ρ.

For Problems 3-7:
    a. Construct a scatter diagram of the data.
    b. State whether or not the variables appear to be correlated.
    c. Compute the sample correlation coefficient.
    d. Test the hypothesis that in the population from which the sample data were drawn no correlation exists.

*3. Y is transportation time in days for goods ordered for our firm from various suppliers. X is the distance in miles.

Supplier	Y	X
1	10	983
2	2	426
3	10	1015
4	11	1763
5	8	416
6	3	283
7	3	124
8	5	674

4.

Y	X
Starting Salary After College ($)	Age
9800	23
10,000	24
10,200	22
12,400	30
11,000	28
9780	25

5.

Y	X
Average Monthly Sales of Company Salespeople	Hours Spent in Formal Sales Training Courses
5583	100
7420	83
12,340	70
4260	90
17,960	25
10,400	35
12,360	40
2420	85
18,960	0
25,862	50
14,920	40
11,360	50
9840	55

6. Y is the average price of selected stocks over randomly selected months. X is the earnings per share for the quarter in which the selected month falls.

Y ($)	X
54	6.25
75	7.33
103	8.16
83	14.24
50	24.23
40	10.13
33	3.14
28	2.98
76	5.18

7. *Y* is the monthly sales for our organization; *X* is the previous month's total advertising budget.

Y	X
50,500	1400
55,710	1400
63,800	1000
45,200	1200
56,000	1500
75,800	1500
93,850	2000

*8. The sales aptitude examination scores for $n = 10$ life insurance salespeople and their annual sales (in millions of dollars of insurance) are provided below.

Salesperson	Sales Y	Score X
Rich	1.1	85
Hank	1.2	72
Johns	1.6	81
White	0.7	64
Green	2.1	84
Jones	2.7	93
Smith	2.4	100
Booker	0.7	76
Zipp	0.6	68
Johnson	0.9	59

a. Calculate the correlation coefficient for the above data.
b. Do you think that the ten salespeople illustrate that the aptitude examination scores are related to annual sales?

9. Is annual rate of return related to the total amount invested? The following portfolios were randomly selected to help answer this question. What is your conclusion? Use acceptable statistical procedures.

Total Investment (1000)	Rate of Return (%)
500	10
120	8
5	7
75	12
40	11
321	15
78	20
480	8
794	7
742	6
40	8
76	10
124	9
853	9
325	18
320	10
710	12
850	11

*10. A security analyst wants to be convinced that the efficiency of capital utilization, expressed by the annual turnover of inventory, actually does have an effect upon a manufacturer's earnings. A sample of five firms is chosen, and the following results are obtained.

Company	Earnings as a Percent of Sales Y	Inventory Turnover (Cost of Goods Sold/Inventory) X
A	11	4
B	9	4
C	15	6
D	14	7
E	12	8

a. Calculate the correlation coefficient for the above data.
b. Do you think that the five firms illustrate that inventory turnover is strongly associated with earnings?

11. Consider the population of 200 weekly observations that are presented as Population (a) below. The independent variable, X, is the average weekly

temperature of Spokane, Washington. The dependent variable, *Y*, is the number of shares of Sunshine Mining Stock traded on the Spokane Exchange in a week. Randomly select data for 16 weeks, and compute the coefficient of correlation. Test the hypothesis that the relationship between temperature and the number of shares traded is not significant. (*Hint:* Make sure your sample is *randomly* drawn from the population. Consult your instructor if you do not know how to do this).

Population (a)

	Y	X		Y	X
(1)	50.00	37.00	(38)	30.00	78.00
(2)	90.00	77.00	(39)	31.00	24.00
(3)	46.00	55.00	(40)	84.00	53.00
(4)	47.00	27.00	(41)	56.00	61.00
(5)	12.00	49.00	(42)	48.00	18.00
(6)	23.00	23.00	(43)	0.00	45.00
(7)	65.00	18.00	(44)	58.00	4.00
(8)	37.00	1.00	(45)	27.00	23.00
(9)	87.00	41.00	(46)	78.00	68.00
(10)	83.00	73.00	(47)	78.00	79.00
(11)	87.00	61.00	(48)	72.00	66.00
(12)	39.00	85.00	(49)	21.00	80.00
(13)	28.00	16.00	(50)	73.00	99.00
(14)	97.00	46.00	(51)	54.00	86.00
(15)	69.00	88.00	(52)	76.00	48.00
(16)	87.00	87.00	(53)	55.00	48.00
(17)	52.00	82.00	(54)	12.00	15.00
(18)	52.00	56.00	(55)	5.00	70.00
(19)	15.00	22.00	(56)	2.00	9.00
(20)	85.00	49.00	(57)	77.00	52.00
(21)	41.00	44.00	(58)	6.00	71.00
(22)	82.00	33.00	(59)	67.00	38.00
(23)	98.00	77.00	(60)	30.00	69.00
(24)	99.00	87.00	(61)	3.00	13.00
(25)	23.00	54.00	(62)	6.00	63.00
(26)	77.00	8.00	(63)	70.00	65.00
(27)	42.00	64.00	(64)	33.00	87.00
(28)	60.00	24.00	(65)	13.00	18.00
(29)	22.00	29.00	(66)	10.00	4.00
(30)	91.00	40.00	(67)	21.00	29.00
(31)	68.00	35.00	(68)	56.00	21.00
(32)	36.00	37.00	(69)	74.00	9.00
(33)	22.00	28.00	(70)	47.00	8.00
(34)	92.00	56.00	(71)	34.00	18.00
(35)	34.00	33.00	(72)	38.00	84.00
(36)	34.00	82.00	(73)	75.00	64.00
(37)	63.00	89.00	(74)	0.00	81.00

(Cont.)

	Y	X		Y	X
(75)	51.00	98.00	(121)	22.00	31.00
(76)	47.00	55.00	(122)	32.00	13.00
(77)	63.00	40.00	(123)	90.00	11.00
(78)	7.00	14.00	(124)	88.00	50.00
(79)	6.00	11.00	(125)	35.00	40.00
(80)	68.00	42.00	(126)	57.00	80.00
(81)	72.00	43.00	(127)	73.00	44.00
(82)	95.00	73.00	(128)	13.00	63.00
(83)	82.00	45.00	(129)	18.00	74.00
(84)	91.00	16.00	(130)	70.00	40.00
(85)	83.00	21.00	(131)	9.00	53.00
(86)	27.00	85.00	(132)	93.00	79.00
(87)	13.00	37.00	(133)	41.00	9.00
(88)	6.00	89.00	(134)	17.00	52.00
(89)	76.00	76.00	(135)	10.00	82.00
(90)	55.00	71.00	(136)	69.00	37.00
(91)	13.00	53.00	(137)	5.00	57.00
(92)	50.00	13.00	(138)	18.00	62.00
(93)	60.00	12.00	(139)	88.00	21.00
(94)	61.00	30.00	(140)	99.00	94.00
(95)	73.00	57.00	(141)	86.00	99.00
(96)	20.00	66.00	(142)	95.00	45.00
(97)	36.00	27.00	(143)	78.00	19.00
(98)	85.00	41.00	(144)	3.00	76.00
(99)	49.00	20.00	(145)	38.00	81.00
(100)	83.00	66.00	(146)	57.00	95.00
(101)	22.00	43.00	(147)	77.00	30.00
(102)	32.00	5.00	(148)	25.00	59.00
(103)	24.00	13.00	(149)	99.00	93.00
(104)	63.00	3.00	(150)	9.00	28.00
(105)	16.00	58.00	(151)	79.00	85.00
(106)	4.00	13.00	(152)	79.00	27.00
(107)	79.00	18.00	(153)	48.00	61.00
(108)	5.00	5.00	(154)	5.00	7.00
(109)	59.00	26.00	(155)	24.00	79.00
(110)	99.00	9.00	(156)	47.00	49.00
(111)	76.00	96.00	(157)	65.00	71.00
(112)	15.00	94.00	(158)	56.00	27.00
(113)	10.00	30.00	(159)	52.00	15.00
(114)	20.00	41.00	(160)	17.00	88.00
(115)	37.00	1.00	(161)	45.00	38.00
(116)	56.00	27.00	(162)	45.00	31.00
(117)	6.00	73.00	(163)	90.00	35.00
(118)	86.00	19.00	(164)	69.00	78.00
(119)	27.00	94.00	(165)	62.00	93.00
(120)	67.00	5.00	(166)	0.00	51.00

(Cont.)

	Y	X		Y	X
(167)	8.00	68.00	(184)	32.00	60.00
(168)	47.00	30.00	(185)	12.00	82.00
(169)	7.00	81.00	(186)	85.00	7.00
(170)	48.00	30.00	(187)	90.00	68.00
(171)	59.00	46.00	(188)	78.00	10.00
(172)	76.00	99.00	(189)	60.00	27.00
(173)	54.00	98.00	(190)	96.00	90.00
(174)	95.00	11.00	(191)	51.00	6.00
(175)	7.00	6.00	(192)	9.00	62.00
(176)	24.00	83.00	(193)	93.00	78.00
(177)	55.00	49.00	(194)	61.00	22.00
(178)	41.00	39.00	(195)	5.00	99.00
(179)	14.00	16.00	(196)	88.00	51.00
(180)	24.00	13.00	(197)	45.00	44.00
(181)	36.00	31.00	(198)	34.00	86.00
(182)	62.00	44.00	(199)	28.00	47.00
(183)	77.00	11.00	(200)	44.00	49.00

12. Consider the population of 140 observations that are presented as Population (b) below. The Marshall Printing Company wishes to estimate the relationship between the number of copies produced by an offset printing technique and the associated direct labor cost. Select a random sample of 20 observations, and determine whether a significant relationship exists between number of copies and total direct labor cost.

Population (b)

	Y*	X**		Y	X		Y	X
(1)	1.0	10	(18)	1.3	70	(35)	1.5	130
(2)	0.9	10	(19)	1.5	70	(36)	1.9	130
(3)	0.8	10	(20)	2.0	70	(37)	1.7	140
(4)	1.3	20	(21)	0.8	80	(38)	1.2	150
(5)	0.9	20	(22)	0.6	80	(39)	1.4	150
(6)	0.6	30	(23)	1.8	80	(40)	2.1	150
(7)	1.1	30	(24)	1.0	90	(41)	0.9	160
(8)	1.0	30	(25)	2.0	100	(42)	1.1	160
(9)	1.4	40	(26)	0.5	100	(43)	1.7	160
(10)	1.4	40	(27)	1.5	100	(44)	2.0	160
(11)	1.2	40	(28)	1.3	110	(45)	1.6	170
(12)	1.7	50	(29)	1.7	110	(46)	1.9	170
(13)	0.9	50	(30)	1.2	110	(47)	1.7	170
(14)	1.2	50	(31)	0.8	110	(48)	2.2	180
(15)	1.3	50	(32)	1.0	120	(49)	2.4	180
(16)	0.7	60	(33)	1.8	120	(50)	1.6	180
(17)	1.0	60	(34)	2.1	120	(51)	1.8	190

(Cont.)

	Y*	X**		Y	X		Y	X
(52)	4.1	190	(81)	2.4	290	(111)	2.6	390
(53)	2.0	190	(82)	2.1	290	(112)	2.5	390
(54)	1.5	200	(83)	1.9	290	(113)	2.7	400
(55)	2.1	200	(84)	2.4	300	(114)	3.1	400
(56)	2.5	200	(85)	2.5	300	(115)	2.4	400
(57)	1.7	220	(86)	2.9	300	(116)	3.0	400
(58)	2.0	220	(87)	2.0	300	(117)	3.4	420
(59)	2.3	220	(88)	1.9	310	(118)	3.5	420
(60)	1.8	220	(89)	2.5	310	(119)	3.1	420
(61)	1.3	230	(90)	2.6	310	(120)	2.9	420
(62)	1.6	230	(91)	3.2	320	(121)	2.8	430
(63)	2.8	230	(92)	2.8	320	(122)	3.3	430
(64)	2.2	230	(93)	2.4	320	(123)	2.5	440
(65)	2.6	230	(94)	2.5	320	(124)	2.8	440
(66)	1.4	240	(95)	2.0	330	(125)	2.4	450
(67)	1.6	240	(96)	2.4	340	(126)	2.6	450
(68)	1.7	240	(97)	2.2	340	(127)	3.0	450
(69)	1.5	250	(98)	2.0	340	(123)	3.4	460
(70)	2.2	250	(99)	2.5	350	(129)	3.0	460
(71)	2.5	250	(100)	2.8	350	(130)	3.3	470
(72)	2.4	260	(101)	2.3	350	(131)	3.4	470
(73)	2.0	260	(102)	2.7	350	(132)	3.1	470
(74)	2.7	260	(103)	2.8	360	(133)	3.6	480
(75)	2.0	270	(104)	3.1	360	(134)	3.0	480
(76)	2.2	270	(105)	2.5	370	(135)	2.9	480
(77)	2.4	270	(105)	2.9	370	(136)	3.2	480
(78)	1.8	280	(107)	2.6	370	(137)	2.6	490
(79)	2.8	290	(108)	3.0	380	(138)	3.8	490
(80)	2.2	290	(109)	3.2	380	(139)	3.3	490
			(110)	2.9	390	(140)	2.9	500

* Y = Total Direct Labor Cost
** X = Copies Produced by an Offset Printing Technique

BIBLIOGRAPHY

HAMBURG, M., *Basic Statistics*, New York: Harcourt, Brace, Jovanovich, Inc., 1974.

HOEL, P., *Elementary Statistics*, Fourth Edition, New York: John Wiley and Sons, Inc., 1976.

LAPIN, L., *Statistics for Modern Business Decisions*, Second Edition, New York: Harcourt, Brace, Jovanovich, Inc., 1978.

LEVIN, R., *Statistics for Management,* Englewood Cliffs, N.J.: Prentice-Hall, Inc., 1978.

MASON, R., *Statistical Techniques in Business and Economics,* Fourth Edition, Homewood, Ill.: Richard D. Irwin, Inc., 1978.

MCALLISTER, H., *Elements of Business and Economic Statistics: Learning by Objectives,* New York: John Wiley and Sons, Inc., 1975.

MENDENHALL, W., AND REINMUTH, J., *Statistics for Management and Economics,* Third Edition, North Scituate, Mass.: Duxbury Press, 1978.

RICHARDS, L. E., AND LACAVA, J. J., *Business Statistics: Why and When,* New York: McGraw-Hill, 1978.

Regression Analysis

4

Introduction

To extend our analysis of the relationship between two variables, let us consider another example. Suppose Mr. Bump observes the selling price and sales volume of milk gallons for ten randomly selected weeks. The data he has collected appear in Table 4.1.

     Mr. Bump first decides to construct a scatter diagram of the data, which appears in Fig. 4–1.

     It appears from this scatter diagram that a definite negative linear relationship exists between Y, the number of milk gallons sold, and X, the price of each gallon. It

TABLE 4.1 *Bump X–Y Data.*

Week	Weekly Sales Level in Thousand of Gallons (Y)	Selling Price (X)
1	10	$1.30
2	6	2.00
3	5	1.70
4	12	1.50
5	10	1.60
6	15	1.20
7	5	1.60
8	12	1.40
9	17	1.00
10	20	1.10

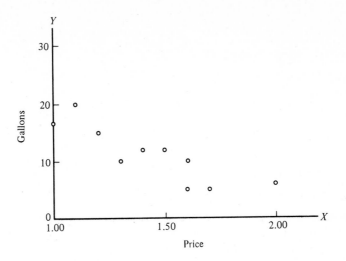

FIGURE 4–1 *Scatter Diagram.*

appears that as price goes up volume goes down. Mr. Bump now wishes to measure the degree of this apparent relationship for which he needs the values in Table 4.2.

From Eq. 3–2 of Chapter 3, the correlation coefficient of this sample data may now be calculated as

$$r = \frac{n \sum XY - (\sum X)(\sum Y)}{\sqrt{n\sum X^2 - (\sum x)^2} \cdot \sqrt{n\sum Y^2 - (\sum Y)^2}}$$

$$= \frac{(10)(149.3) - (14.4)(112)}{\sqrt{(10)(21.56) - 14.4^2} \cdot \sqrt{(10)(1488) - 112^2}}$$

$$= \frac{1493 - 1612.8}{\sqrt{215.6 - 207.36} \cdot \sqrt{14{,}880 - 12{,}544}}$$

TABLE 4.2 *X–Y Data Values.*

	Y	X	X Y	X^2	Y^2
n = 10	10	1.30	13.0	1.69	100
	6	2.00	12.0	4.00	36
	5	1.70	8.5	2.89	25
	12	1.50	18.0	2.25	144
	10	1.60	16.0	2.56	100
	15	1.20	1.80	1.44	225
	5	1.60	8.0	2.56	25
	12	1.40	16.8	1.96	144
	17	1.00	17.0	1.00	289
	20	1.10	22.0	1.21	400
Totals	112	14.4	149.3	21.56	1,488

$$= \frac{-119.8}{\sqrt{8.24} \cdot \sqrt{2336}}$$

$$= \frac{-119.8}{(2.87)(48.33)} = \frac{-119.8}{138.7} = -0.86$$

$$r = -0.86$$

The sample of ten data points has revealed a sample correlation coefficient of $-.86$, a fairly strong negative linear relationship between Y and X. Thus, Mr. Bump may tentatively conclude that as the price of a gallon of milk goes up the number of gallons sold goes down. The question that may occur to him next is "How much does the volume drop as price is raised?" This question suggests drawing a straight line through the data points displayed on the scatter diagram. After this line has been drawn, the slope of the line will show the average decrease in Y for each one dollar increase in X.

Regression Line

Mr. Bump might actually draw a straight line through the data points, attempting to "fit" the line to the points as closely as possible. However, a more correct procedure is to find the equation of the line that best fits the points. This straight line is of the form: $Y_R = b_0 + bX$. The first term in this equation, b_0, is called the Y-intercept since it is the value that Y takes on when X is equal to zero. The second term, b, is called the slope of the straight line since it represents the amount of change in Y when X increases by one unit (recall the discussion of line slope in Chapter 3). What Mr. Bump wishes to do, then, is to compute the values for b_0 and b.

First, it is necessary to define precisely what is meant by a line that best fits the collected data points. Many definitions are possible, but the definition almost universally used in regression analysis is as follows:

The line that best fits a collection of X-Y data points is that line minimizing the sum of the squared distances from the points to the line as measured in the vertical, or Y, direction.

The method that finds values for b_0 and b under this definition is called the *Method of Least Squares*. Finding the equations for b_0 and b requires the use of calculus. The derivation of these two equations appears in the Appendix with the following results.

$$b = \frac{n\Sigma\, X\, Y - \Sigma\, X\Sigma\, Y}{n\Sigma\, X^2 - (\Sigma\, X)^2} \qquad \text{(4-1)}$$

$$b_0 = \frac{\Sigma\, Y}{n} - \frac{b\Sigma\, X}{n} \qquad \text{(4-2)}$$

The computations for the data presented in Table 4.2 are

$$b = \frac{(10)(149.3) - (14.4)(112)}{(10)(21.56) - (14.4)^2} = \frac{119.8}{8.24} = -14.54$$

$$b_0 = \frac{112}{10} - (-14.54)\left(\frac{14.4}{10}\right) = 11.2 + 14.54(1.44) = 32.14$$

Thus, the equation of the straight line that best fits the collected data points, under the method of least squares, is

$$Y_R = b_0 + bX$$
$$Y_R = 32.14 - 14.54\, X \qquad \text{(4-3)}$$

This equation is called the *sample regression equation*. Mr. Bump may now wish to interpret the values in this equation. The Y-intercept, b_0, is that value Y takes on when X is equal to zero. A strict interpretation would suggest that the average number of gallons sold when $X = 0$ (that is, if the price of a gallon of milk were zero) is 32,140 gallons. This interpretation does not agree with common sense since we would expect that much more milk would be "sold" if it were free. The problem illustrated here involves predicting a value for Y based on an X value about which we have collected no sample evidence. That is, our sample points do not involve any having an X value at or near zero. In this case, as in many regression analysis cases, a useful interpretation of the Y-intercept is not possible.

The slope value, b, may be interpreted as the average change in Y that occurs when X increases by one. In this example, Y decreases by an average of 14.54 (that is, 14,540 fewer gallons are sold) when X increases by one (the cost of a gallon of milk is raised by $1). Each dollar increase in a gallon of milk reduces the quantity purchased by an average of 14,540 gallons; or, to put this statement in more meaningful units, the sample evidence indicates that each increase of one cent in a gallon of milk reduces the quantity purchased by an average of 145.4 gallons.

These relationships may be illustrated by drawing the best fit straight line through the scatter diagram of data points, as shown in Fig. 4–2.

Notice that the vertical distances from the points to the line have been shown as dotted lines. If these distances were squared and added,

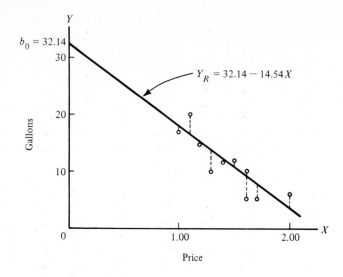

$b_0 = 32.14$

$Y_R = 32.14 - 14.54X$

FIGURE 4–2 *Regression Line.*

this sum would be the lowest possible for any line that could be drawn through the points. Any other line that might be drawn through the points would have a higher sum of squared distances. In accordance with the least-squares procedure, then, this line represents the best possible fit to the ten sample data points.

At this point it should be noted that the regression line we have calculated is correctly termed the *sample* regression line because it is the line that best fits a *sample* of data points randomly drawn from the population of all such data points. As usual in statistical procedures, we distinguish between the population of data values and a sample of data values.

In order to keep these two groups clearly separated, different notation is used to describe the X–Y relationships that exist.

Population	*Sample*
Correlation Coefficient = ρ	Correlation Coefficient = r
Population Regression Model:	Sample Regression Equation:
$Y = \beta_0 + \beta X + \varepsilon$	$Y_R = b_0 + b X$

The population and sample correlation coefficients were discussed in Chapter 3. The sample regression equation, as discussed above, is the equation of the straight line that best fits the observed sample data points. Lying behind the sample data points is the X–Y relationship of the entire population, represented by the population regression model. This model suggests that each value of Y in the population is equal to an intercept value (β_0) plus a constant (β) times its X value, plus an error term (ε). The error terms are thus the differences between the actual population Y values and the values represented by the population regression equation [$\varepsilon = Y - (\beta_0 + \beta X)$].

Having computed the sample regression line equation, Mr. Bump might next be interested in measuring the extent to which the sample data points are dispersed around the sample regression line. In particular, he might wish to measure the typical distance from a data point to the regression line as measured in the Y direction. This concept of measuring dispersion is similar to the notion of standard deviation used to measure the dispersion of data values around their mean. In regression analysis the measurement is called the *standard error of estimate* and is represented by the symbol, $s_{y \cdot x}$. The standard error of estimate is equal to

$$s_{y \cdot x} = \sqrt{\frac{\Sigma(Y - Y_R)^2}{n - 2}} \qquad (4\text{-}4)$$

Note the similarity between this calculation and the sample standard deviation calculation in simple descriptive statistics. In the numerator are the measurements between the actual data values (Y) and the "average" or "expected" value of the variable (Y_R) as determined by the sample regression line. These distances are squared and added, divided by degrees of freedom, and the square root taken. (Note that two degrees of freedom are lost because two population parameters are being estimated by sample data values, namely, b_0 and b.) The standard error thus measures the "typical" distance from a data point to the sample regression line. A regression analysis that has a small standard error involves data points very close to the regression line, and one with a large standard error involves data points widely dispersed around the line. For computation purposes Eq. (4-4) can be converted to

$$s_{y \cdot x} = \sqrt{\frac{\Sigma Y^2 - b_0 \Sigma Y - b \Sigma XY}{n - 2}} \qquad (4\text{-}5)$$

In our example, the standard error becomes

$$s_{y \cdot x} = \sqrt{\frac{1488 - (32.14)(112) + (14.54)(149.3)}{8}}$$

$$= \sqrt{\frac{59.14}{8}} = \sqrt{7.39} \approx 2.72$$

$$s_{y \cdot x} = 2.72$$

The standard error is a measurement of the typical vertical distance from the sample data points to the sample regression line. It can be used to compare the dispersion of data points around the regression line in this situation to the dispersion of data points in other situations. It is used by experienced analysts to judge the extent to which the sample data points may be summarized by the best fit regression line. Also, if it is assumed that the population of data points are normally distributed around the population regression line, $s_{y \cdot x}$ can be used as an estimate of the standard deviation of that normal distribution. The importance of making such a normality assumption is discussed later in this chapter.

Predicting Y

Our next task is to estimate the value that Y will take on for a given value of X. To obtain a *point prediction*, the regression equation is used. The given value of X is placed in the equation, and the predicted value of Y can then be found. For instance, suppose Mr. Bump wished to estimate the quantity of milk that would be sold if the price were set at \$1.63. From Eq. (4–3)

$$Y_R = 32.14 - 14.54\,X$$

$$= 32.14 - 14.54\,(1.63)$$

$$Y_R = 8.440 \qquad \text{or } 8440 \text{ gallons}$$

Note that this estimate is the value of Y_R; that is, it represents the point on the regression line where $X = 1.63$. Of course, we realize the data points that generated the regression line are dispersed around that line, as measured by $s_{y \cdot x}$. In order to make an *interval prediction* of Y when $X = 1.63$, this dispersion must be taken into account. In addition, a second factor must be considered before making such a prediction.

It was stated earlier that the calculated regression line was a sample regression line since it was computed from a random sample of 10 data points, not from all data points in the population. Other random samples of 10 would produce different sample regression lines similar to the case where many samples drawn from a population have different means. In order to make an interval prediction for Y, it is necessary to consider both the dispersion of sample data points around the sample regression line and the dispersion of many sample regression lines around the true population regression line. The *standard error of the forecast* measures the variability of predicted values of Y around the true value of Y for a given value of X. It takes into account both of the above factors. The standard error of the forecast is

$$S_f = S_{y \cdot x} \sqrt{1 + \frac{1}{n} + \frac{(X - \bar{X})^2}{\Sigma(X - \bar{X})^2}} \qquad \textbf{(4-6)}$$

Notice that $s_{y \cdot x}$ is one term in this standard error since the first term under the radical sign is one. The other factors are measuring the variability of sample regression lines around the true regression line. Also, notice that the particular value of X being used appears in Eq. (4-6). In other words, the forecast error *depends on* the value of X for which a forecast is desired. The lowest possible forecast error is for $X = \bar{X}$ since the third term under the radical equals zero, $(X - \bar{X})^2 = 0$. The farther X is from $\bar{X}$, the larger the forecast error. Pictorially, Mr. Bump's 95% prediction interval for various values of X would look similar to Fig. 4-3.

More specifically, the standard error of the forecast is calculated as follows for $X = 1.63$.

$$S_f = 2.72 \sqrt{1 + \frac{1}{10} + \frac{(1.63 - 1.44)^2}{0.8240}}$$

$$= 2.72 \, (1.066)$$

$$S_f = 2.90$$

NOTE: In the above calculation, $\Sigma(X - \bar{X})^2$ was determined as shown in Table 4-3.

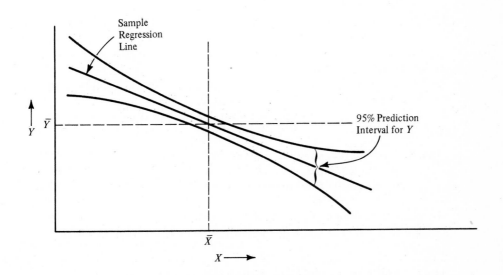

FIGURE 4-3 *Prediction Interval.*

TABLE 4.3   *Calculation of $\Sigma(X - \bar{X})^2$*

X	$(X - \bar{X})^2$
1.30	0.0196
2.00	0.3136
1.70	0.0676
1.50	0.0036
1.60	0.0256
1.20	0.0576
1.60	0.0256
1.40	0.0016
1.00	0.1936
1.10	0.1156

$$\Sigma(X - \bar{X})^2 = .8240$$

A 95% prediction interval for Y when $X = 1.63$ can now be calculated using Eq. (4–7), if the sample size is sufficiently large.

$$Y_R \pm ZS_f \qquad (4\text{-}7)$$

It should be noted that important assumptions are being made when an interval prediction is needed. In fact, the entire regression analysis procedure rests on the following basic assumptions:

1. The population of Y values are normally distributed about the population regression line.
2. The dispersion of population data points around the population regression line remains constant everywhere along the line. That is, the population variance does not become larger or smaller as the X value of the data points increases.*
3. The Y values are independent of each other. This assumption implies a random sample of X-Y data points.**
4. A linear relationship exists between X and Y in the population.

Actually, the interval prediction given by Eq. (4–7) is only approximately correct for our example. In order to use the Z value from the normal curve table correctly, the sample size cannot be small. As a rule of thumb we require a sample size of at least 30 to use the normal table. Since Mr. Bump has collected only 10 data points, it is more correct to compute an interval prediction using the t distribution. The interval becomes

---

*See Fig. 7–1 for a graphic display of this assumption.

**Problems can arise if independence does not exist. Chapter 7 discusses this problem.

$$Y_R \pm t S_f \quad \text{for small sample sizes (for } t \text{ table: } df = n - 2) \qquad \textbf{(4-8)}$$

$$8.44 \pm 2.306 \, (2.90)$$

$$8.44 \pm 6.69$$

1.75 to 15.13   or: 1750 gallons to 15,130 gallons

The formula in Eq. (4–8) produces a somewhat wider interval than if the normal curve value were used, reflecting the presence of a small sample size.

Another important point is that to predict beyond the range of observed data is unwise. This means that Mr. Bump is justified in trying to predict Y when $X = 1.63$ because some of the original X values are near 1.63. On the other hand, it would not be wise to predict Y when $X = 3.00$. No data have been collected for X values nearly this large, and for this reason any prediction involving such an X value would be highly suspect. In order to estimate quantity sold when price per unit is three dollars, we have to assume that the linear model is still valid. We may have good reason to make this assumption, but we have no direct evidence to support it.

Coefficient of Determination

We next consider a most useful statistic that can be calculated from the sample data. This statistic is known as the *coefficient of determination*. Consider Fig. 4–4, which shows a sample regression line along with one of the ten data points.

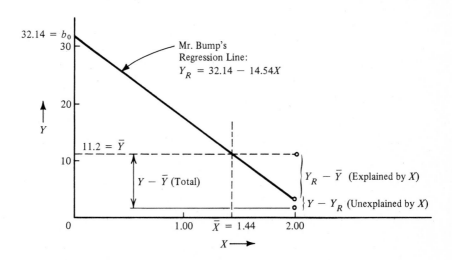

FIGURE 4-4   *Explained and Unexplained Variation.*

In considering the single data point that lies below the regression line, we would first "expect" that its Y value would be equal to the average of all Y values, namely, $\bar{Y}$. The vertical distance between Y and $\bar{Y}$ shown on the above diagram thus becomes the total difference or deviation that we must attempt to explain. Part of this vertical distance is readily explainable. We would expect the Y value to be equal to $\bar{Y}$ only if the X value of the observation were equal to $\bar{X}$. However, this is not the case. The X value of this observation is considerably higher than $\bar{X}$. Thus, we understand why the Y value of this observation might have moved from $\bar{Y}$ down to Y_R. It is because the X value of the observation is greater than $\bar{X}$. The vertical distance $Y_R - \bar{Y}$ is, therefore, "explained" by the movement in X, while the vertical distance $Y - Y_R$ is "unexplained" by the movement in X.

More specifically, in Mr. Bump's example, consider the data point with a large X value ($X = 1.70$, $Y = 5$). For this data point

$$Y_R = 32.14 - 14.54\,(1.70)$$

$$= 32.14 - 24.72 = 7.422$$

Thus:

$$\bar{Y} = 11.2$$

$$Y_R = 7.422$$

$$Y = 5$$

These values appear in Fig. 4–5.

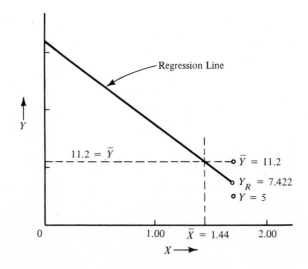

FIGURE 4-5 *Predicting Y.*

In this case the distance from $\bar{Y}$ to Y_R is *explained* by the movement of X from $\bar{X}$ (1.44) to its actual value (1.70), as we expected from our knowledge of the relationship between Y and X ($r = -.86$). In other words, the movement of X from 1.44 to 1.70 has explained the movement of Y from 11.2 to 7.422, but has *not explained* its movement from 7.422 to 5.00.

To find the portion of the total deviation that is explained by X for any observation, it is necessary to divide the explained deviation by the total deviation as follows.

$$\text{Percent of Total Deviation Explained by } X = \frac{Y_R - \bar{Y}}{Y - \bar{Y}}$$

and

$$\text{Percent of Total Deviation Unexplained by } X = \frac{Y - Y_R}{Y - \bar{Y}}$$

Of course, we wish to consider *all* the data points, not just one. Also, the calculation for all the data points is made with squared distances, not straight distances. This is done so that the final result will have a useful interpretation, as will be shown.

The symbol for the sample coefficient of determination is r^2 and this value is defined as:

$$r^2 = \frac{\Sigma(Y_R - \bar{Y})^2}{\Sigma(Y - \bar{Y})^2} = \frac{Explained\ Deviation}{Total\ Deviation}$$

or

$$r^2 = 1 - \frac{\Sigma(Y - Y_R)^2}{\Sigma(Y - \bar{Y})^2} \tag{4-9}$$

$$r^2 = 1 - \frac{Unexplained\ Deviation}{Total\ Deviation}$$

Equation (4–9) is the usual form for defining r^2, and states the percent of the variability in Y that is explained by variability in X is 100% minus the percent unexplained by X. The value r-squared (r^2) thus becomes a most important value in any regression analysis since it shows the extent to which the variability of Y and X are related. In the example involving Mr. Bump's milk vs. price data, r^2 can be calculated using the following equivalent computational formula.

$$r^2 = \frac{b_0 \Sigma Y + b \Sigma XY - n\bar{Y}^2}{\Sigma Y^2 - n\bar{Y}^2} \tag{4-10}$$

$$r^2 = \frac{(32.14)(112) - (14.54)(149.3) - (10)(11.2)^2}{1488 - (10)(11.2)^2}$$

$$r^2 = \frac{3599.68 - 2170.82 - 1254}{1488 - 1254} = \frac{174.9}{234} = 0.747$$

On the basis of this r^2 value, Mr. Bump can make the following statements:

1. Seventy-five percent of the variability in the quantity of milk sold can be explained by the variability in milk price.
2. Twenty-five percent of the variability in the quantity of milk sold *cannot* be explained by the variability in milk price. This portion of the variability in milk volume must be explained by factors that have not been identified in this regression analysis (for example, weather, amount of advertising, availability of substitute products, and so forth).

Note that the value for r^2 is exactly the square of the value for r, the coefficient of correlation computed earlier in this chapter (disregarding rounding errors); that is,

Coefficient of Determination = (Coefficient of Correlation)^2

$r^2 = (r)^2$

$.75 = (-.86)^2$

$.75 = .75$ *(Approximately, Due to Rounding Errors)*

Then, why is it necessary to identify both these values in a regression analysis? The answer is that each of these coefficients has an advantage over the other. The advantage of the coefficient of correlation (r) is that both positive and negative relationships are revealed. In the case of the data that Mr. Bump has collected a negative relationship exists ($r = -.86$). In other cases a positive relationship might be revealed by the value for r. As we shall see in the next chapter, it is important to identify relationships that exist between certain pairs of variables when confronted with a large collection of variables, and it is necessary to know whether positive or negative relationships exist. Note that when the coefficient of correlation is squared the value is always positive and the nature of the relationship is lost.

The advantage of the coefficient of determination (r^2) is that it has a very useful interpretation. The value for r^2 measures the *percent* of the variability in Y, which is explained by variability in X. This is a most useful interpretation, making r^2 the most frequently consulted statistic in regression analysis.

Figure 4–6 illustrates the two extreme cases for r^2.

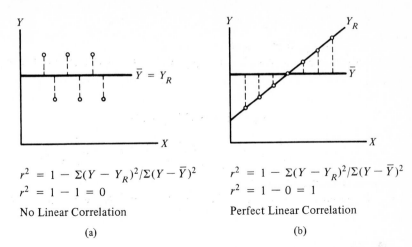

$$r^2 = 1 - \Sigma(Y - Y_R)^2/\Sigma(Y - \bar{Y})^2$$
$$r^2 = 1 - 1 = 0$$

No Linear Correlation

(a)

$$r^2 = 1 - \Sigma(Y - Y_R)^2/\Sigma(Y - \bar{Y})^2$$
$$r^2 = 1 - 0 = 1$$

Perfect Linear Correlation

(b)

FIGURE 4–6   *Extreme Values of* r^2.

In Chapter 3, we noted that the sample coefficient of correlation, r, has a counterpart in the population, namely, ρ (rho). Likewise, the population of all X–Y data points possesses a coefficient of determination, ρ^2 (rho-squared). As always, we must keep in mind that the sample information produces sample statistics that only allow us to make inferences about the relationships that exist between X and Y among all the population data points.

In Chapter 3, we tested the null hypothesis,

$$H_0: \rho = 0$$

Another statistical test that we might consider is

$$H_0: \beta = 0$$

where β is the slope of the true population regression line.

Failing to reject this null hypothesis means that, in spite of the fact the sample evidence has produced a non-zero value for b, the evidence is not strong enough to reject the notion that in the population of all data points the regression line is flat. Note that such a statement is equivalent to stating that $\rho = 0$. A population of data points that had a flat regression line would also have a zero correlation coefficient. How could β be zero while b is non-zero? Consider Fig. 4–7 where a population of data points is shown from which a sample of five has been taken (sampled data points are indicated by x).

As this scatter diagram suggests, if we take enough sample data points, it will become obvious that the population of data points has a

75

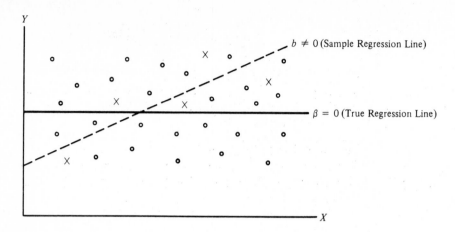

FIGURE 4–7 *Population and Sample Data Points.*

regression line with a flat slope. That is, the true correlation coefficient is zero. However, in our random sample of five data points we happened to select points that lie fairly close to an upward trending regression line. We might erroneously conclude from this evidence that X and Y are related in a positive linear way. However, if we test the hypothesis that $\beta = 0$ or test the hypothesis that $\rho = 0$, we will probably not be able to reject either of them.

Incidentally, these two tests are equivalent; that is, they each produce the same value for the t statistic, as shown in Table 4.4. Why might one test be preferrred over the other? It depends on which test is most meaningful to the analyst in a particular situation. Sometimes the emphasis is on the population correlation coefficient, in which case it is desirable to test the hypothesis that $\rho = 0$. In other cases, the emphasis may be on the slope of the true population regression line, and a test of the hypothesis that $\beta = 0$ is in order. Each hypothesis states that no linear relationship exists between X and Y in the population of data points, and each test produces the same conclusion in a given situation. For Mr. Bump's data, the tests appear as shown in Table 4.4.

From the t table for $n - 2$ degrees of freedom,

$$t_{.01, (df = 8)} = 3.355$$

$$t_{.05, (df = 8)} = 2.306$$

Therefore, Mr. Bump is able to reject the following null hypothesis: The population regression line has a flat slope ($\beta = 0$). Alternatively, he might reject this null hypothesis: The population correlation coefficient is zero ($\rho = 0$).

TABLE 4.4 *Hypotheses Tests.*

H_0: $\rho = 0$		H_0: $\beta = 0$	
$S_r = \sqrt{\dfrac{1 - r^2}{n - 2}}$	(4-11)	$S_b = \dfrac{S_{y \cdot x}}{\sqrt{\Sigma(X - \bar{X})^2}}$	(4-12)
$t = \dfrac{r - \rho}{S_r}$	(4-13)	$t = \dfrac{b - B}{S_b}$	(4-14)
$t = \dfrac{-0.86 - 0}{\sqrt{\dfrac{1 - 0.74}{8}}} = \dfrac{-0.86}{0.18}$		$t = \dfrac{-14.54 - 0}{2.72/\sqrt{0.824}} = \dfrac{-14.54}{3.00}$	
$t = -4.8$		$t = -4.8$	

NOTE: The values used in the above calculations were all computed earlier in this chapter.

Let us now consider two special situations that illustrate the importance of testing a hypothesis regarding the population, as well as considering the value of r^2:

Situation: Suppose $n = 1000$ and $r^2 = .10$.
The following hypothesis is rejected: H_0: $\beta = 0$; however, the regression is not considered useful.

Reason: The extremely large sample size produces a very accurate estimate of ρ^2, the population coefficient of determination. We are able to reject the notion that this coefficient is equal to zero. However, the relationship between X and Y, while we are confident it exists, is very weak ($r^2 = .10$). Therefore, we have established with small chance of error that a weak relationship exists in the population between X and Y; and we are, therefore, not interested in pursuing the regression analysis.

Situation: Suppose $n = 3$ and $r^2 = .95$.
The following hypothesis cannot be rejected: H_0: $\beta = 0$

Reason: The three data points lie nearly on a straight line. However, this is an extremely small sample size, not constituting enough evidence to make a positive statement about the population of all data points. We are not able to reject the null hypothesis even though the value for r^2 is quite high. More sample evidence needs to be collected before meaningful statements about the population can be made.

77

Residuals

Mr. Bump's analysis began with only knowledge of ten weekly sales volume quantities (the Y variable). If no further information were available, he might have employed the mean of Y ($\bar{Y}$) as the predictor for each weekly sales volume. If this were done, he would have generated certain errors, one for each prediction made. These errors are called *residuals*. By estimating the Y values with $\bar{Y}$, Mr. Bump would minimize estimation errors over a long period of time since the mean sales volume, 11,200 gallons, is used as the best estimator of each week's sales volume. The errors sum to zero because the mean is the mathematical center of the distribution of Y. The 10 predictions and the 10 errors would appear as shown in Table 4.5.

TABLE 4.5 *Residuals.*

Actual Y	Predicted Y ($\bar{Y}$)	Residual ($Y - \bar{Y}$)	$(Y - \bar{Y})^2$
10	11.2	−1.2	1.44
6	11.2	−5.2	27.04
5	11.2	−6.2	38.44
12	11.2	0.8	0.64
10	11.2	−1.2	1.44
15	11.2	3.8	14.44
5	11.2	−6.2	38.44
12	11.2	0.8	0.64
17	11.2	5.8	33.64
20	11.2	8.8	77.44
		Sum = 0	233.60

In addition to a table of residuals, Table 4.5 also squares the residuals and sums them. This is done so that the total amount of error can be measured; because there are both positive and negative errors the sum of the actual errors is always zero. The value is called the *sum of the squared residuals*, and represents the total variability of Y values around their mean. It is this total variability that Mr. Bump wishes to reduce by introducing knowledge of a related variable, X. The formula for the sum of the squared residuals around the mean of Y is

$$\Sigma(Y - \bar{Y})^2 \tag{4-15}$$

The sum of the squared residuals can be changed to a variance by dividing it by the appropriate degrees of freedom. Since one population parameter (μ) is being estimated by a sample statistic ($\bar{Y}$), one degree of freedom is lost. The appropriate degrees of freedom is, thus, $n - 1$; and the total variance of Y around its mean becomes

$$s_y^2 = \frac{\Sigma(Y - \bar{Y})^2}{n - 1} \qquad \textbf{(4-16)}$$

$$s_y^2 = \frac{233.6}{9} = 25.96$$

Note the following important point: This variance of Y values has been computed by using $\bar{Y}$ as the best estimator for each week's Y value. That is, no information about the related variable X has been used. When Mr. Bump brings in information about X, a lower variance of Y should result because X is correlated with Y, and more accurate predictions should be possible.

Specifically, Mr. Bump will use the calculated regression equation to predict Y. Since he established a relationship between X and Y on the basis of the sample data points ($r = -.86$), the regression line should generate more accurate predictions for Y than when $\bar{Y}$ was used to predict the Y values. If Mr. Bump predicts Y values using this regression equation, residuals will still exist, but we expect them to be smaller. Likewise, the sum of the squared residuals should be smaller and the variance of Y values around the regression line should be smaller. Table 4.6 presents this analysis of residuals.

TABLE 4.6 *Residuals.*

X	Y	Predicted Y (Y_R) (Using $Y_R = 32.14 - 14.54X$)	Residual ($Y - Y_R$)	$(Y - Y_R)^2$
1.30	10	13.238	−3.238	10.48
2.00	6	3.060	2.940	8.64
1.70	5	7.422	−2.422	5.87
1.50	12	10.330	1.670	2.79
1.60	10	8.876	1.124	1.26
1.20	15	14.692	0.308	0.09
1.60	5	8.876	−3.876	15.02
1.40	12	11.784	0.216	0.05
1.00	17	17.600	−0.600	0.36
1.10	20	16.146	3.854	14.85
			Sum: 0	59.41

The sum of the squared residuals is reduced from 233.6 to 59.41 because the errors now involve the variability of the Y values around the regression line instead of around $\bar{Y}$. In other words, knowledge of the related variable X reduces the prediction error, just as Mr. Bump might expect through his knowledge of the sample correlation coefficient between X and Y. The variance of Y around the predicted values is

$$s_{y \cdot x}^2 = \frac{\Sigma(Y - Y_R)^2}{n - 2} \qquad (4\text{-}17)$$

$$s_{y \cdot x}^2 = \frac{59.41}{8} = 7.43 \qquad \text{(Note that this is the square of the standard error of estimate, } s_{y \cdot x})$$

Of the original error, what percent has Mr. Bump been able to explain through knowledge of the related variable X? This value is the coefficient of determination, r^2.

$$r^2 = 1 - \frac{\Sigma(Y - Y_R)^2}{\Sigma(Y - \bar{Y})^2} \qquad (4\text{-}18)$$

$$r^2 = 1 - \frac{59.41}{233.6} = 1 - 0.25 = 0.746$$

This, of course, is the same r^2 value obtained earlier, and indicates that knowledge of X allows Mr. Bump to explain 74.6% of the variability of Y around its mean. Also, 25.4% of the variability in Y is *not* explained by knowledge of X.

The relationship between total deviation, explained deviation, and unexplained deviation is as follows:

Total Deviation =	*Explained Deviation*	+ *Unexplained Deviation*
$\Sigma(Y - \bar{Y})^2 =$	$\Sigma(Y_R - \bar{Y})^2$	$+ \ \Sigma(Y - Y_R)^2$
$233.6 =$	174.2	$+ \ 59.4$
$233.6 =$	233.6	

Computer Output

Mr. Bump's regression analysis problem (from Table 4.1) is run on a computer regression program to produce the output presented in Table 4.7. In order to understand clearly the terminology employed on the computer output, definitions and computations are presented below. These definitions and calculations are keyed to Table 4.7.

1. CORRELATION X vs. $Y = -.86$ The simple correlation coefficient indicates the relationship between X and Y, or price and sales respectively.

TABLE 4.7 *Computer Output for Bump Regression Example.*

VARIABLE NO.	MEAN	STANDARD DEVIATION	CORRELATION X VS Y	REGRESSION COEFFICIENT	STD. ERROR OF REG.COEF.	COMPUTED T VALUE
2	1.44000	0.30258	-0.86 (1)	-14.54 (2)	3.00 (3)	-4.84 (4)

DEPENDENT						
1	11.20000	5.09466				

INTERCEPT	32.14 (5)	MULTIPLE CORRELATION 0.86 (7)
STD. ERROR OF ESTIMATE	2.725 (6)	R SQUARED 0.746 (8)
		CORRECTED R SQUARED 0.714 (9)

ANALYSIS OF VARIANCE FOR THE REGRESSION (14)

SOURCES OF VARIATION	DEGREES OF FREEDOM	SUM OF SQUARES	MEAN SQUARES	F VALUE
ATTRIBUTABLE TO REGRESSION	1	174.175	174.175	23.448
DEVIATION FROM REGRESSION	8	59.425 (10)	7.428	
TOTAL	9	233.600 (11)		

CORRELATION MATRIX: 2 BY 2 (13)

VAR.	1	2
1	1.000	-0.863
2	-0.863	1.000

TABLE OF RESIDUALS

CASE NO.	Y VALUE	Y ESTIMATE	RESIDUAL
1	10.00000	13.23543	-3.23543 (12)
2	6.00000	3.05824	2.94176
3	5.00000	7.41989	-2.41989
4	12.00000	10.32765	1.67235
5	10.00000	8.87376	1.12624
6	15.00000	14.68932	0.31068
7	5.00000	8.87376	-3.87376
8	12.00000	11.78154	0.21846
9	17.00000	17.59706	-0.59706
10	20.00000	16.14317	3.85683

2. REGRESSION COEFFICIENT $= -14.54$ This is the change in Y (sales) when X (price) increases by one unit (b). When price increases \$1, sales decrease by 14,450 units.

3. STANDARD ERROR OF REGRESSION COEFFICIENT $= 3.0$ This is the standard deviation of the sampling distribution of b, or regression coefficient values.

$$s_b = \frac{s_{y \cdot x}}{\sqrt{\Sigma(X - \bar{X})^2}} = \frac{2.72}{\sqrt{0.824}} = \frac{2.72}{0.908} = 3.00$$

4. COMPUTED T VALUE $= -4.84$ The computed T value is used to test whether the population regression coefficient β is significantly different from zero.

$$T = \frac{b - \beta}{s_{y \cdot x}} \sqrt{\Sigma(X - \bar{X})^2} = \frac{-14.54}{2.72} = \sqrt{0.824}$$

$$T = -5.346(0.908) = -4.85 \text{ (rounding error)}$$

5. INTERCEPT $= 32.14$ This is the Y intercept (b_0). Therefore, the entire regression equation is:

$$Y_R = 32.14 - 14.54\,X$$

6. STANDARD ERROR OF ESTIMATE $= 2.725$ The standard error of the estimate indicates that the Y values fall typically about 2.725 from the regression line.

$$s_{y \cdot x} = \sqrt{\frac{\Sigma(Y - Y_R)^2}{n - 2}} = \sqrt{\frac{59.425}{10 - 2}} = \sqrt{7.428} = 2.725$$

7. MULTIPLE CORRELATION $= .86$ The multiple correlation coefficient is the square root of R^2 and indicates the degree of relationship between X and Y, but not the kind of relationship.

$$R^2 = .74$$
$$\sqrt{R^2} = \sqrt{.74}$$
$$R = .86$$

8. R-SQUARED $= .746$ The regression line explains 74.6% of the sales volume variance.

$$R^2 = 1 - \frac{\Sigma(Y - Y_R)^2}{\Sigma(Y - \bar{Y})^2} = 1 - \frac{59.4}{233.6}$$

$$R^2 = 1 - 0.254 = 0.746$$

9. CORRECTED R-SQUARED $= .714$ The R^2 is adjusted for the appropriate degrees of freedom.

$$R_c^2 = 1 - \cfrac{\cfrac{\Sigma(Y - Y_R)^2}{n-2}}{\cfrac{\Sigma(Y - \bar{Y})^2}{n-1}} = 1 - \cfrac{\cfrac{59.425}{8}}{\cfrac{233.6}{9}} = 1 - \cfrac{7.428}{25.956}$$

$$R_c^2 = 1 - 0.286 = 0.714$$

10. SUM OF SQUARES DEVIATION FROM REGRESSION $= 59.425$ The sum of squared residuals is the difference between the actual Y and the predicted $Y(Y_R)$ squared and summed (sometimes referred to as the error sum of squares).

$$\Sigma(Y - Y_R)^2 = 59.425$$

11. SUM OF SQUARES TOTAL $= 233.6$ This is the sum of the squared deviations from the mean.

$$\Sigma(Y - \bar{Y})^2 = 233.6$$

12. RESIDUALS   Residuals measure the difference between what Y actually is and what we predict it to be using the regression equation. For example,

Case 1: $(Y - Y_R) = (10 - 13.23543) = -3.23543$
Case 2: $(Y - Y_R) = (6 - 3.05824) \ \ = 2.94176$

13. CORRELATION MATRIX   This is a matrix giving the correlation between all variables in the analysis. Since only two variables are involved, there is only one correlation coefficient $(-.863)$.

14. ANALYSIS OF VARIANCE The F value in this ANOVA table tests the null hypothesis that the regression is not significant; that is, the reduction in the error sum of squares from 233.6 to 59.425 is due to chance. A high F value will reject this hypothesis, suggesting a *significant* regression. The F value ($23.448 = 174.175/7.428$) becomes larger as a larger portion of the total error sum of squares is explained by the regression. In this case the tabulated F value ($df_n = 1$, $df_d = 8$, $\alpha = .01$) is 11.26. Thus, we may reject the hypothesis of no significant regression at the 1% significance level. The appropriate degrees of freedom in any regression analysis ANOVA are $k - 1$, $n - k$, and $n - 1$ for attributable-to-regression, deviation-from-regression, and total, respectively, where k is the number of regression constants computed from sample data (b's).

PROBLEMS

1. Consider the population of observations on temperature and shares traded presented in Chapter 3, Problem 11. Draw a random sample of data pairs and:

   a. Construct a scatter diagram.
   b. Compute the sample correlation coefficient.
   c. Determine the sample regression line equation.
   d. Plot the regression line on the scatter diagram.
   e. Compute the standard error of estimate.
   f. Compute the standard error of forecast for $X = 20$.
   g. Compute the sample coefficient of determination and interpret its value.
   h. Test the hypothesis that the slope of the regression line that passes through the entire population of data is zero.
   i. Compute the residual for each of the sampled data points and plot them.
   j. Make a point and a 95% confidence interval estimate for the number of shares traded if the average weekly temperature is estimated to be 50° next week.

2. Consider the population of observations on number of copies and direct labor cost presented in Chapter 3, Problem 12. Draw a random sample of 20 data pairs and perform the analysis in Problem 1 for parts (a) through (i) (exclude f).

   a. Make a point and a 90% confidence interval estimate for the direct labor cost if the project involves 250 copies.

*3.

Y	X
$1250	$41
1380	54
1425	63
1425	54
1450	48
1300	46
1400	62
1510	61
1575	64
1650	71

$X = $ Weekly Advertising Expenditures
$Y = $ Weekly Sales

   a. Does a significant relationship exist between advertising expenditures and sales?
   b. State the prediction equation.
   c. Predict sales for an advertising expenditure of $50.

    d. What percent of the variance can we explain with the prediction equation?

    e. State the amount of unexplained variance.

    f. State the amount of total variance.

4. The times required to check out customers in a supermarket and the corresponding value of purchases are shown in the following table.

Time Required For Checkout (minutes)	Value of Purchase (dollars)
3.6	30.6
4.1	30.5
0.8	2.4
5.7	42.2
3.4	21.8
1.8	6.2
4.3	40.1
0.2	2.0
2.6	15.5
1.3	6.5

Answer (a), (b), (e), and (f) from Problem 3 using this data. Give a point and a 99% confidence interval estimate for Y if $X = 3.0$.

*5. A study done to show the relationship of income to education produced the following results.

Group	Average Number of Years of Education X	Average Annual Income (thousands of dollars) Y
1	3	3
2	4	4
3	5	5
4	7	7
5	6	9
6	9	11
7	11	13
8	12	20
9	16	35
10	15	40
11	21	50

Determine if the linear relationship is significant between income and years of education. Compute the sample regression equation. Compute r^2 and interpret its value.

6. A farming cooperative has undertaken an investigation to determine the nature of the relationship between yield per acre of a particular crop and the intensity of application of a fertilizer compound. The results are shown in the table below.

Tract	Yield Per Acre (thousands of bushels) Y	Tons of fertilizer X
A	7	11
B	8	21
C	10	24
D	12	31
E	9	30
F	10	36
G	15	41
H	13	50

a. Calculate the regression equation.
b. Predict yield when 25 tons of fertilizer are used.
c. Test H_0: $\beta = 0$
d. Compute r^2.

7. Information is supplied by a mail-order business for 12 cities.

City	Number of Mail Orders Received (thousands) Y	Number of Catalogs Distributed (thousands) X
A	24	6
B	16	2
C	23	5
D	15	1
E	32	10
F	25	7
G	38	15
H	18	3
I	35	11
J	34	13
K	15	2
L	32	12

a. Determine whether a significant linear relationship exists between these two variables. (Test at the .025 significance level.)
b. Determine the regression line.
c. Calculate the standard error of estimate.

    d. What percent of the mail order variable variance is explained by the catalogs' distributed variable?

    e. Predict the number of mail orders received when 10 thousand catalogs are distributed.

    f. Test to determine whether the regression coefficient is significantly different from zero. (Use the .02 significance level.)

    g. Calculate the explained variance for the Y variable.

*8. In a regression of investment on the interest rate, the following results were observed during 10 years.

Yearly Investment (thousands of $)	Average Interest Rate (percentage)
1060	4.8
940	5.1
920	5.9
1110	5.1
1590	4.8
2050	3.8
2070	3.7
2030	4.5
1780	4.9
1420	6.2

    a. Is the relationship between these variables significant?

    b. Can an effective prediction equation be developed?

    c. If the average interest rate is 4 percent five years from now, can we estimate yearly investment?

    d. Calculate and interpret r^2.

    e. Discuss correlation and causation in this example.

9. The personnel manager of a company wants to find a measure that can be used to predict weekly sales. As an experimental project, six of the regular salespeople were asked to complete the Norse Sales Aptitude Test. The manager reasoned that if the relationship between the test scores and weekly sales were high, the test might be used to select new salespeople. The test scores and the weekly sales of the six people were as shown in the following table.

Salesperson	Weekly Sales (thousands)	Norse Test Score
M.N.	10	6.2
A.D.	15	10.1
O.I.	8	2.9
S.B.	7	3.2
N.D.	12	8.5
J.J.	5	2.4

Use appropriate statistical procedures to prepare a recommendation for the personnel manager.

10. Some investors feel that since AT&T (American Telephone and Telegraph) is such a large utility its earnings per common share should be related to GNP (gross national product), using the latter as a predictor of the former.

Year	GNP (billions of current dollars)	ATT Earnings Per Share (dollars)
1961	520.1	$ 0.82
1962	560.3	0.86
1963	590.5	0.88
1964	632.4	1.02
1965	684.9	1.08
1966	747.6	1.18
1967	789.7	1.22

Based on the above data, can the EPS of AT&T be predicted by GNP? What is the prediction equation? Present an interval estimate for Y when $X = 800$. Test H_0: $\beta = 0$. Summarize the above investigation in a report to investors.

*11. The ABC Investment Company is in the business of making bids on investments offered by various firms that desire additional financing. ABC has tabulated its bid on the last 25 issues bid on in terms of the bid's percentage of par value. The bid of ABC's major competitor, as a percentage of par value, is also tabulated on these issues. ABC now wonders if it is using the same rationale in preparing bids as is its competitor. In other words, could ABC's bid be used to predict the competitor's bid? If not, then the competitor must be evaluating issues differently. The data are as follows:

Issue	ABC Bid	Competitor Bid
1	99.035	100.104
2	104.358	105.032
3	99.435	99.517
4	96.932	95.808
5	98.904	98.835
6	101.635	101.563
7	100.001	101.237
8	98.234	99.123
9	93.849	94.803
10	99.412	100.063
11	99.949	99.564
12	104.012	103.889
13	99.473	99.348
14	100.542	99.936

Issue	ABC Bid	Competitor Bid
15	96.842	95.834
16	99.200	99.863
17	101.614	102.010
18	99.501	99.432
19	100.898	99.965
20	97.001	96.838
21	100.025	100.804
22	103.014	104.300
23	98.702	99.010
24	101.834	100.936
25	102.903	103.834

    a. To what extent are the two firms using the same rationale in preparing their bids?

    b. Forecast the competitor's bid if ABC bids 101% of par value. Give both a point and an interval prediction under the assumption that the above data constitute the entire *population* of bid data.

    c. Under (b) above, what is the probability of ABC winning this particular bid (lowest bid wins)?

    d. If the above data constituted a random *sample* of bid data rather than the entire population, what changes would be necessary in parts (b) and (c)? Answer the question in (c), assuming the data are from a random sample.

12. Evaluate the following statements:

    a. "A high r^2 means a significant regression."

    b. "A very large sample size in a regression problem will always produce useful results."

13. In a regression problem the following two null hypotheses are considered:

    a. H_0: $\rho = 0$

    b. H_0: $\beta = 0$

Explain whether one, the other, neither, or both might be tested, and explain why.

14. Many analysts consider a scatter diagram to be an important first step in analyzing an $X-Y$ relationship. Explain why this might be so.

15. A large computer firm is considering the possibility that computer sales could be closely correlated with gross private domestic investment. What conclusion would you reach after examining the following 16 years' data?

Year	Gross Private Domestic Investment (billions)	Computer Sales (millions)
1960	74.8	13.2
1961	69.0	14.4
1962	83.0	15.9
1963	87.1	18.3

Year	Gross Private Domestic Investment (billions)	Computer Sales (millions)
1964	93.0	27.3
1965	112.0	29.6
1966	121.3	41.6
1967	116.0	46.8
1968	126.3	42.8
1969	139.6	52.1
1970	140.8	56.7
1971	160.0	51.7
1972	188.3	61.1
1973	220.0	73.6
1974	215.0	91.2
1975	183.7	85.8

BIBLIOGRAPHY

DRAPER, N. R., AND SMITH, H., *Applied Regression Analysis*, New York: John Wiley and Sons, Inc., 1966.

DUNN, O. J., AND CLARK, V. A., *Applied Statistics: Analysis of Variance and Regression*, New York: John Wiley and Sons, Inc., 1974.

HAMBURG, M., *Basic Statistics*, New York: Harcourt, Brace, Jovanovich, Inc., 1974.

HOEL, P., *Elementary Statistics*, Fourth Edition, New York: John Wiley and Sons, Inc., 1976.

LAPIN, L., *Statistics for Modern Business Decisions*, Second Edition, New York: Harcourt, Brace, Jovanovich, Inc., 1978.

LEVIN, R., *Statistics for Management*, Englewood Cliffs, N.J.: Prentice-Hall, Inc., 1978.

MASON, R., *Statistical Techniques in Business and Economics*, Fourth Edition, Homewood, Ill.: Richard D. Irwin, Inc., 1978.

MCALLISTER, H., *Elements of Business and Economics Statistics: Learning by Objectives*, New York: John Wiley and Sons, Inc., 1975.

MENDENHALL, W., AND REINMUTH, J., *Statistics for Management and Economics*, Third Edition, North Scituate, Mass.: Duxbury Press, 1978.

RICHARDS, L. E., AND LaCAVA, J. J., *Business Statistics: Why and When*, New York: McGraw-Hill, 1978.

Multiple Regression

5

Introduction

In simple regression the relationship between an independent and dependent variable is investigated. The relationship between two variables oftentimes allows a person to predict accurately the dependent variable based on knowledge of the independent variable. Unfortunately, most real life situations are not so simple. More than one independent variable is usually necessary in order to predict a dependent variable accurately. When more than one independent or predictor variable is used, the problem becomes one of multiple regression analysis. The basic concepts remain the same; we simply use more than one independent variable in order to predict the dependent variable.

Predictor Variables

As an example, let us return to our problem in which sales volume of gallons of milk is estimated from knowledge of price per gallon. Mr. Bump is faced with the problem of making a prediction that is not entirely accurate. He can explain almost 75 percent of the total variance of the sales volume of gallons of milk sold. This leaves 25 percent $(1 - R^2)$ of the total variation unexplained. In other words, based on the sample evidence Mr. Bump knows 75 percent of what he must know to predict sales volume perfectly. In order to do a more accurate job of estimation, he needs to find another predictor variable, which will enable him to explain more of the total variance. If Mr. Bump can reduce the unexplained variation, his estimate will involve less error and more accuracy.

A search must be conducted for another independent variable that is related to sales volume of gallons of milk. However, this new independent or predictor variable cannot relate too highly with the independent variable (price per gallon) already in use. If the two independent variables are highly related to each other, they will explain the same variation, and the addition of the second variable will not improve the prediction. In fields such as econometrics and applied statistics, there is a great deal of concern with this problem of intercorrelation among independent variables, often referred to as *collinearity*. The simple solution to the problem of two highly related independent variables is merely not to use both of them together. The collinearity problem will be discussed further later in this chapter.

To summarize, the attributes of a good predictor variable are twofold:

1. A good predictor variable is related to the dependent variable.
2. A good predictor variable is *not* highly related to any other independent variable.

Correlation Matrix

Mr. Bump decides that advertising expense might help improve his estimate of weekly sales volume. He investigates the relationships between advertising expense, sales volume, and price per gallon by examining a *correlation matrix*. The matrix is constructed by computing the simple correlation coefficients between each combination of pairs of variables. An example is illustrated in Table 5.1. The correlation coefficient that indicates the relationship between variables 1 and 2 is represented as r_{12}. Notice that the first subscript ($r_{①2}$) refers to the row and the second subscript ($r_{1②}$) refers to the column. This standardized approach allows us to determine,

TABLE 5.1 *Correlation Matrix.*

Variables	1	2	3
1	r_{11}	r_{12}	r_{13}
2	r_{21}	r_{22}	r_{23}
3	r_{31}	r_{32}	r_{33}

at a glance, the relationship between any two variables. Of course, the relationship between variables 1 and 2 (r_{12}) is exactly the same as for variables 2 and 1 (r_{21}). Therefore, only half the matrix is necessary. Also, the primary diagonal will always contain ones since it always relates a variable with itself (r_{11}, r_{22}, r_{33}); and a variable is perfectly and linearly related to itself.

Mr. Bump runs his data on the computer and receives the correlation matrix shown in Table 5.2. (Most multiple regression computer programs provide a correlation matrix.) An investigation of the relationships between advertising expense, sales volume, and price per gallon indicates that the new independent variable should contribute to improved prediction. The correlation matrix shows that advertising expense is highly related (r_{13} = .89) positively to the dependent variable, sales volume, and moderately related (r_{23} = −.65) negatively to the independent variable, price per gallon. This combination of relationships should permit advertising expense to explain some of the total variance of sales volume that is not already being explained by price per gallon. As we shall see, when both price per gallon and advertising expense are used to estimate sales volume, the R^2 increases to 93.2%.

TABLE 5.2 *Computer Correlation Matrix.*

Variables	Sales 1	Price 2	Advertising 3
1. Sales	1.00	−0.86	0.89
2. Price		1.00	−0.65
3. Advertising			1.00

The analysis of the correlation matrix is an important initial step in the solution of any problem involving multiple independent variables.

Multiple Regression Equation

In simple regression the dependent variable can be represented by Y, and the independent variable by X. In multiple regression analysis Xs with subscripts are used to represent the independent variables. The dependent variable is still represented by Y, and the independent variables are represented by X_2, X_3, X_n. Based on this system of notation, Mr. Bump's new regression equation is written

$$Y_R = b_0 + b_2 X_2 + b_3 X_3 \qquad (5\text{-}1)$$

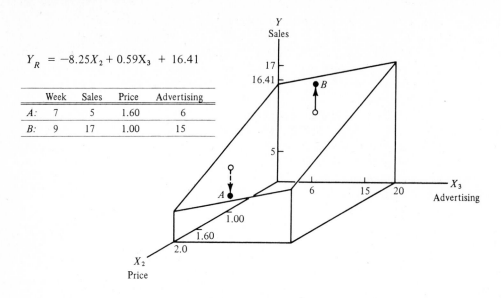

$$Y_R = -8.25X_2 + 0.59X_3 + 16.41$$

Week	Sales	Price	Advertising
A: 7	5	1.60	6
B: 9	17	1.00	15

FIGURE 5-1 *Multiple Regression Plane.*

where: Y_R = the volume of gallons sold
b_2, b_3 = net regression coefficients (the best set of weights for the two independent variables in order to achieve maximum prediction)
X_2 = price per gallon
X_3 = advertising expense (hundreds of dollars)
b_0 = constant or Y-intercept

The analysis uses the method of least squares to obtain the best fitting three-variable linear regression equation. Whereas in the two-variable problem, the least-squares method produced the best fitting straight line, in this three-variable problem the method is used to obtain the best fitting plane (see Fig. 5-1). The points are plotted in three dimensions along the Y, X_2, and X_3 axes. The points fall above and below the plane in such a way that $\Sigma(Y - Y_R)^2$ is a minimum. The b_2 and b_3 values are derived as the best set of weights that minimize the sum of the squared distances between the data points and the multiple regression plane. In the previous example involving two variables, two equations resulted from the minimization process. Now we have three equations that must be solved in order to determine the values of b_2, b_3, and b_0.*

---

*As illustrated in the appendix, a function of the form

$$F(b_2, b_3, b_0) = \Sigma(Y - b_0 - b_2 X_2 - b_3 X_3)^2$$

is minimized by the calculus method of taking partial derivatives with respect to b_0, b_2, and b_3, and equating these derivatives.

$$\Sigma Y = nb_0 + b_2 \Sigma X_2 + b_3 \Sigma X_3$$

$$\Sigma X_2 Y = b_0 \Sigma X_2 + b_2 \Sigma X_2^2 + b_3 \Sigma X_2 X_3 \qquad \text{(5-2)}$$

$$\Sigma X_3 Y = b_0 \Sigma X_3 + b_2 \Sigma X_2 X_3 + b_3 \Sigma X_3^2$$

The computations of the required summations are shown in Table 5.3. Substituting into Eq. (5–2) gives

$$112 = 10b_0 + 14.4b_2 + 114b_3$$

$$149.3 = 14.4b_0 + 21.56b_2 + 155.3b_3$$

$$1480 = 114b_0 + 155.3b_2 + 1522b_3$$

Solving the three equations simultaneously, Mr. Bump obtains

$$b_2 = -8.2476$$

$$b_3 = 0.5851$$

$$b_0 = 16.4064$$

Substituting in Eq. (5–1), we now write the multiple regression equation as

$$Y_R = 16.41 - 8.25X_2 + 0.59X_3$$

TABLE 5.3   *Computations for Linear Multiple Regression Analysis.*

Week	Sales (thousands) Y	Price Per Gallon X_2	Advertising (hundreds) of dollars X_3	$X_2 Y$	$X_3 Y$	$X_2 X_3$	Y^2	X_2^2	X_3^2
1	10	$1.30	9	13	90	11.7	100	1.69	81
2	6	2.00	7	12	42	14.0	36	4.00	49
3	5	1.70	5	8.5	25	8.5	25	2.89	25
4	12	1.50	14	18	168	21.0	144	2.25	196
5	10	1.60	15	16	150	24.0	100	2.56	225
6	15	1.20	12	18	180	14.4	225	1.44	144
7	5	1.60	6	8	30	9.6	25	2.56	36
8	12	1.40	10	16.8	120	14.0	144	1.96	100
9	17	1.00	15	17	255	15.0	289	1.00	225
10	20	1.10	21	22	420	23.1	400	1.21	441
TOTAL:	112	14.40	114	149.3	1480	155.3	1488	21.56	1522
MEAN:	11.2	1.44	11.4						

This equation can now be used for the estimation of next week's sales. If plans call for a price per unit of $1.50 and advertising expenditures of $1000, the prediction is 9930 gallons; that is,

$$Y_R = 16.41 - 8.25X_2 + 0.59X_3$$

$$Y_R = 16.41 - 8.25(1.5) + 0.59(10)$$

$$Y_R = 9.93 \text{ (thousands of gallons)}$$

In our example the analysis for three variables can be performed on a hand calculator. With more than three variables, however, the analysis becomes increasingly complicated since the number of equations to be solved increases with each new independent variable. The best approach is to use one of the numerous multiple regression computer programs that are available. The Biomedical Computer Program (BMDP) and Statistical Package for the Social Sciences (SPSS Regression) are two of the most popular sources. Because of the cost and tedious labor involved in multiple regression analysis when a computer program is not used, the analyst's ability to test and experiment with the variables is severely limited. Therefore, it is highly recommended that a computer program be used to solve multiple regression problems. The analyst gains a wider range of choice in variable selection, the addition and deletion of variables, variable transformations, and in testing curvilinear as well as linear relationships.

Regression Coefficients

In the last chapter we discussed the interpretation of b_0 and b in the regression equation. We now consider the interpretation of b_0, b_2, and b_3 in the multiple regression equation. The value b_0 is again the Y-intercept. However, now it is interpreted as the value of Y_R when both X_2 and X_3 are equal to zero. The b_2 and b_3 values are referred to as net regression coefficients. Each measures the average change in Y per unit change in the relevant independent variable. However, since we are measuring the simultaneous influence of all independent variables on Y, the net effect of X_2 (or any other X) must be measured apart from any influence of other variables. We say, therefore, that b_2 measures the average change in Y per unit change in X_2, holding the other independent variables constant.

In our present example, the b_2 value of -8.25 indicates that each increase of one cent in a gallon of milk when advertising expenditures are held *constant* reduces the quantity purchased by an average of 82.5 gallons. Similarly, the b_3 value of 0.59 means that if advertising expenditures are increased by one-hundred dollars when price per gallon is held constant, then sales volume will increase an average of 590 gallons.

To illustrate these influences, an example is observed where price is to be \$1.00 per gallon and \$1000 is to be spent on advertising.

$$Y_R = 16.41 - 8.25X_2 + 0.59X_3$$

$$Y_R = 16.41 - 8.25(1.00) + 0.59(10)$$

$$Y_R = 16.41 - 8.25 + 5.9$$

$$Y_R = 14.06 \text{ or } 14,060 \text{ gallons}$$

We predict sales to be 14,060 gallons of milk. What is the effect on sales of a one-cent price increase if we still spend $1000 on advertising?

$$Y_R = 16.41 - 8.25(1.01) + 0.59(10)$$

$$Y_R = 16.41 - 8.3325 + 5.9$$

$$Y_R = 13.9775$$

Note that sales decrease by 82.5 gallons ($14.06 - 13.9775 = 0.0825$). What is the effect on sales of a one-hundred dollar increase in advertising if price remains constant at $1.00?

$$Y_R = 16.41 - 8.25(1.00) + 0.59(11)$$

$$Y_R = 16.41 - 8.25 + 6.49$$

$$Y_R = 14.65$$

Note that sales increase by 590 gallons ($14.65 - 14.06 = 0.59$).

Statistical Inference in Multiple Regression

When the measures used in developing a multiple regression equation represent a probability sample from some specific population, it is possible to make statistical inferences about parameters found in the population multiple regression equation.

$$Y = \beta_0 + \beta_2 X_2 + \beta_3 X_3 + \varepsilon$$

For instance, sample data are used to develop a sample multiple regression equation in the form

$$Y_R = b_0 + b_2 X_2 + b_3 X_3$$

where b_0, b_2, and b_3 are efficient, linear, unbiased estimates of the corresponding population parameters B_0, B_2, and B_3. Since sample data are generally used, we are usually interested in making inferences about population parameters.

Certain assumptions underlie this procedure, namely:

1. The Y values are normally distributed about the multiple regression plane.

2. The dispersion of points around the regression plane remains constant everywhere on the plane.
3. The Y values are independent of each other.
4. A linear relationship exists between each X.

Residuals

In the last chapter a residual was defined as the difference between what is actually observed and what is estimated by the regression equation $(e = Y - Y_R)$. The multiple regression equation for each past weekly sales volume is

$$Y = b_0 + b_2 X_2 + b_3 X_3 + e \qquad (5\text{-}3)$$

where
$$\begin{aligned}
Y &= \text{actual weekly sales volume in gallons} \\
b_2, b_3 &= \text{net regression coefficients} \\
X_2 &= \text{price per gallon} \\
X_3 &= \text{advertising expense (hundreds of dollars)} \\
b_0 &= \text{constant} \\
e &= \text{residual [difference between the actual } Y \text{ value} \\
&\quad \text{and our estimate of } Y(Y_R)]
\end{aligned}$$

If Y_R is substituted for $(b_0 + b_2 X_2 + b_3 X_3)$ in Eq. (5-3), Mr. Bump obtains

$$Y = Y_R + e$$

or

$$e = Y - Y_R$$

If he substitutes the data for the first week into Eq. (5-1), an estimate for that week's sales of 10,950 gallons of milk is obtained.

$$Y_R = 16.4064 - 8.2476 X_2 + 0.5851 X_3$$
$$Y_R = 16.4064 - 8.2476(1.30) + 0.5851(9)$$
$$Y_R = 10.9504$$

However, he already knows that sales were 10,000 gallons during that week. His estimate missed by 950 gallons. In other words, the residual from this prediction was 950 gallons.

$$e = Y - Y_R$$
$$e = 10.000 - 10.950$$
$$e = -.950$$

TABLE 5.4 *Residuals from the Full Model.*

X_2	X_3	Y	Predicted Y (Y_R) Using $Y_R = 16.4064$ $-8.2476 X_2 + .5851 X_3$	Residual ($Y - Y_R$)	$(Y - Y_R)^2$
1.30	9	10	10.9504	−0.95041	0.903279
2.00	7	6	4.0069	1.99311	3.972487
1.70	5	5	5.3110	−0.31097	0.096702
1.50	14	12	12.2264	−0.22639	0.051252
1.60	15	10	11.9867	−1.98673	3.947095
1.20	12	15	13.5305	1.46953	2.159518
1.60	6	5	6.7208	−1.72083	2.961256
1.40	10	12	10.7108	1.28925	1.662166
1.00	15	17	16.9353	0.06471	0.004187
1.10	21	20	19.6211	0.37888	0.143550
				SUM: = 0	15.901493

Table 5.4 illustrates the concept of the residual for each of the ten data points. The b_2 and b_3 values are derived as the best set of weights that minimize the sum of the squared distances between the data points and the multiple regression plane. When the residuals are summed [$\Sigma(Y - Y_R)$] for all ten data points, the column sums to zero $\Sigma(Y - Y_R) = 0$. When the errors are squared and summed [$\Sigma(Y - Y_R)^2$], the sum of squares is a minimum value $\Sigma(Y - Y_R)^2 = 15.901$. No other b values can be found for these data points that will produce a sum of squared residuals that is less than 15.901.

When Mr. Bump used only price per gallon to estimate quantity of gallons sold, the sum of the square residuals $\Sigma(Y - Y_R)^2$ was 59.4. When price per gallon and advertising expense were used as predictor variables, the sum of the squared residuals was reduced to 15.9. Mr. Bump can now explain 93.2 percent of the sales volume variance through his knowledge of the relationships between price per gallon, advertising expense, and quantity sold.

*Total Deviation = Explained Deviation + Unexplained Deviation**

$$\Sigma(Y - \bar{Y})^2 = \Sigma(Y_R - \bar{Y})^2 + \Sigma(Y - Y_R)^2$$

$$233.6 = 217.7 + 15.9$$

$$R^2 = \frac{\Sigma(Y_R - \bar{Y})^2}{\Sigma(Y - \bar{Y})^2} = \frac{217.7}{233.6} = 0.932 \quad \text{or 93.2 percent}$$

---

*Deviation is used to simplify the example. If the deviations are divided by the appropriate degrees of freedom, we have variances.

$$R^2 = 1 - \frac{\Sigma(Y - Y_R)^2}{\Sigma(Y - \bar{Y})^2} = 1 - \frac{15.9}{233.6} = 1 - 0.068 = 0.932$$

In summary:

Variables Used to Explain Variance of Y	R^2	$\Sigma(Y - Y_R)^2$
None	0	233.6
Price	0.75	59.4
Price and Advertising Expense	0.93	15.9

Standard Error of Estimate

Just as in simple regression, the standard error of estimate is the standard deviation of the residuals. It measures the typical scatter of Y values around the regression plane. The standard error of estimate is written:

$$S_{y \cdot x_2 x_3} = \sqrt{\frac{\Sigma(Y - Y_R)^2}{n - k}} \qquad (5-4)$$

where: $S_{y \cdot x_2 x_3}$ = the standard error of estimate of the dependent variable Y regressed against the two independent variables X_2 and X_3
  Y = actual weekly sales volume in gallons
  Y_R = the volume of gallons estimated sold from the regression equation
  n = the number of observations
  k = the number of linearly independent parameters to be estimated in the multiple regression equation (b's)

In Mr. Bump's example the standard error becomes

$$S_{y \cdot x_2 x_3} = \sqrt{\frac{15.901493}{10 - 3}} = \sqrt{2.27} = 1.51$$

That is, if sales volumes are normally distributed around the regression plane, about two-thirds (68%) of the quantities should fall within 1510 of the quantity estimated from the regression plane.

Computer Output

The computer output for the Bump example is presented in Table 5.5. Examination of this output leads to the following observations:

1. The regression coefficients are -8.2476 for price and 0.5851 for advertising expense. The regression equation is $Y_R = 16.4064 - 8.2476X_2 + .5851X_3$
2. The regression equation explains 93.2% of the sales volume variance.

TABLE 5.5 *Computer Output for Bump Multiple Regression Example.*

VARIABLE	MEAN	STANDARD DEVIATION	CORRELATION X VS Y	REGRESSION COEFFICIENT	STD. ERROR OF REG.COEF.	COMPUTED T VALUE
2	1.44000	0.30258	-0.86349	-8.24760 (1)	2.19605	-3.75565 (4)
3	11.40000	4.97103	0.89150	0.58510 (1)	0.13367	4.37716 (4)
DEPENDENT						
1	11.20000	5.09466				

INTERCEPT	16.40639 (1)	MULTIPLE CORRELATION	0.96536
STD. ERROR OF ESTIMATE	1.50719 (3)	R SQUARED	0.93193 (2)
		CORRECTED R SQUARED	0.91248

ANALYSIS OF VARIANCE FOR THE REGRESSION

SOURCES OF VARIATION	DEGREES OF FREEDOM	SUM OF SQUARES	MEAN SQUARES	F VALUE
ATTRIBUTABLE TO REGRESSION	2	217.699	108.849	47.917 (7)
DEVIATION FROM REGRESSION	7	15.901 (5)	2.272	
TOTAL	9	233.600		

CORRELATION MATRIX: 3 BY 3

VAR.	1	2	3
1	1.000	-0.863	0.891
2	-0.863	1.000	-0.654
3	0.891	-0.654	1.000

TABLE OF RESIDUALS (6)

CASE NO.	Y VALUE	Y ESTIMATE	RESIDUAL
1	10.00000	10.95041	-0.95041
2	6.00000	4.00689	1.99311
3	5.00000	5.31097	-0.31097
4	12.00000	12.22639	-0.22639
5	10.00000	11.98673	-1.98673
6	15.00000	13.53047	1.46953
7	5.00000	6.72083	-1.72083
8	12.00000	10.71075	1.28925
9	17.00000	16.93529	0.06471
10	20.00000	19.62112	0.37888

3. The standard error of the estimate indicates that the standard deviation of Y values around the regression plane is 1.501 gallons.
4. In the regression chapter we tested the regression coefficient to determine whether it was different from zero. Both regression coefficients in this equation are important, as indicated by the computed t values of -3.76 and 4.38 (since from the t table for 7 degrees of freedom, $t_{.01} = 3.499$).
5. The sum of squares deviation from regression (15.901) computation was demonstrated in Table 5.4. This is the sum of the squared residuals $[\Sigma(Y - Y_R)^2]$.
6. The residuals were also demonstrated in Table 5.4.
7. The regression is significant since the computed F value in the ANOVA is greater than the tabulated F value (for $df_n = 2$ and $df_d = 7$, $F_{.01} = 9.55$).

Dummy Variables

Suppose we wish to investigate how well a particular aptitude test predicts job performance. Eight women and seven men have taken the test, which

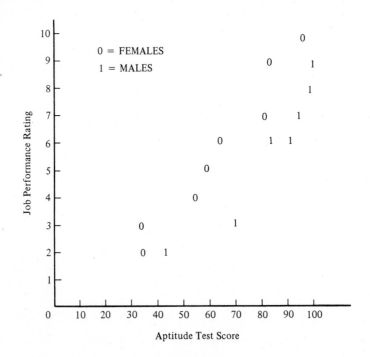

FIGURE 5-2

measures manual dexterity in using their hands with tiny objects. Each then went through a month of intensive training as electronics assemblers, followed by a month at actual assembly, during which their productivity was evaluated by an index having values ranging from 0 to 10 (0 means unproductive). The data are shown in Table 5.6. A scatter diagram is presented in Fig. 5–2. Each female worker is represented by a zero and each male by a one. It is immediately evident that the relationship of this aptitude test to job performance follows two distinct patterns—one applying to women and the other to men.

It is sometimes necessary to determine how a dependent variable is related to an independent variable when a *qualitative* factor is influencing the situation. We accomplish this by creating a dummy variable. There are many ways to identify quantitatively the classes of a qualitative variable. We shall use the values 0 and 1.

The dummy variable technique is illustrated in Fig. 5–3. The data points for females are shown as zeros, while the ones represent males. Two parallel lines are constructed for the scatter diagram. The top one fits the data for females, while the bottom line fits the male data points.

TABLE 5.6   *Electronics Assemblers Dummy Variable Example*

Subject	Job Performance Rating Y	Aptitude Test Score X_2	Sex X_3
1	5	60	0 (F)
2	4	55	0 (F)
3	3	35	0 (F)
4	10	96	0 (F)
5	2	35	0 (F)
6	7	81	0 (F)
7	6	65	0 (F)
8	9	85	0 (F)
9	9	99	1 (M)
10	2	43	1 (M)
11	8	98	1 (M)
12	6	91	1 (M)
13	7	95	1 (M)
14	3	70	1 (M)
15	6	85	1 (M)
	87	1093	

$\bar{Y}_F$ = *Mean Female Job Performance Rating* = 5.75

$\bar{Y}_M$ = *Mean Male Job Performance Rating* = 5.86

$\bar{X}_F$ = *Mean Female Aptitude Test Score* = 64

$\bar{X}_M$ = *Mean Male Aptitude Test Score* = 83

103

Each of these lines was obtained through the solution of the multiple regression equation

$$Y_R = b_0 + b_2 X_2 + b_3 X_3 \qquad\qquad \textbf{(5-5)}$$

where $\quad X_2 =$ test score

$$X_3 \begin{cases} = 0 \text{ for females} \\ = 1 \text{ for males} \end{cases}$$

The single equation is seen to be equivalent to the following two equations.

$$Y_R = b_0 + b_2 X_2 \qquad \text{(for females)}$$

$$Y_R = b_0 + b_2 X_2 + b_3 \text{ (for males)}$$

Notice that b_3 represents the effect of a male on job performance and b_2 represents the effect of aptitude test score differences (the b_2 value is assumed to be the same for males and females). The important point is that one multiple regression equation, Eq. (5-5), will yield the two estimated lines shown in Fig. 5-3. The top line is the estimate for females, and the lower line for males. We may envision X_3 as a "switching" variable that is "on" when an observation is made for a male, and "off" for a female.

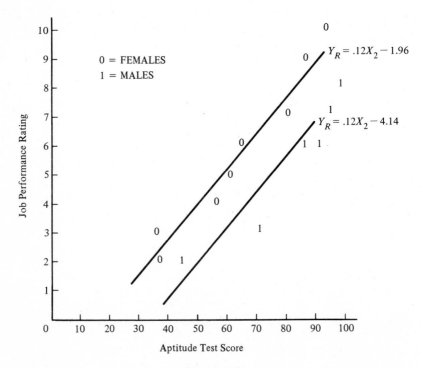

Figure 5-3

The estimated multiple regression equation is shown on the computer output, Table 5.7

$$Y_R = -1.96 + 0.12X_2 - 2.18X_3$$

For the two values (0 and 1) of X_3, the equation provides

$$Y_R = -1.96 + 0.12X_2 - 2.18(0)$$

$$Y_R = -1.96 + 0.12X_2 \quad \text{(for females)}$$

and

$$Y_R = -1.96 + 0.12X_2 - 2.18(1)$$

$$Y_R = -4.14 + 0.12X_2 \quad \text{(for males)}$$

We may interpret these equations in the following way. The regression coefficient value $b_2 = .12$, which is the slope of each of the lines, is the estimated average increase in performance rating for each 1 unit increase

TABLE 5.7 *Performance Rating Output.*

VARIABLE NO.	MEAN	STANDARD DEVIATION	CORRELATION X VS Y	REGRESSION COEFFICIENT	STD. ERROR OF REG.COEF.	COMPUTED T VALUE
2	72.86665	22.90311	0.876	0.12041	0.01015	11.86
3	0.46667	0.51640	0.021	-2.18072	0.45035	-4.84

DEPENDENT

| 1 | 5.80000 | 2.59670 | | | | |

INTERCEPT		-1.95646		MULTIPLE CORRELATION		0.96
STD. ERROR OF ESTIMATE		0.78627		R SQUARED		0.92
				CORRECTED R SQUARED		0.91

ANALYSIS OF VARIANCE FOR THE REGRESSION

SOURCES OF VARIATION	DEGREES OF FREEDOM	SUM OF SQUARES	MEAN SQUARES	F VALUE
ATTRIBUTABLE TO REGRESSION	2	86.981	43.491	70.349
DEVIATION FROM REGRESSION	12	7.419	0.618	
TOTAL	14	94.400		

CORRELATION MATRIX: 3 BY 2

VAR.	1	2	3
1	1.000	0.876	0.021
2	0.876	1.000	0.428
3	0.021	0.428	1.000

in aptitude test score. This applies to both males and females. The other regression coefficient, $b_3 = -2.18$, applies only to males. If a male has taken the test, our estimated job performance rating is lowered by 2.18 units when the aptitude score is held constant.

An examination of the means of the Y and X_2 variables, classified by sex, helps us understand this result. Table 5.6 shows that the mean job performance ratings for males, 5.86, and females, 5.75, were approximately equal. However, the males scored significantly higher (83) on the aptitude test than the females (64). Therefore, if two applicants, one male and one female, took the aptitude test and both scored 70, the female's estimated job performance rating would be 2.18 points higher than the male's.

FEMALE

$$Y_R = -1.96 + 0.12X_2$$
$$Y_R = -1.96 + 0.12\,(70)$$
$$Y_R = 6.44$$

MALE

$$Y_R = -4.14 + 0.12X_2$$
$$Y_R = -4.14 + 0.12\,(70)$$
$$Y_R = 4.26$$

A look at the correlation matrix in Table 5.7 provides some interesting insights. A high linear relationship exists between job performance and the aptitude test, $r_{12} = .88$. Through our knowledge of this relationship we can explain 77 percent of the variance of the job performance rating variable ($.88^2 = .77$). The correlation coefficient, $r_{13} = .02$, indicates practically no relationship between sex and job performance. This conclusion is also evident when one considers the fact that the mean performance ratings for males and females are nearly equal (5.86 versus 5.75). At first glance, one might conclude that knowledge of whether an applicant is male or female is not useful information. However, the moderate relationship, $r_{23} = .43$, between sex and aptitude test score indicates that the test might discriminate between sexes. Males seem to do better on the test than females (83 versus 64). Perhaps some element of strength is required on the test that is not required on the job. When both test results and sex are used to estimate job performance, 92 percent of the variance is explained. This result suggests that both variables make a valuable contribution to predicting performance. The aptitude test explains 77 percent of the variance, and sex used in conjunction with the aptitude test results adds another 15 percent. Actually, an F test could be used to determine if the sex variable is making a contribution to the prediction equation or if the increase in R^2 could have been caused by sampling error.

Why can we not do just as well by calculating two separate linear regression equations, splitting the observations into separate samples for males and females? If the sample sizes are large, this would be more desirable than using dummy variables. We would then have lines with different slopes, reflecting the possibility that males increase or decrease their job performance at a different rate. However, in this illustration the number of males observed was small, thereby creating a situation with the possibility of considerable error in doing a separate regression analysis for each sex.

Collinearity

Collinearity refers to the situation in which independent variables in a multiple regression equation are highly intercorrelated. Collinearity can cause problems with respect to the following aspects of an analysis:

1. A regression coefficient that is positive in sign in a two-variable regression equation may change to a negative sign in a multiple regression equation containing other independent variables with which it is highly interrelated. (The change could be reversed, negative to positive).
2. Estimates of the regression coefficients fluctuate markedly from sample to sample.
3. Multiple regression is often used as an interpretative tool to evaluate the relative importance of various independent variables. When predictor variables are intercorrelated, they explain the same variance in the estimation of the dependent variable. For this reason it is extremely difficult to separate out the individual influences of each of the independent variables.

A multiple regression equation is developed, based on the data presented in Table 5.8. Food expenditure is estimated from a knowledge of its relationship with the variables income and family size. A quick examination of the correlation matrix for these three variables in Table 5.9 leads to the following conclusions:

1. Both income and family size are positively related to food expenditures, and have potential as good predictor variables ($r_{12} = .88$ and $r_{13} = .74$).
2. Income and family size are highly interrelated, and will probably be explaining the same portion of food expenditure variance ($r_{23} = .87$).

TABLE 5.8   *Collinearity Example.*

Family	*Yearly Food Expenditures (hundreds of dollars)* Y	*Yearly Income (thousands of dollars)* X₂	*Family Size* X₃
A	24	11	6
B	8	3	2
C	16	4	1
D	18	7	3
E	24	9	5
F	23	8	4
G	11	5	2
H	15	7	2
I	21	8	3
J	20	7	2

TABLE 5.9   *Food Expenditures: Predicted by Income and Family Size.*

VARIABLE NO.	MEAN	STANDARD DEVIATION	CORRELATION X VS Y	REGRESSION COEFFICIENT	STD ERROR OF REG.COEF.	COMPUTED T VALUE
2	6.9	2.38	.884	2.28	0.81261	2.80
3	3.0	1.56	.737	-0.41	1.23603	-0.33

DEPENDENT

1	18.0	5.5				

INTERCEPT	3.52		MULTIPLE CORRELATION		.886
STD. ERROR OF ESTIMATE	2.89		R SQUARED		0.785
			CORRECTED R SQUARED		0.723

CORRELATION MATRIX

	EXPENDITURES	INCOME	SIZE
EXPENDITURES	1.00	.88	.74
INCOME		1.00	.87
SIZE			1.00

The computer output for this example is presented in Table 5.9. The multiple regression equation is

$$Y_R = 3.52 + 2.28X_2 - 0.41X_3$$

Notice the negative regression coefficient, -0.41, for the family size (X_3) variable.

This coefficient suggests that an increase of one person in a family when yearly income is held constant *decreases* estimated yearly food expenditures by 41 dollars, regardless of whether the family earns $10,000 or $20,000. This is not logical, especially when we observe in the correlation matrix that the family size and food consumption are *positively* related, $r_{13} = .74$. Notice also when income alone is used to estimate food expenditures 78.1 percent, $(.884)^2$, of the variance is explained. When we add family size, the R^2 only increases to 78.5 percent. Evidently, family size is explaining the same variance as income, which is suggested originally by the correlation matrix.

When extreme collinearity exists, no acceptable way is available to perform multiple regression analysis using the given set of independent variables. Two suggested solutions are: (1) to use only one of the highly interrelated variables in the final equation, or (2) to create and use a new variable that is a combination of the two highly intercorrelated variables.

Selecting the Best Regression Equation

How does one develop a multiple regression equation to estimate a variable of interest? The first step involves the selection of a complete set of potential independent or predictor variables. Any variable that might add to the accuracy of the estimation is included. In the selection of a final equation we are usually faced with the dilemma of providing the most accurate prediction for the smallest cost. In other words, when we choose predictor variables to include in the final equation we must evaluate them using the following two opposed criteria:

1. We want our equation to include as many predictor variables as possible so that our estimates will be as accurate as possible. Whenever a new predictor variable is added to a multiple regression equation, the R^2 either remains unchanged or increases. As long as our sample is sufficiently large, an n of 10 for every independent variable used in the equation, every new predictor variable has the potential of improving our estimation.
2. Since it costs money to obtain and monitor information on a large number of Xs, the equation should include as few predictors as possible. The simplest equation is, therefore, the best equation.

The selection of the best regression equation usually results from a compromise between these extremes. Since no unique statistical procedure exists for developing this compromise, personal judgment will be a necessary part of any solution.

After a lengthy list of potential predictors has been compiled, the second step is to screen out the independent variables that do not seem appropriate. An independent variable: (1) may not be fundamental to the problem (it should have some plausible causality between the dependent and an independent variable), (2) may be subject to large measurement errors, (3) may duplicate other independent variables (collinearity), or (4) may be difficult to measure accurately (accurate data are unavailable or costly).

The third and final step is to shorten the list of predictors so as to obtain a "best" selection of independent variables. In this section several techniques currently in use are discussed. None of the search procedures can be said to yield the "best" set of independent variables. Indeed, there is often no unique "best" set. To add to the confusion, the various techniques do not all necessarily lead to the same final prediction equation. The entire variable-selection process is extremely subjective. For this reason the correlation matrix should be analyzed as a first step before any automatic procedure is used. The primary advantage of automatic search procedures is that the analyst can focus his judgments on the pivotal areas of the problem.

Multiple Regression Example

In order to demonstrate various search procedures, we shall use a simple example that has five potential independent variables.

The personnel manager of the Zurenko Pharmaceutical Company is interested in predicting whether a particular applicant will become a good salesperson. She decides to use the first month's sales as the dependent variable (Y), and chooses to analyze the following independent variables.

$$X_2 = \textit{Selling Aptitude Test}$$

$$X_3 = \textit{Age (years)}$$

$$X_4 = \textit{Anxiety Test Score}$$

$$X_5 = \textit{Experience (years)}$$

$$X_6 = \textit{High School G.P.A.}$$

The personnel manager collects the data shown in Table 5.10, and assigns the task of obtaining the "best" set of independent variables for predicting sales ability to her analyst (us).

TABLE 5.10 *Zurenko Pharmaceutical Company Example.*

One Month's Sales (Units)	Selling Aptitude Test Score	Age (years)	Anxiety Test Score	Previous Selling Experience (years)	H.S. G.P.A.
44	10	22.1	4.9	0	2.4
47	19	22.5	3.0	1	2.6
60	27	23.1	1.5	0	2.8
71	31	24.0	0.6	3	2.7
61	64	22.6	1.8	2	2.0
60	81	21.7	3.3	1	2.5
58	42	23.8	3.2	0	2.5
56	67	22.0	2.1	0	2.3
66	48	22.4	6.0	1	2.8
61	64	22.6	1.8	1	3.4
51	57	21.1	3.8	0	3.0
47	10	22.5	4.5	1	2.7
53	48	22.2	4.5	0	2.8
74	96	24.8	0.1	3	3.8
65	75	22.6	0.9	0	3.7
33	12	20.5	4.8	0	2.1
54	47	21.9	2.3	1	1.8
39	20	20.5	3.0	2	1.5
52	73	20.8	0.3	2	1.9
30	4	20.0	2.7	0	2.2
58	9	23.3	4.4	1	2.8
59	98	21.3	3.9	1	2.9
52	27	22.9	1.4	2	3.2
56	59	22.3	2.7	1	2.7
49	23	22.6	2.7	1	2.4
63	90	22.4	2.2	2	2.6
61	34	23.8	0.7	1	3.4
39	16	20.6	3.1	1	2.3
62	32	24.4	0.6	3	4.0
78	94	25.0	4.6	5	3.6

Our first step is to obtain a correlation matrix for all the variables from a computer program. This matrix will provide us with essential knowledge about the basic relationships between the variables.

Examination of the correlation matrix in Table 5.11 reveals that the selling aptitude test, age, experience, and GPA are positively related to sales ability and have potential as good predictor variables. The anxiety test score shows a low negative correlation with sales, and is probably not an important predictor. Further analysis indicates that GPA and age, and experience and age, are intercorrelated. It is precisely the presence

TABLE 5.11 *Correlation Matrix.*

	(1) SALES	(2) TEST	(3) AGE	(4) ANX	(5) EXP	(6) GPA
(1) SALES	1.000	.676	.798	−.296	.550	.622
(2) TEST		1.000	.228	−.222	.350	.318
(3) AGE			1.000	−.287	.540	.695
(4) ANX				1.000	−.279	−.244
(5) EXP					1.000	.312
(6) GPA						1.000

of these interrelationships that we must deal with in attempting to find the "best" possible set of explanatory variables.

It is our task to decide which of the following procedures to use: (1) all possible regressions, (2) backward elimination, or (3) stepwise regression.

1. All Possible Regressions

This procedure calls for the investigation of all possible regression equations that involve the potential independent variables. We start with an equation with no independent variables, and proceed to analyze every possible combination in order to select the best "set" of predictors.

Different criteria for comparing the various regression equations may be used with the "all possible regressions" approach. We shall discuss only the R^2 technique. The procedure first requires the fitting of every possible regression model that involves the dependent variable and any number of independent variables. Since each independent variable can either be, or not be, in the equation (two possible outcomes), and this is true for every independent variable; there are altogether 2^i equations (where i equals the number of independent variables). If there are eight independent variables to consider ($i = 8$), then $2^i = 256$ equations must be examined.

The second step in the procedure is to divide the equations into sets according to the number of parameters to be estimated.

Example $Y = \beta_0 + \beta_2 X_2 + \beta_3 X_3 + \varepsilon$

where β_0, and β_2, and β_3 are parameters*

---

* "β_0" is used so that the population parameters are easy to count. Actually, instead of "β_0", the parameter involves the requirement that the points ($\bar{Y}, \bar{X}_2, \bar{X}_3$) lie on the multiple regression plane.

All possible regression runs for the Zurenko Pharmaceutical Company example are presented in Table 5.12. Notice that Table 5.12 is divided into six sets of regression equation outcomes. This breakdown coincides with the number of parameters contained in each equation.

TABLE 5.12 R^2 *Values for All Possible Regressions for Zurenko Pharmaceutical Example.*

Independent Variables Used	Number of Parameters	Degrees of Freedom	R^2
None	1	29	0
X_2	2	28	.457
X_3	2	28	.637
X_4	2	28	.088
X_5	2	28	.302
X_6	2	28	.387
X_2, X_3	3	27	.8948
X_2, X_4	3	27	.479
X_2, X_5	3	27	.569
X_2, X_6	3	27	.641
X_3, X_4	3	27	.642
X_3, X_5	3	27	.657
X_3, X_6	3	27	.646
X_4, X_5	3	27	.324
X_4, X_6	3	27	.409
X_5, X_6	3	27	.527
X_2, X_3, X_4	4	26	.8951
X_2, X_3, X_5	4	26	.8948
X_2, X_3, X_6	4	26	.8953
X_2, X_4, X_5	4	26	.575
X_2, X_4, X_6	4	26	.646
X_2, X_5, X_6	4	26	.701
X_3, X_4, X_5	4	26	.659
X_3, X_4, X_6	4	26	.650
X_3, X_5, X_6	4	26	.669
X_4, X_5, X_6	4	26	.531
X_2, X_3, X_4, X_5	5	25	.8951
X_2, X_3, X_4, X_6	5	25	.8955
X_2, X_3, X_5, X_6	5	25	.8953
X_2, X_4, X_5, X_6	5	25	.701
X_3, X_4, X_5, X_6	5	25	.671
X_2, X_3, X_4, X_5, X_6	6	24	.8955

Step three involves the selection of the "best" set of independent variable (or variables) for each parameter grouping. The equation with the highest R^2 is considered "best." The "best" equation from each set is presented in Table 5.13.

TABLE 5.13   *Best Regression Equations for Zurenko Pharmaceutical Example.*

Number of Parameters	Independent Variables	D.F.	R^2	F
1	None	29	0	
2	X_3	28	.637	48.980
3	X_2, X_3	27	.8948	66.220
4	X_2, X_3, X_6	26	.8953	0.124
5	X_2, X_3, X_4, X_6	25	.8955	0.054
6	X_2, X_3, X_4, X_5, X_6	24	.8955	0

Step four involves making the subjective decision, "Which equation is the best?" On one hand we desire the highest R^2 possible; on the other hand, we want the simplest equation possible. It should also be noted that an n of 10 for each independent variable used is desirable, but not essential. The "all possible regressions" approach assumes that n exceeds the number of parameters.

We are attempting to find the point where adding additional independent variables is not worthwhile because it leads to a very small increase in R^2. Our example (Table 5.13) clearly indicates that adding variables after test (X_2) and age (X_3) accomplishes very little. Therefore, our final equation is

$$Y_R = b_0 + b_2 X_2 + b_3 X_3$$

and explains 89.48 percent of the variance.

The "all possible regressions" procedure is best summed up by Draper and Smith,

> In general the analysis of all regressions is quite unwarranted. While it means that the statistician has looked at all possibilities it also means he has examined a large number of regression equations which intelligent thought would often reject out of hand. The amount of computer time used is wasteful and the sheer physical effort of examining all the computer printouts is enormous when more than a few variables are being examined. Some sort of selection procedure which shortens this task is preferable.*

---

* Draper, N. R., and Smith, H., *Applied Regression Analysis*, New York: John Wiley and Sons, 1966, p. 167.

2. Backward Elimination

The backward elimination method is an improvement over the "all possible regressions" method because it attempts to examine only the "best" set of independent variables. The basic steps in the procedure are:

1. All the independent variables are included in a full model regression equation.
2. Each variable or set of variables can be analyzed by dropping them from the full model. This approach employs the following logic. If you want to know how valuable something is to you, do without it. For example, if you want to know how valuable your pants are, go to school without them. If you want to determine whether an independent variable is important, drop it out of the full model.
3. A partial F-test value is calculated to determine whether the dropped variable or set of variables is making an important contribution to explaining the dependent variable variance.

The variance ratio test or partial F-test involves the unbiased estimate of the variance explained by the different models, *divided* by the unbiased estimate of the unexplained or error variance.

The F statistic formula is

$$F = \frac{(R_F^2 - R_R^2) \,/\, (K_F - K_R)}{(1 - R_F^2) \,/\, (N - K_F)} \tag{5-6}$$

where:
R_F^2 = the R^2 for the full model
R_R^2 = the R^2 for the restricted model that is being tested
K_F = the number of linearly independent parameters to be estimated in the full model
K_R = the number of linearly independent parameters to be estimated in the restricted model
N = sample size
$R_F^2 - R_R^2$ = percent of total variance explained by the variables or variable dropped out of the full model
$1 - R_F^2$ = percent of total variance that is not explained by the full model

We analyze the Zurenko Pharmaceutical Company example using the backward elimination method.

1. A regression model containing all the independent variables is run. The $R^2 = .8955$ is significant, as determined by the F-test. If this R^2 were not significant, more variables would be added to create a new full model.

$$Y_R = b_0 + b_2X_2 + b_3X_3$$
$$+ b_4X_4 + b_5X_5 + b_6X_6 \qquad R_F^2 = 0.8955 \qquad K_F = 6$$
$$Y_R = b_0 \text{ (where } b_0 = \bar{Y}) \qquad R_R^2 = 0.0000 \qquad K_R = 1$$

$$F = \frac{(R_F^2 - R_R^2)/(K_F - K_R)}{(1 - R_F^2)/(N - K_F)} = \frac{(0.8955 - 0)/(6 - 1)}{(1 - 0.8955)/(30 - 6)}$$

$$F = \frac{0.1791}{0.004354} = 41.13 \qquad \text{.05 level critical } F_{5,24} = 2.62$$

2. The correlation matrix, Table 5.11, is examined in order to determine which variable to eliminate first. Age should be the best predictor variable because it is highly related with the dependent variable, $r_{13} = 0.798$.

3. A restricted model that does not contain the variable age is compared against the full model.

$$Y_R = b_0 + b_2X_2 + b_3X_3$$
$$+ b_4X_4 + b_5X_5 + b_6X_6 \qquad R_F^2 = 0.8955 \qquad K_F = 6$$
$$Y_R = b_0 + b_2X_2 + b_4X_4$$
$$+ b_5X_5 + b_6X_6 \qquad R_R^2 = 0.7014 \qquad K_R = 5$$

$$F = \frac{(0.8955 - 0.7014)/(6 - 5)}{(1 - 0.8955)/(30 - 6)} = \frac{0.1941}{0.004354} = 44.58$$

Since the R^2 drops dramatically, 19.41 percent, when age is eliminated from the full model, we conclude that this variable is making a contribution to the prediction of sales. The large F ratio confirms this conclusion.

4. Table 5.14 presents the results when each of the independent variables is dropped from the full model. Both the age and test variables make contributions to the prediction of sales, and should be included in the final equation.

TABLE 5.14 *Backward Elimination R^2 for Zurenko Pharmaceutical Example.*

Variable Dropped	R_R^2	Drop in R^2	Computed F	Critical F (.05 level)	Important Contribution
Test (X_2)	.6705	.2250	51.68	4.26	Yes
Age (X_3)	.7014	.1941	44.58	4.26	Yes
Anx (X_4)	.8953	.0002	0.05	4.26	No
Exp (X_5)	.8955	.0000	0.00	4.26	No
GPA (X_6)	.8951	.0004	0.09	4.26	No

Notice that we arrive at the same conclusion as with the "all possible regressions" procedure.

The backward elimination method is a satisfactory procedure that does not require as much computational time as the "all possible regressions" procedure. The technique is particularly useful to researchers who are interested in analyzing variables, and not in the estimating equation. This method is slightly inferior to stepwise regression when the analyst's task is to develop the "best" possible prediction equation.

3. Stepwise Regression

The stepwise regression search procedure adds one independent variable at a time to the model, one "step" at a time. A large number of independent variables can be handled on the computer in one run using this procedure. Essentially, this approach computes a sequence of regression equations, at each step adding or deleting an independent variable. In other words, the computer program enters variables in single steps from best to worst provided that they meet the statistical criteria established. The independent variable that explains the greatest amount of variance in the dependent variable will enter first. The next variable to enter explains the greatest amount of variance in conjunction with the first, and so on. The variable that explains the greatest amount of variance unexplained by the variables already in the model enters the equation at each step. It should be pointed out that some stepwise programs allow an independent variable, entered into the equation at an early stage, to be eliminated subsequently because of the relationships between it and other variables added to the model at later stages. To check on this the partial F statistic for each variable in the regression equation at any stage of computation is evaluated and compared with a predetermined critical point chosen from the appropriate F distribution. This provides a check on the contribution made by each variable as though it was the most recent variable entered, irrespective of when it actually entered the equation. Any variable that does not contribute is removed from the model.

Example   We solve the Zurenko example step-by-step as a stepwise regression program might operate.

1. Examine the correlation matrix in Table 5.11. Which variable is most highly related with the dependent variable, sales? *Age* shows a high relationship ($r_{13} = .798$). This variable explains the greatest percentage of variance $R^2 = (.798)^2 = .6368$ in the dependent variable, and will be entered first.
2. The model using age is compared with the model using no independent variables. (The mean of Y is the predictor.)

117

$$Y_R = b_0 + b_3 X_3 \qquad\qquad R_F^2 = 0.6368 \qquad K_F = 2$$

$$Y_R = b_0 \text{ (where } b_0 = \bar{Y}) \qquad\qquad R_R^2 = 0.0000 \qquad K_R = 1$$

$$F = \frac{(R_F^2 - R_R^2)/(K_F - K_R)}{(1 - R_F^2)/(N - K_F)} = \frac{(0.6368 - 0)/(2 - 1)}{(1 - 0.6368)/(30 - 2)} = 49.09$$

Therefore, the age variable is making a contribution to the prediction of sales.

3. We enter the variable *Test* into the equation next because it is highly related to sales, $r_{12} = .676$, and not related to age, $r_{23} = .228$. The R^2 increases to .8948.

4. The model using age and test is compared with the model using only age.

$$Y_R = b_0 + b_2 X_2 + b_3 X_3 \qquad\qquad R_F^2 = 0.8948 \qquad K_F = 3$$

$$Y_R = b_0 + b_3 X_3 \qquad\qquad R_R^2 = 0.6368 \qquad K_R = 2$$

$$F = \frac{(0.8948 - 0.6368)/(3 - 2)}{(1 - 0.8948)/(30 - 3)} = \frac{0.2580}{0.003896} = 66.22$$

Therefore, the test variable in conjunction with age is making a contribution to the prediction of sales.

5. We enter the variable GPA into the equation next because it is highly related to sales, $r_{16} = .622$. However, GPA is also highly related to age, $r_{36} = .695$, and will probably explain the same dependent variable variance. The R^2 only increases to .8953.

6. The model using age, test, and GPA is compared with the model using only age and test.

$$Y_R = b_0 + b_2 X_2 + b_3 X_3 + b_6 X_6 \qquad\qquad R_F^2 = 0.8953 \qquad K_F = 4$$

$$Y_R = b_0 + b_2 X_2 + b_3 X_3 \qquad\qquad R_R^2 = 0.8948 \qquad K_R = 3$$

$$F = \frac{(0.8953 - 0.8948)/(4 - 3)}{(1 - 0.8953)/(30 - 4)} = \frac{0.0005}{0.004027} = 0.124$$

(Critical value of F at the $\alpha = .05$ level $F_{1,26} = 4.22$) Therefore, the GPA variable in conjunction with the age and test variables is not making a contribution to the prediction of sales.

7. The example is ended at this point. Table 5.15 shows a summary of the completed stepwise regression analysis. Notice that we arrived at the same conclusion as with the "all possible regressions" procedure and "backward elimination method."

Stepwise regression is the best of the search procedures when the analyst's task is to develop the best prediction equation. It is easy to

TABLE 5.15   *Stepwise Summary Table for Zurenko Pharmaceutical Example.*

Independent Variables	D.F.	R^2	Increase In R^2	Partial F
None	29	0	0	
X_3	28	.6368	.6368	48.98
X_2, X_3	27	.8948	.2580	66.22
X_2, X_3, X_6	26	.8953	.0005	0.124
X_2, X_3, X_4, X_6	25	.8955	.0002	0.054

use because the computer program does almost all of the work. Unfortunately, this technique is easily abused by "amateur" statisticians because it is relatively automatic. Sensible judgment is sometimes not used in the initial selection of variables and/or the critical examination of the residuals. The completion of a stepwise regression run implies a "best" set of independent variables. However, if the initial list of explanatory variables includes none that are highly related to the dependent variable, this "best" set will be virtually useless.

One commonly used computer package that contains a stepwise regression program is the *Statistical Package For The Social Sciences* (SPSS). Table 5.16 illustrates the usage of the SPSS stepwise multiple regression program* on the data for the Zurenko Pharmaceutical example.

Computer Output Definitions and Computations

In order to clearly understand the terminology employed on the computer output, definitions and computations are presented below. These definitions and calculations are keyed to Table 5.16 (Step Number 3 G.P.A.) when G.P.A. is added to the model. The equation at this point is

$$Y_R = b_0 + b_2 X_2 + b_3 X_3 + b_6 X_6$$

$$K = 4 \text{ (the number of parameters to be estimated)}$$

1.   MULTIPLE R = 0.94621

The multiple R is a simple correlation coefficient r between Y and Y_R

**Statistical Package for the Social Sciences*, Second Edition, New York: McGraw-Hill Book Company, 1975, p. 345.

TABLE 5.16 *Stepwise Regression.*

DEPENDENT VARIABLE ..

VARIABLE(S) ENTERED ON STEP NUMBER 1 ..   AGE

		ANALYSIS OF VARIANCE	DF	SUM OF SQUARES	MEAN SQUARE	F
MULTIPLE R	0.79814	REGRESSION	1	2303.68306	2303.68306	49.14086
R SQUARE	0.63703	RESIDUAL	28	1312.61694	46.87918	
ADJUSTED R SQUARE	0.63703					
STANDARD ERROR	3.84684					

------- VARIABLES IN THE EQUATION-------   ------VARIABLES NOT IN THE EQUATION------

VARIABLE	B	BETA	STD ERROR B	F	VARIABLE	BETA IN	PARTIAL	TOLERANCE	F
AGE	6.96799	0.79814	0.99400	49.141	TEST	0.52141	0.84272	0.94815	66.162
(CONSTANT)	-100.85252				ANX	-0.07296	-0.11601	0.91775	0.368
					EXPR.	0.16813	0.23496	0.70887	1.578
					GPA	0.13026	0.15555	0.51757	0.669

* *

VARIABLE(S) ENTERED ON STEP NUMBER 2 ..   TEST

		ANALYSIS OF VARIANCE	DF	SUM OF SQUARES	MEAN SQUARE	F
MULTIPLE R	0.94594	REGRESSION	2	3235.88151	1617.94076	114.83249
R SQUARE	0.89480	RESIDUAL	27	380.41849	14.08957	
ADJUSTED R SQUARE	0.89105					
STANDARD ERROR	3.75361					

------- VARIABLES IN THE EQUATION-------   ------VARIABLES NOT IN THE EQUATION------

VARIABLE	B	BETA	STD ERROR B	F	VARIABLE	BETA IN	PARTIAL	TOLERANCE	F
AGE	5.93145	0.67941	0.55964	112.333	ANX	0.01653	0.04812	0.89186	0.060
TEST	0.19973	0.52141	0.02456	66.162	EXPR	0.00143	0.00357	0.65463	0.000
(CONSTANT)	-86.79156				GPA	-0.03221	-0.06956	0.49070	0.126

* * * * * * * * * * * *   MULTIPLE REGRESSION * * * * * * * * * * * *

DEPENDENT VARIABLE ..   SALES

VARIABLE(S) ENTERED ON STEP NUMBER 3 ..   GPA

		ANALYSIS OF VARIANCE	DF	SUM OF SQUARES	MEAN SQUARE	F
(1) MULTIPLE R	0.94621	REGRESSION	3	3237.72227	1079.24076	(9) 74.12021
(2) R SQUARE	0.89531	RESIDUAL	26	378.57773	14.56068	
(3) ADJUSTED R SQUARE	0.88324	(5)		(7)		
(4) STANDARD ERROR	3.81585	(6)		(8)		

VARIABLE LIST 1
REGRESSION LIST 1

-------- VARIABLES IN THE EQUATION --------   ------ VARIABLES NOT IN THE EQUATION ------

VARIABLE	B	BETA	STD ERROR B	F
AGE	(10) 6.11597	(11) 0.70055	(12) 0.77006	63.079
TEST	0.20181	0.52684	0.02564	61.967
GPA	-0.59225	-0.03221	1.66570	(13) 0.126
(CONSTANT)	-89.41502			

VARIABLE	BETA IN	PARTIAL	TOLERANCE	F
ANX	(14) 0.01586	(15) 0.04627	(16) 0.89114	(17) 0.054
EXPR	-0.00364	-0.00896	0.63391	0.002

* *

VARIABLE(S) ENTERED ON STEP NUMBER 4 .. ANX

MULTIPLE R   0.94633
R SQUARE   0.89554
ADJUSTED R SQUARE 0.88343
STANDARD ERROR   3.88725

ANALYSIS OF VARIANCE

	DF	SUM OF SQUARES	MEAN SQUARE	F
REGRESSION	4	3238.53278	809.63320	53.58017
RESIDUAL	25	377.76722	15.11069	

-------- VARIABLES IN THE EQUATION --------   ------ VARIABLES NOT IN THE EQUATION ------

VARIABLE	B	BETA	STD ERROR B	F
AGE	6.14698	0.70410	0.79581	59.662
TEST	0.20278	0.52936	0.02645	58.788
GPA	-0.58107	-0.03160	1.69756	0.117
ANX	0.11333	0.01586	0.48934	0.054
(CONSTANT)	-90.49218			

VARIABLE	BETA IN	PARTIAL	TOLERANCE	F
EXPR	-0.00140	-0.00343	0.62476	0.000

F-LEVEL OR TOLERANCE-LEVEL INSUFFICIENT FOR FURTHER COMPUTATION

DEPENDENT VARIABLE .. SALES

SUMMARY TABLE

VARIABLE	MULTIPLE R	R SQUARE	RSP CHANGE	SIMPLE R	B	BETA
AGE	0.79814	0.63703	0.63703	0.79814	6.14698	0.70410
TEST	0.94594	0.89480	0.25778	0.67612	0.20278	0.52936
GPA	0.94621	0.89531	0.00051	0.62178	-0.58107	-0.03160
ANX	0.94623	0.89554	0.00022	-0.29586	0.11333	0.01586
(CONSTANT)					-90.49218	

$$R^2 = 0.89531$$

$$\sqrt{R^2} = \sqrt{0.89531}$$

$$R = 0.94621$$

2. R SQUARE = 0.89531

The R^2 indicates the percentage of dependent variable (sales) variance explained by the multiple regression equation, using independent variables age, test, and G.P.A.

$$R^2 = 1 - \frac{\Sigma(Y + Y_R)^2}{\Sigma(Y - \bar{Y})^2}$$

$$R^2 = 1 - \frac{378.58}{3616.30}$$

$$R^2 = 1 - 0.104687$$

$$R^2 = 0.89531$$

3. ADJUSTED R SQUARE = 0.88324

The R^2 adjusted for the appropriate degrees of freedom.

$$R_c^2 = 1 - \frac{\dfrac{\Sigma(Y - Y_R)^2}{n - k}}{\dfrac{\Sigma(Y - \bar{Y})^2}{n - 1}} = 1 - \frac{\dfrac{378.58}{30 - 4}}{\dfrac{3616.3}{30 - 1}}$$

$$R_c^2 = 1 - \frac{14.56}{124.7} = 1 - 0.11676$$

$$R_c^2 = 0.88324$$

4. STANDARD ERROR = 3.81585

The standard error of the estimate is the standard deviation of the residuals or the typical scatter of Y values around the regression plane.

$$S_{y \cdot x_2 x_3 x_6} = \sqrt{\frac{\Sigma(Y - Y_R)^2}{n - k}} = \sqrt{\frac{378.58}{30 - 4}} = \sqrt{14.56} = 3.81585$$

5. SUM OF SQUARES REGRESSION = 3237.72

The sum of squares explained or accounted for by the regression plane is the difference between the mean of Y ($\bar{Y}$) and the predicted Y (Y_R) squared and summed.

$$\Sigma(\bar{Y} - Y_R)^2 = 3237.72$$

6. **SUM OF SQUARES RESIDUAL = 378.58**

The sum of squared residuals is the difference between the actual Y and the predicted $Y(Y_R)$ squared and summed (sometimes referred to as the error sum of squares).

$$\Sigma(Y - Y_R)^2 = 378.58$$

7. **MEAN SQUARE REGRESSION = 1079.24**

This is the amount of variance explained by the regression plane.

$$\frac{\Sigma(\bar{Y} - Y_R)^2}{k - 1} = \frac{3237.72}{4 - 1} = 1079.24$$

8. **MEAN SQUARE RESIDUAL = 14.56**

The unexplained or error variance is the variance of the residuals or the typical scatter of Y values around the regression plane squared.

$$S^2_{y \cdot x_2 x_3 x_6} = \frac{\Sigma(Y - Y_R)^2}{N - k} = \frac{378.58}{30 - 4} = 14.56$$

9. **F = 74.12**

The F ratio or variance ratio test involves the unbiased estimate of explained variance divided by the unbiased estimate of error variance. The model containing age, test, and G.P.A. is compared against the model that uses the mean of Y ($\bar{Y}$).

$$F = \frac{(R_F^2 - R_R^2)/(K_F - K_R)}{(1 - R_F^2)/(N - K_F)} = \frac{(0.89531 - 0)/(4 - 1)}{(1 - 0.89531)/(30 - 4)} = 74.12$$

10. The prediction equation for the run using the predictor's age, test, and G.P.A. is

$$Y_R = -89.41502 + 0.20181\,X_2 + 6.11597\,X_3 - 0.59225\,X_6$$

where: X_2 = test
X_3 = age
X_6 = G.P.A.

The b_3 for the variable age equals 6.11597. This regression coefficient indicates that an increase of one year in the age of applicants with the same test score and G.P.A. increases sales by 6.1 units.

11. **BETA for the Variable AGE = 0.70055**

The regression coefficient B is in standard score form (Standardized regression coefficient).

12. **STD ERROR B = 0.77006**

The standard error of the regression coefficient is the sampling error (standard deviation) associated with using the regression coefficient b_2 as an estimate of the population parameter B_2.

13. **$F = .126$**

   This is the partial F ratio that tests the variance explained by adding G.P.A. to the model.

$$F = \frac{(R_F^2 - R_R^2)/(K_F - K_R)}{(1 - R_F^2)/(N - K_F)} = \frac{(0.89531 - 0.89480)/(4 - 3)}{(1 - 0.89531)/(30 - 4)}$$

$$F = \frac{0.00051}{0.00403} = 0.126$$

where: $R_F^2 = 0.89531$ $\quad Y_R = b_0 + b_2 X_2 + b_3 X_3 + b_6 X_6 \quad$ $K_F = 4$

$\qquad\qquad R_R^2 = 0.89480$ $\quad Y_R = b_0 + b_2 X_2 + b_3 X_3 \qquad\quad$ $K_R = 3$

14. **BETA**

   This is the standardized regression coefficient that will enter the standard score regression equation if the anxiety variable enters the model.

15. **PARTIAL for the Variable ANX = 0.04627**

   The partial correlation coefficient involves the computation of a correlation coefficient for the dependent variable as acted upon by one independent variable while the remaining variables are held constant. The partial coefficient gives an indication of the relative importance of each of the variables not yet in the regression equation. It indicates which variable would have the greatest affect in reducing unexplained variance if added to the model.

16. **TOLERANCE for the Variable ANX = 0.89114**

   The proportion of the variance is of the anxiety variable not explained by the independent variables already in the regression equation (age, test, and G.P.A.). The tolerance of 0.89114 indicates that 89.1 percent of the variance of the anxiety variable is unexplained by the predictors already entered in the equation.

17. **$F = 0.054$**

   This is the partial F ratio that tests the variance explained by adding ANX to the model.

$$F = \frac{(R_F^2 - R_R^2)/(K_F - K_R)}{(1 - R_F^2)/(N - K_F)} = \frac{(0.89554 - 0.89531)/(5 - 4)}{(1 - 0.89554)/(30 - 5)}$$

$$F = \frac{0.00023}{0.0041784} = 0.054$$

where: $R_F^2 = 0.89554$ $Y_R = b_0 + b_2X_2 + b_3X_3 + b_4X_4 + b_6X_6$ $K_F = 5$
       $R_R^2 = 0.89531$ $Y_R = b_0 + b_2X_2 + b_3X_3 + b_6X_6$ $K_R = 4$

Overfitting

Overfitting involves the selection of a model that matches the eccentricities of the sample data under analysis. When such a model is applied to new sets of data selected from the same population, it does not perform in nearly the same manner.

Overfitting is more likely to occur when the sample size is small. This is especially true if a large number of independent variables are included in the model. Experience has indicated that sample size should include an n of 10 for each independent variable (If we have 4 independent variables, we need a sample size of at least 40).

One way to guard against overfitting is to develop the model from one part of the data and then to apply the results to another segment. If the model takes into account primarily the eccentricities of the particular sample from which it has been developed, this should show up when the estimating errors from the two sets are compared. If a comparable measure of the average squared error $[\Sigma(Y - Y_R)^2]/(n - k)$ is substantially larger from the set that used the model to estimate new observations, we would know that overfitting occurred. Question 13 in the Problems Section of this chapter provides an opportunity to apply this technique.

Summary

Multiple regression measures the simultaneous effect of more than one independent variable upon one dependent variable. Independent variables contribute to the prediction of a dependent variable if they are related to it, but not to each other. A net regression coefficient measures the average change in the dependent variable per unit change in the relevant independent variable. Because of the cost and tedious labor involved in multiple regression analysis, computer programs are frequently used.

PROBLEMS

1. Most computer solutions for multiple regression begin with a correlation matrix. This should be the first step when analyzing a problem that involves more than one independent variable. Answer the following questions concerning this correlation matrix.

Correlation Matrix

Variable Number	1	2	3	4	5	6
1	1.00	0.55	0.20	−0.51	0.79	0.70
2		1.00	0.27	0.09	0.39	0.45
3			1.00	0.04	0.17	0.21
4				1.00	−0.44	−0.14
5					1.00	0.69
6						1.00

a. Why are all the entries on the primary diagonal equal to one?

b. Why is the bottom half of the matrix below the primary diagonal blank?

c. If variable 1 is the dependent variable, which independent variables have the highest degree of relationship with variable 1?

d. What kind of relationship exists between variables 1 and 4?

e. Does this correlation matrix show any evidence of collinearity?

f. In your opinion, which variable or variables will be included in the best prediction model? Explain why.

g. If the problem is run on a stepwise program, which variable will be entered first?

*2. Beer sales at the Shapiro One-Step Store are analyzed using temperature and number of people (21 or over) on the street as predictor variables. A regression is run using the following variables:

$$Y = Number\ of\ Six\text{-}Packs\ of\ Beer\ Sold\ Each\ Day$$

$$X_2 = High\ Temperature$$

$$X_3 = Traffic\ Count$$

A random sample of 20 days are selected. The partial computer output yields the following data:

CORRELATION MATRIX: 3 BY 3

VAR.	1	2	3
1	1.000	0.827	0.822
2	0.827	1.000	0.680
3	0.822	0.680	1.000

VARIABLE NO.	MEAN	STANDARD DEVIATION	REGRESSION COEFFICIENT	STD. ERROR OF REG. COEF.
2	64.09999	17.46243	0.78207	0.22694
3	537.54980	195.59874	0.06795	0.02026

```
DEPENDENT

    1           59.95000    27.45038

INTERCEPT      -26.70621
```

ANALYSIS OF VARIANCE FOR THE REGRESSION

SOURCE OF VARIATION	DEGREES OF FREEDOM	SUM OR SQUARES	MEAN SQUARES	F VALUE
ATTRIBUTABLE TO REGRESSION	2	11589.03500	5794.51560	36.11064
DEVIATION FROM REGRESSION	17	2727.91400	160.46553	
TOTAL	19	14316.94900		

    a. Analyze the correlation matrix.
    b. Test the significance of the net regression coefficients at the .01 significance level.
    c. Estimate the volume of beer sold if the high temperature is 60 degrees and the traffic count is 500 people.
    d. Calculate the R^2, and interpret its meaning in terms of this problem.
    e. Calculate the standard error of estimate.
    f. Explain how beer sales are affected by an increase of one degree in the high temperature.
    g. State your conclusions for this analysis concerning the accuracy of the prediction equation and also the contributions of the predictor variables.

3. Define, discuss, and give an example of each of the following terms:
    a. *collinearity*
    b. *dummy variable*
    c. *backward elimination*
    d. *stepwise regression*
    e. *net regression coefficient*

*4. The sales manager of a large automotive parts distributor, Hartman Auto Supplies, wants to develop a model to estimate as early as May the total annual sales of a region. If regional sales can be predicted, then the total sales for the company can be estimated. The number of retail outlets in the region stocking the company's parts and the number of automobiles registered for each region as of May 1 are the two predictor variables investigated. The data appears below:

Region	Annual Sales (millions) Y	Number of Retail Outlets X_2	Number of Automobiles Registered (millions) X_3
1	52.3	2011	24.6
2	26.0	2850	22.1
3	20.2	650	7.9

Region	Annual Sales (millions) Y	Number of Retail Outlets X_2	Number of Automobiles Registered (millions) X_3
4	16.0	480	12.5
5	30.0	1694	9.0
6	46.2	2302	11.5
7	35.0	2214	20.5
8	3.5	125	4.1
9	33.1	1840	8.9
10	25.2	1233	6.1
11	38.2	1699	9.5

a. Analyze the correlation matrix.
b. How much error is involved in the prediction for region 1?
c. Estimate the annual sales for Region 12, given 2500 retail outlets and 20.2 million automobiles registered
d. Discuss the accuracy of the estimate made in part (c).
e. Show how the standard error of estimate was computed.
f. Give an interpretation of the net regression coefficients. Are these regression coefficients valid?
g. How can this regression equation be improved?

5. The sales manager of Hartman Auto Supplies decides to investigate a new independent variable, personal income by region. The data for this new variable are presented below:

Region	Personal Income (billions)
1	98.5
2	31.1
3	34.8
4	32.7
5	68.8
6	94.7
7	67.6
8	19.7
9	67.9
10	61.4
11	85.6

a. Does personal income by region make a contribution to the prediction of sales?
b. Estimate annual sales for Region 12 for personal income of 40 billion, using all three predictor variables.

   c. Discuss the accuracy of the estimate made in part (b).

   d. Which predictor variables would you include in your final prediction model? Why?

*6. The Nelson Corporation decides to analyze the variation in sales performance for a random sample of 14 salespeople. The salespeople are interviewed and given an aptitude test. Also, an index of effort expended is calculated for each salesperson on the basis of a ratio of the mileage on his/her company car to the total mileage projected for adequate coverage of his/her sales territory. Regression analysis yields the following results.

$$Y_R = 16.57 + \underset{(0.05)}{0.65} \ X_2 + \underset{(1.69)}{20.6} \ X_3$$

The quantities in parentheses are the standard errors of the net regression coefficients. The standard error of estimate is 3.56. The standard deviation of the sales variable is $s_y = 16.57$. The variables are

$$Y = \textit{Sales Performance (thousands)}$$

$$X_2 = \textit{Aptitude Test Score}$$

$$X_3 = \textit{Effort Index}$$

   a. Are the net regression coefficients significantly different from zero at the .01 significance level?

   b. Interpret the net regression coefficient for the effort index.

   c. Calculate a corrected R-squared.

   d. Estimate the sales performance for a salesperson who has an aptitude test score of 75 and an effort index of 0.5.

   e. Calculate the sum of the squared residuals, $\Sigma(Y - Y_R)^2$.

   f. Calculate the total sum of squares, $\Sigma(Y - \bar{Y})^2$.

   g. Calculate R-squared and interpret what it means in terms of this problem.

7. The Profit Corporation administers a thirty minute test in order to aid in the selection of salespeople for an expensive training program. The test is an achievement test designed to measure knowledge of leisure-time activities and current events. The applicant is also asked if he or she graduated from college, and the response is recorded as a one (1) if they graduated and a zero (0) if not. In order to evaluate the effectiveness of this approach, sales records for the past three months are checked for 15 salespeople chosen at random. This data along with test scores and college graduate information are presented below.

3 Month Sales (units)	Test Score	College Graduate
690	26	1 (G)
950	30	1 (G)
265	7	0
325	15	0

3 Month Sales (units)	Test Score	College Graduate
410	10	1 (G)
685	25	0
430	15	0
290	10	0
705	19	1 (G)
275	11	0
325	16	0
290	9	0
555	14	1 (G)
600	22	0
810	23	1 (G)

a. Plot the data using zeros and ones.
b. State the equation that would be used for prediction purposes.
c. How effective is the prediction equation?
d. Interpret the net regression coefficients.
e. Estimate the three-month sales of a person who graduated from college and scored 25 on the test.
f. Graph the two separate equations; i.e., one equation for college graduates and one equation for non-graduates.
g. Discuss the contribution of both predictor variables to the final estimation of sales.

*8. Mr. Palmer, the owner of a mobile home sales lot, wishes to predict gross sales. He randomly selects data for 40 months on the following four variables.

X_2 = Number of Salesmen Employed
X_3 = Average Monthly Temperatures
X_4 = Number of Different Mobile Lines in Inventory During the Month
X_5 = Advertising Expenditures

Gross Sales (thousands) Y	Number of Salesmen X_2	Average Temperatures X_3	Number of Lines X_4	Advertising X_5
$ 54.3	5	16.3	6	$ 716
79.9	7	26.1	9	792
57.1	5	35.9	8	492
89.3	7	46.2	8	650
115.0	11	57.4	15	865
126.0	12	65.2	16	1293
76.5	10	67.4	7	790
81.1	7	67.1	7	802
56.7	6	59.8	8	484

Gross Sales (thousands) Y	Number of Salesmen X_2	Average Temperatures X_3	Number of Lines X_4	Advertising X_5
138.8	11	43.7	16	1501
47.9	7	36.3	5	326
42.5	7	29.4	4	202
39.4	5	25.9	5	215
68.9	5	36.3	10	609
60.3	7	37.0	10	600
87.7	8	41.6	13	764
46.9	6	54.9	6	304
44.2	6	66.2	8	252
84.4	8	72.5	5	746
64.1	5	70.2	8	629
115.3	11	54.2	8	1044
40.7	5	44.9	4	158
79.2	5	36.0	7	716
39.5	4	27.9	5	176
14.7	4	31.8	6	102
24.1	5	33.6	4	209
117.3	10	35.2	11	1501
67.9	7	45.3	9	631
73.2	10	56.3	11	692
63.7	10	58.2	6	618
36.1	7	69.7	5	140
58.6	5	74.1	6	544
97.2	7	55.2	11	901
41.8	5	44.2	4	100
93.9	6	35.4	9	862
21.8	5	25.8	2	175
17.3	3	22.6	4	111
65.9	6	30.7	7	594
32.4	4	41.4	7	131
61.1	6	42.0	9	589

a. Analyze the correlation matrix.
b. Discuss the importance of each predictor variable.
c. Which regression equation should Mr. Palmer use to estimate gross sales if he wishes to include all of the statistically significant predictor variables? Use the .01 significance level.
d. Which regression equation would you advise Mr. Palmer to use? Why?
e. Is collinearity a problem in the equation chosen in part (c), and, if so, what effects might it have?
f. Estimate gross sales, given

- 4 salesmen employed,
- 40° average temperature for the month,

131

- 5 different mobile lines in inventory, and
- $750 advertising expenditures.

     [Note: Use the equation you selected in part (d)]
  g. Discuss the accuracy of this prediction.

9. The Print & Run Advertising Agency decides to analyze the effectiveness of each of their four production departments. The agency wants to know if all, or any, of the four departments contributed to the gross sales of the business firms that used the agency during 1971.

- The four production departments within the agency are: (1) newspaper advertising, (2) magazine advertising, (3) television advertising, and (4) radio advertising.
- Each department is self-contained and does all the work for that particular type of media.
- The regression analysis is developed by using each department as a predictor variable and by using the gross sales of each firm as the dependent variable.
- The sales figure is the gross dollar amount of sales, for the year 1971, for each company in the analysis. The 41 firms used in the analysis are randomly picked from the total firms that used the services of the agency during the year 1971.

Firm	Total Sales	Newspaper Advertising	Magazine Advertising	Television Advertising	Radio Advertising
1	20.50	4.09	2.87	4.00	1.09
2	10.70	1.36	0.78	0.68	1.03
3	7.00	0.39	0.25	0.89	0.30
4	28.00	2.07	2.16	2.27	1.50
5	30.00	2.57	1.19	0.00	1.40
6	13.50	1.26	0.41	2.08	0.45
7	17.00	4.43	1.73	6.26	0.00
8	28.00	1.01	0.28	1.70	0.40
9	22.00	2.30	7.20	7.40	0.00
10	15.00	2.61	1.50	5.16	1.40
11	10.00	0.89	0.23	1.44	0.35
12	11.50	0.15	1.62	0.56	0.70
13	30.00	3.45	5.21	1.30	9.34
14	99.00	0.57	0.21	2.30	0.40
15	10.00	1.16	0.32	0.00	2.40
16	11.50	2.48	2.79	0.00	1.75
17	38.50	9.98	4.90	6.82	2.97
18	8.50	2.03	0.74	1.34	0.80
19	7.00	0.00	1.93	3.19	0.77
20	33.00	4.00	7.81	6.72	3.00
21	14.00	4.42	1.04	2.74	0.55
22	8.00	0.12	0.17	0.28	1.70
23	30.00	1.54	6.93	3.90	5.70
24	15.00	0.47	0.10	0.22	5.00

Firm	Total Sales	Newspaper Advertising	Magazine Advertising	Television Advertising	Radio Advertising
25	18.00	0.60	1.30	2.70	0.40
26	30.00	3.27	4.34	2.10	1.70
27	13.00	1.03	1.27	0.50	2.14
28	10.50	1.05	0.12	0.94	0.00
29	9.80	0.55	0.30	0.00	2.35
30	22.00	0.39	0.01	7.00	5.00
31	11.00	2.24	1.64	1.38	0.60
32	45.50	8.88	3.52	9.20	0.53
33	9.00	2.37	1.07	0.37	1.40
34	10.00	0.65	0.77	1.14	2.03
35	10.00	0.48	1.52	0.00	2.93
36	18.50	2.66	2.64	1.69	0.41
37	7.50	0.29	0.72	0.60	0.35
38	17.50	3.14	1.72	2.32	0.60
39	9.50	0.10	1.03	0.52	2.75
40	20.50	3.03	0.33	0.12	0.78
41	8.00	0.29	0.18	2.14	1.73

NOTE: All data is in millions and each column is the amount spent by each firm.

    a. Analyze the effectiveness of each of the four production departments.

    b. Analyze the effectiveness of each production department *variable* as a predictor of a firm's total sales using the backward elimination method. (Use the .01 significance level.)

    c. Does the analysis show any evidence of collinearity; and, if so, how does this affect the analysis?

    d. Predict the gross dollar sales for a company that budgets one million for advertising and that contracts with Print & Run to have it divided between the departments equally. Use the full model.

    e. Discuss the accuracy of your prediction in part d.

    f. What regression equation would you use to predict a firm's sales?

10. A researcher is interested in determining what variables influence a person's prejudice toward outgroups. She decides to investigate social class, dogmatism, and authoritarianism. Twenty-two persons are selected randomly and are classified as either working class (1) or middle-upper class (0). Each participant is given instruments and the following data are collected: (Test at the .05 significance level.)

Attitude Toward Outgroup Y	Social Class X_2	Dogmatism X_3	Authoritarianism X_4
9	0	8	5
5	1	8	4
10	0	7	3
2	0	4	2

Attitude Toward Outgroup Y	Social Class X_2	Dogmatism X_3	Authoritarianism X_4
8	1	7	4
2	1	5	2
6	1	5	9
1	1	4	1
5	0	5	10
2	1	3	1
9	0	5	9
4	1	6	3
10	0	9	8
4	1	4	4
7	0	8	6
7	0	6	5
6	1	8	6
7	0	4	7
3	1	6	3
3	1	3	5
8	0	2	7
7	0	3	7

Discuss the relative contributions of the three independent variables to the prediction of attitude toward outgroups.

11. Ms. Haight, a real estate broker, wishes to estimate the importance of four factors in determining the prices of lots. She accumulates data on price, area, elevation, and slope, and rates the view for 50 lots. She runs the data on a correlation program and obtains the following matrix.

Correlation Matrix

Variable	Price	Area	Elevation	Slope	View
Price	1.00	.59	.66	.68	.88
Area		1.00	.04	.64	.41
Elevation			1.00	.13	.76
Slope				1.00	.63
View					1.00

Ms. Haight runs the data on a stepwise multiple regression program.
a. Determine which variable would enter the model first, second, third, and last.
b. Which variable or variables will be included in the best prediction equation?

*12. Mr. Smith, the manager of a real estate office, assigns Stu Ross, a recent college graduate, the task of developing a more scientific approach to fixing an accurate price for the resale of residential property. Stu surveys the information provided by the Multiple Listing Exchange and decides to include the following variables in a multiple regression equation.

134

$$Y = Price$$

$$X_2 = Number\ of\ Bedrooms$$

$$X_3 = Number\ of\ Bathrooms$$

$$X_4 = Number\ of\ Showers$$

$$X_5 = Number\ of\ Fireplaces$$

$$X_6 = Size\ of\ Basement\ in\ Percent\ of\ Main\ Floor\ Square\ Feet$$

$$X_7 = Number\ of\ Cars\ That\ Could\ Be\ Sheltered$$

$$X_8 = Square\ Feet\ of\ Floor\ Space$$

Stu ran the data on the SPSS stepwise, multiple regression program, and obtained the results that follow for a sample of 70 listings.

CORRELATION MATRIX

	PRICE	BED	BATH	SHOWER	FIRE	BASE	CARS	FLOOR
PRICE	1.00	0.47	0.76	0.67	0.70	0.18	0.52	0.87
BED	0.47	1.00	0.44	0.31	0.47	0.22	0.22	0.54
BATH	0.76	0.44	1.00	0.74	0.67	0.03	0.43	0.70
SHOWER	0.67	0.31	0.74	1.00	0.70	0.29	0.45	0.56
FIRE	0.70	0.47	0.67	0.70	1.00	0.36	0.40	0.59
BASE	0.18	0.22	0.03	0.29	0.36	1.00	0.29	0.11
CARS	0.52	0.22	0.43	0.45	0.40	0.29	1.00	0.44
FLOOR	0.87	0.54	0.70	0.56	0.59	0.11	0.44	1.00

MULTIPLE REGRESSION

DEPENDENT VARIABLE .. PRICE
VARIABLE(S) ENTERED ON STEP NUMBER 1 .. FLOOR

		ANALYSIS OF VARIANCE	DF	SUM OF SQUARES	MEAN SQUARE	F
MULTIPLE R	0.87					
R SQUARE	0.76	REGRESSION	1	8915044631.78	8915044631.78	226.8
ADJUSTED R SQUARE	0.76	RESIDUAL	68	2672873582.50	39306964.44	
STANDARD ERROR	6269.52					

--------VARIABLES IN THE EQUATION-----

VARIABLE	8	STD ERROR B	F
FLOOR	21.80	1.44	226.8
(CONSTANT)	-3057.89		

--------VARIABLES NOT IN THE EQUATION----

VARIABLE	PARTIAL	TOLERANCE	F
BED	-0.00	0.69	0.0
BATH	0.41	0.49	13.6
SHOWER	0.45	0.68	17.5
FIRE	0.45	0.64	17.6
BASE	0.18	0.98	2.3
CARS	0.29	0.79	6.5

* *

```
MULTIPLE REGRESSION

VARIABLE(S) ENTERED ON STEP NUMBER 2..        FIRE
```

MULTIPLE R	0.90	ANALYSIS OF VARIANCE	DF	SUM OF SQUARES	MEAN SQUARE	F
R SQUARE	0.81	REGRESSION	2	9472387587.70	4736193793.85	150.0
ADJUSTED R SQUARE	0.81	RESIDUAL	67	2115530626.57	31575083.97	
STANDARD ERROR	5619.17					

```
-------VARIABLES IN THE EQUATION--------    -------VARIABLES NOT IN THE EQUATION-----
```

VARIABLE	B	STD ERROR B	F	VARIABLE	PARTIAL	TOLERANCE	F
FLOOR	17.71	1.62	119.4	BED	-0.12	0.66	1.0
FIRE	4003.02	952.79	17.6	BATH	0.25	0.39	4.7
(CONSTANT)	-1993.21			SHOWER	0.27	0.47	5.4
				BASE	0.01	0.84	0.0
				CARS	0.24	0.76	4.0

```
* * * * * * * * * * * * * * * * * * * * * * * * * * * * * * * * * * * * * * * * *

DEPENDENT VARIABLE ..    PRICE
VARIABLE(S) ENTERED ON STEP NUMBER 3..    SHOWER
```

MULTIPLE R	0.91	ANALYSIS OF VARIANCE	DF	SUM OF SQUARES	MEAN SQUARE	F
R SQUARE	0.83	REGRESSION	3	9633622491.30	3211207497.10	108.4
ADJUSTED R SQUARE	0.82	RESIDUAL	66	1954295722.98	29610541.25	
STANDARD ERROR	5441.55					

```
-------VARIABLES IN THE EQUATION-------    -------VARIABLES NOT IN THE EQUATION-----
```

VARIABLE	B	STD ERROR B	F	VARIABLE	PARTIAL	TOLERANCE	F
FLOOR	16.75	1.62	106.2	BED	-0.08	0.64	0.4
FIRE	2591.39	1103.30	5.5	BATH	0.15	0.31	1.6
SHOWER	2753.47	1179.98	5.4	BASE	-0.01	0.83	0.0
(CONSTANT)	-2577.12			CARS	0.19	0.73	2.5

```
* * * * * * * * * * * * * * * * * * * * * * * * * * * * * * * * * * * * * * * * *

VARIABLE(S) ENTERED ON STEP NUMBER 4..    CARS
```

MULTIPLE R	0.91	ANALYSIS OF VARIANCE	DF	SUM OF SQUARES	MEAN SQUARE	F
R SQUARE	0.83	REGRESSION	4	9707899599.40	2426974899.85	83.9
ADJUSTED R SQUARE	0.83	RESIDUAL	65	1880018614.88	28923363.30	
STANDARD ERROR	5378.04					

```
MULTIPLE REGRESSION

-------VARIABLES IN THE EQUATION-------    -------VARIABLES NOT IN THE EQUATION-------
```

VARIABLE	B	STD ERROR B	F	VARIABLE	PARTIAL	TOLERANCE	F
FLOOR	16.15	1.64	96.2	BED	-0.07	0.64	0.3
FIRE	2501.19	1091.88	5.2	BATH	0.15	0.31	1.5
SHOWER	2352.52	1192.74	3.8	BASE	-0.05	0.80	0.1
CARS	1504.04	938.55	2.5				
(CONSTANT)	-3334.60						

```
* * * * * * * * * * * * * * * * * * * * * * * * * * * * * * * * * * * * * * * * *
```

```
DEPENDENT VARIABLE..       PRICE
VARIABLE(S) ENTERED ON STEP NUMBER 5..      BATH
MULTIPLE R          0.91   ANALYSIS OF VARIANCE  DF   SUM OF SQUARES   MEAN SQUARE     F
R SQUARE            0.84   REGRESSION             5   9752267915.43   1950453583.08  68.0
ADJUSTED R SQUARE   0.83   RESIDUAL              64   1835650298.85     28682035.91
STANDARD ERROR   5355.56
-------VARIABLES IN THE EQUATION-------   -------VARIABLES NOT IN THE EQUATION-------
VARIABLE       B      STD ERROR B     F   VARIABLE    PARTIAL    TOLERANCE        F
FLOOR       15.13         1.83      67.9  BED          -0.08       0.64         0.5
FIRE      2242.77      1106.99       4.1  BASE          0.00       0.68         0.0
SHOWER    1620.55      1325.56       1.4
CARS      1473.45       934.95       2.4
BATH      2259.81      1816.94       1.5
(CONSTANT) -4445.72
* * * * * * * * * * * * * * * * * * * * * * * * * * * * * * * * * * * * * * * * * *
VARIABLE(S) ENTERED ON STEP NUMBER 6..      BED
MULTIPLE R          0.91   ANALYSIS OF VARIANCE  DF   SUM OF SQUARES   MEAN SQUARE     F
R SQUARE            0.84   REGRESSION             6   9767043276.12   1627840546.02  56.3
ADJUSTED R SQUARE   0.83   RESIDUAL              63   1820874938.15     28902776.79
STANDARD ERROR   5376.13
-------VARIABLES IN THE EQUATION-------   -------VARIABLES NOT IN THE EQUATION-------
VARIABLE       B      STD ERROR B     F   VARIABLE    PARTIAL    TOLERANCE        F
FLOOR       15.59         1.95      63.7  BASE          0.02       0.66         0.0
FIRE      2452.55      1149.32       4.5
SHOWER    1469.45      1347.33       1.1
CARS      1438.22       939.83       2.3
BATH      2359.81      1829.27       1.6
BED       -724.39      1013.15       0.5
(CONSTANT) -2888.55
MULTIPLE REGRESSION

DEPENDENT VARIABLE ..       PRICE
VARIABLE(S) ENTERED ON STEP NUMBER 7 ..      BASE
MULTIPLE R          0.91   ANALYSIS OF VARIANCE  DF   SUM OF SQUARES   MEAN SQUARE     F
R SQUARE            0.84   REGRESSION             7   9767830524.81   1395404360.68  47.5
ADJUSTED R SQUARE   0.82   RESIDUAL              62   1820087689.46     29356253.05
STANDARD ERROR   5418.14

-------VARIABLES IN THE EQUATION-------

VARIABLE       B      STD ERROR B      F
FLOOR       15.62         1.97       62.5
FIRE      2391.35      1217.09        3.8
SHOWER    1409.56      1406.25        1.0
CARS      1399.06       976.90        2.0
BATH      2490.49      2008.89        1.5
BED       -756.92      1040.21        0.5
```

```
BASE           3.83      23.42        0.0
(CONSTANT)  -3152.47
```

★ ★

DEPENDENT VARIABLE ..   PRICE

SUMMARY TABLE

VARIABLE	MULTIPLE R	R SQUARE	RSQ CHANGE	SIMPLE R	B
FLOOR	0.877	0.769	0.769	0.877	15.62
FIRE	0.904	0.817	0.048	0.701	2391.35
SHOWER	0.911	0.831	0.013	0.675	1409.56
CARS	0.915	0.837	0.006	0.522	1399.06
BATH	0.917	0.841	0.003	0.761	2490.49
BED	0.918	0.842	0.001	0.479	-756.92
BASE	0.918	0.842	0.000	0.189	3.83
(CONSTANT)					-3152.47

a. Analyze the correlation matrix.

b. Which variables will enter the model first and second?

The following questions refer to step number 2 in Problem 12:

c. What is the simple correlation coefficient between Y and Y_R?

d. What percentage of the *price* variable variance is being explained by this model?

e. Two-thirds or 68% of the prices should fall within what distance of the price estimated from the regression plane?

f. Show how the $F = 150$ was calculated.

g. Interpret the meaning of the F ratio in part (f) in terms of the variables involved.

h. State the regression equation that would be used to estimate price for this model.

i. Interpret the regression coefficient for the floor space variable for this model.

j. What is the standard deviation of the sampling distribution associated with using the regression coefficient $b_8 = 17.71$ as an estimate of the population parameter B_8?

k. Show how the partial F ratio, 17.6, was calculated.

l. Interpret the meaning of the F ratio in part (k) in terms of the variables involved.

m. Which variable will have the greatest effect in reducing unexplained variance if added to this model?

n. What proportion of the variance of the bedroom variable is not explained by the independent variables already in the regression equation?

o. Show how the standard error of estimate was calculated for this model.

p. Show how the corrected R_c^2 was calculated for this model.

The following questions refer to the entire computer output:

q. Which model should Stu use to predict the price of lots? Base this decision on the .01 level of significance.

r. Would Stu's decision change for part (q) if he used the .05 level of significance? If so, how?

s. Estimate the price of a lot for a home that has 3 bedrooms, 3 bathrooms, 2 showers, 1 fireplace, no basement, a 2-car garage, and 1800 square feet of floor space. Use the equation you selected in part (q).

13. In this problem our objective is to build a model relating median family income to one or more independent variables. The variables are:

Y = *Median Family Income*

X_2 = *Weekly Earnings of Production Workers in Manufacturing Industries*

X_3 = *Median Monthly Housing Rent*

X_4 = *Non-White Population* (thousands)

X_5 = *The Percent of Occupied Households with 1.01 or More Persons Per Room.*

The following population of 200 standard Metropolitan Statistical Areas is obtained from the *Statistical Abstract, 1972.*

a. Choose a random sample of 40 areas and develop a good regression model to estimate median family income.

b. Investigate the contribution of each independent variable to the prediction of median family income.

c. Since a population of 200 is available, new random samples can be drawn. You can then validate the model developed in part (a). In order to test the predictive power of your model, draw a sample of 10 new statistical areas. Use this data and your equation to predict median family income. Now compare your estimates of median income, Y_R, with the actual median income, Y. Evaluate the accuracy of your model by calculating $\Sigma(Y - Y_R)^2$ for the 10 new areas.

Areas	Median Family Income Y	Weekly Earnings X_2	Median Rent X_3	Non-white Population X_4	% Households 1.01 Or More Persons Per Room X_5
1	11047	167	99	56	5.9
2	11056	173	97	60	5.6
3	11049	169	95	57	5.8
4	11038	163	92	52	6.1
5	11051	170	96	58	5.7
6	10655	149	77	27	4.4
7	10647	142	74	25	4.8
8	10639	140	72	29	5.1
9	10662	153	80	29	4.1
10	10659	151	79	28	4.3
11	9013	115	88	15	10.5
12	9022	119	90	17	9.9

Areas	Median Family Income Y	Weekly Earnings X_2	Median Rent X_3	Non-white Population X_4	% Households 1.01 Or More Persons Per Room X_5
13	9008	111	85	12	10.8
14	9019	117	89	16	10.2
15	9011	114	87	18	10.6
16	12295	152	138	39	6.1
17	12236	198	135	36	6.9
18	12251	155	141	42	5.8
19	12233	147	133	34	6.6
20	12249	159	140	41	5.6
21	10695	131	98	314	7.6
22	10701	139	101	320	7.3
23	10683	127	95	309	7.9
24	10698	133	100	316	7.9
25	10690	129	97	312	7.8
26	8272	117	60	72	10.8
27	8265	113	57	68	11.1
28	8279	120	63	75	10.5
29	8258	111	55	66	11.3
30	8280	121	69	76	10.9
31	9288	114	104	36	9.1
32	9291	116	106	37	8.9
33	9277	110	99	33	9.4
34	9294	118	108	39	8.8
35	9280	111	101	34	9.3
36	8937	151	77	29	11.3
37	8930	148	75	26	11.6
38	8942	154	79	31	11.0
39	8928	146	74	25	11.7
40	8945	155	80	32	10.8
41	10577	142	96	501	7.1
42	10582	195	99	510	6.8
43	10585	196	100	515	6.7
44	10572	190	93	496	7.3
45	10570	139	92	992	7.4
46	9627	101	76	82	11.2
47	9622	168	73	79	11.9
48	9618	166	71	79	11.7
49	9630	173	78	89	11.0
50	9635	175	80	87	10.8
51	9136	169	64	68	10.0
52	9190	171	66	70	9.8
53	9132	166	61	65	10.2
54	9143	172	67	72	9.6
55	9130	169	60	63	10.3
56	10033	136	85	4	5.1

Areas	Median Family Income Y	Weekly Earnings X_2	Median Rent X_3	Non-white Population X_4	% Households 1.01 Or More Persons Per Room X_5
57	10028	132	83	3	5.4
58	10039	139	87	6	4.9
59	10025	130	82	2	5.5
60	10040	140	88	7	4.8
61	8295	186	59	219	9.5
62	8301	139	56	223	9.2
63	8307	142	58	225	9.0
64	8290	133	52	216	9.7
65	8288	131	51	214	9.8
66	10430	159	77	118	5.3
67	10425	157	75	115	5.5
68	10420	155	73	113	5.7
69	10435	162	79	120	5.1
70	10490	169	81	122	4.9
71	10249	153	76	22	6.2
72	10255	155	78	24	6.0
73	10245	151	74	20	6.9
74	10260	157	80	26	5.8
75	10240	149	72	18	6.6
76	7818	123	74	96	11.6
77	7820	125	75	97	11.5
78	7822	126	76	99	11.4
79	7824	128	77	100	11.3
80	7826	129	78	101	11.2
81	8669	168	69	15	7.6
82	8665	166	63	15	7.8
83	8663	165	62	14	7.9
84	8661	163	61	14	8.0
85	8659	162	60	13	8.2
86	9832	104	77	96	8.0
87	9835	107	79	98	7.8
88	9840	109	81	100	7.6
89	9830	103	76	95	8.1
90	9828	102	75	94	8.2
91	8513	117	69	99	8.3
92	8510	115	62	48	8.5
93	8506	112	60	47	8.7
94	8517	119	66	50	8.1
95	8520	120	67	51	7.9
96	11931	148	116	1306	8.2
97	11935	150	118	1309	8.0
98	11940	152	120	1312	7.4
99	11945	159	122	1315	7.7
100	11950	156	129	1317	7.6

Areas	Median Family Income Y	Weekly Earnings X_2	Median Rent X_3	Non-white Population X_4	% Households 1.01 Or More Persons Per Room X_5
101	10257	147	81	156	9.3
102	10252	195	80	155	9.5
103	10247	144	79	153	9.6
104	10242	143	78	152	9.8
105	10237	191	77	151	9.9
106	11407	155	95	393	5.5
107	11398	153	94	340	5.6
108	11395	152	93	338	5.7
109	11410	157	96	345	5.4
110	11414	158	97	347	5.3
111	7475	85	65	70	11.4
112	7980	87	66	71	11.2
113	7485	89	67	73	11.1
114	7490	83	64	69	11.6
115	7465	81	63	67	11.7
116	10460	145	91	110	5.9
117	10457	193	89	108	6.0
118	10454	192	88	107	6.1
119	10450	140	86	105	6.3
120	10448	139	85	109	6.4
121	8000	155	69	15	17.1
122	8005	157	70	15	16.9
123	8010	159	71	16	16.7
124	8015	161	72	16	16.5
125	8020	163	73	17	16.3
126	10405	122	110	261	8.6
127	10400	120	108	258	8.7
128	10395	118	106	255	8.8
129	10910	129	112	269	8.5
130	10915	126	119	267	8.9
131	10504	163	92	13	6.9
132	10508	166	94	13	6.8
133	10513	168	96	14	6.6
134	10500	161	90	12	7.1
135	10496	159	88	11	7.2
136	11234	173	94	96	6.1
137	11239	175	96	98	6.0
138	11231	172	93	95	6.2
139	11241	176	97	99	5.9
140	11228	170	92	99	6.3
141	10777	146	105	67	5.4
142	10770	143	103	66	5.5
143	10780	147	106	68	5.3
144	10768	142	102	66	5.6

Areas	Median Family Income Y	Weekly Earnings X_2	Median Rent X_3	Non-white Population X_4	% Households 1.01 Or More Persons Per Room X_5
145	10783	149	107	69	5.2
146	10682	152	98	13	6.0
147	10690	153	99	13	6.0
148	10693	155	100	19	5.9
149	10696	156	101	15	5.9
150	10699	158	102	15	5.8
151	12117	181	94	780	7.8
152	12115	179	93	779	7.8
153	12113	178	92	778	7.9
154	12110	176	91	776	7.9
155	12108	175	90	774	8.0
156	8906	133	69	3	7.5
157	8910	134	70	3	7.4
158	8913	135	71	4	7.4
159	8902	132	68	3	7.6
160	8900	131	68	2	7.6
161	7792	87	72	15	18.6
162	7779	84	70	13	18.9
163	7776	83	69	13	19.0
164	7795	88	73	16	18.5
165	7798	89	74	16	18.4
166	9363	143	69	9	6.0
167	9366	144	69	9	5.9
168	9369	145	70	10	5.8
169	9360	142	68	8	6.0
170	9357	141	68	8	6.1
171	9332	154	94	3	5.9
172	9330	153	93	3	6.0
173	9334	155	95	3	5.8
174	9328	152	92	3	6.1
175	9336	156	95	4	5.7
176	8983	135	71	14	8.9
177	8980	134	70	14	9.0
178	8977	133	69	13	9.1
179	8974	132	69	13	9.2
180	8971	131	68	12	9.2
181	11172	188	108	63	8.9
182	11175	189	109	63	8.8
183	11178	190	109	64	8.7
184	11180	191	110	64	8.7
185	11182	192	111	65	8.6
186	11010	148	93	20	6.4
187	11005	146	92	20	6.5
188	11015	150	94	21	6.3

Areas	Median Family Income Y	Weekly Earnings X_2	Median Rent X_3	Non-white Population X_4	% Households 1.01 Or More Persons Per Room X_5
189	11002	145	91	19	6.6
190	11018	151	95	21	6.2
191	10101	136	92	88	8.3
192	10094	134	91	87	8.4
193	10092	133	91	87	8.4
194	10108	137	93	89	8.2
195	10110	138	93	89	8.2
196	8622	128	80	40	11.1
197	8625	129	81	40	11.0
198	8619	127	74	40	11.2
199	8628	130	82	41	10.9
200	8760	160	82	30	10.1

BIBLIOGRAPHY

BOLCH, B. W., AND HUANG, C. J., *Multivariate Statistical Methods for Business and Economics*, Englewood Cliffs, N.J.: Prentice-Hall, Inc., 1974.

DRAPER, N. R., AND SMITH, H., *Applied Regression Analysis*, New York: John Wiley and Sons, Inc., 1966.

KLEINBAUM, D. G., AND KUPPER, L. L., *Applied Regression Analysis and Other Multivariate Methods,* North Scituate, Mass: Duxbury Press, 1978.

MILLER, R. B., AND WICHERN, D. W., *Intermediate Business Statistics*, New York: Holt, Rinehart, and Winston, 1977.

NETER, J., AND WASSERMAN, W. *Applied Linear Statistical Models*, Homewood, Ill.: Richard D. Irwin, Inc., 1974.

SPURR, W. A., AND BONINI, C. P., *Statistical Analysis for Business Decisions,* Homewood, Ill.: Richard D. Irwin, Inc., 1973.

WONNACOTT, T. H., AND WONNACOTT, R. J., *Introductory Statistics for Business and Economics,* New York: John Wiley and Sons, Inc., 1977.

Time Series Analysis

Introduction

Regression and correlation analyses are concerned with the functional linear relationship between two variables. Knowledge of the independent variable, X, is used to predict the dependent variable, Y. In time series analysis the independent variable is time. The variable under study (Y) is one that takes on different values over time. Thus, any variable classified chronologically is a time series. The time periods may be years (see example, Table 6.2), quarters, months, weeks, and, in some cases, days or hours. Time series are analyzed to discover past patterns of growth and change that can be used to predict future patterns and needs for business operations. Time series analysis does not provide the answer to what the future holds, but it is valuable in the forecasting process and helps to reduce errors in forecasts.

Publications such as the Statistical Abstract of the United States, the Survey of Current Business, the Monthly Labor Review, the Federal Reserve Bulletin, and the annual reports of corporations contain time series of all types. Historical data—typically reported on a monthly, quarterly, or annual basis, and covering prices, production, sales, employment, unemployment, hours worked, fuel used, energy produced, earnings, and so on—fill the pages of these and other business and economic publications.

A careful analysis of what has happened helps us to understand the past, to observe important trends and patterns, and to use the data to make reasonable predictions of the future. It is important that we understand what has happened and that we use historical evidence and sound judgment to make intelligent plans to meet the demands of the future.

Forecasts are not made just for the sake of forecasting; that is, they are not ends in themselves. Forecasts are made in order to assist management in determining alternative strategies.

Long-term forecasts are usually considered as being more than one year into the future; 5-, 10-, and even 20–year predictions are common. Long-range predictions are essential to allow sufficient time for the procurement, manufacturing, sales, finance, and other departments of a company to develop plans for possible new plants, financing, development of new products, and new methods of assembly.

Forecasting the level of sales, both short-term and long-term, is almost dictated by the very nature of business organizations in the United States. Competition for the consumer's dollar, stress on earning a profit for the stockholders, and a desire to produce a larger and larger share of the market are some of the prime motivating forces in business. Thus, a statement of the goals of management, called forecasts, is considered necessary in order to have the raw materials, production facilities, and staff available to meet the projected demand.

The alternative, of course, is not to plan ahead. In a dynamic business environment, however, this lack of planning might be disastrous. An electronics firm that ignored the trend to color television and solid-state circuitry a few years ago would no doubt have lost most of its market share by now.

Forecasts may be based only on the judgment of management. This is common in small firms. The management of a small firm is concerned mainly with day-to-day problems. It seldom has the time to make an extensive study of the market, the effect of governmental actions on the firm, the sales of competition, and other factors that must be considered in making a forecast; and many managers do not have the specialized knowledge necessary to make forecasts based on quantitative data. Many large firms, however, have planning departments (sometimes called statistical departments or control departments), which are constantly making and revising both long-range and short-range forecasts. Their activities involve all departments—accounting, finance, procurement, production, advertising, personnel, and sales.

This is not to suggest, however, that judgment is not a factor in making forecasts. What *is* important is that statistical forecasting techniques are available that, when supplemented with management's experience, will provide a better basis for decision making than would result from decisions based on judgment alone.

Several reasons support why subjective considerations are so important in time series analysis. First, a generally satisfactory probability approach to such analysis has not yet been found. Second, some purely subjective evaluations would be necessary in making forecasts even if a suitable probability approach to time series analysis were available. Whenever we examine the past to obtain clues about the future—as is the case when we use time series analysis as an aid to forecasting—the past is relevant only to the extent that causal conditions previously in effect continue to hold in the period ahead. In economic and business activity, causal conditions seldom remain constant from period to period. Rather, the multitude of causal factors at work tends to be constantly shifting so that the connection between the past, present, and future must be continually reevaluated.

While the techniques of time series analysis do not eliminate subjective evaluations, they do make a useful contribution by providing a conceptual approach to forecasting. Forecasts are made with the aid of a set of specific formal procedures, and judgments are indicated explicitly.

Decomposition

One principal approach to the analysis of time-series data involves the attempt to identify the component factors that influence each of the periodic values in the series. This identification procedure is called the decomposition of a time series. In turn, these components are identified so that the time series can be projected into the future, and are used for both short-run and long-run forecasting.

Three components are found in an annual time series; namely, secular trend, cyclical variations, and irregular fluctuations. An additional component, called seasonal variation, is found in short-term time series data classified by quarters, months, or weeks.

Trend. This is the long-term component in a time series, and underlies the growth (or decline) in the series. The trend can be described by a straight line or a curve. The basic forces producing or affecting the trend of a series are: population change, price change, technological change, and productivity increases.

Cyclical. The cyclical component is a series of irregular wave-like fluctuations or cycles of more than one year's duration due to changing economic conditions. It is the difference between the expected values of a variable (trend) and the actual values—the residual variation fluctuating around the trend.

Irregular. The irregular component is composed of random fluctuations that are caused by unpredictable or nonperiodic events such as weather changes, strikes, wars, rumors of wars, elections, and the passage of legislative bills.

Seasonal. These fluctuations are typically found in data classified as quarterly, monthly, or weekly. Seasonal variation refers to a pattern of change that recurs regularly over time. This movement is completed within the duration of a year, and repeats itself year after year.

In order to study the components of a time series, a consideration of the mathematical relationships of the components is necessary. The approach used most frequently is to treat the original data of a time series as a product of the components; that is, an annual series is a product of trend, cyclical, and irregular fluctuations, expressed symbolically as $T \times C \times I$. In data where seasonal variations are present, the composition is $T \times C \times S \times I$. In this multiplicative composition, T is measured in the units of the actual data; and the other components (C, S, and I) are index values.

$$\textit{Long-Term} \qquad Y = TCI \qquad \textbf{(6-1)}$$

$$\textit{Short-Term} \qquad Y = TSCI \qquad \textbf{(6-2)}$$

where: Y = Actual value
T = Trend
C = Cyclical
I = Irregular
S = Seasonal

Before we examine the individual components of a time series, let us look at the problem caused by data measured in dollar values.

Price Deflation

Several of the series on production, sales, and other economic cases contain data available only in terms of dollar values. These data are affected by both the physical quantity of goods and their prices. Inflation and widely varying prices over time can cause analysis problems. It is desirable in these instances to express dollar values in terms of "constant dollars." Frequently, it is necessary to know how much of the change in dollar values represents a real change in physical quantity, and how much is due to change in price due to inflation. Price indexes can be utilized to this end. Quantities can be estimated by dividing the dollar values by the prices of the goods in order to eliminate price change effects. Since value is a product of quantity "times" price, value divided by price equals quantity. This relationship can be represented mathematically as

$$PQ = V$$

$$\frac{PQ}{P} = \frac{V}{P} \qquad \qquad \textbf{(6-3)}$$

$$Q = \frac{V}{P}$$

This adjustment is called *price deflation*, or expressing a series in terms of "constant dollars."

The deflating process is relatively simple. The use of an index number computed from the prices of the commodities whose values are to be deflated is desired. For example, shoe store sales should be deflated by an index of shoe prices, not by a general price index.

In deflating dollar values that represent more than one type of commodity, we should develop the price index by combining the appropriate price indexes together in the proper mix. For example, Mr. Burnham wishes to study the long-term growth of the Burnham Furniture Store. The long-term trend of his business should be evaluated using the physical volume of sales. If this cannot be done, price changes reflected in dollar sales will follow no consistent pattern and will merely obscure the real growth pattern. If sales dollars are to be used, actual dollar sales need to be divided by an appropriate price index.

The Consumer Price Index is not suitable because it contains elements such as rents, foods, and personal services not sold by the store; but some components of this index may be appropriate. Mr. Burnham is aware that 70% of sales are from furniture and 30% from appliances. He can, therefore, multiply the CPI retail furniture component by .70, multiply the appliance component by .30, then add to get a combined price index. Table 6.1 illustrates this approach where the computations for 1970 are

$$111.6(.70) + 105.3(.30) = 109.7$$

Dividing sales for 1970 by this appropriate price index gives deflated sales in dollars of 1967 purchasing power.

$$Q = \frac{V}{P} = \frac{42.1}{1.097} = 38.4$$

Table 6.1 shows that while actual sales gained steadily from 1970 to 1977, physical volume remained rather stable. Evidently the sales

TABLE 6.1   *Burnham Furniture Sales (1970–1977).*

Year	Burnham Sales (thousands)	Retail Furniture Price Index (1967 = 100)	Retail Appliance Price Index (1967 = 100)	Price Index* (1967 = 100)	Deflated Sales** (thousands of 1967 dollars)
1970	42.1	111.6	105.3	109.7	38.4
1971	47.2	117.2	108.5	114.6	41.2
1972	48.4	124.2	109.8	119.9	40.4
1973	50.6	128.3	114.1	124.0	40.8
1974	55.2	136.1	117.6	130.6	42.3
1975	57.9	139.8	122.4	134.6	43.0
1976	59.8	145.7	128.3	140.5	42.6
1977	60.7	156.2	131.2	148.7	40.8

*Constructed for furniture (weight 70%) and appliance (weight 30%).
**Sales divided by price index times 100.

increases were due to price markups that were generated, in turn, by the inflationary tendency of the economy.

Trend

Secular trends are the basic long-term movements in a time series that can be described by a straight line or curve. The basic forces producing or affecting the trend of a series are: population change, price change, technological change, and productivity increases.

The total retail sales of a community may rise each year for several years because its population continues to grow. Moreover, the sales in current dollars may be pushed upward because of general increases in prices of retail goods—even if the physical volume of goods sold does not change.

Technological change may cause a time series to move generally upward or downward. The development and improvement of the automobile, accompanied by improvements in roads, has increased gasoline sales. The same automobile, however, produced in increasing volumes, caused a downward trend in the production of horse-drawn wagons and buggies.

Productivity increases, which, in turn, may be due to technological change, give an upward slope to many time series. Any measure of total output, such as manufacturers' sales, are affected by changes in productivity.

Before measuring the trend of a time series, one must know the purpose for measuring it. Basically the purposes are twofold, to project the trend and/or to eliminate it from the original data. Knowledge of the purpose guides the analyst in his/her choice of method and in the length of the time series to be used for the measurement. If projection is the purpose for measurement, it is important to know the projection date. A trend projection for twenty years may require the use of a time series of longer duration than a projection for five years.

In trend analysis the independent variable is time. The analyst should chart the data on both arithmetic and semi-log scales before choosing the method of measurement. By doing this, the analyst gets an additional guide for choosing the trend equation because the general shape of the trend is apparent. If a plot of the series indicates basically a straight-line movement on the arithmetic scale, the analyst will probably fit a straight trend line to the data. If a curved trend is revealed, the analyst can determine which of the several trend formulae gives a most appropriate curve. If the data plotted on semilogarithmic paper indicate a constant rate of growth, he/she may compute a straight trend line for the logarithms of the original data.

A chart of the data and a statement of purpose for measuring the trend do not always enable the analyst to make a final choice of trend formula. Sometimes two or more trends must be computed and plotted with the original data to see which fits the time series best.

What constitutes a "best" fit is a matter of judgment. The trend that fits best is the one that best does the job the analyst has to do. No methods are superior for measuring trends. Sometimes a trend drawn freehand through a time series is sufficient to reveal a picture of the general shape and direction of the series. To draw a freehand trend properly, however, the analyst must be able to recognize the major cycles and seasonal fluctuations through which the trend must pass. Sometimes this is hard to do unless he/she is very familiar with the particular series being analyzed. Most analysts, therefore, choose an objective method that can be stated as an equation in order to avoid the subjective decisions required for the freehand method.

The method most widely used to describe straight-line trends is called the "least squares" method. This approach computes the line that best fits a group of points mathematically in accordance with a stated criterion.* The trend equation is $Y_R = b_0 + bX$

where: Y_R = the predicted trend value for the Y variable for a selected coded time period (X)

b_0 = the value of the trend when $X = 0$

b = the average increase or decrease in Y_R (trend) for each increase of one period of X

X = any value of time that is selected

---

*As discussed in Chapter 4, the least squares method minimizes the sum of the squared distances from the data points to the trend line measured in the vertical direction.

Table 6.2 provides actual data for the registration of new passenger cars in the United States from 1951 to 1975. The data are plotted and graphed as shown in Fig. 6-1. Although there are some large variations in the series, registration of new passenger cars is increasing by a fairly constant *amount* each year. Therefore, a straight-line (linear) trend is investigated.

TABLE 6.2   *Registration of New Passenger Cars in the United States* (1951–1975).*

Year	Annual Registrations (millions)
1951	5.061
1952	4.158
1953	5.739
1954	5.535
1955	7.170
1956	5.955
1957	5.982
1958	4.655
1959	6.041
1960	6.577
1961	5.855
1962	6.939
1963	7.557
1964	8.065
1965	9.314
1966	9.009
1967	8.357
1968	9.404
1969	9.447
1970	8.388
1971	9.831
1972	10.409
1973	11.351
1974	8.701
1975	8.168

*Alaska is included beginning with 1958, and Hawaii is included beginning with 1959.
Source of data: Department of Commerce, Survey of Current Business.

When computing a least squares trend equation using the *long method,* we use the same formulae and computations as for a regression equation. First, the years are coded beginning with $X = 0$, representing the first time period (1951)—as shown in Table 6.3. Next, the slope is computed using the slope formula.

$$b = \frac{N \Sigma XY - \Sigma X \Sigma Y}{N \Sigma X^2 - (\Sigma X)^2}$$

152

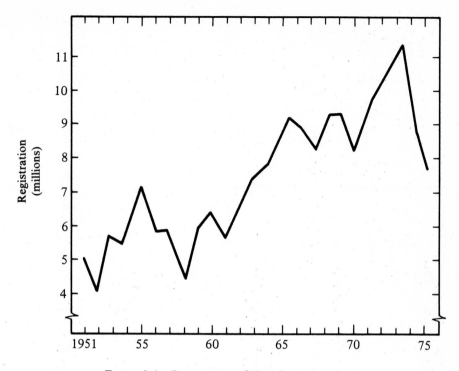

FIGURE 6–1   *Registration of New Passenger Cars.*

$$b = \frac{25(2546.717) - (300)(187.668)}{25(4900) - (300)^2}$$

$$b = \frac{63{,}667.925 - 56{,}300.4}{122{,}500 - 90{,}000}$$

$$b = \frac{7367.525}{32{,}500}$$

$$b = 0.22669$$

The slope is now inserted in the constant formula in order to solve for b_0

$$b_0 = \frac{\Sigma Y}{N} - b \frac{\Sigma X}{N}$$

$$b_0 = \frac{187.668}{25} - 0.22669 \frac{300}{25}$$

$$b_0 = 7.507 - 2.720$$

$$b_0 = 4.787$$

The trend equation is, thus, $Y_R = 4.787 + .22669X$ (origin: July 1, 1951; 1 unit of $X = 1$ year).

In 1951 the trend was projected to be 4.787 million (since $X = 0$). Each year new passenger car registrations increased an average of .22669 million or 226,690. Figure 6–2 shows the trend equation fitted to the actual data.

The *long method* just explained is not ordinarily used to calculate trend values by hand because the same results can be obtained more quickly using either a *short method* or the computer. In the short method the calculations are easier because the years are coded so that the X values

TABLE 6.3   *Long Method For Fitting a Least-Squares Straight Line.*

Year	Registrations in Millions (Y)	Year Coded for $X = 0$ in 1951 (X)	X^2	XY
1951	5.061	0	0	0
1952	4.158	1	1	4.158
1953	5.739	2	4	11.478
1954	5.535	3	9	16.605
1955	7.170	4	16	28.680
1956	5.955	5	25	29.775
1957	5.982	6	36	35.892
1958	4.655	7	49	32.585
1959	6.041	8	64	48.328
1960	6.577	9	81	59.193
1961	5.855	10	100	58.550
1962	6.939	11	121	76.329
1963	7.557	12	144	90.684
1964	8.065	13	169	104.845
1965	9.314	14	196	130.396
1966	9.009	15	225	135.135
1967	8.357	16	256	133.712
1968	9.404	17	289	159.868
1969	9.447	18	324	170.046
1970	8.388	19	361	159.372
1971	9.831	20	400	196.620
1972	10.409	21	441	218.589
1973	11.351	22	484	249.722
1974	8.701	23	529	200.123
1975	8.168	24	576	196.032
Totals	187.668	300	4900	2,546.717

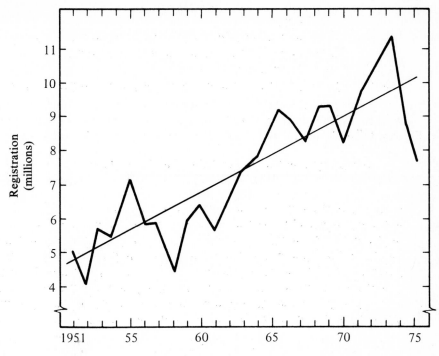

FIGURE 6–2 *Least Squares Trend for Registration of New Passenger Cars.*

will add to zero. When $\Sigma X = 0$, the formulae are shortened, and the computations are greatly simplified.

$$b = \frac{N \Sigma XY - \Sigma X \Sigma Y}{N \Sigma X^2 - (\Sigma X)^2} \qquad \text{Now let } \Sigma X = 0$$

$$b = \frac{N \Sigma XY - 0 \ \Sigma Y}{N \Sigma X^2 - (0)^2}$$

$$b = \frac{N \Sigma XY}{N \Sigma X^2}$$

$$b = \frac{\Sigma XY}{\Sigma X^2} \qquad\qquad\qquad\qquad\qquad \textbf{(6–4)}$$

$$b_0 = \frac{\Sigma Y}{N} - b \frac{\Sigma X}{N} \qquad \Sigma X = 0$$

$$b_0 = \frac{\Sigma Y}{N} - b\frac{0}{N} \qquad\qquad (6\text{-}5)$$

$$b_0 = \frac{\Sigma Y}{N}$$

Table 6.4 illustrates the new passenger car registration problem as worked by the short method. First, a year is selected to represent the origin so that the ΣX will equal zero. Next, the slope is computed.

TABLE 6.4   *Short Method for Fitting a Least-Squares Straight Line.*

Year	Registrations (millions)	X	X^2	XY
1951	5.061	−12	144	−60.732
1952	4.158	−11	121	−45.738
1953	5.739	−10	100	−57.390
1954	5.535	−9	81	−49.815
1955	7.170	−8	64	−57.360
1956	5.955	−7	49	−41.685
1957	5.982	−6	36	−35.892
1958	4.655	−5	25	−23.275
1959	6.041	−4	16	−24.164
1960	6.577	−3	9	−19.731
1961	5.855	−2	4	−11.710
1962	6.939	−1	1	−6.939
1963	7.557	0	0	0
1964	8.065	1	1	8.065
1965	9.314	2	4	18.628
1966	9.009	3	9	27.027
1967	8.357	4	16	33.428
1968	9.404	5	25	47.020
1969	9.447	6	36	56.682
1970	8.388	7	49	58.716
1971	9.831	8	64	78.648
1972	10.409	9	81	93.681
1973	11.351	10	100	113.510
1974	8.701	11	121	95.711
1975	8.168	12	144	98.016
Totals	187.668	0	1300	294.701

$$b = \frac{\Sigma XY}{\Sigma X^2}$$

$$b = \frac{294.701}{1300}$$

156

$$b = 0.22669$$

Then, the constant is computed.

$$b_0 = \frac{\Sigma Y}{N}$$

$$b_0 = \frac{187.668}{25}$$

$$b_0 = 7.507$$

Thus, the trend equation is $Y_R = 7.507 + .227X$. (Origin: July 1, 1963; 1 unit of $X = 1$ year). The equation arrived at using the short method is the same as when the long method was used with an adjustment for the shift in the origin.

$$Y_R = 7.507 + .227X \qquad (X = 0 \text{ represents } 1963)$$

$$Y_R = 4.787 + .227X \qquad (X = 0 \text{ represents } 1951)$$

In 1963 the long method (Table 6.3) uses an X coded value of 12. Substituted into the appropriate equation

$$Y_R = 4.787 + 0.22669X$$

$$Y_R = 4.787 + 0.22669(12)$$

$$Y_R = 7.507$$

In 1963 the short method (Table 6.4) uses an X coded value of 0. Substituted into the appropriate equation

$$Y_R = 7.507 + 0.22669X$$

$$Y_R = 7.507 + 0.22669(0)$$

$$Y_R = 7.507$$

If the appropriate coded X values are used, the final trend solution is precisely the same using either method.

Table 6.5 illustrates a generally preferred way to calculate trend values by the short method when an even number of years is being analyzed. The procedure is exactly the same as that for an odd number of years except that X in the equation $Y_R = b_0 + bX$ is defined as the number of half-year periods from the trend origin. In Table 6.5 the trend origin is January 1, 1965. The -1 value for 1964 represents the six-month period before the origin; that is, from January 1, 1965, back to July 1, 1964. The -3 for 1963 is the eighteen month period (3 half-year periods) before the trend origin, from January 1, 1965, to July 1, 1963. The positive X values represent the number of half-year periods from the trend origin to the middle of the years after the trend origin.

TABLE 6.5   *Value of Shipments of Metal-Working Machinery from Manufacturing Plants, United States, 1962–1967*

(Short Method—Even Number of Years)

Year	Shipments (millions of dollars) Y	X	X^2	XY	Trend Y_R
1962	43	−5	25	−215	29.45
1963	58	−3	9	−174	60.07
1964	82	−1	1	−82	90.69
1965	112	1	1	112	121.31
1966	137	3	9	411	151.93
1967	204	5	25	1020	182.55
Total	636	0	70	1072	

Step 1: $b_0 = \dfrac{\Sigma Y}{N}$

Step 3: $Y_R = b_0 + bX$

$b = \dfrac{\Sigma XY}{\Sigma X^2}$

$Y_R = 106 + 15.31 X$

Step 4: $Y_R (1962) = 106 + 15.31(-5) = 29.45$

Step 2: $b_0 = \dfrac{636}{6} = 106$

Step 5: $15.31 \times 2 = 30.62 = $ *Increase per Year*

$b = \dfrac{1072}{70} = 15.31$

Step 6: $Y_R (1972) = 106 + 15.31(15) = 335.65$

One could let X represent the number of years, but then the X values would read −2.5, −1.5, −0.5, 0.5, 1.2, 2.5, etc. This would necessitate the use of two-digit figures and decimals, which would be an inconvenience in performing the calculations.

Also, one may ask why the X values are measured to the middle of each year. This is done because a trend value is an "average" value that represents the entire year, and the middle of a year represents the entire year better than any other point in time. Another important reason for having a common reference point (middle of each time period) is that the interpretation of b depends on a "one unit increase in X." If the reference point were different for each time period, this type of statement would be meaningless. A one unit increase would mean different things between different time periods.

The value of b calculated from Table 6.5 is 15.31. This means that the average increase in the value of shipments of metal working machinery during each six-month period for the years 1962–1967 was $15.31 million. The average increase per year, of course, was $30.62 million. To use the equation $Y_R = 106 + 15.31X$ (origin: Jan. 1, 1965; 1 unit of $X = \frac{1}{2}$ year) to make estimates and projections, we must substitute for X the number of half-year periods from the trend origin, January 1, 1965, to the middle of the year for which we want to find a trend value. Step 6, for example, shows the calculation for 1972. In this calculation the middle of 1972 is 15 half-year periods from the trend origin.

Although the least squares trend line is probably used more often than any other to describe the long-term growth of a time series, the use of curved trends is sometimes necessary for a logical description of change. A large variety of equations are available to compute trends for curves.

1. Second Degree Parabola

The equation is

$$Y_R = b_0 + b_2 X + b_3 X^2 \tag{6-6}$$

where: Y_R = the predicted trend value for the Y variable for a selected X coded year

       b_0 = the value of the trend when $X = 0$ (origin)

       b_2 = the weight given the X variable

       b_3 = the weight given the X^2 variable

       X = any value of time that is selected

The formulae that are used when the X variable is coded so that $\Sigma X = 0$, are

$$b_3 = \frac{N \Sigma X^2 Y - \Sigma X^2 \Sigma Y}{N \Sigma X^4 - (\Sigma X^2)^2} \tag{6-7}$$

$$b_2 = \frac{\Sigma X Y}{\Sigma X^2} \tag{6-8}$$

$$b_0 = \frac{\Sigma Y - b_3 \Sigma X^2}{N} \tag{6-9}$$

The use of these three formulae is demonstrated in Table 6.6 where the trend for the number of miles of railroad track operated is analyzed from 1910 through 1970. Figure 6-3 illustrates the first step of our analysis, which is to plot the data. Next, a decision is made to investigate the

TABLE 6.6   *Miles of Railroad Track Operated (1910–1970)*

Year	Y	X	X^2	X^4	XY	X^2Y	Y_R
1910	352	−6	36	1296	−2112	12672	371.76
1915	391	−5	25	625	−1955	9775	386.38
1920	407	−4	16	256	−1628	6512	398.02
1925	418	−3	9	81	−1254	3762	406.68
1930	430	−2	4	16	−860	1720	412.36
1935	419	−1	1	1	−419	419	415.06
1940	406	0	0	0	0	0	414.78
1945	398	1	1	1	398	398	411.52
1950	396	2	4	16	792	1584	405.28
1955	391	3	9	81	1173	3519	396.06
1960	382	4	16	256	1528	6112	383.86
1965	371	5	25	625	1855	9275	368.68
1970	360	6	36	1296	2160	12960	350.52
Total:	5121		182	4550	−322	68708	

$$b_2 = \frac{\Sigma XY}{\Sigma X^2} = \frac{-322}{182} = -1.77$$

$$b_3 = \frac{N\Sigma X^2 Y - \Sigma X^2 \Sigma Y}{N\Sigma X^4 - (\Sigma X^2)^2} = \frac{13(68708) - (182)(5121)}{13(4550) - (182)^2} = -1.49$$

$$b_0 = \frac{\Sigma Y - b_3 \Sigma X^2}{N} = \frac{5121 - (-1.49)(182)}{13} = 414.78$$

$Y_R = 414.78 - 1.77X - 1.49X^2$ (origin: July 1, 1940; 1 unit of $X = 5$ years)

$Y_R (1970) = 414.78 - 1.77(6) - 1.49(6)^2$

$Y_R (1970) = 350.52$

parabolic equation as the best fitting trend model. The computations for b_0, b_2, and b_3 are demonstrated in Table 6.6. Note that X is coded so that one unit of X represents a five-year period, and $X = 0$ refers to July 1, 1940. The equation $Y_R = 414.78 - 1.77X - 1.49X^2$ (origin: July 1, 1940; 1 unit of $X = 5$ years) fits the data points fairly well, as indicated by Fig. 6–4. In order to draw this curve, the first step is to determine the line of symmetry. This is the line that divides the parabola exactly in half. The computation is shown in Eq. (6–10):

$$X = \frac{-b_2}{2b_3}$$

$$X = \frac{-(-1.77)}{2(-1.49)} = \frac{1.77}{-2.98} = -0.59$$

(6–10)

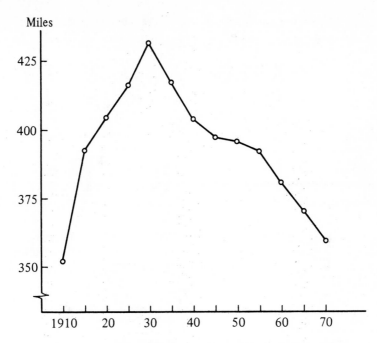

FIGURE 6–3   *Miles of Railroad Track Operated (1910–1970).*

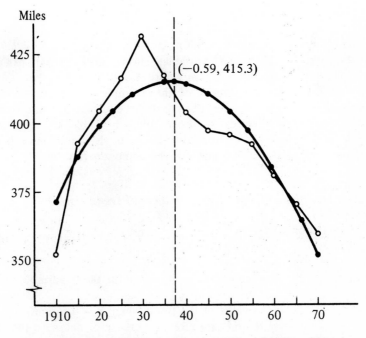

FIGURE 6–4   *Parabolic Curve Fitted to Miles of Railroad Track.*

Next, the point where the curve changes direction is determined by substituting the X value -0.59 into the parabolic equation. The calculation is

$$Y_R = 414.78 - 1.77X - 1.49X^2$$

$$Y_R = 414.78 - 1.77(-0.59) - 1.49(-0.59)^2$$

$$Y_R = 414.78 + 1.04 - 0.52$$

$$Y_R = 415.3$$

The curve rises until 1937 ($X = -0.59$), when it reaches a maximum value of 415.3 and then begins to decrease. The maximum point is $(-0.59, 415.3)$. Since the curve is symmetrical around this value, the rest of the points are fairly easy to calculate (see Table 6.6).

In order to evaluate how well the curve fits the data, the standard error of estimate is computed. This calculation is shown below.

$$S_{y \cdot x} = \sqrt{\frac{\Sigma(Y - Y_R)^2}{n - 3}}$$

$$S_{y \cdot x} = \sqrt{\frac{1417.59}{13 - 3}}$$

$$S_{y \cdot x} = \sqrt{141.76} \qquad\qquad \text{(6-11)}$$

$$S_{y \cdot x} = 11.9$$

The typical distance from each point to the curve is 11.9.

The Y, X, and X^2 variables shown in Table 6.6 can be run on a regression computer program where X and X^2 are independent variables. Table 6.7 shows the results of the example for the operating miles of railroad track. Notice that the parabolic equation and the standard error of estimate are identical to those found in Table 6.5. Actually, we do not need to code X so that the $\Sigma X = 0$. It would have been simpler to use 1910 as the $X = 0$ year for the computer run.

2. Logarithmic Straight Line (Exponential Trend Curve)

The equation is

$$Y_R = b_0 \, b^X \qquad\qquad \text{(6-12)}$$

where: Y_R = the predicted trend value for the Y variable for a selected X coded year

b_0 = the value of the trend when $X = 0$ (origin)

b = the constant rate of increase or decrease (constant multiplier)

TABLE 6.7   *Computer Output for Miles of Railroad Track Operated.*

COMPUTER OUTPUT FOR MILES
OF RAILROAD TRACK OPERATED

VARIABLE NO.	MEAN	STANDARD DEVIATION	CORRELATION X VS Y	REGRESSION COEFFICIENT	STD. ERROR OF REG. COEF.	COMPUTED T VALUE
2	0	3.89	-0.30	-1.76922	0.88255	-2.0
3	14	12.92	-0.83	-1.49150	0.26610	-5.6

DEPENDENT

1	393.92	23.17

INTERCEPT   414.80371

MULT. CORR.   0.883   R-SQUARE   0.780

STD. ERR.   11.906

ANALYSIS OF VARIANCE FOR THE REGRESSION

SOURCE OF VARIATION	DEGREES OF FREEDOM	SUM OF SQUARES	MEAN SQUARES	F VALUE
ATTRIBUTABLE TO REGRESSION	2	5023.31	2511.65	17.71
DEVIATION FROM REGRESSION	10	1417.60	141.76	
TOTAL	12	6440.91		

TABLE OF RESIDUALS

CASE NO.	Y VALUE	Y ESTIMATE	RESIDUAL
1	352.00000	371.72460	-19.72461
2	391.00000	386.36206	4.63794
3	407.00000	398.01611	8.98389
4	418.00000	406.68774	11.31226
5	430.00000	412.37597	17.62402
6	419.00000	415.08105	3.91895
7	406.00000	414.80371	-8.80371
8	398.00000	411.54272	-13.54272
9	396.00000	405.29907	-9.29907
10	391.00000	396.07226	-5.07227
11	382.00000	383.86254	-1.86255
12	371.00000	368.66992	2.33008
13	360.00000	350.49389	9.50610

X = any value of time that is selected

This equation produces trend values that plot as a curve on arithmetic paper and as a straight line on semi-log paper. A straight line on semi-log paper results because the equation produces a trend that increases by a constant percentage *rate*. See the Appendix for a complete discussion of semilogarithmic graphs. In logarithm form the equation is

$$\text{Log } Y_R = \log b_0 + X \log b \qquad (6\text{-}13)$$

where the log Y_R values are calculated first, and from these the Y_R values are determined.

The formulae that are used when the X variable is coded so that $\Sigma X = 0$, are

$$\log b = \frac{\Sigma X \log Y}{\Sigma X^2} \qquad (6\text{-}14)$$

$$\log b_0 = \frac{\Sigma \log Y}{N} \qquad (6\text{-}15)$$

The use of these two formulae is demonstrated in Table 6.8, where

TABLE 6.8   *Growth of Mutual Fund Salespeople (1969–1975).*

Year	Number of Salespeople Y	log Y*	X	X²	X log Y	log Y_R	Y_R
1969	13	1.1139	−3	9	−3.3417	1.1093	12.9
1970	17	1.2304	−2	4	−2.4608	1.2305	17.0
1971	22	1.3424	−1	1	−1.3424	1.3517	22.5
1972	29	1.4624	0	0	0	1.4729	29.7
1973	42	1.6232	1	1	1.6232	1.5941	39.3
1974	50	1.6990	2	4	3.3980	1.7153	51.9
1975	69	1.8388	3	9	5.5164	1.8365	68.6
Total	242	10.3101	0	28	3.3927		

*These are common logs (base 10).

$$\log b = \frac{\Sigma X \log Y}{\Sigma X^2} = \frac{3.3927}{28} = 0.1212$$

Antilog $(0.1212) = 1.32$ or 32% per year

$$\log b_0 = \frac{\Sigma \log Y}{N} = \frac{10.3101}{7} = 1.4729$$

Antilog $(1.4729) = 29.7$

$$Y_R = b_0 b^x = 29.7\,(1.32)^x$$

$$\log Y_R = \log b_0 + X \log b = 1.4729 + X(.1212)$$

$$\log Y_R\,(1975) = 1.4729 + 3(0.1212) = 1.8365$$

Antilog $(1.8365) = 68.6$

the trend in growth of mutual fund salespeople is analyzed. The first step is to plot the data, as illustrated in Fig. 6–5.

Based on this graph a decision is made to investigate the exponential as the best fitting curve. The calculations needed to compute b_0 and b are shown in Table 6.8. The equation $Y_R = 29.7(1.32)^X$ (origin: July 1, 1972; 1 unit of X = 1 year) fits the data extremely well as indicated by the plot on a semi-log scale (Fig. 6–6). The 1.32 value for b means that, on the average, the number of mutual fund salespeople in any one

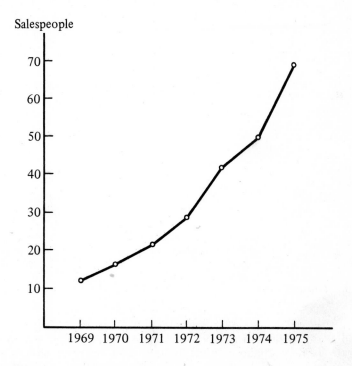

Salespeople

FIGURE 6–5 *Growth of Mutual Fund Salespeople (1965–1975).*

year was 132% of the number in the previous year. The average rate of increase per year during the seven-year period was 32%. This constant *rate* of change shows up as a straight line when graphed on a semi-log scale, as illustrated by Fig. 6–6.

The Y and X variables shown in Table 6.8 can be read into a regression computer program that makes the transformation and fits the log Y to X. The results are shown in Table 6.9. Therefore, if we take the antilog of the regression coefficient (0.12116), we find the constant rate is 1.32 or 132%.

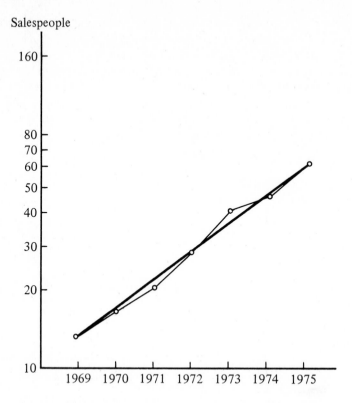

Salespeople

FIGURE 6–6   *Semi-Log Trend for Mutual Fund Salespeople.*

3.   Growth Curves

Growth curves of the Gompertz or logistic type represent the tendency of many industries and product lines to grow at a declining percentage rate as they mature. If the plotted data reflect a situation where sales begin low, then as the product catches on, sales boom and finally ease off as saturation is reached, the Gompertz curve might be appropriate. Figure 6–7 shows the general shape of a Gompertz growth curve when

TABLE 6.9   *Computer Output for Growth of Mutual Fund Salespeople.*

Variable Number	Mean	Standard Deviation	Correlation X vs. Y	Regression Coefficient	Std. Error of Reg. Coef.	Computed T Value
2	0	2.1603	0.9999	0.12116	0.00809	99.18
Dependent						
1	1.4729	0.2622				
Intercept	1.4729					
R-Square	0.99675					

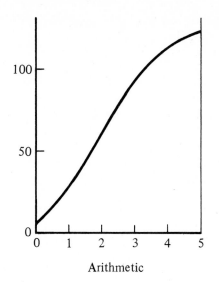

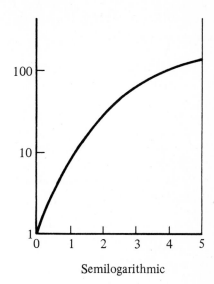

Arithmetic   Semilogarithmic

FIGURE 6–7   *Gompertz Growth Curves.*

plotted on both arithmetic and semilogarithmic scales. The computations for the Gompertz curve are extremely complex and are not within the scope of this text. Specialized books on time series analysis should be consulted for calculation procedures.*

, In deciding which trend to use, we must know the purpose for computing the trend. For example, if the purpose is to obtain an estimate of expenditures for a future year, a knowledge of the basic forces producing or affecting the trend is needed. The right choice of a trend is a matter of judgment and, therefore, requires experience and common sense on the part of the analyst. The line or curve that "best" fits a set of data points might not make sense when projected as the trend of the future.

Cyclical

Whereas the analysis of trend has direct practical value for long-term forecasting, the analysis of the cyclical component, taken by itself, is of dubious forecasting value for the management of an organization. The cyclical component represents wavelike movements on the time-series graph,

---

*For a description of the mathematical methods to fitting growth curves, see CROXTON, F. E., COWDEN, D. J., AND BOLCH, B. W., *Practical Business Statistics,* 14th ed., Englewood Cliffs, N. J.: Prentice-Hall, 1969, pp. 332–338; or MAKRIDAKIS, S. AND WHEELWRIGHT, S. C., *Interactive Forecasting* (Vol. 1), Palo Alto, California: The Scientific Press, 1977, pp. 100–104.

but the cyclical movements are longer in duration and less predictable than the seasonal movements. Economists have given extensive attention to the analysis of business cycles and their causes, but it is not our purpose to consider the numerous theories addressed to this problem. For the managers who must make operating decisions, it appears more fruitful to base cyclical expectations on the particular factors that underlie cyclical fluctuations in their industry (e.g., inventory levels), rather than to anticipate cyclical fluctuations based on the assumed mathematical characteristics of the movements themselves. Because both the cyclical and irregular components of the time series are determined by the use of the residual method described below, they are combined for discussion purposes in this section.

The essence of the classical approach in identifying the cyclical and irregular components of the time series is to eliminate or average out the effects of the trend from a time series, thus leaving the cyclical and irregular components. Since these components constitute that which remains after such adjustments, the method is referred to as the *residual method.*

The specific steps included in the residual method are dependent upon whether the analysis begins with monthly, quarterly, or annual time-series data. If the data are monthly, or quarterly, then the effects of both the trend and seasonal components have to be removed. If the data are annual, then only the effects of the trend component are removed.

Though the use of annual data results in a simpler computational procedure, it does not make possible the identification of the short-term irregular variations, but only of those that are long-term and intertwined with the cyclical variations themselves. For this reason, when annual data are used as the basis for the decomposition, no attempt is usually made to separate the cyclical and irregular components that remain. Symbolically, then, the decomposition of an annual time series is represented as

$$\frac{Y}{T} = \frac{TCI}{T} = CI \qquad (6\text{--}16)$$

In determining the relative effect of the cyclical component in each annual value, we accept the Y_R value as an accurate indication of trend; the discrepancy (residual) is treated as the cyclical component. Thus, as indicated in Table 6.10, each cyclical relative is computed by dividing the actual registration for each year (Y) by the expected registration (Y_R), and multiplying by 100 so that the ratio is in percentage form.

In order to study the cyclical movements represented in Table 6.10 over time, it is useful to portray them graphically as in Fig. 6–8. From this figure it would appear that the cyclical movements associated with new car registrations are neither of regular duration nor very predictable.

Of course, though Fig. 6–8 is called a cycle chart, it actually reflects

TABLE 6.10 *Computation of Cyclical Relatives for New Car Registrations (1951–1975).*

Year	Registrations Y	Expected Registrations Y_R	Cyclical Relative $CI = \dfrac{Y}{Y_R} \ (100)$
1951	5.061	4.787	105.72
1952	4.158	5.014	82.93
1953	5.739	5.240	109.52
1954	5.535	5.467	101.24
1955	7.170	5.694	125.93
1956	5.955	5.920	100.58
1957	5.982	6.147	97.31
1958	4.655	6.374	73.03
1959	6.041	6.601	91.51
1960	6.577	6.827	96.34
1961	5.855	7.054	83.00
1962	6.939	7.281	95.31
1963	7.571	7.507	100.66
1964	8.065	7.734	104.28
1965	9.314	7.961	117.00
1966	9.009	8.187	110.03
1967	8.357	8.414	99.32
1968	9.404	8.641	108.83
1969	9.447	8.867	106.53
1970	8.388	9.094	92.23
1971	9.831	9.321	105.47
1972	10.409	9.547	109.02
1973	11.351	9.774	116.13
1974	8.701	10.001	87.00
1975	8.168	10.228	79.86

the effect of two influences on the time-series values, that is, those associated with both the cyclical and the long-term irregular components. The separation of these two influences, if it were to be attempted, would be dependent upon the analyst's judgment regarding the nature of the real cyclical influences.

To the extent that Fig. 6–8 actually represents cyclical movements in new car registrations, the data for 1955, 1964, and 1973 represent peaks of cyclical movements; and the data for 1958 and 1975 represent cyclical bottoms.

In order to use this information to forecast the future cyclical pattern of new car registrations, a complete understanding of the reasons for the peaks and bottoms is essential. What variables affect new car registrations? How does the economy affect new car registrations? A thorough analysis of these factors is necessary in order to forecast the cyclical pattern.

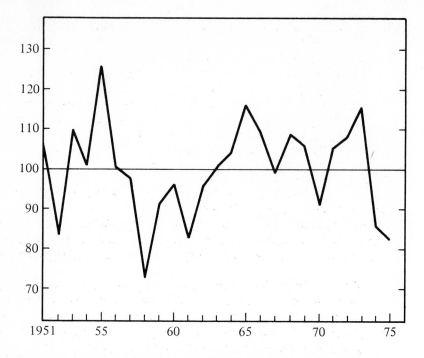

FIGURE 6–8   *Car Registration Cyclical Chart.*

One way to investigate cyclical patterns is through the study of business indicators. A business indicator is a business related time series that is used to help assess the general state of the economy, particularly with reference to the business cycle. Many business people and economists systematically follow the movements of such statistical series to obtain economic and business information in the form of an unfolding picture that is up-to-date, comprehensive, relatively objective, and capable of being read and understood with a minimum expenditure of time.

The most important list of statistical indicators originated during the sharp business setback of 1937–1938. The Secretary of the Treasury, Henry Morgenthau, requested the National Bureau of Economic Research (NBER) to devise a system that would signal when the setback was nearing an end. Under the leadership of Wesley Mitchell and Arthur F. Burns, NBER economists selected 21 series that, based on past performance, promised to be fairly reliable indicators of business revival. Since then the Bureau has revised the list several times. The most recent list, consisting of 26 indicators, appears in Table 6.11.

The NBER has found that certain statistical time series may be useful as direct indicators of cyclical expansions and contractions in business activity. After continuous study of business cycles, it has been learned

TABLE 6.11   *Cyclical Indicator Table Cyclical Indicators (NBER Short List).*

Leading Indicators:

   Average hourly workweek, production
      workers, manufacturing
   Average weekly initial claims, state
      unemployment insurance
   Index of net business formation
   New orders, durable goods industries
   Contracts and orders, plant and equipment
   Index of new building permits, private
      housing units
   Change in book value, manufacturing
      and trade inventories
   Index of industrial materials prices
   Index of stock prices, 500 common stocks
   Corporate profits after taxes (quarterly)
   Index: ratio, price to unit labor
      cost, manufacturing
   Change in consumer installment debt

Roughly Coincident Indicators:

   GNP in current dollars
   GNP in 1958 dollars
   Index of industrial production
   Personal income
   Manufacturing and trade sales
   Sales of retail stores
   Employees on nonagricultural payrolls
   Unemployment rate, total

Lagging Indicators:

   Unemployment rate, persons unemployed
      15 weeks or over
   Business expenditures, new plant and equipment
   Book value, manufacturing and trade inventories
   Index of labor cost per unit of output
      in manufacturing
   Commercial and industrial loans outstanding
      in large commercial banks
   Bank rates on short-term business loans

Source: U.S. Department of Commerce.

that all areas of the economy do not expand simultaneously during expansions, nor do all contract concurrently during periods of contraction. A study of individual economic time series and their relation to this general cyclical movement indicates that the timing of most series conforms only loosely—and in some series not at all—to that of the business cycle. Exceptions to this general statement, however, do exist. The Bureau has identified 26 statistical indicators, 12 classified as leading, 8 as coincident, and 6 as lagging, that have proven to be useful as indicators of business conditions. Up-to-date figures for these series are published monthly in *Business Condition Digest* by the U.S. Department of Commerce, and weekly in *Statistical Indicator Reports* by Statistical Indicator Associates.

For the guidance of forecasters and other users, each series in the National Bureau list has been evaluated and scored by the Bureau in terms of the following elements: (1) extent to which the series measures or represents an activity having a key role in the cyclical process; (2) statistical accuracy and dependability of the series; (3) degree of conformity of the series to historical business cycles; (4) consistency with which the series has moved in some specific phase (leading, coincident, or lagging) with cyclical movement in the economy; (5) degree of smoothness—i.e., relative absence of persistent major irregular fluctuations; and (6) timeliness of publication.* The series selected for the short list (Table 6.11) all have high scores and involve little duplication in coverage.

Three groups of indicators have been identified: those that provide advance warning of probable change in economic activity, the leading indicators; those that reflect the current performance of the economy, the coincident indicators; and those that confirm changes previously signaled, the lagging indicators.

1. LEADING INDICATORS. In practice, the leading series are studied to help in anticipating cyclical turning points. Examples include hiring rates, construction contracts, new orders for durable goods, and formation of new business enterprises. These indicators move ahead of turns in the business cycle, primarily because decisions to expand or curtail output take time to produce influences.

2. COINCIDENT INDICATORS. The coincident series are those whose movements coincide roughly with, and provide a measure of, the current performance of economic activity. Gross National Product, personal income, employment, industrial production, and wholesale prices are examples. These indicators are comprehensive in coverage and tell us whether the economy is currently experiencing a recession or a slowdown, a boom, or an inflation.

3. LAGGING INDICATORS. The fluctuations of these series usually follow those of the coincident indicators. Examples are long-term unemploy-

---

*MOORE, G. H., AND SHISKIN, J., *Indicators of Business Expansions and Contractions*, New York: National Bureau of Economic Research, 1967, pp. 8–28.

ment, the yield on mortgage loans, labor cost per unit of output, and expenditures on new plant and equipment.

One of the major difficulties with an indicator is the determination of when it has reached a cyclical turning point. The fluctuating component of economic and business series contains short-term irregular movements in addition to cyclical ones. Thus, weekly, monthly, or quarterly data plotted on a chart typically have the ragged, saw-tooth appearance that was evident in Fig. 6–8. Consequently, it is difficult to identify cyclical turning points near the time they occur. Remember that the turning points come into existence only as the consequence of a following decline or gain in the cyclical component. Hence, several months may go by before a genuine cyclical upturn or downturn in a leading series is finally identified with any assurance.

Another problem in using the cyclical-indicator approach arises because no uniformity occurs in the length of time by which a given leading indicator precedes cyclical turns in the economy; instead, considerable variability can be noted in the lead time from cycle to cycle. Consequently, the leading indicators may signal that a recession or recovery can be expected some time in the future, but they provide less help in establishing the timing of the turn. Analysis of the coincident and lagging indicators is frequently helpful in this connection; for instance, if leading indicators have signaled a cyclical downturn analysts will begin to look very carefully for signs of weakening in the coincident indicators. In practice, then, effective use of the cyclical-indicator approach requires continuous evaluation of series in all three timing groups.

Still another difficulty is that the indicators occasionally give "false signals", that is, they signal a turning point that does not materialize. Sometimes such signals are due to factors that can be identified in advance, such as a major strike, so that the signals are discounted. In other cases it has been impossible to distinguish false signals from accurate ones until after the fact.

In summary, business indicators have proven to be most useful in forecasting turning points, especially where most other methods tend to break down. Indicators have their limitations; however, over the test of time they have performed as well as any method.

In their article entitled "Early Warning Signals for Economy," in *Statistics: A Guide to Business and Economics,* Geoffrey H. Moore and Julius Shiskin have this to say on the usefulness of statistical indicators:

It seems clear from the record that business cycle indicators are helpful in judging the tone of current business and short-term prospects. But because of their limitations, the indicators must be used together with other data and with full awareness of the background of business and consumer confidence and expectations, governmental policies, and international events. We also must anticipate that the indicators will often be difficult to interpret, that interpretations will sometimes vary among analysts, and that the signals they give will not always be correctly interpreted.

Indicators provide a sensitive and revealing picture of the ebb and flow of economic tides that a skillful analyst of the economic, political, and international scene can use to improve his chances of making a valid forecast of short-run economic trends. If the analyst is aware of their limitations and alert to the world around him, he will find the indicators useful guideposts for taking stock of the economy and its needs.*

In order to explain the cyclical pattern of the new car registration variable shown in Fig. 6–8, several factors are investigated. If the passenger registration variable is logically related to the economy, roughly coincident indicators that provide a measure of current performance of economic activity should provide assistance in forecasting. Many indicator series are forecasted by experts, and these forecasts are often available in published sources. If such forecasts are available, and if the forecasts have a good record of reliability, they might provide a basis for forecasting new passenger car registrations.

Figure 6–8 clearly indicates that the registration variable is related to the economy. When new passenger car registrations bottomed out in 1952, 1958, 1961, 1970, and 1974–75, the economy was depressed. When registrations peaked in 1955, 1965, 1968, and 1973, the economy was healthy.

Another variable that might provide some forecasting assistance is the new car price index. Logically, when prices are up, registrations should be down; and when prices are down registrations should be up. The new car price index is adjusted for trend to eliminate the effects of inflation and is graphed with new passenger car registrations for the purpose of comparison. Figure 6–9 indicates that the two variables are inversely related. Thus, knowledge of proposed price policies should help us forecast new passenger car registrations.

The discussion so far shows how the factors that create variation in a time series can be separated and studied individually. Analysis is the procedure for taking the time series apart; synthesis is a process of putting it back together. In order to understand the new passenger car registration variable, the individual components are analyzed. The decomposition of the year 1975 was accomplished by determining the trend and cyclical components.

Example T = *Trend*   (1975) = 10.228   (See Table 6.10)

          CI = *Cyclical*   (1975) = 79.86   (See Table 6.10)

---

*MOORE, G. H., AND SHISKIN, J., "Early Warning Signals for the Economy," *Statistics: A Guide to Business and Economics,* San Francisco: Holden-Day, Inc., 1976, p. 81.

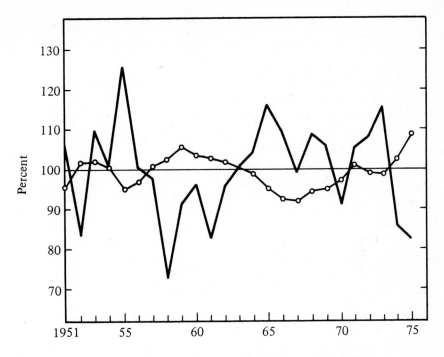

FIGURE 6–9 *Car Registration and Price Index Cyclical Relatives.*

In order to put the series back together we return to the original multiplicative model and substitute the appropriate components.

Example

$$Y = TCI$$

$$Y(1975) = 10.228 \times 0.7986$$

$$Y(1975) = 8.168 \text{ (See Table 6.10)}$$

Now we are in a position to forecast. It is apparent that the multiplicative model approach can be used to provide a forecast for 1976. All we need are accurate estimates for the trend and cyclical–irregular components.

The trend estimate is determined by using the appropriate trend equation, in this case, $Y_R = 4.787 + 0.22669X$. Since $X = 0$ represents July 1, 1951, the X coded value representing 1976 is 25 (See Table 6.3).

Example   Trend for 1976.

$$Y_R = 4.787 + 0.22669X$$

$$Y_R = 4.787 + 0.22669(25)$$

175

$$Y_R = 4.787 + 5.667$$

$$Y_R = 10.454$$

Next, the cyclical relative must be estimated on a subjective basis. All the information that the analyst has gathered concerning the cyclical pattern of new car registrations is taken into consideration. Business indicators are studied and used whenever helpful. Leading indicators are investigated for the short-term cycle, and if any are found they are analyzed.

The cyclical–irregular index for new car registrations has dropped below 80 in 1975 (see Table 6.10). Will it continue to drop or will it bottom out and turn upward? In the past the cyclical relative has never dropped for more than three years in succession. Will this pattern continue? What is the past performance record of this variable in election years? Will gasoline shortages occur in 1976? How does the economy affect new car registrations? Will the economy continue to improve? Will the Bicentennial celebration have an effect? Analysts must answer numerous questions about the past and present performance of a variable. They must also anticipate the effects of recent events and new variables that have never been encountered in the past.

The actual cyclical–relative index that is used depends on whether the analyst feels that new-car registrations will continue to drop, level off, or turn upward (See Fig. 6–8). The important aspect of the *CI* estimate is to get the direction correct. The actual index that is used is not as critical as getting the direction right.

Since economic indicators pointed to a healthier economy in 1976, a decision was made to forecast an upturn for the cyclical–irregular relative. In order to demonstrate the completion of this example, a cyclical–irregular index of 89 is employed:

Example   Forecast for 1976.

$$Y = TCI$$

$$Y(1976) = 10.454 \times 0.89$$

$$Y(1976) = 9.304$$

The multiplicative time series model $Y = TCI$ has been suggested as a long-term forecasting tool. The importance of the individual components dictates the model's usefulness. How well does the trend equation fit the time series data? If the fit is poor, then the cyclical variation is the most important component. It is extremely difficult to estimate *CI* for more than a year or two into the future. Therefore, any long-term forecast of such a variable is risky at best. If the trend equation does a good job of fitting past data, a five-or ten-year projection into the future is reasonable. As long as the trend growth or decline is expected to remain consistent with past performance, an accurate forecast can be anticipated.

The seasonal component in a time series is measured in the form of an index number for each segment of the year being studied. The interpretation of this index number, which represents the extent of seasonal influence for a particular segment of the year, involves a comparison of the measured or expected values for that segment (month, quarter, etc.) with the overall average for all the segments of the year. Thus, a seasonal index of 100 for a particular month indicates that the expected time-series value for that month is exactly one-twelfth of the total for the annual period centered at that month. A seasonal index of 110 for another month would indicate that the expected value for that month is 10 percent greater than one-twelfth of the annual total. A monthly index of 80 indicates that the expected level of activity that month is 20 percent less than one-twelfth of the total activity level for the year. Thus, a monthly index number indicates the expected ups and downs in monthly levels of activity, with effects due to trend T, cyclical C, and irregular I time-series components removed.

Seasonal Variation

Whereas the analysis of trend has implications for long-term managerial planning, the analysis of the seasonal component of a time series has more immediate short-term implications. Manpower and marketing plans, for example, must take into consideration expected seasonal patterns in the employment market and in consumer purchases. The identification of the seasonal component in a time series differs from trend analysis in at least two ways.

1. First, whereas trend is determined directly from all available data, the seasonal component is determined by eliminating the other components from the data so that only the seasonal component remains.
2. Second, whereas trend is represented by one best-fitting line, or equation, it is necessary to compute a separate seasonal value for each month (or quarter, week, etc.) of the year, usually in the form of an index number. As was true for trend analysis, several methods of measuring seasonal variation have been developed; most of the seasonal index computations now used are variations of the ratio-to-moving-average method.

In the analysis of new car registrations the monthly data for the years 1969 through 1975 are used as the basis for the analysis of the seasonal component, rather than the monthly data for the entire 1951–1975 time period. One reason for this reduction in data is to simplify the computations in this illustration. However, another more important reason emerges. If the seasonal pattern of new-car purchases has shifted signifi-

TABLE 6.12 Registration of New Passenger Cars Monthly Data (1969–1970).

Year	Month	Registrations (in thousands) (a)	Twelve-Month Moving Total (b)	Two-Year Moving Total of Column (b) (c)	Twelve-Month Centered Moving Average (d)	Percent of Twelve-Month Centered Moving Average (e)
1969	Jan.	653				
	Feb.	608				
	March	681				
	Apr.	876				
	May	889				
	June	842	(2) →9,448			
	July	815	9,409	(3) →18,857	(4) →785.71	(5) →103.73
	Aug.	719	9,379	18,788	782.83	91.85
	Sept.	733	9,439	18,818	784.08	93.48
	Oct.	956	9,331	18,770	782.08	122.24
	Nov.	758	9,226	18,557	773.21	98.03
	Dec.	913	9,285	18,511	771.29	118.37
1970	Jan.	619	9,308	18,593	774.71	79.90
	Feb.	578	9,272	18,580	774.17	74.66
	March	741	9,151	18,423	767.63	96.53
	Apr.	768	8,914	18,065	752.71	102.03
	May	784	8,693	17,607	733.63	106.87
	June	901	8,387	17,080	711.67	126.60
	July	838	8,356	16,743	697.63	120.12
	Aug.	683	8,396	16,752	698.00	97.25
	Sept.	612	8,475	16,871	702.96	87.06
	Oct.	719	8,555	17,030	709.58	101.33
	Nov.	537	8,621	17,176	715.67	75.03
	Dec.	607	8,631	17,252	718.83	84.44

(1) appears in column (a); registrations from Jan. 1969 (653) through June 1969 (842) bracketed.

Handwritten notes: 815 / 785.71 = 815/785.71; "monthly"; "1 34"

cantly in recent years, using the entire 1951–1975 period for the seasonal analysis would result in poorer projections of expected seasonal patterns for 1976 than using the data for only 1969–1975.

Table 6.12 presents the monthly new car registrations, in thousands, for the period from January, 1969 through December, 1970 to illustrate the beginning of the ratio-to-moving-average computations. The first step when using monthly data is to compute a twelve-month moving average (using quarterly data, a four-quarter moving average would be computed). Because all of the months of the year are included in this moving average, effects due to the seasonal component itself are removed, leaving only the effects due to long-term trend, cyclical, and irregular components in the moving averages.

The steps for computing seasonal indexes by the ratio-to-moving average method are given below and shown in Table 6.12.

1. Compute the twelve-month moving totals and place the total for January, 1969 through December, 1969 opposite July 1, 1969.
2. In order to have the subsequent averages located at the center of each month, compute a two-year moving total.
3. Since the two-year total contains the data for 24 months (January, 1969 once; February, 1969–December, 1969 twice; and January, 1970, once) this total is centered (opposite) July 15, 1969. (9448 + 9409 = 18,857)
4. Divide the two-year moving total by 24 in order to obtain the twelve-month centered moving average. [(18,857/24) = 785.71]
5. The ratio-to-moving average is calculated by dividing the actual value for each month by the twelve-month centered moving average and multiplying by 100 so that the ratio is an index number in the form of a percentage. $[S = TSCI/TCI = 815.00/785.71(100) = 103.73]$

Next, determine the average percentage ratio for each month by computing some kind of average. Table 6.13 shows the use of the modified mean method. This approach involves eliminating the highest and lowest values, and averaging the remaining indexes.

From Table 6.13 the computation of the modified mean for January would be as shown below.

Modified Mean		
79.90		Eliminate the highest (87.86) and
80.69	80.69	lowest (79.90), and average the rest.
81.54	81.54	
81.87	81.87	$329.25 \div 4 = 82.31$
85.15	85.15	
87.86	329.25	

TABLE 6.13 Seasonal Variation. Calculation of Seasonal Indexes Using Percent of Twelve-Month Moving Average

Month	1969	1970	1971	1972	1973	1974	1975	Modified Month Mean	Adjusted Seasonal Index Mean · 1.007148
Jan.		79.90	81.87	81.54	87.86	80.69	85.15	82.31	82.9
Feb.		74.66	85.63	80.44	88.33	75.09	89.00	82.37	83.0
Mar.		96.53	111.70	97.07	104.47	84.80	96.08	98.54	99.2
Apr.		102.03	112.91	96.00	101.36	92.35	87.42	97.94	98.6
May		106.87	109.37	110.68	111.04	99.09	98.36	106.50	107.3
Jun.		126.60	113.01	111.53	112.52	112.34	109.08	112.35	113.2
Jul.	103.73	120.12	98.98	100.42	117.55	120.80		110.46	111.2
Aug.	91.85	97.85	95.33	107.07	106.54	117.12		101.70	102.4
Sept.	93.48	87.06	95.97	91.73	91.21	102.08		93.10	93.8
Oct.	122.24	101.33	112.51	98.28	105.88	107.54		106.82	107.6
Nov.	98.03	75.03	112.87	100.55	105.36	89.56		98.37	99.1
Dec.	118.37	84.44	105.95	104.43	106.98	86.77		101.03	101.8
								1191.48	1200.0

Finally, determine the seasonal indexes by multiplying each of the average ratios by a value such that the sum of all twelve monthly indexes is equal to exactly 1200. Since this multiplier should be greater than 1 if the total of the averages before adjustment is less than 1200, the multiplier is defined as

$$\frac{1200}{Actual\ Total}$$

Table 6.13 shows the computation for the new passenger car registration data.

$$\frac{1200}{1191.48} = 1.007148$$

The final column of Table 6.13 lists the computed seasonal index values for each month, determined by making the adjustment (multiplying by 1.007148). In scanning these values, it is obvious that the seasonal peak in the number of new car registrations occurs in the early summer months, and the seasonal low occurs in the months of January and February.

Weather plays an important role in the explanation of the seasonal pattern of this variable. New car registrations tend to be up in good weather months such as June and July and down in bad weather months such as January and February. The peak in October is probably caused by the introduction of new car models. The low for September, perhaps, reflects consumer's lack of money after summer vacations and the tendency of people to wait for the new models.

The results of a seasonal variation analysis can be used in a number of ways: (1) to schedule production; (2) to de-seasonalize sales; (3) to evaluate current sales, production, and shipments; and/or (4) to forecast monthly sales.

Seasonally Adjusted Data

A large number of economic indicators appear in each issue of *The Survey of Current Business*. Many of these contain *seasonally adjusted data* to enable users of the index to see patterns that are independent of seasonal variations. Removal of seasonal variations helps clarify basic strengths or weaknesses in the data. For example, new car registrations might increase by 15% from September to October. Is this an indication that new car sales are headed for a banner quarter? The question can be answered more accurately if the seasonal fluctuations in new car registrations are known. Table 6.13 indicates that a sharp increase from September to October is typical. Perhaps an adjustment for seasonal increase would demonstrate that all of the increase is due to seasonal factors.

If the original monthly values of a time series are divided by their corresponding seasonal indexes, the resulting data are said to be de-seasonalized, or adjusted for seasonal variation. Since the resulting values still include the trend, cyclical, and irregular movements, the process of deseasonalizing data can be algebraically represented by

$$\frac{TSCI}{S} = TCI \qquad (6\text{-}17)$$

Table 6.14 lists the seasonally adjusted data for new car registrations. These values were calculated by dividing the actual monthly values of Table 6.12 by the seasonal indexes of Table 6.13, and by multiplying the result by 100. Because the effect of the seasonal component has been removed from these data, notice that in this table the number of new car registrations for June of each year, a high registration month, is not markedly higher than for September, a low registration month. Thus, the data of Table 6.14 have had the effect of the seasonal component removed, but still include the effects of the trend, cyclical, and irregular components. The seasonally adjusted data (TCI) are shown in the third column of Table 6.14.

Example for January, 1969.

$$Y = 658$$

$$S = 0.829 \text{ (Table 6.13)}$$

$$Y = TSCI$$

$$Y/S = TCI$$

$$\frac{658}{0.829} = 793.71$$

Monthly or Quarterly Trend Values

In order to compute trend values for monthly data, two approaches are available. The least-squares procedure illustrated in Table 6.14 can be used with the monthly data to arrive at a monthly trend equation. This approach is tedious and time consuming, however, unless a computer is used. It also might not provide a true indication of the variable's trend since only the most recent data are considered. Trend was defined as, "the long-term component in a time series that underlies the growth (or decline) in the series." In conjunction with this definition the best approach to the development of a monthly trend equation seems to be to use the long-term trend equation already computed. Fortunately, trend values for monthly data can be obtained quite easily by computing the values of b_0 and b in annual terms and then by converting these to monthly values.

In order to change the equation from annual to monthly, the following four steps need to be accomplished:

TABLE 6.14 *Time Series Analysis—Trend, Seasonal, Cyclical, and Irregular —Current and Forecast—*

TIME SERIES ANALYSIS--TREND, SEASONAL, CYCLICAL, AND IRREGULAR
----CURRENT AND FORECAST----

PERIOD		DATA Y	REGRESSION T	SEAS. ADJ TCI	CI	C	I
1969	JAN	658.00	730.23	793.71	108.69		
	FEB	608.00	731.80	732.88	100.15		
	MAR	681.00	733.38	686.21	93.57	107.16	87.32
	APR	876.00	734.95	888.11	120.84	105.58	114.45
	MAY	889.00	736.53	828.81	112.53	105.36	106.80
	JUN	842.00	738.10	744.13	100.82	105.59	95.48
	JUL	815.00	739.67	732.62	99.05	102.47	96.66
	AUG	719.00	741.25	701.97	94.70	103.84	91.20
	SEP	733.00	742.82	781.75	105.24	104.18	101.01
	OCT	956.00	744.40	888.64	119.38	108.38	110.15
	NOV	758.00	745.97	765.06	102.56	109.38	93.77
	DEC	913.00	747.54	897.26	120.03	106.89	112.29
1970	JAN	619.00	749.12	746.67	99.67	102.86	96.90
	FEB	578.00	750.69	696.72	92.81	103.01	90.10
	MAR	741.00	752.27	746.66	99.26	98.36	100.91
	APR	768.00	753.84	778.62	103.29	99.46	103.85
	MAY	784.00	755.41	730.92	96.76	100.76	96.03
	JUN	901.00	756.99	796.27	105.19	98.45	106.84
	JUL	838.00	758.56	753.29	99.31	94.93	104.61
	AUG	683.00	760.14	666.83	87.72	93.09	94.23
	SEP	612.00	761.71	652.71	85.69	86.23	99.37
	OCT	719.00	763.28	668.34	87.56	81.93	106.87
	NOV	537.00	764.86	542.00	70.86	82.86	85.52
	DEC	607.00	766.43	596.53	77.83	85.08	91.48
1971	JAN	588.00	768.01	709.28	92.35	89.00	103.77
	FEB	618.00	769.58	744.93	96.80	97.08	99.71
	MAR	820.00	771.15	826.27	107.15	101.98	105.07
	APR	848.00	772.73	859.73	111.26	104.26	106.71
	MAY	850.00	774.30	792.45	102.34	103.73	98.67
	JUN	911.00	775.88	805.11	103.77	102.12	101.61
	JUL	814.00	777.45	731.72	94.12	101.73	92.51
	AUG	791.00	779.02	772.27	99.13	103.56	95.73
	SEP	800.00	780.60	853.21	109.30	107.14	102.01
	OCT	938.00	782.17	871.91	111.47	110.70	100.70
	NOV	945.00	783.75	953.80	121.70	112.09	108.58
	DEC	894.00	785.32	878.58	111.88	111.32	100.50
1972	JAN	692.00	786.89	834.73	106.08	110.45	96.04
	FEB	690.00	788.47	831.72	105.49	107.37	98.24
	MAR	840.00	790.04	846.42	107.14	107.43	99.73
	APR	830.00	791.62	841.48	106.30	107.65	98.75
	MAY	954.00	793.19	889.41	112.13	106.35	105.43
	JUN	964.00	794.76	851.95	107.19	108.12	99.14
	JUL	877.00	796.34	788.35	99.00	108.85	90.95
	AUG	948.00	797.91	925.55	116.00	107.19	108.21
	SEP	824.00	799.49	878.81	109.92	109.04	100.81
	OCT	895.00	801.06	831.94	103.85	112.97	91.93
	NOV	926.00	802.63	934.63	116.44	114.60	101.61
	DEC	971.00	804.21	954.26	118.66	117.78	100.74

183

TABLE 6.14 *Continued*

PERIOD		DATA Y	REGRESSION T	SEAS. ADJ. TCI	CI	C	I
1973	JAN	829.00	805.78	999.98	124.10	121.88	101.83
	FEB	843.00	807.36	1016.15	125.86	122.83	102.47
	MAR	998.00	808.93	1005.63	124.32	123.46	100.69
	APR	969.00	810.50	982.40	121.21	121.86	99.46
	MAY	1061.00	812.08	989.16	121.81	121.01	100.66
	JUN	1069.00	813.65	944.74	116.11	119.58	97.10
	JUL	1103.00	815.23	991.50	121.62	116.60	104.30
	AUG	980.00	816.80	956.79	117.14	113.10	103.57
	SEP	816.00	818.37	870.27	106.34	111.72	95.18
	OCT	920.00	819.95	855.18	104.30	108.32	96.29
	NOV	889.00	821.52	897.28	109.22	103.70	105.32
	DEC	876.00	823.10	860.89	104.59	99.50	105.12
1974	JAN	643.00	824.67	775.62	94.05	94.49	99.54
	FEB	585.00	826.24	705.16	85.34	89.71	95.13
	MAR	651.00	827.82	655.98	79.24	85.17	93.04
	APR	698.00	829.39	707.65	85.32	83.37	102.34
	MAY	730.00	830.97	680.57	81.90	84.47	96.96
	JUN	801.00	832.54	707.89	85.03	87.64	97.02
	JUL	843.00	834.11	757.79	90.85	88.64	102.49
	AUG	814.00	835.69	794.72	95.10	88.68	107.24
	SEP	709.00	837.26	756.16	90.31	86.33	104.62
	OCT	741.00	838.84	688.79	82.11	81.84	100.34
	NOV	610.00	840.41	615.68	73.26	79.12	92.60
	DEC	586.00	841.98	575.89	68.40	77.89	87.82
1975	JAN	570.00	843.56	687.56	81.51	76.58	106.44
	FEB	590.00	845.13	711.18	84.15	75.81	111.00
	MAR	635.00	846.71	639.85	75.57	76.55	98.72
	APR	581.00	848.28	589.03	69.44	75.53	91.94
	MAY	657.00	849.85	612.52	72.07	74.82	96.33
	JUN	736.00	851.43	650.45	76.40	76.52	99.83
	JUL	765.00	853.00	687.67	80.62	81.05	99.47
	AUG	736.00	854.58	718.57	84.09	83.95	100.16
	SEP	739.00	856.15	788.15	92.06	83.54	110.20
	OCT	799.00	857.72	742.70	86.59	83.97	103.12
	NOV	633.00	859.30	638.90	74.35		
	DEC	725.00	860.87	712.50	82.76		
1976	JAN		862.45				
	FEB		864.02				
	MAR		865.59				
	APR		867.17				
	MAY		868.74				
	JUN		870.32				
	JUL		871.89				
	AUG		873.46				
	SEP		875.04				
	OCT		876.61				
	NOV		878.19				
	DEC		879.76				

REGRESSION FORECAST = 1.574000 X PERIOD + 730.23

1. The slope and constant need to be converted from annual values to monthly values. This is accomplished by dividing b_0 and b by 12, (divide by 4 if quarterly data are used). When the data are cumulative or the annual figures are averages, this step is omitted. In other words, the monthly or quarterly data *must* add to the annual totals in order for this step to apply.

2. Are the annual and monthly or quarterly data recorded in the same type of units? If the answer to this question is yes, omit this step. If the answer is no, convert the annual data to monthly by moving the decimal point accordingly.
3. Convert the X value from annual to monthly by dividing by 12. Convert from annual to quarterly by dividing the X value by 4.
4. Shift the origin to the middle of the first month of data, usually January 15. If quarterly data are employed, shift to the middle of the first quarter, usually February 15.

To illustrate this procedure, the annual equation developed in Table 6.3 for the new car registration problem is converted to a monthly equation.
The equation was

$$Y_R = 4.787 + 0.22669X$$

where: 1 unit of X represented 1 year
$X = 0$ represented July 1, 1951

Step 1:   To change the scale of the equation from annual totals to monthly totals, we divide b_0 and b by 12.

$$Y_R = \frac{4.787}{12} + \frac{0.22669}{12}X$$

$$Y_R = 0.3989 + 0.01889X$$

Step 2:   Are the annual and monthly data recorded in the same type of units? Since the annual data are recorded in millions of registrations and the monthly data in thousands, the answer to this question is *no*.

For forecasting the monthly registration figures in terms of *thousands* of units instead of millions of units, the equation is modified to read

$$Y_R = 398.9 + 18.89X$$

Step 3:   The X in the equation still refers to units in terms of years. The X is converted so that it represents months by dividing it by 12; thus,

$$Y_R = 398.9 + 18.89\frac{X}{12}$$

$$Y_R = 398.9 + 1.574X$$

Step 4:   Finally, in order to let $X = 0$ represent the first month of the monthly data, January 15, 1969, instead of July 1, 1951, the origin must be shifted. This step is particularly useful because the data are centered in each month. In order to move forward from July 1, 1951 to January 15, 1969; 210.5 months must be added to the X coded value. The final monthly trend equation is

$$Y_R = 398.9 + 1.574 \, (X + 210.5)$$

$$Y_R = 398.9 + 1.574X + 331.33$$

$$Y_R = 730.23 + 1.574X$$

where: Y_R = expected monthly trend values
X = monthly values with 0 located at January 15, 1969

Short Term Cyclical and Irregular

The cyclical and irregular variations can now be calculated from the short-term analysis. Since the data have been seasonally adjusted,

$$\frac{TSCI}{S} = TCI$$

these de-seasonalized values can now be divided by the appropriate monthly trend values.

$$\frac{TCI}{T} = CI$$

The CI is shown in column 4 of Table 6.14.

Example   for January, 1969.

$$Y = 658$$

$$S = 0.829 \text{ (Table 6.13)}$$

$$T = 730.23 \text{ (Table 6.14)}$$

$$\frac{TSCI}{S} = \frac{658}{0.829} = 793.71$$

$$\frac{TCI}{T} = \frac{793.71}{730.23} (100) = 108.69$$

After the data have been adjusted for seasonal and trend influences, the cyclical and irregular variation is analyzed. With annual data the CI is investigated as one entity; however, with monthly data the *C* and the *I* can be separated. This is possible due to the short-term effects of irregular variations. A moving average is developed to smooth out the irregularities. The computational procedure is simple and illustrated in Table 6.15.

TABLE 6.15   *Computational Procedure for Five Month Moving Average.*

COMPUTATIONAL PROCEDURE FOR
5 MONTH MOVING AVERAGE

		CI	5 MONTH MOVING TOTAL	C
1969	JAN	108.69		
	FEB	100.15		
	MAR	93.57	535.78	107.16
	APR	120.84	527.91	105.58
	MAY	112.53	526.81	105.36
	JUN	100.82		
	JUL	99.05		

The five-month moving averages entered in column 5 of Table 6.14 (labeled *C*) presumably reflect only the effect of the short-term cyclical component. If the residual variations of Table 6.14 indeed represent the cyclical effect in the time series, it appears that throughout the 1971–1973 period the cycle was well above that expected, and during 1974 and 1975 new car registrations were seriously depressed. Leading indicators can now be investigated.

Finally, the identification of the short-term irregular component is accomplished by dividing each of the values already adjusted for seasonal and trend (Table 6.14) *CI* by the values representing the effect of only the cyclical (Table 6.14) *C*, and multiplying by 100. The resulting index number helps to identify the relative contribution of the irregular component in the monthly values of the time series, as illustrated in column 6 of Table 6.14 (labeled *I*). In terms of algebraic representation, the irregular component has been segregated in the following manner:

$$\frac{CI}{C} = I \qquad (6\text{-}18)$$

187

Example   for March, 1969.

$$CI = 93.57$$

$$C = 107.16$$

$$I = \frac{CI}{C}(100) = \frac{0.9357}{1.0716}(100) = 87.32$$

The irregular variations in a time series, especially those that are sizable, can usually be explained. For example, according to Table 6.14 a definite irregularity occurred in November and December of 1970. This was caused by a major strike against General Motors by the United Auto Workers, which lasted from September 15 to November 20. Production was cut in half by the strike. Another irregular drop was caused by wage problems and strikes in November and December of 1974.

The decomposition of the new car registration variable is now complete. The short-term monthly data have been separated into components.

Example T = *Trend*   (October, 1975) = 857.72 (See Table 6.14)
S = *Seasonal*   (October)   = 107.6 (See Table 6.13)
C = *Cyclical*   (October, 1975) = 83.97 (See Table 6.14)
I = *Irregular*   (October, 1975) = 103.12 (See Table 6.14)

In order to put the series back together, we return to the original multiplicative model and substitute the appropriate components.

Example $Y = TSCI$

$$Y \text{ (Oct., 1975)} = (857.72)(1.076)(0.8397)(1.0312)$$

$$Y \text{ (Oct., 1975)} = 799 \text{ (See Table 6.14)}$$

Short-Term Forecasting

The multiplicative model $Y = TSCI$ can be used to develop the short-term forecast for January, 1976. Again, each individual component must be estimated on an accurate basis.

1. Trend

The monthly trend estimate is determined by using the appropriate monthly trend equation, in this case $Y_R = 730.23 + 1.574X$. Since $X = 0$ represents January 15, 1969, the X coded value representing January, 1976 is 84.

Example　　　　Trend for January, 1976.

$$Y_R = 730.23 + 1.574X$$

$$Y_R = 730.23 + 1.574 (84)$$

$$Y_R = 730.23 + 132.216$$

$$Y_R = 862.45 \text{ (See Table 6.14)}$$

2. Seasonal

The adjusted seasonal index for the month of January 82.9 was computed in Table 6.13.

3. Cyclical

The cyclical relative must be estimated subjectively using all the gathered information on the cyclical pattern. Leading indicators are especially valuable. The long-term cyclical estimate must be considered. In order to demonstrate the completion of this example, a cyclical index of 87 is estimated.

4. Irregular

The irregular index must also be estimated from past experience. Since irregular fluctuations are oftentimes random variations, an estimate of 100 will commonly be used. Occasionally we can identify past irregularities, but cannot predict them. In this situation an estimate of 100 will again be useful. Finally, some instances help us anticipate irregularities from past experience. We may be able to predict a strike or some governmental action. When this is the case, an estimate can be developed for the irregular index. In this example Table 6.14 indicates that no major irregularities have occurred during previous Januarys. Therefore, an estimate of 100 is appropriate.

Example　　　　Forecast for January, 1976.

$$Y = TSCI$$

$$(Y, \text{Jan.}, 1976) = 862.45 \times 0.829 \times 0.87 \times 1.00$$

$$(Y, \text{Jan.}, 1976) = 622.02$$

In actual practice the importance of individual components dictates their usage in short-term forecasting. If a variable is extremely seasonal, the seasonal variation analysis will provide important, if not complete, input into the forecasting process. If a dependable leading indicator is discovered, the short-term forecast might be totally based upon it. Hence, if one component dominates the analysis, it alone might provide a practical, accurate forecast.

Summary

Forecasting is a necessary task for a business in order to budget time and resources. Forecasts provide a plan, however tentative, for the business to follow in order to achieve its objectives and remain competitive.

Forecasting methods are many and varied. Traditionally, forecasting has been quite subjective, without relying on rigorous mathematical forecasting models. The use of mathematical forecasting models for time series has been suggested in this chapter since these models can be:

1. designed to track the specific components (long-term trend, cyclical, and seasonal effects) within the time series under study; and
2. adapted to conform to the intuitive knowledge of the business about the time series.

The last point is especially important; it implies that the ingenuity of the business statistician is an essential factor in the selection of an appropriate forecasting model.

The ultimate criterion for the value of a time series forecasting model is how well it forecasts the future. Forecasting models are always based on the assumption that past behavior of the time series accurately reflects its future behavior. Dormant variables and other factors may cause a time series to react differently in the future than it has ever reacted before. Thus, a model that "fits" the sample data may well be a poor model to forecast the future behavior of the time series.

Thus, statistical analysis provides only a starting point in the analysis of a time series and the adoption of a forecasting scheme. Statistical and mathematical models are limited and cannot provide a complete solution to forecasting as long as uncertainty exists.

Time Series Analysis Case

Ms. Love,* an analyst for the Wheeler Electric Range Corporation, is assigned the task of forecasting corporation sales. She determines that

---

*Marilyn Jean Love developed this time series analysis case while completing her B.A. degree at Eastern Washington University.

Wheeler sales typically represent 3 percent of nationwide electric range sales. If Ms. Love can successfully estimate sales at the national level, she will be able to forecast Wheeler Corporation sales for 1976.

Household electric ranges are not a product that goes out of style quickly. They are a durable good whose useful life averages between 10 and 15 years. Therefore, replacement sales are very important. People who purchase ranges tend to be either first-time buyers, remodelers, or new feature seekers. Whatever the reason for buying an electric range, sales have varied over time, and Ms. Love decides to investigate the various time series components. The nationwide electric range sales in thousands for 1959–75 are presented in Table 6.16.

TABLE 6.16   *Electric Range Sales (Thousands).*

1959	1687
1960	1495
1961	1530
1962	1675
1963	1870
1964	1965
1965	2075
1966	2029
1967	1910
1968	2307
1969	2342
1970	2362
1971	2714
1972	3232
1973	3430
1974	2925
1975	2014

Trend

As shown on Fig. 6–10, household electric range sales (over $2\frac{1}{2}$ K.W.) have been growing at a fairly even amount over the past 17 years. This increased growth in sales can be attributed to many factors. One of the most important variables affecting the trend is population growth. The population of the United States has increased from approximately 180 million in 1959 to 212 million in 1975. As the population grows, the need for electric ranges also grows. The number of people in the 25–39 age bracket is of special interest because they spend the most on household appliances. The number of people in the 25–39 age bracket has been increasing steadily and is expected to grow by 23 percent between 1974 and 1980, as compared to a 6 percent expected increase in the total population.

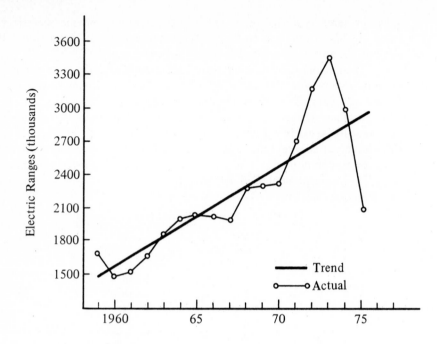

FIGURE 6–10   *Trend for Electric Ranges.*

The income level of the population has also been steadily increasing. People have been able to replace older model ranges with better, more efficient ones. They have had enough income to buy new models to match new kitchen improvements, even when their old model was still in working condition.

The long-term growth movement for electric ranges can best be described by the linear trend model, $Y_R = 1389.12 + 91.15X$ (origin: July 1, 1958; 1 unit of $X = 1$ year). There were an expected 1,389,120 ranges sold in 1958, and the average amount of increase since then has been 91,150 per year. This trend model explains only 9 percent, $R^2 = .09$, of the sales variable variance. While the linear model does accurately indicate the growth movement of electric range sales, other factors will need to be analyzed in order to forecast accurately.

Cyclical and Irregular

The fluctuations in the growth of electric range sales can be attributed largely to the fluctuations in the economy. The cyclical movement in the

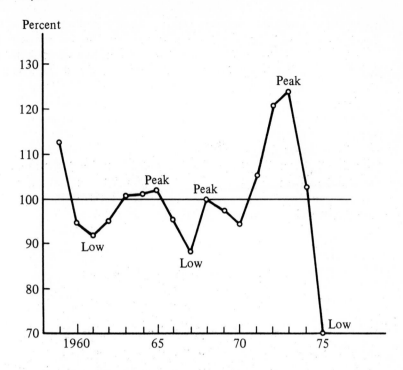

FIGURE 6–11 *Cyclical for Electric Ranges.*

number of electric ranges sold over time is shown in Fig. 6–11. A peak time for sales is in 1965. The increasing amount of installment credit granted to lower incomes and the rising incomes from the healthy economy greatly increased demand for electric ranges. Kitchen remodeling was growing

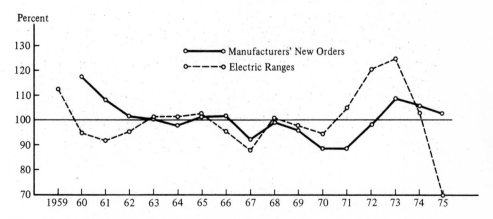

FIGURE 6–12 *Electric Ranges Related to Manufacturers' New Orders.*

in popularity and manufacturers were greeting consumers with new styles. Besides the healthy economy, the many electric ranges bought right after the Second World War had come to the end of their 10-to-15 year life cycles and were ready to be replaced. In 1968 and 1973, electric range sales also peaked. In these years the economy was doing well. The effect of the expanding market for mobile homes and apartments starting in 1971 can be seen in Fig. 6–11. The enriched demand caused electric range sales to move upward.

The low points in electric range sales all occurred when the economy was suffering—1967, 1969, 1970, 1974, and 1975 were time periods when the economy was depressed. Also in 1967, electric range imports from Europe and Japan were especially high. This increase in imports together with the depressed economy greatly decreased sales.

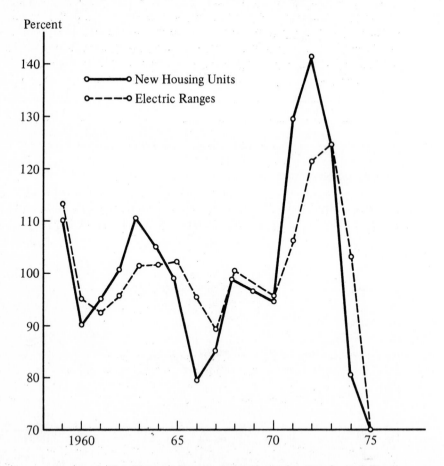

FIGURE 6–13 *Electric Ranges Related to the Number of New Housing Units Started.*

TABLE 6.17 *Electric Range Sales Trend Analysis and Cyclical Results.*

Year	Data	Regression	Cyclical
1959	1687.00	1480.31	113.96
1960	1495.00	1571.47	95.13
1961	1530.00	1662.62	92.02
1962	1675.00	1753.77	95.51
1963	1870.00	1844.92	101.36
1964	1965.00	1936.07	101.49
1965	2075.00	2027.23	102.36
1966	2029.00	2118.38	95.78
1967	1910.00	2209.53	86.44
1968	2307.00	2300.68	100.27
1969	2342.00	2391.83	97.92
1970	2362.00	2482.99	95.13
1971	2714.00	2574.14	105.43
1972	3232.00	2665.29	121.26
1973	3430.00	2756.44	124.44
1974	2925.00	2847.59	102.72
1975	2014.00	2938.74	68.53
1976		3029.90	
1977		3121.05	
1978		3212.20	
1979		3303.35	
1980		3394.50	

$Y_R = 1389.12 + 91.15X$ (origin: July 1, 1958; 1 unit of X = 1 year)

Figure 6–12 shows a coincidental indicator, the new orders for household durables. The cyclical pattern of this indicator is related to the cyclical pattern for electric ranges sold. Knowledge of new orders for household durables might help anticipate movement in electric range sales.

The cyclical for new housing starts tends to lead the cyclical for electric range sales, as indicated by Fig. 6–13. The low sales of 1961, 1967, and 1971 might have been predicted by the decreased number of housing units started in 1960, 1966, and 1970. In 1973 and 1974, housing starts were dropping drastically. This is shown in the sharp decline of electric range sales in 1974 and 1975. New housing starts should prove to be an effective leading indicator, and should be investigated on a monthly basis.

Long-Term Forecast

The trend analysis, presented in Table 6.17 indicates that 3,029,900 electric ranges are expected to be sold in 1976. Ms. Love feels that this quantity is extremely high considering that the economy is just beginning to recover from a deep recession. In 1975 the number of *housing units started* dropped. This means that sales in 1976 can be expected to drop below 1975 electric range sales. Toward the end of 1975, *housing units started* begin to increase so Ms. Love does not expect a drastic decrease. In fact, since the economy was expected to improve and the number of *housing units started* was on the increase, Ms. Love chooses a cyclical relative index of 80 for the year 1976. Her final forecast is

$$Y = TCI$$

$$Y(1976) = (3029.9)(0.80)$$

$$Y(1976) = 2423.92 \text{ thousand}$$

Since this represents a forecast of nationwide electric range sales, Ms. Love takes 3 percent and projects sales for Wheeler Corporation to be 72,718 in 1976.

Seasonal Variation

Examination of the adjusted seasonal indexes in Table 6.18 show a considerable amount of seasonal variation in the sale of electric ranges. The 1st quarter sales are low due mainly to a lack of money. Leftover Christmas expenses, income taxes, car licenses, and insurance premiums all cut down on the amount people have available to spend on a major appliance. Electric range sales improve during the spring months due to numerous sales promotions and the improved money situation of most people. August is a good month because new housing units that were started in the spring are now completed and must be furnished. October is the best month because new housing units that were started in the summer are now completed. October is also a time when fall sales are prevalent. December is a low month because people spend on Christmas and not on household appliances unless they give them as presents.

TABLE 6.18   *Adjusted Seasonal Indexes.*

January	92.1	July	101.5
February	84.8	August	107.2
March	97.3	September	101.6
April	100.5	October	114.5
May	104.4	November	99.6
June	105.1	December	91.3

Cyclical

Figure 6–14 shows the cyclical variations in the monthly data for electric range sales and for the number of housing units started. The cyclical variation shows an increase between 1971 and 1973. New *housing units started* increased until the latter part of 1972. The increase in the number of new *housing units started* led the growing electric range sales by about 2 months. In July, 1971, the electric range cyclical started increasing at a faster rate. This was due to the increase in the mobile home market during the summer months. In November of 1972, the number of *housing units started* dropped off quickly. They rose slightly in the early part of 1973 only to drop steadily downward until February of 1975. Electric range sales followed the same pattern. In the beginning of 1973, electric range sales started declining just like the *housing units started*. The decline was drastic until April of 1975. However, the number of *housing units started* did not always lead by a constant time period. It usually led by at least 1 or 2 months for upturns and downturns.

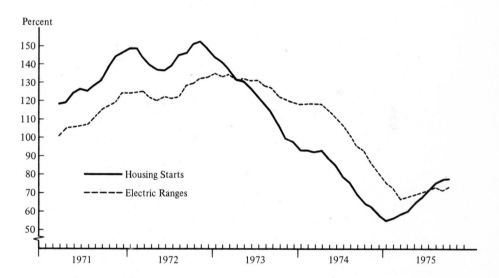

Figure 6–14 *Electric Ranges Related to Number of New Housing Units Started.*

Another reason for the decline in electric range sales is an increasing amount of younger and older segments of the population eating away from home. Retirees and young marrieds with larger incomes and more free time are traveling and eating out rather than preparing food at home. In addition, fast food and similar type operators are catering to the average family, offering appetizing meals at a price comparable to the cost of preparing a meal at home. As a result, electric range sales decrease.

Irregularities

The irregular component in time series analysis helps explain random fluctuations caused by nonpredictable events. In 1971, 1972, and 1973, the irregularities in the number of household electric ranges sold are very slight (see Table 6.20 column I). In 1974, the high in December may have been caused by new and more attractive styles of electric ranges offered to consumers during that year. Two styles introduced were the new stay-clean oven and the space-age range control. These new styles were probably bought as Christmas presents because they were so practical and attractive. The new stay-clean oven required little or no cleaning and did not become greasy. Another reported advantage of the oven was that several items could be cooked simultaneously since a constant temperature was maintained throughout the oven. Food cooked in the hot-air oven was said to be especially juicy due to less moisture being lost through evaporation.

TABLE 6.19 *Short Term Forecast for Wheeler Electric Range Corporation*

	T	$\ast$	S	$\ast$	C	$\ast$	I	$=$	Forecast National	Wheeler
Jan.	241.41		0.921		.77		1.00		171.20	5.14
Feb.	242.05		0.848		.78		1.00		160.10	4,80
Mar.	242.68		0.973		.79		1.00		186.54	5.60
Apr.	243.31		1.005		.80		1.00		195.62	5.87
May	243.95		1.044		.81		1.00		205.75	6.17
June	244.58		1.051		.82		1.00		210.78	6.32
July	245.21		1.015		.83		1.00		206.58	6.20
Aug.	245.84		1.072		.84		1.00		221.37	6.64
Sept.	246.48		1.016		.85		1.00		212.86	6.39
Oct.	247.11		1.145		.86		1.00		243.33	7.30
Nov.	247.74		0.996		.86		1.00		212.20	6.37
Dec.	248.38		0.913		.87		1.00		197.29	5.92
									2,423.62	72.72

The space-age range control was an unveiled electric range that brought computer technology into the kitchen to simplify cooking operations. A flat glass control panel on the range featured unique touch points—similar to modern elevator touch buttons—to control all operations on the range. Digital readouts were incorporated into the electronic controls. These two new attractive styles encouraged the giving of electric ranges as Christmas gifts.

Short-Term Forecasting

Ms. Love uses the model $Y = TSCI$ to forecast monthly sales. The long-term trend equation is converted so that it can be used with monthly data.

TABLE 6.20 *Short-Term Computer Output.*

SHORT-TERM COMPUTER OUTPUT

PERIOD		DATA	REGRESSION	SEAS. ADJ.			
		Y	T	TCI	CI	C	I
1971	JAN	163.00	203.43	176.92	86.97		
	FEB	179.00	204.07	210.99	103.39		
	MAR	224.00	204.70	230.28	112.50	100.82	111.58
	APR	212.00	205.33	210.84	102.68	105.07	97.73
	MAY	212.00	205.97	203.04	98.58	106.16	92.87
	JUN	235.00	206.60	223.53	108.19	106.45	101.63
	JUL	229.00	207.23	225.52	108.82	107.35	101.38
	AUG	254.00	207.86	236.95	113.99	111.53	102.21
	SEP	227.00	208.50	223.40	107.15	114.88	93.27
	OCT	286.00	209.13	249.86	119.48	117.27	101.88
	NOV	261.00	209.76	262.17	124.98	119.58	104.52
	DEC	232.00	210.40	254.11	120.78	124.65	96.89
1972	JAN	244.00	211.03	264.84	125.50	124.49	100.81
	FEB	238.00	211.66	280.53	132.54	125.09	105.96
	MAR	245.00	212.30	251.87	118.64	125.42	94.60
	APR	274.00	212.93	272.50	127.98	121.90	104.99
	MAY	273.00	213.56	261.47	122.43	120.05	101.98
	JUN	243.00	214.19	231.14	107.91	122.04	88.42
	JUL	269.00	214.83	264.91	123.31	121.77	101.27
	AUG	297.00	215.46	277.06	128.59	122.52	104.96
	SEP	278.00	216.09	273.59	126.61	128.39	98.61
	OCT	313.00	216.73	273.45	126.17	129.75	97.24
	NOV	297.00	217.36	298.33	137.25	132.33	103.72
	DEC	259.00	217.99	283.69	130.14	132.81	97.98
1973	JAN	285.00	218.63	309.35	141.50	135.07	104.76
	FEB	240.00	219.26	282.89	129.02	133.42	96.71
	MAR	294.00	219.89	302.24	137.45	134.41	102.26
	APR	286.00	220.52	284.44	128.98	131.16	98.34
	MAY	312.00	221.16	298.82	135.12	132.27	102.15
	JUN	292.00	221.79	277.74	125.23	129.46	96.73
	JUL	304.00	222.42	299.38	134.60	129.53	103.91

PERIOD		DATA	REGRESSION	SEAS. ADJ			
		Y	T	TCI	CI	C	I
	AUG	295.00	223.06	275.20	123.37	128.29	96.17
	SEP	294.00	223.69	289.34	129.35	126.82	101.99
	OCT	331.00	224.32	289.17	128.91	122.33	105.37
	NOV	264.00	224.96	265.18	117.88	120.88	97.52
	DEC	231.00	225.59	253.02	112.16	119.43	93.91
1974	JAN	242.00	226.22	262.67	116.11	118.23	98.21
	FEB	235.00	226.85	277.00	122.10	118.38	103.15
	MAR	272.00	227.49	279.63	122.92	118.55	103.68
	APR	272.00	228.12	270.51	118.58	118.05	100.45
	MAY	270.00	228.75	258.59	113.04	115.21	98.12
	JUN	274.00	229.39	260.62	113.62	110.93	102.42
	JUL	252.00	230.02	248.17	107.89	106.87	100.95
	AUG	251.00	230.65	234.15	101.52	101.82	99.70
	SEP	231.00	231.29	227.34	98.29	95.59	102.82
	OCT	233.00	231.92	203.56	87.77	92.99	94.39
	NOV	191.00	232.55	191.85	82.50	86.15	95.76
	DEC	202.00	233.18	221.25	94.88	80.27	118.21
1975	JAN	145.00	233.82	157.39	67.31	75.83	88.76
	FEB	137.00	234.45	161.48	68.88	72.84	94.57
	MAR	150.00	235.08	154.21	65.60	66.42	98.76
	APR	160.00	235.72	159.13	67.51	67.89	99.44
	MAY	155.00	236.35	148.45	62.81	68.79	91.31
	JUN	186.00	236.98	176.92	74.66	69.68	107.13
	JUL	177.00	237.62	174.31	73.36	71.59	102.47
	AUG	179.00	238.25	166.98	70.09	73.47	95.39
	SEP	187.00	238.88	184.04	77.04	71.59	107.61
	OCT	198.00	239.51	172.98	72.22	73.66	98.05
	NOV	156.00	240.15	156.70	65.25		
	DEC	184.00	240.78	201.54	83.70		
1976	JAN		241.41				
	FEB		242.05				
	MAR		242.68				
	APR		243.31				
	MAY		243.95				
	JUN		244.58				
	JUL		245.21				
	AUG		245.84				

PERIOD	DATA	REGRESSION	SEAS. ADJ
	Y	T	TCI
SEP		246.48	
OCT		247.11	
NOV		247.74	
DEC		248.38	

REGRESSION FORECAST = 0.633000 X PERIOD + 203.433940

The monthly trend equation shown in Table 6.20 is $Y_R = 203.434 + 0.633X$ (origin: Jan. 15, 1971; 1 unit of $X = 1$ month). The adjusted seasonal indexes for each month are presented in Table 6.18. A cyclical index is estimated for each month based on knowledge of the leading indicator and past experience. Finally, the irregular index is estimated as 100 for each month since it is practically impossible to anticipate any monthly irregularities for 1976.

Conclusion

Ms. Love found that the cyclical variable is the most important long-term component. This means that it will be very difficult for Wheeler Corporation to forecast more than one year in the future. If the trend were the most important component, long-term projections would be possible. Both seasonal and cyclical variations are extremely important components for the preparation of short-term forecasts. Since *housing units started* usually lead electric range sales by 2 months, revised short-term forecasts should be prepared each month. This constant-revision approach should improve the short-term forecasting accuracy greatly.

PROBLEMS

*1. Use the following information to answer the questions below.

$$Y_R = 400 + 15X$$

$$Y = \text{Annual Sales in Units}$$

201

$$X = 0 \text{ Represents July 1, 1968}$$

$$1 \quad \text{unit of } X = 1 \quad \text{year}$$

a. If 1975 is the last year of the data and the short-cut method is used, how many years of data are used to determine the trend equation?

b. Estimate sales for 1977.

c. What is the average increase in sales per year?

d. What were the expected sales for 1965?

2. Use the following information to answer the questions below.

$$Y_R = 100 + 5X$$

$$Y = \text{Annual Sales in Thousands of Dollars}$$

$$X = 0 \text{ Represents January 1, 1970}$$

$$1 \quad \text{unit of } X = \tfrac{1}{2} \text{ year}$$

a. If 1975 is the last year of the data and the short-cut method is used, how many years of data are used to determine the trend equation?

b. Estimate sales for 1978.

c. What is the average increase in sales per year?

d. What were the expected sales for 1971?

3. Use the following information to answer the questions below.

$$Y_R = 88.4 + 3.9X + 0.4X^2$$

$$Y = \text{Factory Sales of Trucks and Buses in the United States in Thousands of Dollars}$$

$$X = 0 \text{ Represents July 1, 1961}$$

$$1 \quad \text{unit of } X = 1 \text{ year}$$

a. Estimate sales for 1973.

b. What were the expected sales for 1958?

c. In what year does the curve change direction (line of symmetry)?

d. What was the minimum or maximum amount of factory sales of trucks and buses in the United States?

e. Is the value in part (d) a minimum or maximum?

*4. Use the following information to answer the questions below.

$$Y_R = 89.8 \, (1.08)^X$$

$$Y = \text{Business Expenditures for Plant and Equipment in the United States in Billions of Dollars}$$

$$X = 0 \text{ Represents July 1, 1972}$$

$$1 \quad \text{unit of } X = 1 \text{ year}$$

a. Estimate sales for 1980.

b. What were the expected sales for 1976?

202

    c. What is the average increase in sales per year?

5. Plot the curve represented by each of the following equations.
    a. $Y_R = 125 + 10X$, where $X = 0$, 1970; $X = 1$ year
    b. $Y_R = 50 - 2X$, where $X = 0$, 1968; $X = \frac{1}{2}$ year
    c. $Y_R = 100\,(1.10)^X$, where $X = 0$, 1969; $X = 1$ year
    d. $\log Y_R = 2.1543 + 0.0428X$, where $X = 0$, 1967; $X = 1$ year
    e. $Y_R = 9.8 - 0.22X + 0.14X^2$, where $X = 0$, 1970; $X = 1$ year

6. The following data are for the per capita retail pounds of beef consumed in the United States from 1963–71.

Year	Per Capita Consumption
1963	70
1964	74
1965	74
1966	77
1967	79
1968	81
1969	82
1970	84
1971	84

    a. Plot the data.
    b. Fit a linear trend equation.
    c. Estimate the expected per capita consumption for 1975 based on the trend.
    d. Compute the standard error of the estimate.
    e. What factor or factors affect the trend of beef consumption?

*7. The following data are for men's sportcoat production.

Year	Sportcoats (thousands of units)
1965	12.3
1966	13.4
1967	13.2
1968	14.2
1969	14.3
1970	11.8
1971	14.4
1972	21.3
1973	21.5
1974	17.6

203

a. Plot the data.
b. Fit a linear trend equation.
c. Estimate expected production for 1975 based on trend.
d. Compute the standard error of the estimate.
e. What factor or factors affect the trend of men's sportcoat production?

8. The following data are for residential construction contracts.

Year	Contracts (millions of dollars)
1968	24.8
1969	25.3
1970	24.0
1971	34.7
1972	45.0
1973	45.7
1974	34.4

a. Plot the data.
b. Fit a linear trend equation.
c. Estimate the expected residential construction contract amount for 1976 based on trend.
d. Compute the standard error of the estimate.
e. What factor or factors affect the trend of residential construction contracts?

*9. The following data are for the employment in the Atwater Spokane Plant.

Year	Employment (thousand of employees)
1970	6.0
1971	7.0
1972	7.4
1973	8.2
1974	7.6
1975	7.1
1976	6.5

a. Plot the data.
b. Find a parabolic trend equation.
c. Estimate the expected number of employees for 1978 based on trend.
d. Compute the standard error of estimate.
e. Compute the maximum point.

*10. The following data are for the sales of Kembel Shoes from 1969–1976.

Year	Sales (thousands of pairs)
1969	10
1970	13
1971	19
1972	23
1973	30
1974	42
1975	55
1976	70

a. Plot the data.
b. Find the exponential trend model.
c. Estimate expected sales for 1977 based on trend.
d. What is the average rate of increase in sales per year?

11. The following data are for the sale of houses in the Spokane, Washington area between 1961 and 1975.

Year	Sales (hundreds of units)
1961	18
1962	20
1963	21
1964	25
1965	32
1966	31
1967	38
1968	47
1969	58
1970	61
1971	54
1972	53
1973	75
1974	69
1975	65

a. Plot the data.
b. Determine the appropriate trend model.
c. Estimate expected sales for 1980 based on the trend.

12. The following data are for the number of U.S. citizens who depart the United States for any country except Canada.

Year	Departures
1950	668
1951	725
1952	886
1953	939
1954	1000
1955	1186
1956	1352
1957	1461
1958	1592
1959	1824
1960	2002
1961	2020
1962	2292
1963	2588
1964	2841
1965	3341
1966	3814
1967	4334
1968	4820
1969	5767
1970	6499

a. Find the appropriate trend model.
b. What is the average increase per year?
c. Estimate the expected number of departures based on the trend for 1975.

*13. The following data are for the number of persons employed in Anthracite Coal Mining in a certain coal region.

Year	Persons Employed (thousands)
1969	84
1970	61
1971	53
1972	20
1973	21
1974	14
1975	12
1976	9

a. Plot the data.
b. Develop the best trend model to use if the number of employed persons is going to decrease by a constant *amount* to 1980.
c. Develop the best trend model to use if the number of employed persons

206

is going to decrease by a constant *rate* to 1980.
d. Develop the best trend model to use if the number of employed persons is going to be increasing in 1977.
e. Estimate based on the trend the expected number of employed persons for 1980 using each of the three models.

14. The following are data for annual merchandise exports in the United States from 1957 to 1968. 1974

Year	Total Volume (billions of dollars)
1957	21
1958	18
1959	18
1960	20
1961	21
1962	21
1963	22
1964	26
1965	27
1966	29
1967	31
1968	34
1969	37
1970	43
1971	43
1972	49
1973	70
1974	97

a. Plot the data.
b. Find a linear trend equation.
c. Find a parabolic trend equation.
d. Which of the two curves fits the data best?
e. Estimate annual merchandise exports for 1975 based on the trend.
f. What factor or factors affect the trend of annual merchandise exports?

15. The following data are for the residential consumption of electric power.

Year	Annual Consumption (billions of kilowatt-hours)
1950	70.1
1951	80.5
1952	90.5
1953	101.2
1954	113.1
1955	125.4

Continued

Year	Annual Consumption (billions of kilowatt-hours)
1956	139.0
1957	152.6
1958	164.8
1959	180.2
1960	196.4
1961	209.0
1962	226.4
1963	241.7
1964	262.0
1965	281.0
1966	306.6
1967	331.5
1968	367.7
1969	407.9
1970	447.8
1971	479.1
1972	511.4
1973	554.2
1974	555.0

    a. Plot the data.
    b. Find the appropriate trend model.
    c. Estimate consumption for 1980 based on the trend.
    d. What is the average increase in sales per year?
    e. What factor or factors affect the trend of residential consumption of electric power?

*16. Using the data presented in question 7 for men's sportcoat production from 1965–74, compute the following components.
    a. The cyclical–irregular (CI) for 1965.
    b. The cyclical–irregular (CI) for 1974.
    c. A forecast of sportcoat production for 1975 if the economy remains about the same as 1974.

17. Using the data presented in question 8 for residential construction contracts from 1968–74, answer the following:
    a. Calculate the cyclical–irregular (CI) for 1972.
    b. Does the cyclical pattern for residential construction contracts appear to be influenced by the economy?
    c. Decompose the 24.8 millions of dollars spent on contracts for 1968 into the two important components.
    d. Forecast the amount that will be spent on contracts for 1976 if the economy is a little better than anticipated by the trend.

18. In preparing a report for the manager of a shoe store, you include the following statistics from last year's sales. Upon seeing them, the president says, "This report confirms what I've been telling you; business is getting better and better." How should your report have been prepared?

Month	Sales (thousands)	Seasonal Index	Month	Sales (thousands)	Seasonal Index
Jan.	111	50	Jul.	166	95
Feb.	104	53	Aug.	149	88
Mar.	177	86	Sep.	180	100
Apr.	180	94	Oct.	205	117
May	201	109	Nov.	235	143
Jun.	187	98	Dec.	255	167

19. Using the data presented in question 9 for employment in the Atwater Spokane Plant from 1970–76, answer the following:
    a. Calculate the cyclical–irregular relative (*CI*) for 1973.
    b. Which component is most important for forecasting employment, trend or cyclical?
    c. Forecast the number of employees for 1978 if the parabolic equation is the appropriate trend model.

*20. The following data are for total industry sales and the sales of the Mills Company.

Year	Industry Sales (millions)	Mills Company Sales (thousands)	Percent of Industry Sales
1969	6.8	11.7	.172%
1970	7.2	12.6	.175%
1971	7.7	13.6	.177%
1972	7.1	12.8	.180%
1973	7.8	14.3	.183%
1974	8.7	16.1	.185%
1975	8.2	15.4	.188%
1976	8.5	16.2	.190%
1977	8.8	17.1	.194%

   a. Determine the appropriate trend equation for the percent of industry sales.
   b. Estimate the percent for 1978.
   c. If economists predict total industry sales of 9 million for 1978, estimate the 1978 sales of Mills Company.
   d. Develop a regression model where total industry sales are the independent variable, and Mills Company sales are the dependent variable.
   e. If a relationship is found in part (d), use the regression equation to estimate the sales of Mills Company for 1978, assuming total industry sales are expected to be 9 million.

     f. Determine the appropriate trend equation for Mills Company Sales.

     g. Estimate the 1978 sales of Mills Company.

     h. Compare the estimates made in parts (c), (e), and (g).

21. The following data are for the Spokane County Business Activity Index and the sale of houses from 1965–75.

Year	Sale of Houses (hundreds of units)	Spokane County Business Activity Index
1965	32	90.0
1966	31	95.8
1967	38	100.0
1968	47	105.8
1969	58	110.0
1970	61	113.3
1971	54	116.5
1972	53	120.2
1973	75	124.2
1974	69	135.0
1975	65	132.0

     a. Calculate the cyclical–irregular relatives for both variables.

     b. How confident would you be if you used the trend estimate to predict the sale of houses in Spokane for 1979?

     c. How confident would you be if you used the trend estimate to predict the Spokane County Business Activity Index for 1979?

     d. Explain your answers for parts (b) and (c).

     e. Is the Spokane County Business Activity Index of any value in forecasting the sale of houses?

     f. Forecast the sale of houses in Spokane for 1976 if the cyclical–irregular index will be 95.

     g. Forecast the sale of houses in Spokane for 1977 if the cyclical–irregular relative will be 102.

22. A retail store has the following index of seasonal variation in sales.

January	63	July	80
February	72	August	70
March	94	September	103
April	111	October	118
May	102	November	125
June	106	December	156

     a. The manager of the store forecasts that sales for the coming year will total $72 million. On the basis of this forecast of total sales, make a forecast of sales for each month.

  b. January sales were 3.5 million. If this is the prevailing level of sales for the remaining 11 months, what will be the total annual sales for this year?

  c. Based on January sales and the seasonal indexes above, what should sales be for the first quarter?

*23. The following index of seasonal variation reflects the changing volume of business of a mountain resort hotel that caters to the family tourist in the summer and the skiing enthusiast during the winter months. No sharp cyclical variations are expected during 1976.

January	115	July	150
February	142	August	154
March	95	September	90
April	38	October	65
May	47	November	80
June	125	December	99

  a. If 500 tourists were at the resort in January, 1976, what is a reasonable estimate for February?

  b. If the monthly trend equation is $Y_R = 255 + 3X$, where $X = 0$ represents January 15, 1971; what is the seasonally adjusted forecast for January, 1977?

  c. What is the average number of new tourists per month?

  d. Based on the trend equation and seasonal indexes, prepare a forecast for each month of 1976.

*24. The following table shows the railroad transportation of steel mill products in thousands of short tons.

Year	Quarter	Short Tons
1971	I	929
	II	950
	III	556
	IV	567
1972	I	730
	II	682
	III	592
	IV	728
1973	I	771
	II	842
	III	775
	IV	841
1974	I	903
	II	876
	III	787

Continued

Year	Quarter	Short Tons
	IV	851
1975	I	969
	II	778
	III	686
	IV	718

a. Compute the adjusted seasonal index for each quarter using both the median and modified mean methods.

b. Compare your results for the two methods used in part (a).

c. Explain the seasonal pattern for the railroad transportation of steel mill products.

*25. The data presented below represents shipments received by the Simpson Manufacturing Company.

   a. Calculate the linear trend for the annual data.

   b. Convert the annual trend equation into a quarterly trend equation.

   c. Calculate the adjusted seasonal indexes using the modified mean method.

   d. Forecast shipments received for each quarter of 1977 based on both the trend and seasonal.

	Shipments (millions of dollars)	
	Y	X
1970	44	0
1971	60	1
1972	85	2
1973	113	3
1974	135	4
1975	203	5
1976	220	6

Year	Quarter	Shipments (millions of dollars)
1973	1	20
	2	25
	3	30
	4	38
1974	1	30
	2	40

Continued

Year	Quarter	Shipments (millions of dollars)
	3	35
	4	30
1975	1	40
	2	50
	3	55
	4	58
1976	1	44
	2	54
	3	59
	4	63

26. The data for magazine advertising revenue is presented below for both annual (1951–70) and monthly (1967–70).

a. Calculate the linear trend for the annual data.

b. Convert the annual trend equation into a monthly trend equation.

c. Calculate the adjusted seasonal indexes using the modified mean method.

d. Forecast magazine advertising revenue for January, 1971.

Year	Millions of Dollars
1951	513.9
1952	553.8
1953	603.1
1954	597.1
1955	657.3
1956	691.7
1957	738.6
1958	693.1
1959	783.8
1960	853.2
1961	831.3
1962	875.3
1963	931.6
1964	996.6
1965	1083.3
1966	1170.5
1967	1161.0
1968	1163.6
1969	1243.4
1970	1186.7

	Monthly Data (millions of dollars)			
	1967	*1968*	*1969*	*1970*
Jan.	68	61	67	70
Feb.	90	82	88	89
Mar.	106	103	108	110
Apr.	111	116	122	112
May	112	112	126	121
June	98	95	99	101
July	69	68	71	71
Aug.	64	67	73	71
Sept.	108	105	113	103
Oct.	119	125	134	124
Nov.	116	132	134	121
Dec.	100	99	107	96

27. Select a leading indicator from the NBER's short list and:
   a. Explain why this indicator leads the business cycle at cyclical turning points.
   b. Discuss this indicator's performance as a barometer of business activity in recent years.

28. What is the present position of the business cycle? Is it expanding or contracting? When will the next turning point occur?

BIBLIOGRAPHY

CROXTON, F. E., COWDER, D. J., AND BOLCH, B. W., *Practical Business Statistics,* Englewood Cliffs, N.J.: Prentice-Hall, 1969.

DANTEN, C. A., AND VALENTINE, L. M., *Business Cycles and Forecasting,* Cincinnati: South-Western Publishing Company, 1974.

MOORE, G. H., AND SHISKIN, J., *Indicators of Business Expansions and Contractions,* New York: National Bureau of Economic Research, 1967.

———— "Early Warning Signals for the Economy," *Statistics: A Guide to Business and Economics,* San Francisco: Holden-Day, Inc., 1976.

SPURR, W. A., AND BONINI, C. P., *Statistical Analysis for Business Decisions,* Homewood, Ill.: Richard D. Irwin, Inc., 1973.

Regression of Time Series Data

7

In business and economics many regression applications involve time series. The regression of monthly, quarterly, or yearly data may be carried out using techniques described in early chapters. However, time series measures cannot be considered probability samples; and, instead, are subject to trends, cycles, seasonal and irregular variations, and random fluctuations. Hence, problems of interpretation often arise.

The basic regression models discussed in Chapters 4 and 5 assume that the residuals, $(Y - Y_R)$, are either uncorrelated random variables or independent normal random variables. Thus, the error terms are assumed to occur in a random manner. This is not a valid assumption to make for most time series because the error terms tend to increase whenever a variable taken from a growing industry is related over time. Error terms get larger because the variable or variables involved tend to grow at a constant *rate* instead of a constant *amount*. The use of logarithms to discount this tendency was illustrated in Chapter 6.

Suppose we are engaged in forward planning for the Carlson Dishwasher Corporation, and wish to establish a quantitative basis for projecting future sales. Since the corporation sells nationwide, United States disposable personal income should relate closely. Table 7.1 shows sales and income for the period 1955–75. We

215

correlate these variables and attempt to use income to predict Carlson sales for 1976.

First, the data are plotted on an arithmetic scale, Fig. 7–1. The relationship is linear, and when our data are run on an appropriate computer program the results shown in Table 7.2 are obtained. The fit is good, and we can explain 90 percent of the sales variable variance by using the linear equation $Y_R = -792 + 4.25517X$. However, close examination of Fig. 7–1 indicates that the residuals violate the constant variance assumption. The residuals are much larger as sales grow over the years. This occurs because the variables are increasing at a constant *rate*. Logarithms are chosen to correct this violation of the theory of least squares.

TABLE 7.1 *Carlson Dishwasher Sales.*

	Carlson Dishwasher Sales (thousands of dollars) Y	Disposable Personal Income (billions of dollars) X	Carlson Dishwasher Sales Lagged One Year
1955	295	273.4	—
1956	400	291.3	295
1957	390	306.9	400
1958	425	317.1	390
1959	547	336.1	425
1960	555	349.4	547
1961	620	362.9	555
1962	720	383.9	620
1963	880	402.8	720
1964	1050	437.0	880
1965	1290	472.2	1050
1966	1528	510.4	1290
1967	1586	544.5	1528
1968	1960	588.1	1586
1969	2118	630.4	1960
1970	2116	685.9	2118
1971	2477	742.8	2116
1972	3199	801.3	2477
1973	3702	903.1	3199
1974	3316	983.6	3702
1975	2702	1076.7	3316

Source: Survey of Current Business.

The two variables, sales and income, are converted to logarithms to the base 10. After this transformation is produced, a linear regression equation is computed. The results are presented in Table 7.3. We now

TABLE 7.2 *Computer Output for Carlson Dishwasher Sales (Linear Fit).*

Table 7-2

COMPUTER OUTPUT FOR
CARLSON DISHWASHER SALES
Linear Fit

VARIABLE NO.	MEAN	STANDARD DEVIATION	CORRELATION X VS Y	REGRESSION COEFFICIENT	STD. ERROR OF REG.COEF.	COMPUTED T VALUE
2	542.85	241.16	0.95	4.25517	0.31627	13.45
DEPENDENT						
1	1517.90450	1078.69840				

INTERCEPT	-792		MULTIPLE CORRELATION	0.951
STD. ERROR OF ESTIMATE	341.1		R SQUARED	0.905
DURBIN-WATSON STATISTIC	0.87		CORRECTED Q SQUARED	0.900

ANALYSIS OF VARIANCE FOR THE REGRESSION

SOURCES OF VARIATION	DEGREES OF FREEDOM	SUM OF SQUARES	MEAN SQUARES	F VALUE
ATTRIBUTABLE TO REGRESSION	1	21061184	21061184	181.018
DEVIATION FROM REGRESSION	19	2210624	116348	
TOTAL	20	23271808		

TABLE OF RESIDUALS

CASE NO.	Y VALUE	Y ESTIMATE	RESIDUAL
1	295	371.36	-76.36
2	400	447.53	-47.53
3	390	513.91	-123.91
4	425	557.32	-132.32
5	547	638.16	-91.16
6	555	694.76	-139.76
7	620	752.20	-132.20
8	720	841.56	-121.56
9	880	921.98	-41.98
10	1050	1067.51	-17.51
11	1290	1217.29	72.71
12	1528	1379.84	148.16
13	1586	1524.94	61.06
14	1960	1710.47	249.53
15	2118	1890.46	227.54
16	2116	2126.62	-10.62
17	2477	2368.74	108.26
18	3199	2617.67	581.33
19	3702	3050.84	651.16
20	3316	3393.38	-77.38
21	2702	3789.54	-1087.54

explain 76 percent of the variance through our usage of the logarithmic line ($\log Y_R = -1.91024 + 1.84297 \log X$). The computations of the two points from which the line is drawn are demonstrated below.

- When $X = 300$, $Y_R = 452$
  $\log Y_R = -1.91024 + 1.84297 \log 300$

TABLE 7.3 *Computer Output for Carlson Dishwasher Sales (Logarithmic Fit).*

COMPUTER OUTPUT FOR CARLSON
DISHWASHER SALES LOGARITHMIC FIT

INTERCEPT	-1.91024	REGRESSION COEFFICIENT	1.84297
STD. ERROR OF ESTIMATE	2.7344	R SQUARE	0.76

DURBIN-WATSON STATISTIC   0.56

TABLE OF RESIDUALS

CASE NO.	Y VALUE	Y ESTIMATE	RESIDUAL
1	2.46982	2.58070	-85.8
2	2.60206	2.63146	-28.0
3	2.59106	2.67322	-81.2
4	2.62839	2.69939	-75.5
5	2.73799	2.74596	-10.1
6	2.74429	2.77702	-43.4
7	2.79239	2.80737	-21.8
8	2.85733	2.85239	8.1
9	2.94448	2.89086	102.2
10	3.02119	2.95609	146.2
11	3.11059	3.01809	247.5
12	3.18412	3.08035	324.8
13	3.20030	3.13212	230.4
14	3.29226	3.19377	397.7
15	3.32592	3.24936	342.3
16	3.32551	3.31690	41.5
17	3.39393	3.38069	74.4
18	3.50501	3.44136	436.1
19	3.56844	3.53709	257.8
20	3.52061	3.60543	-715.2
21	3.43168	3.67782	-2060.4

$\log Y_R = -1.91024 + 1.84297 \ (2.4771)$
$\log Y_R = -1.91024 + 4.56522$
$\log Y_R = 2.65498$
Antilog $2.65498 = 452$

- When $X = 1000$, $Y_R = 4{,}155$
$\log Y_R = -1.91024 + 1.84297 \log 1000$
$\log Y_R = -1.91024 + 1.84297 \ (3.0000)$
$\log Y_R = -1.91024 + 5.52891$
$\log Y_R = 3.6186$
Antilog $3.6186 = 4155$

Figure 7–2 illustrates the logarithmic line drawn on a semilogarithmic scale. Notice, we have solved our problem. The residuals are now uniformly

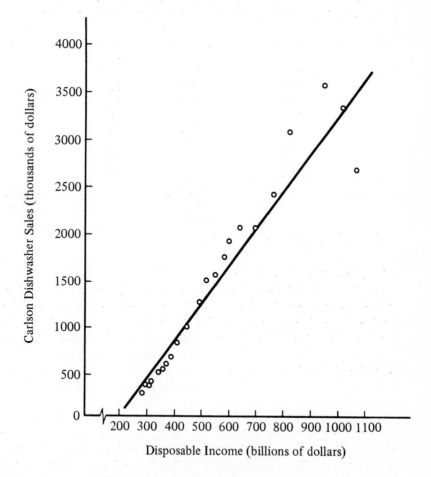

FIGURE 7–1 *Carlson Dishwasher Sales Linear Fit.*

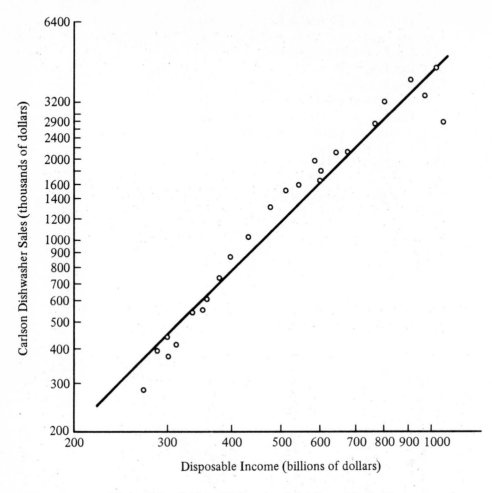

FIGURE 7-2   *Carlson Dishwasher Sales Logarithmic Fit.*

dispersed around the line. They are not gradually increasing with the growth of the dishwasher industry.

The second problem with time series data is their movement in cycles rather than in a purely random fashion. This phenomenon often causes runs of several successive negative or positive errors in a row. An examination of Fig. 7–2 illustrates this point. The first seven residuals (1955–61) are negative, while the next twelve (1962–73) are in the positive direction. Each year's value is dependent or related to that of the preceding year, rather than being independent of it. This fact should not surprise us. Consider, for example, a price series. If successive observations from one year to the next were indeed independent of one another, we would be living in a chaotic economy. In such a world prices would be determined

220

like numbers drawn from a random number table. Knowledge of the price in one year would not influence the price in the next year.

Economic data ordered in a time series can seldom be regarded as a random sample. An observation on price, inventory, production, stocks, and other economic variables in a given time period is usually correlated with (dependent on) the value of that same variable in the previous time period. The term *autocorrelation* is used to describe this situation. The residuals ($Y - Y_R$) are not independent from one observation to the next. Knowledge of the error in one year *helps* one anticipate the error in the next year.

Consider the time series data illustrated in Fig. 7–3, which plots some fictitious time series. The straight line is a regression line with respect to time. The difficulty is immediately obvious. From 1965–1968 the residuals ($Y - Y_R$) are all positive, while from 1969–73 they are negative. For 1975 we anticipate a positive error. It is easy for us to predict the direction of each successive residual.

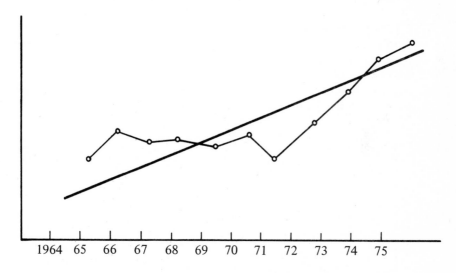

FIGURE 7–3   *Positive Autocorrelation.*

Problem of Autocorrelation

A major cause of positively autocorrelated residuals in business and economics is the omission of one or more key variables from the model. When the time-sequenced effects of these "missing" variables are positively related, the residuals tend to be positively autocorrelated in the regression equation because they include the effects of the missing variable or variables. This usually means that an important part of the variation of the dependent variable has not been explained. The best solution to this problem is to search for other explanatory variables to include in the model. Suppose, for example, that average yearly price and sales of a product are related over a period of 35 years. If population size has an important effect on the magnitude of sales, its omission from the equation may lead to the residuals being positively autocorrelated. This occurs because the effect of population on sales is likely to be positively correlated over time.

If the residuals in a regression equation are positively autocorrelated, the use of the least-squares procedure poses several problems as follows.

1. The regression coefficient may be quite unreliable.
2. The standard error of estimate may seriously underestimate the variability of the error terms.
3. The confidence intervals and tests employing the t and F distributions are no longer strictly applicable.
4. The standard error of the regression coefficient may underestimate the variability of the estimated regression coefficient.

Figure 7–4 illustrates the presence of positive autocorrelation in a model with a single independent variable. The residual associated with the first observation indicated by $(Y - Y_R)$ on the graph happens to be positive. This leads to a series of five positive error terms and a series of four negative residuals. Notice the estimated regression slope is lower than the true slope. The least-squares fitted regression line fits the observed

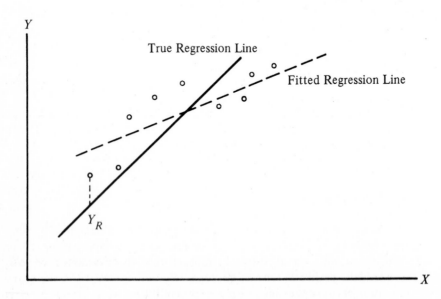

FIGURE 7–4 *Autocorrelation Example.*

sample data points more closely than does the true regression line. This leads to an R^2 that is artificially high. Furthermore, the standard error of the estimate will be smaller than the true standard error. The success of the regression procedure will be overstated if the least-squares standard error of the estimate is used to perform statistical tests.

Durbin-Watson Test for Autocorrelation

One approach that is used frequently to determine if autocorrelation is present is the Durbin-Watson test. The test involves the determination of whether or not the autocorrelation parameter ρ shown in Eq. 7–1 is zero:

$$Y_t = \beta_0 + \beta X_t + \varepsilon_t$$

$$\varepsilon_t = \rho e_{t-1} + d_t \qquad (7\text{--}1)$$

where: ρ = the autocorrelation parameter that measures the correlation between residuals

d_t = disturbances or independent random variables

Notice that each error term in (7–1) consists of a fraction of the previous error term when $\rho > 0$, plus a new disturbance term d_t. If $\rho = 0$, $\varepsilon_t = d_t$, then the error terms are independent since the disturbances are independent.

The hypotheses to be considered are

$$H_0: \quad \rho = 0$$

$$H_1: \quad \rho > 0$$

The alternative hypothesis is $\rho > 0$ since residuals in time series applications tend to show positive correlation.

The first step in the computations is to fit the least-squares regression line to the data. Next the residuals are calculated, and the Durbin-Watson statistic is computed in the following manner.

$$DW = \frac{\sum\limits_{t=2}^{n} (e_t - e_{t-1})^2}{\sum\limits_{t=1}^{n} e_t^2} \qquad (7\text{--}2)$$

where: e_t = the error or difference between the point and the line

e_{t-1} = the error or difference between the point and the line for the previous time period

223

$$\sum_{t=2}^{n}(e_t - e_{t-1})^2 =$$ the difference between the present residual and the previous residual squared and summed for all observations

$$\sum_{t=1}^{n}e_t^2 =$$ each of the residuals squared and then summed

Although an exact testing procedure is unavailable, Durbin and Watson have provided lower (L) and upper (U) bounds such that a value of DW that falls outside these bounds tends to indicate the presence of autocorrelation. The decision rules are:

- If $DW > U$, conclude H_0.
- If $DW < L$, conclude H_1.
- If DW lies within the lower and upper bounds $(L < DW < U)$, conclude that the test is inconclusive.

The critical bounds for L and U are found in the appendix. In order to find the appropriate L and U, one needs to know the sample size, level of significance, and the number of independent variables. When inconclusive results are found, more observations are needed. With time series data this may not be possible so that Durbin and Watson* give an approximate test that requires at least 40 observations.

The actual computations showing the implementation of Eq. (7–2) are demonstrated in Table 7.4. The data are from the Carlson Dishwasher Sales example (Table 7.1). The residuals column was taken from the computer output, Table 7.2. The computations for the other three columns for 1956 are demonstrated below.

$$(e_t - e_{t-1}) = (-47.53 - -76.36) = 28.83$$
$$(e_t - e_{t-1})^2 = 28.83^2 = 831.17$$
$$e_t^2 = -47.53^2 = 2259.1$$

The Durbin-Watson statistic is computed as

$$DW = \frac{\sum_{t=2}^{n}(e_t - e_{t-1})^2}{\sum_{t=1}^{n}e_t^2} = \frac{1,926,035.14}{2,210,641.78} = 0.87$$

---

*DURBIN, J., AND WATSON, G. S., "Testing for Serial Correlation in Least-Squares Regression II." *Biometrika*, Vol. 38 (1951), pp. 159–78

TABLE 7.4   *Durbin-Watson Calculations for Carlson Dishwasher Sales Example.*

Year	Sales Y	Income X	Residuals e_t	$(e_t - e_{t-1})$	$(e_t - e_{t-1})^2$	e_t^2
1955	295	273.4	−76.36	—	—	5,830.85
1956	400	291.3	−47.53	28.83	831.17	2,259.10
1957	390	306.9	−123.91	−76.38	5,833.90	15,353.69
1958	425	317.1	−132.32	−8.41	70.73	17,508.58
1959	547	336.1	−91.16	41.16	1,694.15	8,310.15
1960	555	349.4	−139.76	−48.60	2,361.96	19,532.86
1961	620	362.9	−132.20	7.56	57.15	17,476.84
1962	720	383.9	−121.56	10.64	113.21	14,776.83
1963	880	402.8	−41.98	79.58	6,332.98	1,762.32
1964	1050	437.0	−17.51	24.47	598.78	306.60
1965	1290	472.2	72.71	90.22	8,139.65	5,286.74
1966	1528	510.4	148.16	75.45	5,692.70	21,951.39
1967	1586	544.5	61.06	−87.10	7,586.41	3,728.32
1968	1960	588.1	249.53	188.47	35,520.94	62,265.22
1969	2118	630.4	227.54	−21.99	483.56	51,774.45
1970	2116	685.9	−10.62	−238.16	56,720.19	112.78
1971	2477	742.8	108.26	118.88	14,132.45	11,720.23
1972	3199	801.3	581.33	473.07	223,795.22	337,944.57
1973	3702	903.1	651.16	69.83	4,876.23	424,009.35
1974	3316	983.6	−77.38	−728.54	530,770.53	5,987.66
1975	2702	1076.7	−1087.54	−1,010.16	1,020,423.23	1,182,743.25
					1,926,035.14	2,210,641.78

This answer checks with the computer output of Table 7.2. Using a .01 level of significance for a sample of 21 and one independent variable,

$$L = 0.97$$

$$U = 1.16$$

Since $DW = .87$ falls below $L = .97$, we reject the null hypothesis and conclude that the residuals are positively autocorrelated ($\rho > 0$).

Notice in Table 7.4 that the adjacent error terms e_t and e_{t-1} tend to be of the same sign and magnitude. When positive autocorrelation exists, the differences $(e_t - e_{t-1})$ tend to be small, leading to a small numerator in the DW statistic.

Solutions to Autocorrelation Problems

A variety of approaches are available to solve the problem of autocorrelation. The best solution is to search for the key variable, or variables, which will explain the portion of dependent variable variance that is not being explained. Other methods involve fitting a regression equation to the percentage changes from year to year, correlating the absolute amounts of change each year, lagging the dependent variable one period and including it as an independent variable, other autoregressive models, and the "rho" correction factor technique. Each approach is demonstrated by example in the following section.

Missing Key Variables

The Billings Corporation wishes to develop a forecasting model for the projection of future sales. Since the corporation has outlets nationwide, disposable personal income is chosen as a possible predictor variable. Table 7.5 shows Billings sales for 1959–76. The disposable personal income data are obtained from Table 7.1.

TABLE 7.5   Billings Corporation Sales.

Year	Billings Sales (millions)	Year	Billings Sales (millions)
1959	8.0	1967	14.6
1960	8.2	1968	16.4
1961	8.5	1969	17.8
1962	9.2	1970	18.6
1963	10.2	1971	20.0
1964	11.4	1972	21.9
1965	12.8	1973	24.9
1966	13.6	1974	27.3
		1975	29.1

A simple regression model is run on the computer using disposable personal income as the independent variable and Billings's sales as the dependent variable. The results are presented in Table 7.6. Using a .01 level of significance for a sample of 17 and one independent variable,

$$L = 0.87$$

$$U = 1.10$$

The Durbin-Watson statistic of 0.72181 indicates that positive autocorrelation exists ($0.72 < 0.87$). Evidently, one or more key variables are missing from the model. An important part of the variation of the sales variable has not been explained. This is probably true even though Table 7.6 indicates that disposable income is explaining 99.5% of the sales variable variance.

The best solution to this dilemma is to search for the missing variable or variables. The unemployment rate (Table 7.8) is added to the model,

226

TABLE 7.6 *Billings Corporation Sales and Disposable Personal Income.*

BILLINGS CORPORATION SALES AND DISPOSABLE PERSONAL INCOME

VARIABLE NO.	MEAN	STANDARD DEVIATION	CORRELATION X VS Y	REGRESSION COEFFICIENT	STD. ERROR OF REG.COEF.	COMPUTED T VALUE
2	600.651	232.361	0.99769	0.029	0.00051	56.9
DEPENDENT						
1	16.029	6.799				

INTERCEPT   -1.505

STD. ERROR OF ESTIMATE   0.47665

DURBIN-WATSON STATISTIC   0.72181

MULTIPLE CORRELATION   0.99769

R SQUARE   0.99539

CORRECTED R SQUARED   0.93684

ANALYSIS OF VARIANCE FOR THE REGRESSION

SOURCE OF VARIATION	DEGREES OF FREEDOM	SUM OF SQUARES	MEAN SQUARES	F VALUE
ATTRIBUTABLE TO REGRESSION	1	736.147	736.147	3240.1
DEVIATION FROM REGRESSION	15	3.408	0.227	
TOTAL	16	739.55		

TABLE OF RESIDUALS

CASE NO.	Y VALUE	Y ESTIMATE	RESIDUAL
1	8.0	8.30671	-0.30671
2	8.2	8.69495	-0.49495
3	8.5	9.08904	-0.58904
4	9.2	9.70206	-0.50206
5	10.2	10.25378	-0.05378
6	11.4	11.25214	0.14786
7	12.8	12.27968	0.52032
8	13.6	13.39480	0.20520
9	14.6	14.39023	0.20977
10	16.4	15.66298	0.73701
11	17.8	16.89778	0.90222
12	18.6	18.51791	0.08209
13	20.0	20.17892	-0.17892
14	21.9	21.88663	0.01337
15	24.9	24.85834	0.04166
16	27.3	27.20825	0.09175
17	29.1	29.92599	-0.82599

and the results of this computer run are presented in Table 7.7. Using a .01 level of significance for a sample of 17 and two independent variables,

$$L = 0.77$$

$$U = 1.25$$

The Durbin-Watson statistic of 1.98 indicates that we seem to have eliminated the autocorrelation problem (1.98 > 1.25). We can use the regression equation $Y_R = 0.014 + 0.03X_2 - 0.35X_3$ to estimate Billings Corporation's

TABLE 7.7 *Billings Sales: Disposable Personal Income and Unemployment Rate.*

BILLINGS SALES: DISPOSABLE PERSONAL INCOME AND UNEMPLOYMENT RATE

VARIABLE NO.	MEAN	STANDARD DEVIATION	CORRELATION X VS Y	REGRESSION COEFFICIENT	STD. ERROR OF REG.COEF.	COMPUTED T VALUE
2	600.651	232.361	0.99769	0.030	0.00025	119.83
3	5.218	1.238	0.24054	-0.350	0.04661	-7.51

DEPENDENT

1	16.02939	6.79869

INTERCEPT	-0.014	MULTIPLE CORRELATION	0.99954
STD. ERROR OF ESTIMATE	0.22018	R-SQUARE	0.99908
DURBIN-WATSON STATISTIC	1.98	CORRECTED R SQUARED	0.99908

ANALYSIS OF VARIANCE FOR THE REGRESSION

SOURCE OF VARIATION	DEGREES OF FREEDOM	SUM OF SQUARES	MEAN SQUARES	F VALUE
ATTRIBUTABLE TO REGRESSION	2	738.876	369.548	7620.5
DEVIATION FROM REGRESSION	14	0.679	0.048	
TOTAL	16	739.555		

TABLE OF RESIDUALS

CASE NO.	Y VALUE	Y ESTIMATE	RESIDUAL
1	8.0	8.06044	-0.06044
2	8.2	8.45610	-0.25610
3	8.5	8.43787	0.06213
4	9.2	9.48244	-0.28244
5	10.2	9.97473	0.22527
6	11.4	11.16708	0.23292
7	12.8	12.45916	0.34085
8	13.6	13.84048	-0.24048
9	14.6	14.85492	-0.25492
10	16.4	16.22194	0.17805
11	17.8	17.51532	0.28468
12	18.6	18.67657	-0.07657
13	20.0	20.01944	-0.01944
14	21.9	21.86472	0.03528
15	24.9	25.13809	-0.23810
16	27.3	27.28798	0.01202
17	29.1	29.04300	0.05701

sales with the knowledge that the error terms are independent. We use expert estimates of disposable personal income (1185 billion dollars) and the unemployment rate (7.8%) in order to predict Billings's sales for 1976 of 32.8 million dollars.

$$Y_R = -0.014 + 0.03 \ (1185.0) - 0.35 \ (7.8)$$

$$Y_R = 32.8$$

Regression of Percentage Changes

Suppose we are engaged in forecasting Sears Roebuck sales. Disposable personal income is again chosen as our independent variable. Table 7.8 shows Sears sales and disposable income for the period 1955-75. The computer output in Table 7.9 indicates that we can explain 99.5% of the Sears sales variance through our knowledge of its relationship with disposable income. Using a .01 level of significance for a sample of 20 and one independent variable,

TABLE 7.8   *Sears Sales, U.S. Disposable Income and Unemployment Rate (1955-75 billions of dollars).*

Year	Sears Sales Y	Disposable Income X_2	Unemployment Rate X_3	Percent Change from Previous Year		
				X_4 ΔY	X_5 ΔX_2	X_6 ΔX_3
1955	3.307	273.4	4.4%	—	—	—
1956	3.556	291.3	4.1	7.5	6.5	−6.8
1957	3.601	306.9	4.3	1.3	5.4	4.9
1958	3.721	317.1	6.8	3.3	3.3	58.1
1959	4.036	336.1	5.5	8.5	6.0	−19.1
1960	4.134	349.4	5.5	2.4	4.0	0
1961	4.268	362.9	6.7	3.2	5.7	21.8
1962	4.578	383.9	5.5	7.3	5.8	−17.9
1963	5.093	402.8	5.7	11.2	6.3	3.6
1964	5.716	437.0	5.2	12.2	8.5	−8.8
1965	6.357	472.2	4.5	11.2	8.1	−13.5
1966	6.769	510.4	3.8	6.5	8.1	−15.6
1967	7.296	544.5	3.8	7.8	6.7	0
1968	8.178	588.1	3.6	12.1	8.0	−5.3
1969	8.844	630.4	3.5	8.1	7.2	−2.8
1970	9.251	685.9	4.9	4.6	8.8	40.0
1971	10.006	742.8	5.9	8.2	8.3	20.4
1972	11.200	801.3	5.6	11.9	7.9	−5.1
1973	12.500	903.1	4.9	11.6	12.7	−12.5
1974	13.101	983.6	5.6	4.6	8.9	14.3
1975	13.640	1076.7	8.5	4.0	9.5	51.8

$$L = 0.95$$

$$U = 1.15$$

The Durbin-Watson statistic of 0.63 indicates positive autocorrelation (0.63 < 0.95). In an attempt to eliminate the relationship between residuals, a regression line is fitted to the percentage changes from year to year, rather than to the actual data. The percent change from previous years

TABLE 7.9   *Sears Sales and Disposable Personal Income.*

SEARS SALES AND DISPOSABLE PERSONAL INCOME

VARIABLE NO.	MEAN	STANDARD DEVIATION	CORRELATION X VS Y	REGRESSION COEFFICIENT	STD. ERROR OF REG.COEF.	COMPUTED T VALUE
2	556.32	239.18	0.995	0.01405	0.00034	41.5
DEPENDENT						
1	7.29	3.38				

INTERCEPT	-0.522	MULTIPLE CORRELATION	0.995
STD. ERROR OF ESTIMATE	0.35	R SQUARE	0.990
DURBIN-WATSON STATISTIC	0.63	CORRECTED R SQUARE	.989

TABLE OF RESIDUALS

CASE NO.	Y VALUE	Y ESTIMATE	RESIDUAL
1	3.55600	3.56950	-0.01350
2	3.60100	3.78863	-0.18763
3	3.72100	3.93192	-0.21092
4	4.03600	4.19881	-0.16281
5	4.13400	4.38564	-0.25164
6	4.26800	4.57527	-0.30727
7	4.57800	4.87026	-0.29226
8	5.09300	5.13575	-0.04275
9	5.71600	5.61616	0.09984
10	6.35700	6.11062	0.24638
11	6.76900	6.64722	0.12178
12	7.29600	7.12622	0.16978
13	8.17800	7.73868	0.43932
14	8.84400	8.33287	0.51113
15	9.25100	9.11248	0.13852
16	10.00600	9.91176	0.09424
17	11.20000	10.73352	0.46648
18	12.50000	12.16351	0.33649
19	13.10100	13.29430	-0.19330
20	13.64000	14.60208	-0.96208

for Sears sales and disposable income (Table 7.8, columns 4 and 5) are regressed, and the computer output is presented in Table 7.10.

The plotted residuals are more randomly distributed, as indicated by the Durbin-Watson statistic of 1.305 (1.305 > 1.15). The various standard errors computed for these percentage changes ($s_{y \cdot x}$, s_b) are more valid than those computed from the original values. This does not mean, of course, that the forecast itself is necessarily more accurate. The R^2, 0.229, is also more valid than the spuriously high value of 0.995 obtained in relating the original series, which both have rising trends. Unfortunately,

TABLE 7.10   *Percent Change from Previous Year of Sears Sales and Disposable Income.*

PERCENT CHANGE FROM PREVIOUS YEAR
SEARS SALES & DISPOSABLE INCOME

VARIABLE NO.	MEAN	STANDARD DEVIATION	CORRELATION X VS Y	REGRESSION COEFFICIENT	STD. ERROR OF REG.COEF.	COMPUTED T VALUE
5	7.285	2.08	0.478	0.815	0.35266	2.3
DEPENDENT						
4	7.375	3.55				
INTERCEPT		1.440		MULTIPLE CORRELATION	0.478	
STD. ERROR OF ESTIMATE		3.20		R SQUARE	0.229	
DURBIN-WATSON STATISTIC		1.305		CORRECTED R SQUARED	0.186	

changes in disposable income explain only 22.9 percent of the variance in yearly percentage changes of Sears sales.

At this point, we turn to our knowledge of multiple regression for help. If we relate the change in Sears sales simultaneously to other variables that affect sales, our estimation accuracy should improve. For example, change in unemployment rate (Table 7.8) is introduced into the model. Table 7.11 shows the computer output results. We can now explain 48.6 percent of the variance in the change of Sears sales. Our Durbin-Watson statistic has improved to 1.84. Thus, no autocorrelation problem is apparent.

We now face the dilemma of whether or not to add more independent variables to our model. We are still *not* explaining 51.4% of the change in the Sears sales variable variance. However, whenever we add a new variable to the model, in order to predict, we must use expert estimates of that variable. It seems possible that the accuracy of our forecast will be decreased by this procedure.

TABLE 7.11   *Percent Change from Previous Year of Sears Sales: Disposable Income and Unemployment Rate.*

PERCENT CHANGE FROM PREVIOUS YEAR
SEARS SALES: DISPOSABLE INCOME & UNEMPLOYMENT RATE

VARIABLE NO.	MEAN	STANDARD DEVIATION	CORRELATION X VS Y	REGRESSION COEFFICIENT	STD. ERROR OF REG.COEF.	COMPUTED T VALUE
5	7.285	2.08	0.478	0.705	0.29850	2.4
6	5.375	22.55	-0.564	-0.080	0.02756	-2.9
DEPENDENT						
4	7.375	3.55				
INTERCEPT		2.669		MULTIPLE CORRELATION	0.697	
STD. ERROR OF ESTIMATE		2.688		R SQUARED	0.486	
DURBIN-WATSON STATISTIC		1.84		CORRECTED R SQUARED	0.426	

If we decide to use the model demonstrated in Table 7.11, expert estimates of both disposable personal income and the unemployment rate will need to be acquired. The prediction procedure is shown below.

	Y	X_2	X_3	X_4 ΔY	X_5 ΔX_2	X_6 ΔX_3
1975	13.640	1076.7	8.5	4.0	9.5	51.8
1976	14.881[6]	1185.0[1]	7.8[2]	9.1[5]	10.1[3]	−8.2[4]

1. Estimate of disposable personal income for 1976.
2. Estimate of unemployment rate for 1976.
3. $(1185.0 - 1076.1) = 108.3$

$$\frac{108.3}{1076.7} = 10.1\%$$

4. $(7.8 - 8.5) = -0.7$

$$\frac{-0.7}{8.5} = -8.2\%$$

5. $Y_R = 2.669 + 0.705X_5 - 0.08X_6$ (Table 7.11)
   $Y_R = 2.669 + 0.705(10.1) - 0.08(-8.2)$
   $Y_R = 9.1\%$. Estimated change or increase in Sears sales.

6. $Y(1975) * \Delta Y(1976) + Y(1975) = Y(1976)$
   $13.640 * 0.091 = 1.241$ increase in Sears sales from 1975 to 1976
   $13.640 + 1.241 = 14.881$ Sears sales predicted for 1976.

Our estimate of Sears sales for 1976 is 14.881 billion dollars. The various standard errors computed for this multiple regression model are valid and can be used to develop confidence intervals. If more accuracy is desired, we can introduce other important variables (population, number of stores, consumption expenditures, and price index) into the model.

Autoregressive Models

One way to solve the autocorrelation problem is to take advantage of the correlation between adjacent observations. This is referred to as an *autoregressive model*. The dependent variable is lagged one or more periods and is used as an independent variable. In the Carlson Dishwasher example sales, Y_T, is lagged one period and is used along with personal income as an independent variable. We refer to this estimated model as a first-order autoregressive model, and it is written

$$Y_{T+1} = b_0 + b_2 X_2 + b_3 X_3 \tag{7-3}$$

where: $X_3 = Y_T$

The data for this model are presented in Table 7.1. Note that one year of data is lost since we did not know Carlson's sales for 1954. Our sample

TABLE 7.12   *Carlson Dishwasher Sales Autoregressive Model.*

CARLSON DISHWASHER SALES AUTOREGRESSIVE MODEL

VARIABLE NO.	MEAN	STANDARD DEVIATION	CORRELATION X VS Y	REGRESSION COEFFICIENT	STD. ERROR OF REG.COEF.	COMPUTED T VALUE
2	2.709	0.179	0.96792	-0.370	0.40752	-0.91
3	3.041	0.348	0.98769	1.127	0.20928	5.38

DEPENDENT

| 1 | 3.089 | 0.331 | | | | |

INTERCEPT		0.666	MULTIPLE CORRELATION	0.98826
STD. ERROR OF ESTIMATE	0.05346		R SQUARED	0.97665
DURBIN-WATSON STATISTIC	1.91897		CORRECTED R SQUARED	0.97390

ANALYSIS OF VARIANCE FOR THE REGRESSION

SOURCES OF VARIATION	DEGREES OF FREEDOM	SUM OF SQUARES	MEAN SQUARES	F VALUE
ATTRIBUTABLE TO REGRESSION	2	2.032	1.016	355.544
DEVIATION FROM REGRESSION	17	0.049	0.003	
TOTAL	19	2.081		

CORRELATION MATRIX: 3 BY 3

VAR.	1	2	3
1	1.000	0.968	0.988
2	0.968	1.000	0.986
3	0.988	0.986	1.000

TABLE OF RESIDUALS

CASE NO.	Y VALUE	Y ESTIMATE	RESIDUAL
1	2.60206	2.53630	0.06576
2	2.59106	2.67722	-0.08616
3	2.62839	2.65926	-0.03087
4	2.73799	2.69196	0.04603
5	2.74429	2.80920	-0.06491
6	2.79239	2.81021	-0.01782
7	2.85733	2.85536	0.00197
8	2.94448	2.92081	0.02368
9	3.02119	3.00590	0.01529
10	3.11059	3.07987	0.03072
11	3.18412	3.16809	0.01603
12	3.20030	3.24054	-0.04024
13	3.29226	3.24639	0.04587
14	3.32592	3.33883	-0.01290
15	3.32551	3.36319	-0.03768
16	3.39393	3.34992	0.04400
17	3.50501	3.41481	0.09020
18	3.56844	3.52075	0.04769
19	3.52022	3.57848	-0.05826
20	3.43168	3.51006	-0.07837

size is 20 instead of 21. The results of running this multiple regression model are presented in Table 7.12. The Durbin-Watson statistic has improved to 1.92. Our estimate of Carlson Dishwasher's sales for 1976 is 2607 thousand dollars:

$$Y_{1975+1} = 0.666 - 0.37X_2 + 1.127X_3$$

where: $X_3 = Y_{1975}$
$Y_{1976} = 0.666 - 0.37(1185) + 1.127(2702)$
$Y_{1976} = 2607$

A check of the correlation matrix in Table 7.12 leads to the conclusion that collinearity might be a problem. The high interrelationship between the independent variables, $r_{23} = .986$, indicates that they are probably explaining the same dependent variable variance. The collinearity problem becomes obvious when the regression coefficient, $b_2 = -.37$, for the disposable personal income variable is analyzed. Since the income variable shows a high positive relationship with sales, $r_{12} = .968$, the regression coefficient cannot possibly be meaningful. The model might be improved if the only independent variable were Carlson Dishwasher sales lagged one period.

Other Autoregressive Models

Since one way to solve autocorrelation problems is to develop a model that recognizes the relationship among the residuals in some appropriate fashion, the following technique can be employed. We originally represented each data point by:

$$Y_t = \beta_0 + \beta X_t + \varepsilon_t \qquad (7\text{-}4)$$

We need to create a new model that recognizes that the error term (ε_t) consists of a fraction of the previous error term, plus some random effect. If we write our error term,

$$\varepsilon_t = \rho\varepsilon_{t-1} + d_t \qquad \text{OR}$$
$$d_t = \varepsilon_t - \rho\varepsilon_{t-1} \qquad (7\text{-}5)$$

where: ρ = represents the correlation between residuals
d_t = random error or disturbance
$d_t = \varepsilon_t$ when $\rho = 0$
then our new model becomes
$$Y_t = \beta_0 + \beta X_t + \rho\varepsilon_{t-1} + d_t \qquad (7\text{-}6)$$

If the residuals are unrelated and ρ is equal to zero, our equation becomes Eq. (7-4).

$$Y_t = \beta_0 + \beta X_t + \rho \varepsilon_{t-1} + d_t$$

$$Y_t = \beta_0 + \beta X_t + 0\varepsilon_{t-1} + d_t$$

$$Y_t = \beta_0 + \beta X_t + d_t, \quad \text{if} \quad d_t = \varepsilon_t$$

$$Y_t = \beta_0 + \beta X_t + \varepsilon_t$$

If the error terms are related and ρ is greater than zero, it is desirable for us to recognize the related structure of the error terms.

If ρ were known, then generalized differencing could be used to adjust the least-squares regression procedure so that the error terms would be independent. To describe this procedure, we utilize the fact that the linear model, Eq. (7–4), holds for all time periods.

In particular,

$$Y_{t-1} = \beta_0 + \beta X_{t-1} + \varepsilon_{t-1} \tag{7-7}$$

Since this is the case, we can transform our equation by multiplying Eq. (7–7) by ρ and by subtracting it from Eq. (7–4).

$$Y_t = \beta_0 + \beta X_t + \varepsilon_t \qquad \text{Eq. (7-4)}$$

$$\rho(Y_{t-1}) = \rho\beta_0 + \rho\beta X_{t-1} + \rho\varepsilon_{t-1} \qquad \rho * \text{Eq. (7-7)}$$

$$Y_t - \rho(Y_{t-1}) = (\beta_0 - \rho\beta_0) + (\beta X_t - \rho\beta X_{t-1}) + (\varepsilon_t - \rho\varepsilon_{t-1})$$

$$Y_t^1 = \beta_0(1 - \rho) + \beta X_t^1 + d_t \tag{7-8}$$

The transformed equation has an error process that is independently distributed with mean equal 0 and constant variance. Thus, ordinary least-squares regression applied to Eq. (7–8) will yield valid estimates of regression parameters. Remember, we have transformed our variables.

$$Y_t^1 = Y_t - \rho Y_{t-1}$$

$$X_t^1 = X_t - \rho X_{t-1} \tag{7-9}$$

First Differences

One commonly used estimation procedure known as *first-differencing* assumes that ρ is equal to 1. If $\rho = 1$, the transformed model Eq. (7–8) becomes

$$Y_t^1 = \beta_0(1 - \rho) + \beta X_t^1 + \varepsilon_t$$

$$Y_t^1 = \beta_0(1 - 1) + \beta X_t^1 + \varepsilon_t \tag{7-10}$$

$$Y_t^1 = \beta X_t^1 + \varepsilon_t$$

Therefore, the regression coefficient β can be estimated using the least-squares method for regression through the origin with the transformed variables.

$$Y_t^1 = Y_t - \rho Y_{t-1}$$
$$X_t^1 = X_t - \rho X_{t-1}$$

Notice that these transformed variables are first differences. This approach is effective in a variety of applications.

For example, Table 7.13 contains the transformed variables Y_t^1 and X_t^1 based on the first differences transformation for our Sears sales example.

TABLE 7.13 *First Differences for Sears Sales Computations of Linear Regression Through Origin.*

Year	Sales Y	Disposable Income X	Y_T'	X_T'	$X_T' Y_T'$	$(X_T')^2$	$(X_T' - bX_T')^2$
1955	3.307	273.4					
1956	3.556	291.3	.249	17.9	4.5	320.4	.0016
1957	3.601	306.9	.045	15.6	.7	243.4	.0189
1958	3.721	317.1	.120	10.2	1.2	104.0	.0000
1959	4.036	336.1	.315	19.0	6.0	361.0	.0086
1960	4.134	349.4	.098	13.3	1.3	176.9	.0033
1961	4.268	362.9	.134	13.5	1.8	182.3	.0006
1962	4.578	383.9	.310	21.0	6.5	441.0	.0041
1963	5.093	402.8	.515	18.9	9.7	357.2	.0864
1964	5.716	437.0	.623	34.2	21.3	1169.6	.0497
1965	6.357	472.2	.641	35.2	22.6	1239.0	.0525
1966	6.769	510.4	.412	38.2	15.7	1459.2	.0012
1967	7.296	544.5	.527	34.1	18.0	1162.8	.0164
1968	8.178	588.1	.882	43.6	38.5	1901.0	.1383
1969	8.844	630.4	.666	42.3	28.2	1789.3	.0293
1970	9.251	685.9	.407	55.5	22.6	3080.3	.0587
1971	10.006	742.8	.755	56.9	43.0	3237.6	.0080
1972	11.200	801.3	1.194	58.5	69.8	3422.3	.2596
1973	12.500	903.1	1.300	101.8	132.3	10363.2	.0119
1974	13.101	983.6	.601	80.5	48.4	6480.3	.1162
1975	13.640	1076.7	.539	93.1	50.2	8667.6	.3028
					542.3	46158.4	1.1681

$$b = \frac{\Sigma X_T' X_T'}{\Sigma (X_T')^2} = \frac{542.3}{46158.4} = 0.0117$$

$$S_b^2 = \frac{\dfrac{\Sigma (y_T' - bX_T')^2}{n-1}}{\Sigma X_T'^2} = \frac{\dfrac{1.1681}{19}}{46158.4} = \frac{0.0614789}{46158.4} = 0.0000013$$

$$S_b = 0.00114$$

The table also contains the computations for estimating the linear regression through the origin. Notice that the estimated regression coefficient $b = .0117$ is similar to that obtained with ordinary least-squares applied to the original variables $b = .014$ (Table 7.9). However, the standard error of the regression coefficient, $s_b = .00114$, is considerably higher than $s_b = .00034$ (Table 7.9). The new standard error of the regression coefficient, $s_b = .00114$, is probably more accurate. The original standard error $s_b = .00034$ for ordinary least-squares applied to the original variables is likely to understate the true standard error due to autocorrelation.

Iterative Approach

The iterative approach also involves the transformation of the original variables.

$$Y_t^1 = Y_t - \rho Y_{t-1}$$
$$X_t^1 = X_t - \rho X_{t-1} \qquad (7\text{-}11)$$

The process is based on the transformed model Eq. (7–8), which can be solved with ordinary least-squares methods. Unfortunately, the transformed model

$$Y_t^1 = \beta_0 (1 - \rho) + \beta X_t^1 + \varepsilon_t$$

cannot be used directly because the autocorrelation parameter ρ needed to obtain the transformed variables in Eq. (7–11) is unknown. However, techniques to estimate ρ have been developed. Several approaches are discussed in *Econometric Models and Economic Forecasts* by Pindyck and Rubinfeld.* These approaches generally utilize the notion that ρ is a correlation coefficient associated with errors of adjacent time periods. The iterative approach does not always work. One reason is that the autocorrelation parameter ρ tends to be underestimated.

Rho Correction

Sometimes no additional variables can be identified to reduce autocorrelation to an insignificant level. When this is the case, estimates from the equation should be modified to reflect the error in the last observation. One approach for phasing out the effect of the last observed error is to calculate a

---

*PINDYCK, R. S., AND RUBINFELD, D. L., *Econometric Models and Economic Forecasts*, New York: McGraw-Hill Book Company, 1976, pp. 108–113.

factor, rho, which is half the difference between the Durbin-Watson statistic and 2.0.

When Sears sales are related to disposable income in Table 7.9, the Durbin-Watson statistic of .63 indicates positive autocorrelation. An examination of the table of residuals shows that the prediction for 1975 was too high.

$$e = Y - Y_R$$

$$-0.962 = 13.64 - 14.602$$

We expect that our estimate for 1976 will also be too high. Using the regression equation in Table 7.9, we estimate Sears sales for 1976 to be 16.068 billion dollars.

$$Y_R = -0.522 + 0.014X_2$$

$$Y_R = -0.522 + 0.014(1185)$$

$$Y_R = 16.068$$

In order to adjust for autocorrelation, the residual for 1975 is multiplied by the rho correction factor and added to the 1976 estimate.

$$Rho = \frac{(2.0 - D.W.)}{2}$$

$$Rho * e_{1975} = Correction\ Factor$$

$$0.685 * -0.962 = -0.66$$

$$Forecast_{1976} = Y_R + Correction\ Factor$$

$$Forecast_{1976} = 16.068 + (-0.66)$$

$$Forecast_{1976} = 15.408$$

(7-12)

The rho correction factor is used when all other approaches fail, and an equation containing related residuals must be used for prediction.

Summary

When regression analysis is applied to time series data, the residuals are frequently correlated. Since regression analysis assumes that residuals are independent, problems arise. The term autocorrelation describes this situation. The R^2 for a model containing autocorrelation is artificially high; furthermore, the standard error seriously underestimates the variability of the residuals, and the regression coefficients become quite inefficient.

A major cause of autocorrelated residuals is the omission of one or more key variables. This omission usually means that an important part of the dependent variable variation has not been explained. When the time-sequenced effects of a missing variable are positively related, the residuals are autocorrelated because they include the effects of the missing variable. The best solution to this problem is to search for the missing variable to include in the model.

Regression of Time Series Case

Prior to 1973 Spokane County, Washington had no up-to-date measurement of general business activity. What is happening in this area as a whole, however, affects every local business, governmental agency, and individual. Plans and policies made by an economic unit would be incomplete without some reliable knowledge about the recent performance of the economy of which the unit is a component part. A Spokane business activity index should serve as a vital input in the formulation of strategies and decisions in private as well as in public organizations.

A business activity index is an indicator of the relative changes in overall business conditions within a specified region. At the national level the Gross National Product (by U.S. Department of Commerce) and the Industrial Production Index (by the Federal Reserve Board) are generally considered excellent indicators. Each of these series is based on thousands of pieces of information—the collecting, editing, and computing of which are costly and time-consuming undertakings. For a local area such as Spokane County, Washington, a simplified version, capable of providing reasonably accurate and current information at moderate cost, is most desirable.

Multiple regression is commonly used to construct a business activity index. There are three essential questions with which the construction of such an index must deal:

1. What are the components of the index?
2. Do these components adequately represent the changes in overall business conditions?
3. What weight should be assigned to each of the chosen components?

Answers to these questions can be obtained through regression analysis.

Dr. Shik Chun Young, Professor of Economics at Eastern Washington University, attempted to develop a business activity index for Spokane County. Dr. Young selected personal income as the dependent variable. At the county level personal income is judged as the best available indicator of local business conditions. Personal income measures the total income received by households before personal taxes are paid. Since productive activities are typically remunerated by monetary means, personal income may, indeed, be viewed as a reasonable proxy for the general economic performance. Why then is it necessary to construct another index if personal income can serve as a good business activity indicator? Unfortunately, personal income data at the county level are estimated by the U.S. Department of Commerce on an annual basis, and are released 16 months too late. Consequently, these data are of little use for short-term planning. Dr. Young's task is to establish an up-to-date business activity index.

The independent variables are drawn from those local data that are readily available on a monthly basis. Currently, about fifty series of such monthly data are available and range from employment, bank activities, and real estate transactions, to electricity consumption. If each series were to be included in the regression analysis, the effort would yield low productivity because only a handful of these series would be expected to be statistically significant. Therefore, some knowledge of the relationship between personal income and the available data is necessary in order to determine which series are to be included in the regression equation. Based on Dr. Young's knowledge of the Spokane economy, the following ten series are selected:

- X_2: *Total Employment*
- X_3: *Manufacturing Employment*
- X_4: *Construction Employment*
- X_5: *Wholesale and Retail Trade Employment*
- X_6: *Service Employment*
- X_7: *Bank Debits*
- X_8: *Bank Demand Deposits*
- X_9: *Building Permits Issued*
- X_{10}: *Real Estate Mortgages*
- X_{11}: *Total Electricity Consumption*

The first step in the analysis is to run the model

$$Y_R = b_0 + b_2 X_2 + b_3 X_3 + ... + b_{11} X_{11} \qquad \text{(7-13)}$$

where:
$$Y = \text{personal income}$$
$$b_0 = \text{the } Y \text{ intercept}$$
$$b_2, b_3, ... \, b_{11} = \text{the coefficients of the respective independent variables.}$$

A brief summary of the regression results follows. The total corrected R^2 is 0.96, which means that the ten variables used together explain 96 percent of the variance in the dependent variable—personal income. However, other regression statistics indicate several problems. First, of these ten independent variables only three have a computed t value significant

240

at the .05 level; namely, total employment, service employment, and total bank debits. Second, the correlation matrix shows a high degree of interdependence among several of the independent variables—the problem of multicollinearity. For example, the total employment and bank debits have a correlation coefficient of 0.88; total electricity consumption and the bank demand deposits, 0.76; and building permit issued and real estate mortgages, 0.68. Third, autocorrelation, as indicated by a Durbin-Watson statistic of 0.91, is present. This is a rather common phenomenon in time-series data where each observation is not independent of the other observations in the same series.

Since one of the basic concepts in statistical inference is the randomness of the observations, Dr. Young chooses to deal with the autocorrelation problem first. The first-difference method is adopted to minimize the interdependence among the observations in each of the time series. The ten independent variables are now measured by the difference between the periods, rather than by the absolute value of each period. To distinguish the sets of data, a new designation for the independent variables is used.

- ΔX_2: *Change in Total Employment*
- ΔX_3: *Change in Manufacturing Employment*
- ΔX_4: *Change in Construction Employment*
- ΔX_5: *Change in Wholesale and Retail Trade Employment*
- ΔX_6: *Change in Service Employment*
- ΔX_7: *Change in Bank Debits*
- ΔX_8: *Change in Demand Deposits*
- ΔX_9: *Change in Building Permits Issued*
- ΔX_{10}: *Change in Real Estate Mortgages*
- ΔX_{11}: *Change in Total Electricity Consumption*

Also, the regression equation to be estimated becomes

$$\Delta Y_R = b_0 + b_2\Delta X_2 + b_3\Delta X_3 + \ldots + b_{11}\Delta X_{11} \qquad (7\text{-}14)$$

where
ΔY = the change in personal income
b_0, = the Y intercept
$b_2, b_3, \ldots b_{11}$ = the regression coefficients of the respective independent variables.

A regression run using this equation, based on the first-difference data, produces a Durbin-Watson statistic of 1.71. It indicates that no serious autocorrelation remains.

The next step is to determine which of the ten variables are significant predictors of the dependent variable. A variety of possible combinations of the ten are regressed against the Y in order to select the best equation. The criteria used in the selection are:

1. A satisfactorily high corrected R_c^2.
2. Low correlation coefficients among the independent variables.
3. Each of the independent variable's regression coefficient being significant at the .05 level.

After careful scrutiny of the regression results, the equation that contains $\Delta X_5, \Delta X_6$, and ΔX_{11} as independent variables best meets the above criteria.

However, it is reasoned that (in addition to commercial and industrial uses) total electricity consumption includes residential consumption, which should not have significant relation to business activity in the near term. To test this hypothesis, the total electricity consumption is subdivided into four variables: ΔX_{12}, change in residential electricity use; ΔX_{13}, change in commercial electricity use; ΔX_{14}, change in industrial electricity use; and ΔX_{15}, change in commercial and industrial use. Each of these four variables, combined with ΔX_5 and ΔX_6, are used to produce the four new regression equations.

Equation	Independent Variables	Dependent Variable
A	$\Delta X_5, \Delta X_6, \Delta X_{12}$	ΔY
B	$\Delta X_5, \Delta X_6, \Delta X_{13}$	ΔY
C	$\Delta X_5, \Delta X_6, \Delta X_{14}$	ΔY
D	$\Delta X_5, \Delta X_6, \Delta X_{15}$	ΔY

Statistical analysis indicates that Equation D is the best. As compared to the earlier equation that contains $\Delta X_5, \Delta X_6$, and ΔX_{11} as independent variables, Equation A is the only one that shows a deterioration in statistical significance. This confirms the notion that commercial and industrial electricity use is a better predictor of personal income than total electricity use, which includes residential electricity use. Therefore, Equation D is selected as the final regression equation, and the results are as follows

$$\Delta Y = -1.86 + 17.10\Delta X_5 + 23.01\Delta X_6 + 0.007\Delta X_{15}$$

$$(4.07) \qquad (5.61) \qquad (0.002)$$

$$N = 15; \qquad R_c^2 = 0.835; \qquad D.W. = 1.769; \qquad F = 26.26$$

The figures in parentheses below the regression coefficients are the standard errors of estimation of the coefficients, all significant at the 0.05 level. The t values of the coefficients are 4.10, 4.20, and 2.97 for ΔX_5, ΔX_6, and ΔX_{15}, respectively. The R_c^2 indicates that nearly 84 percent of the variance in change in personal income is explained by the three independent variables. The $D.W.$ statistic shows that autocorrelation is not a problem. In addition, the correlation coefficient matrix demonstrates a low level of interdependence among the three independent variables.

	ΔX_5	ΔX_6	ΔX_{15}
ΔX_5	1.000	0.452	0.113
ΔX_6	0.452	1.000	0.122
ΔX_{15}	0.113	0.122	1.000

For index construction purposes, the independent variables in the final regression equation become the index components. The weights of the components can be determined from the regression coefficients. (Recall that the regression coefficient represents the change in the dependent variable from a unit change in the independent variable.) However, since the variables in the regression equation do not have the same unit of measurement (for example, ΔY is measured in thousand dollars and ΔX_{15} in thousand kilowatt hours), the regression coefficients must be transformed into relative terms. This is accomplished by computing their β coefficients.

$$\beta = b \left(\frac{s}{s_y} \right)$$

where b is the independent variable regression coefficient, s the independent variable's standard deviation, and s_y the dependent variable's standard deviation. The values of all these statistics are typically available from the regression computer output. Hence, the standardized coefficients of the three independent variables are

$$\beta_5 = 0.4959$$
$$\beta_6 = 0.4833$$
$$\beta_{15} = 0.3019$$
$$Total = 1.2811$$

Finally, due to the necessity that the sum of the weights in an index must be 100 percent, the above coefficients are recalculated for this purpose as follows.

Component	Weight
ΔX_5	0.3871
ΔX_6	0.3772
ΔX_{15}	0.2357
Total	1.0000

After the components and their respective weights have been determined, the index can be obtained by the following steps:

243

1. Compute the percentage change of each component since the base period.
2. Multiply the percentage change by the appropriate weight.
3. Sum the weighted percentage changes obtained in step (2).

   The completed Spokane County Activity Index is compared to U.S. GNP in Constant Dollars Index (1967 = 100) in Fig. 7–5.

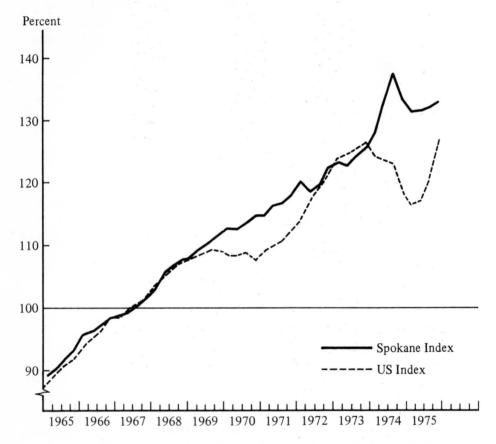

FIGURE 7–5 *Spokane County Business Activity Index and U.S. GNP in Constant Dollars Index. (1967 = 100)*

QUESTIONS TO BE ANSWERED

1. Dr. Young chose to solve the autocorrelation problem first. Would it have been better to eliminate multicollinearity first and then tackle autocorrelation?
2. How does the small sample size affect the analysis?

3. Should the regression done on the first differences have been through the origin?

4. Is there any potential for the usage of lagged data?

5. What conclusions can be drawn from a comparison of the Spokane County Business Activity Index and the Gross National Product Index?

PROBLEMS

1. Explain the term "autocorrelation."
   a. Discuss the factors that cause autocorrelation.
   b. Discuss the problems that exist when a regression model contains autocorrelation.
   c. Discuss the various approaches to the elimination of autocorrelation.

2. Thompson Airlines has determined that 5 percent of the total number of U.S. Domestic Airline Passengers fly on Thompson planes. Because of this relationship, you are given the task of forecasting the number of passengers who will fly on Thompson Airlines in 1965. The data are presented below.

Year	Number of Passengers (millions)	Year	Number of Passengers (millions)
1952	22.8	1964	61.9
1953	26.1	1965	69.9
1954	29.4	1966	79.9
1955	34.5	1967	96.3
1956	37.6	1968	109.0
1957	40.3	1969	116.0
1958	39.5	1970	117.2
1959	45.4	1971	124.9
1960	46.3	1972	136.6
1961	45.8	1973	144.8
1962	48.0	1974	147.9
1963	54.6		

a. Develop a time series regression model using time as the independent variable and the number of passengers as the dependent variable.
b. Are the error terms for this model dispersed in a uniform manner?
c. Transform the number of passengers variable so that the error terms will be uniformly dispersed.
d. Run the transformed model developed in part (c).
e. Are the error terms independent for the model run in part (d)?
f. If the error terms are dependent, what problems are involved with using this model?
g. Estimate the number of Thompson Airlines passengers for 1975.

3. The Thomas Furniture Company concludes that production scheduling can be improved by developing an accurate method of predicting quarterly sales. The company analyst, Mr. Estes, decides to investigate the relationship between housing construction permits and furniture sales in the Spokane area. Estes feels that permits will lead sales by one or two quarters. In addition he wonders if seasons affect furniture sales. Mr. Estes decides to consider another independent variable:

$$X_3 = \begin{cases} 0 \text{ if first or second quarter sales} \\ 1 \text{ if third or fourth quarter sales} \end{cases}$$

	Quarter	Sales (thousands) Y	Permits X_2
1973	3		19
	4		3
1974	1	120	35
	2	80	11
	3	400	11
	4	200	16
1975	1	75	32
	2	120	10
	3	270	12
	4	155	21
1976	1	120	72
	2	150	31
	3	660	19
	4	270	14
1977	1	200	75
	2	280	41
	3	800	17
	4	320	10

a. Develop a regression model that uses housing construction permits as the predictor variable.
b. Test this model for autocorrelation.
c. Develop a regression model that uses both permits and the seasonal effect.
d. Is the multiple regression model better than the simple regression model? (Test at the .05 significance level.)
e. Does your best model contain an autocorrelation problem? If so, how might it be corrected?
f. Estimate Thomas Furniture Company sales for 1978 by quarter.

4. The data below show seasonally adjusted quarterly sales for the Dickson Corporation and for the entire industry for the most recent 20 quarters.

	Quarter	Dickson Sales (thousands) Y	Industry Sales (millions) X_2
1973	1	83.8	31.8
	2	85.6	32.5
	3	87.8	33.2
	4	86.1	32.4
1974	1	89.6	33.8
	2	91.0	34.3
	3	93.9	35.3
	4	94.6	35.7
1975	1	96.4	36.4
	2	96.0	36.3
	3	98.2	37.1
	4	97.2	36.6
1976	1	100.1	37.6
	2	102.6	38.3
	3	105.4	39.3
	4	107.9	40.2
1977	1	110.1	41.1
	2	111.1	41.4
	3	110.1	41.1
	4	111.1	41.4

a. Fit the linear regression model, obtain the residuals, and plot them against time. What do you find?

b. Calculate the Durbin-Watson statistic, and determine whether autocorrelation exists.

c. Estimate the regression coefficient B_2 by the first differences approach.

d. Estimate the standard error of the regression coefficient by the first differences approach.

e. Are your estimates using the first differences approach more accurate?

*5. A study is done in an attempt to relate personal savings and personal income (in billions of dollars) for the time period 1935–54. The data are presented below.

Year	Personal Savings Y	Personal Income X
1935	2	60
1936	4	69
1937	4	74
1938	1	68
1939	3	73
1940	4	78
1941	11	96

Continued

Year	Personal Savings Y	Personal Income X
1942	28	123
1943	33	151
1944	37	165
1945	30	171
1946	15	179
1947	7	191
1948	13	210
1949	9	207
1950	13	279
1951	18	257
1952	19	273
1953	20	288
1954	19	290

a. Evaluate the simple regression model where personal income is used to predict personal savings. Specifically, (1) test the regression coefficient for significance ($\alpha = .01$); (2) test the personal income variable's contribution to the prediction of personal savings using the F test ($\alpha = .01$); (3) test for autocorrelation; and (4) how can the model be improved?

b. Develop a dummy variable X_3 for war years. Let $X_3 = 0$ for peacetime and $X_3 = 1$ for wartime. The war years are considered to be 1941–45. Run this multiple regression model, and evaluate the results. Specifically, (1) test to determine if knowledge of war years makes a significant contribution to the prediction of personal savings ($\alpha = .01$); (2) test for autocorrelation; (3) is the multiple regression model better than the simple regression model?

BIBLIOGRAPHY

DURBIN, J., AND WATSON G. S., "Testing for Serial Correlation in Least Squares Regression II." *Biometrika*, Vol. 38 (1951), pp. 159–78.

JOHNSTON, J., *Econometric Methods*, New York: McGraw-Hill Book Co., 1963.

MAKRIDAKIS, S., AND WHEELWRIGHT, S. C., *Interactive Forecasting*, Palo Alto, Calif. The Scientific Press, 1977.

——— *Forecasting Methods & Applications*, New York: John Wiley and Sons, 1978.

MILLER, R. B., AND WICHERN, D. W., *Intermediate Business Statistics*, New York: Holt, Rinehart, and Winston, 1977.

NETER, J., AND WASSERMAN, W., *Applied Linear Statistical Models*, Homewood, Ill.: Richard D. Irwin, Inc., 1974.

PINDYCK, R. S., AND RUBINFELD, D. L., *Econometric Models and Economic Forecasts*, New York: McGraw-Hill Book Company, 1976.

Other Forecasting Models

8

A tremendous emphasis is being placed on the improvement of decision making in both business and government organizations. Since we exist in an environment influenced by time, it has become a common goal to allocate available time among competing resources in some optimal manner. This can be accomplished, in part, through accurate forecasting. Twenty years ago managers made their decisions largely on their own feelings and intuition about the industry. Now they are supplementing this "feel for the industry" with both simple and sophisticated forecasting techniques.

Naïve Models

The simplest naïve models assume that recent periods are the best predictors of the future. The simplest model is

$$X_{T+1} = X_T \qquad (8-1)$$

Thus, if X stands for quarterly sales of saws, this model forecasts sales for the next quarter to be the same as the present quarter. The sales of saws is shown for the Acme Tool Company in Table 8.1. Our forecast for the first quarter of 1977 is

TABLE 8.1 *Sales of Saws for the Acme Tool Company (1971–1976).*

Year	Quarter	T	Sales
1971	1	1	500
	2	2	350
	3	3	250
	4	4	400
1972	1	5	450
	2	6	350
	3	7	200
	4	8	300
1973	1	9	350
	2	10	200
	3	11	150
	4	12	400
1974	1	13	550
	2	14	350
	3	15	250
	4	16	550
1975	1	17	550
	2	18	400
	3	19	350
	4	20	600
1976	1	21	750
	2	22	500
	3	23	400
	4	24	650

$$X_{24+1} = X_{24}$$
$$X_{25} = 650$$

What if a definite trend exists in the series being forecast? Investigation of Table 8.1 shows that a trend probably does exist, and if we use Eq. (8–1) our projections will be consistently low. The best approach would seem to incorporate the trend into the forecasting model. If this is the case, our model becomes

$$X_{T+1} = X_T + (X_T - X_{T-1}) \tag{8-2}$$

This model takes into account the amount of change that occurred between this period and last. Our forecast for the first quarter of 1977 using this model is

$$X_{24+1} = X_{24} + (X_{24} - X_{24-1})$$
$$X_{25} = X_{24} + (X_{24} - X_{23})$$
$$X_{25} = 650 + (650 - 400)$$

$$X_{25} = 650 + 250$$

$$X_{25} = 900$$

For some purposes the rate of change may be more appropriate than the absolute amount, and then the model is

$$X_{T+1} = X_T \frac{X_T}{X_{T-1}} \tag{8-3}$$

Our forecast for the first quarter of 1977 using this model is

$$X_{24+1} = X_{24} \cdot \frac{X_{24}}{X_{24-1}}$$

$$X_{25} = X_{24} \cdot \frac{X_{24}}{X_{23}}$$

$$X_{25} = 650 \cdot \frac{650}{400}$$

$$X_{25} = 1056$$

It would probably be better if the forecaster used an *average* of past absolute changes or rates of change in preparing the forecast.

Visual inspection of the data in Table 8.1 indicates that seasonal variation seems to exist. Sales in the fourth quarter are typically larger than any of the other quarters. If the seasonal pattern is strong, then the appropriate model might be

$$X_{T+1} = X_{T-3} \tag{8-4}$$

Equation (8–4) states that next quarter the variable will take on the same value it did in the corresponding quarter one year ago. Our forecast for the first quarter of 1977 is

$$X_{24+1} = X_{24-3}$$

$$X_{25} = X_{21}$$

$$X_{25} = 750$$

The major weakness of this approach is that it ignores everything that has occurred since last year and also any trend pattern. The ways of introducing more recent information are numerous. For example, we can combine approaches and take into consideration both seasonal and trend variations. One possible model is

$$X_{T+1} = X_{T-3} + \frac{(X_T - X_{T-1}) + \ldots + (X_{T-3} + X_{T-4})}{4} \tag{8-5}$$

251

where the X_{T-3} term forecasts the seasonal patterns and the remaining term averages the amount of change for the past 4 quarters (trend). Our forecast for the first quarter of 1977 using this model is

$$X_{24+1} = X_{24-3} + \frac{(X_{24} - X_{24-1}) + \ldots + (X_{24-3} - X_{24-4})}{4}$$

$$X_{25} = X_{21} + \frac{(X_{24} - X_{23}) + (X_{23} - X_{22}) + (X_{22} - X_{21}) + (X_{21} - X_{20})}{4}$$

$$X_{25} = 750 + \frac{(650 - 400) + (400 - 500) + (500 - 750) + (750 - 600)}{4}$$

$$X_{25} = 750 + 37.5$$

$$X_{25} = 787.5$$

It is apparent that the number and complexity of naïve models possible is limited only by the ingenuity of the analyst.

Exponential Smoothing

Exponential smoothing is a procedure for continually revising an estimate in the light of more recent experiences. This method is based on averaging (smoothing) past values of a series in a decreasing (exponential) manner. The observations are weighted, with more weight being given to the more recent observations. The weights used are A for the most recent observation, $A(1 - A)$ for the next most recent, $A(1 - A)^2$ for the next, and so forth. This weighting system can be written as

$$F_T = AX_T + (1 - A)F_{T-1} \qquad \text{(8-6)}$$

where: F_T = the exponentially smoothed value in period T; the fore-casted value made at time T for the next period

A = the smoothing constant ($0 \le A \le 1$)

X_T = the actual value of the series in period T

F_{T-1} = the average experience of the series smoothed to period $T - 1$

In an effort to better interpret A, Eq. (8-6) can be rewritten as

$$F_T = AX_T + (1 - A)F_{T-1}$$

$$F_T = AX_T + F_{T-1} - AF_{T-1} \qquad \text{(8-7)}$$

$$F_T = F_{T-1} + A(X_T - F_{T-1})$$

We see that exponential smoothing is simply the old forecast (F_{T-1}) "plus"

A "times" the error $(X_T - F_{T-1})$ in the old forecast.

The smoothing constant A serves as the weighting factor. The actual value of A determines the extent to which the most current observation is to influence the forecasted value. When A is close to 1, the new forecast will include a substantial adjustment for any error that occurred in the preceding forecast. Conversely, when A is close to 0, the new forecast will be very similar to the old one. We can think of F_T as a linear combination of all past observations with weights given these past observations that decrease geometrically with the age of the data. The speed at which past values lose their importance depends upon the value of A, as demonstrated in Table 8.2.

TABLE 8.2 *Comparison of Smoothing Constants.*

Time Period	$A = 0.1$ Calculations	Weight	$A = 0.6$ Calculations	Weight
T		0.100		0.600
$T - 1$	0.9×0.1	0.090	0.4×0.6	0.240
$T - 2$	$0.9 \times 0.9 \times 0.1$	0.081	$0.4 \times 0.4 \times 0.6$	0.096
$T - 3$	$0.9 \times 0.9 \times 0.9 \times 0.1$	0.073	$0.4 \times 0.4 \times 0.4 \times 0.6$	0.038
$T - 4$	$0.9 \times 0.9 \times 0.9 \times 0.9 \times 0.1$	0.066	$0.4 \times 0.4 \times 0.4 \times 0.4 \times 0.6$	0.015
All Others		0.590		0.011
Total		1.000		1.000

The value assigned to A is critical in the analysis. If it is desired that predictions be stable and random variations smoothed, a small A is required. If a rapid response to a real change in the pattern of observations is desired, a larger value of A is appropriate. The usual method of estimating A is an iterative procedure that minimizes

$$\Sigma(F_{T-1} - X_T)^2 \quad \text{or} \quad \Sigma(\hat{F}_T - X_T)^2 \qquad \textbf{(8-8)}$$

Forecasts are computed for A equal to 0.1, 0.2, ..., 0.6; and the sum of the squared forecast errors is computed. The value of A producing the smallest error is then chosen for use in generating future forecasts.

The exponential smoothing technique is demonstrated in Table 8.3 for smoothing constants of 0.1 and 0.6. The exponentially smoothed series that uses $A = 0.1$ is computed by initially setting $F_1 = 500$ and then:*

1. $F_T = AX_T + (1 - A)F_{T-1}$

   $F_2 = 0.1(350) + (1 - 0.1)500$

   $F_2 = 485$

---

*Numbers 1–5 are shown in parentheses in Table 8.3.

2. $F_3 = 0.1(250) + 0.9(485)$

   $F_3 = 462$

The forecast error is calculated in the following manner:

3. $e_T = F_{T-1} - X_T$

   $e_2 = 500 - 350$

   $e_2 = 150$

4. $e_3 = 485 - 250$

   $e_3 = 235$

5. The forecasted sales for the 1st quarter of 1977 using a smoothing constant of 0.1 is 470.

Note how stable the smoothed values are for the smoothing constant 0.1. Conversely, the values fluctuate widely when an $A = 0.6$ is used. On the basis of minimizing Eq. (8–8), the smoothing constant 0.6 is better. However, the other smoothing constants have not been investigated; nor has the trend or seasonal variation of the data been taken into consideration.

$$A = 0.1 \qquad \Sigma(F_{T-1} - X_T)^2 = 587{,}505$$
$$A = 0.6 \qquad \Sigma(F_{T-1} - X_T)^2 = 509{,}698$$

Exponential Smoothing Adjusted for Trend

Exponentially smoothed averages will always lag behind a steadily rising or falling linear trend. Therefore, the trend must be estimated and the series adjusted accordingly. One convenient approach is Holt's Two Parameters Linear Exponential Smoothing Method. The three equations used in this model are:

1. Update the exponentially smoothed series.

$$F_T = AX_T + (1 - A)(F_{T-1} + T_{T-1}) \qquad \textbf{(8-9a)}$$

2. Update the trend estimate.

$$T_T = B(F_T - F_{T-1}) + (1 - B)T_{T-1} \qquad \textbf{(8-9b)}$$

3. Forecast P periods into the future.

$$\hat{F}_{T+P} = F_T + PT_T \qquad \textbf{(8-9c)}$$

TABLE 8.3 *Exponentially Smoothed Sales for the Acme Tool Company.*

Time Period	Actual Value X_T	Smoothed Value $F_T (A = .1)$	Forecast Error e_T	Smoothed Value $F_T (A = .6)$	Forecast Error e_T
1	500	500	—	500	—
2	350	485 (1)	150 (3)	410	150
3	250	462 (2)	235 (4)	314	160
4	400	456	62	366	−86
5	450	455	6	416	−84
6	350	445	105	376	66
7	200	421	245	270	176
8	300	409	121	288	−30
9	350	403	59	325	−62
10	200	383	203	250	125
11	150	360	233	190	100
12	400	364	−40	316	−210
13	550	383	−186	456	−234
14	350	380	33	392	106
15	250	367	130	307	142
16	550	385	−183	453	−243
17	550	402	−165	511	−97
18	400	402	2	444	121
19	350	397	52	388	96
20	600	417	−203	515	−212
21	750	450	−333	656	−235
22	500	455	−50	562	156
23	400	450	−95	465	12
24	650	470 (5)	200	576	−185

where:
F_T = the exponentially smoothed value in period T
A = the smoothing constant
X_T = the actual value of the series
F_{T-1} = the average experience of the series smoothed to period $T - 1$
B = the smoothing constant for the trend estimate
T_T = the trend estimate
T_{T-1} = the average experience of the trend estimate smoothed to period $T - 1$
P = periods to be forecasted into the future
$\hat{F}_{T+P}$ = forecast for P periods into the future

The first equation, Eq. (8–9a), is very similar to the original single exponential smoothing equation, Eq. (8–6), except that a term has been added for the trend (T_{T-1}). The trend estimate is calculated by taking the difference between two successive exponential smoothing values ($F_T - F_{T-1}$). Since successive values have been smoothed for randomness, their difference constitutes an estimate of the trend in the data. A second smoothing constant, B, is used to smooth the trend estimate. Equation (8–9b) shows that the estimate of the trend $(F_T - F_{T-1})$ is multiplied by B and then added to the old estimate of the trend (T_{T-1}), multiplied by $(1 - B)$. Equation (8–9b) is similar to Eq. (8–9a), except that the smoothing is done for the trend rather than the actual data. The result of Eq. (8–9b) is a smoothed trend excluding any randomness. Equation (8–9c) shows the forecast for P periods into the future. The trend estimate (T_T) is multiplied by the number of periods to be forecasted (P), and then the product is added to the current level of the data smoothed (F_T) to eliminate randomness. Table 8.4 illustrates this procedure with the Acme Tool Company data. To begin the computations we need two estimated initial values, namely, the initial smoothed value and the initial trend value. The initial smoothed

TABLE 8.4 *Exponentially Smoothed Sales for the Acme Tool Company Adjusted for Trend.*

Time Period $+$	Actual Value X_T	Smoothed Value F_T	Trend Estimate T_T	Forecast F_T	Forecast Error e_T
1	500	500	0	500	
2	350	455(1)	−4.5(2)	450.5(3)	150
3	250	390.4	−10.5	379.9	200.5(4)
4	400	385.9	−9.9	376.0	−20.1
5	450	398.2	−7.7	390.5	74.0
6	350	378.4	−8.9	369.5	40.5
7	200	318.7	−14.0	304.7	169.5
8	300	303.3	−14.1	289.2	4.7
9	350	307.4	−12.3	295.1	−60.8
10	200	266.6	−15.2	251.4	95.1
11	150	221.0	−18.2	202.8	101.4
12	400	262.0	−12.3	259.7	−197.2
13	550	346.8	−2.6	344.2	−290.3
14	350	345.9	−2.4	343.5	−5.8
15	250	315.5	−5.2	310.3	93.5
16	550	382.2	−2.0	380.2	−239.7
17	550	431.1	3.1	434.2	−169.8
18	400	423.9	2.1	426.0	34.2
19	350	403.2	−0.2	403.0	76.0
20	600	462.1	5.7	467.8	−197.0
21	750	552.5	14.2	566.7	−282.2
22	500	546.7	12.2	558.9	66.7
23	400	511.2	7.4	518.6	158.9
24	650	558.0	11.3	569.3(5)	−131.4
25				580.6(6)	
26				591.9(7)	
27				603.2(8)	

value is usually estimated by averaging a few past observations of the series. The initial trend value is estimated by using the slope of the trend equation obtained from past data. If past data are not available, zero is used as the initial estimate.

The value for A is similar to the smoothing model (Eq. 8–6), and smooths the data to eliminate randomness. The smoothing constant B is like A except that it smooths the trend in the data. Both smoothing constants remove randomness by weighting past values.

The technique is demonstrated in Table 8.4 for an $A = 0.3$ and $B = 0.1$. The computations leading to the forecast for period three are shown below:*

1. $F_T = A X_T + (1 - A)(F_{T-1} + T_{T-1})$

   $F_2 = 0.3 X_2 + (1 - 0.3)(F_{2-1} + T_{2-1})$

   $F_2 = 0.3(350) + 0.7(500 + 0)$

   $F_2 = 455$

2. $T_T = B(F_T - F_{T-1}) + (1 - B) T_{T-1}$

   $T_2 = 0.1(F_2 - F_{2-1}) + (1 - 0.1) T_{2-1}$

   $T_2 = 0.1(455 - 500) + 0.9(0)$

   $T_2 = -4.5$

3. $\hat{F}_{T+P} = F_T + PT_T$

   $\hat{F}_{2+1} = F_2 + 1T_2$

   $\hat{F}_3 = 455 + 1(-4.5)$

   $\hat{F}_3 = 450.5$

The forecast error is calculated in the following manner:

4. $e_T = \hat{F}_T - X_T$

   $e_3 = \hat{F}_3 - X_3$

   $e_3 = 450.5 - 250$

   $e_3 = 200.5$

The forecasted sales for each quarter of 1977 are shown below.

First quarter

5. $\hat{F}_{T+P} = F_T + PT_T$

---

*Numbers 1–8 are shown in Parentheses in Table 8.4.

$$\hat{F}_{24+1} = F_{24} + 1(T_{24})$$
$$\hat{F}_{25} = 558 + 1(11.3)$$
$$\hat{F}_{25} = 569.3$$

Second quarter

6. $\hat{F}_{24+2} = F_{24} + 2(T_{24})$
$$\hat{F}_{26} = 558 + 2(11.3)$$
$$\hat{F}_{26} = 580.6$$

Third quarter

7. $\hat{F}_{27} = 558 + 3(11.3) = 591.9$

Fourth quarter

8. $\hat{F}_{28} = 558 + 4(11.3) = 603.2$

In order to evaluate the model, Eq. (8–8) is applied; when

$$A = 0.3$$
$$B = 0.1$$
$$\Sigma(\hat{F}_T - X_T)^2 = 512,577$$

It does not appear as if the trend estimate improves the accuracy of our forecasts. However, other combinations of A and B constants might improve the result.

Exponential Smoothing Adjusted for Trend and Seasonal Variation

Examination of the data for saw sales of Acme Tool Company, Table 8.1, indicates that sales are consistently better during the first and fourth quarters, and worse during the third quarter. A seasonal pattern appears to exist. Winter's Three Parameter Linear and Seasonal Exponential Smoothing model, an extension of Holt's model, might improve our forecasts. One additional equation is used in order to estimate seasonality. This seasonality estimate is given as a seasonal index (see Chapter 6), and is calculated with Eq. (8–10b). Equation (8–10b) shows that the estimate of the seasonal index (X_T/F_T) is multiplied by B and then added to the old seasonal estimate (S_{T-P}), multiplied by $(1 - B)$. The reason why X_T is divided by F_T is to express the value as an index, rather than in absolute terms, so that it can be averaged with the seasonal index smoothed to period $T - 1$.

The four equations used in Winter's model are:

1. Update the exponentially smoothed series.

$$F_T = A \frac{X_T}{S_{T-P}} + (1 - A)(F_{T-1} + T_{T-1}) \qquad \text{(8–10a)}$$

2. Update the seasonality estimate.

$$S_T = B \frac{X_T}{F_T} + (1 - B)S_{T-P} \qquad \text{(8–10b)}$$

3. Update the trend estimate.

$$T_T = C(F_T - F_{T-1}) + (1 - C)T_{T-1} \qquad \text{(8–10c)}$$

4. Forecast P periods in the future.

$$\hat{F}_{T+P} = (F_T + PT_T) S_T \qquad \text{(8–10d)}$$

where: F_T = the exponentially smoothed value in period T
A = the smoothing constant
X_T = the actual value of the series
F_{T-1} = the average experience of the series smoothed to period $T - 1$
B = the smoothing constant for the seasonality estimate
S_T = the seasonality estimate
S_{T-P} = the average experience of the seasonality estimated smoothed to period $T - P$
C = the smoothing constant for the trend estimate
T_T = the trend estimate
T_{T-1} = the average experience of the trend estimate smoothed to period $T - 1$
P = number of seasons per year (monthly or quarterly)
$\hat{F}_{T+P}$ = forecast for P periods into the future

Equation (8–10a) updates the smoothed series. A slight difference in Eq. (8–10a) distinguishes it from the corresponding one in Holt's model, Eq. (8–9a). In Eq. (8–10a), X_T is divided by S_{T-P}, which adjusts X_T for seasonality, thus removing the seasonal affects that might exist in the original data X_T.

After the seasonality estimate and trend estimate have been smoothed in Eqs. (8–10b) and (8–10c), a forecast is obtained with Eq. (8–10d). It is almost the same as the corresponding formula, Eq. (8–9c), used to obtain a forecast in Holt's model. The difference is that this estimate for the future period, $T + P$, is multiplied by S_{T-P+1}. This is the last seasonal index available, and, therefore, is used to adjust the forcast for seasonality.

This technique is demonstrated in Table 8.5. Initial values of A

$= 0.4, \; B = 0.3, \; C = 0.1, \; F = 400, \; T = 0, \; S1 = 1, \; S2 = 1, \; S3 = 1,$ and $S4 = 1$ were used to develop the forecast for 1977. The computations for first quarter 1971 are shown below.

1. Update the exponentially smoothed series.

$$F_T = A \frac{X_T}{S_{T-P}} + (1 - A)(F_{T-1} + T_{T-1})$$

$$F_1 = 0.4 \frac{500}{1.0} + 0.6(400 + 0)$$

$$F_1 = 440$$

2. Update the seasonality estimate.

$$S_T = B \frac{X_T}{F_T} + (1 - B) S_{T-P}$$

$$S_1 = 0.3 \frac{500}{440} + 0.7(1.0)$$

$$S_1 = 1.041$$

3. Update the trend estimate.

$$T_T = C(F_T - F_{T-1}) + (1 - C) T_{T-1}$$

$$T_1 = 0.1(440 - 400) + 0.9(0)$$

$$T_1 = 4$$

4. Forecast P periods in the future.

$$\hat{F}_{T+P} = (F_T + PT_T) S_T$$

$$\hat{F}_{1+4} = [440 + 4(4)] \; 1.041$$

$$\hat{F} = 475$$

The forecast for first quarter 1972 is 475. Since actual sales were 450, the error is 25.

5. $e_T = \hat{F}_T - X_T$

$$e_T = 475 - 450$$

$$e_T = 25$$

Table 8.5 shows the computer output for this problem. The error squared and summed $\Sigma(\hat{F}_T - X_T)^2$ equals 326,150. This is an improvement over the model that used only the trend estimate.

Another approach to the determination of this model's accuracy

TABLE 8.5 *Acme Tool Example Computations for Exponential Smoothing Adjusted for Trend and Seasonal Variation.*

Time Period	Actual Value X_t	Smoothed Value $F_T (A = .4)$	Seasonal Adjustment $S_T (B = .3)$	Trend Adjustment $T_T (C = .1)$	Forecasted Value F_{T+1} or $\hat{F}_T$	Forecasting Error $\hat{F}_T - X_T$
1970						
1			1.0			
2			1.0			
3			1.0			
4		400	1.0	0		
1971						
1	500	440 (1)	1.04 (2)	4 (3)	400	100
2	350	406	0.96	0	400	−50
3	250	344	0.92	−6	400	−150
4	400	363	1.03	−4	400	0
1972						
1	450				475 (4)	+25 (5)

Computer Output Forecast of 1977, Sales and Forecast Accuracy.

Initial Values — A = 0.400, B = 0.300, C = 0.100, F = 400, T = 0, S1 = 1.00, S2 = 1.00, S3 = 1.00, and S4 = 1.00.

QUARTER =

YEAR	SALES	FRCST	S	SALES	FRCST	S	SALES	FRCST	S	SALES	FRCST	S	F	T
1971	500.	400.	1.04	350.	400.	0.96	250.	400.	0.92	400.	400.	1.03	363.	−4.
1972	450.	475.	1.08	350.	390.	0.95	200.	294.	0.83	300.	359.	1.02	300.	−8.
1973	350.	415.	1.10	200.	353.	0.89	150.	235.	0.79	400.	272.	1.14	283.	−6.
1974	550.	303.	1.22	350.	197.	0.90	250.	133.	0.76	550.	294.	1.20	408.	6.
1975	550.	460.	1.24	400.	355.	0.90	350.	274.	0.76	600.	520.	1.22	476.	10.
1976	750.	569.	1.29	500.	426.	0.91	400.	372.	0.75	650.	630.	1.21	550.	12.

$\Sigma(F_T - X_T)^2 = 326150$

Forecast

QUARTER =	1	2	3	4
1977	764.	552.	453.	723.

Final Values — F = 550.0, T = 12.00, S1 = 1.29, S2 = 0.91, S3 = 0.75, S4 = 1.21

is to see how well it forecasted 1976. Table 8.6 shows the actual values (X_T) compared to our forecasted values $(\hat{F}_T)$. To evaluate the forecasting model, we need some indication of the average error that can be expected over time. If we add up the e_T column, we find that it sums close to zero, because we add both positive and negative errors. We can avoid this problem by disregarding the "plus" or "minus" sign and by computing the mean absolute deviation (MAD).

TABLE 8.6   *Forecast Errors for Acme Tool Exponential Smoothing Forecast.*

Quarter	Actual Value	Forecast	Error	Squared Error
	X_T	$\hat{F}_T$	$(\hat{F}_T - X_T)$	$(\hat{F}_T - X_T)^2$
1	750	569	−181	32761
2	500	426	−74	5476
3	400	372	−28	784
4	650	630	−20	400
				$\Sigma(\hat{F}_T - X_T)^2 = 39421$

$$MSE = \frac{\Sigma(\hat{F}_T - X_T)^2}{N} = \frac{39421}{4} = 9855 \qquad MAD = \frac{\Sigma|\hat{F} - X_T|}{N} = \frac{303}{4} = 75.75$$

$$MAD = \frac{\Sigma|\hat{F}_T - X_T|}{N} \qquad (8\text{-}11)$$

The mean absolute deviation for the Acme Tool forecast equals 75.75.

$$MAD = \frac{\Sigma|\hat{F} - X_T|}{N} = \frac{303}{4} = 75.75$$

An alternative method for evaluating a forecast is to square each of the individual errors and to compute the mean of the squared values summed. This is called the mean-squared error.

$$MSE = \frac{\Sigma(\hat{F}_T - X_T)^2}{N} \qquad (8\text{-}12)$$

The mean-squared error for the Acme Tool forecast equals 9855.25.

$$MSE = \frac{\Sigma(\hat{F}_T - X_T)^2}{N} = \frac{39421}{4} = 9855.25$$

The difficult aspect of using exponential smoothing adjusted for trend and seasonal variation is choosing the best smoothing constants.

TABLE 8.7 Sales of Saws for the Acme Tool Company: Seasonal Variation (1971–76).

Quarter	1971	1972	1973	1974	1975	1976	Modified Quarter Mean	Adjusted Seasonal Index Mean * 1.011730
1		126.32	136.59	146.67	122.22	134.83	132.58	134.1
2		103.70	76.19	86.15	85.33	87.91	86.47	87.5
3	67.80	64.00	50.00	58.82	70.00		63.54	64.3
4	110.34	106.67	116.36	127.54	111.63		112.78	114.1
							395.36	400.0

263

Fortunately, computer programs such as the one illustrated in Table 8.5, allow the analyst to try various combinations quickly.

TABLE 8.8 *Sales of Saws for the Acme Tool Company: Trend, Cyclical, and Irregular (1971–76).*

SALES OF SAWS FOR THE ACME TOOL COMPANY
TREND, CYCLICAL, AND IRREGULAR
(1971-76)

PERIOD		DATA Y	REGRESSION T	SEAS. ADJ. TCI	CI	C	I
1971	1	500.00	286.83	372.77	129.96		
	2	350.00	297.40	400.09	134.53	130.26	103.28
	3	250.00	307.96	388.89	126.28	123.62	102.15
	4	400.00	318.53	350.56	110.06	112.76	97.60
1972	1	450.00	329.09	335.49	101.94	109.93	92.73
	2	350.00	339.66	400.09	117.79	102.86	114.52
	3	200.00	350.22	311.11	88.83	93.17	95.35
	4	300.00	360.79	262.92	72.87	77.32	94.25
1973	1	350.00	371.36	260.94	70.27	67.67	103.84
	2	200.00	381.92	228.62	59.86	63.19	94.73
	3	150.00	392.49	233.33	59.45	68.76	86.46
	4	400.00	403.05	350.56	86.98	81.85	106.26
1974	1	550.00	413.62	410.04	99.14	93.48	106.05
	2	350.00	424.18	400.09	94.32	94.30	100.02
	3	250.00	434.75	388.89	89.45	97.34	91.90
	4	550.00	445.31	482.03	108.24	95.88	112.90
1975	1	550.00	455.88	410.04	89.95	98.74	91.09
	2	400.00	466.44	457.24	98.03	100.70	97.34
	3	350.00	477.01	544.45	114.14	106.67	107.00
	4	600.00	487.57	525.85	107.85	111.41	96.80
1976	1	750.00	498.14	559.15	112.25	110.82	101.29
	2	500.00	508.70	571.56	112.36	114.81	97.86
	3	400.00	519.27	622.23	119.83	113.23	105.82
	4	650.00	529.83	569.67	107.52		
1977	1		540.40				
	2		550.96				
	3		561.53				
	4		572.09				

REGRESSION FORECAST =   10.565 X PERIOD + 286.83

264

Time Series Forecasting Example

Forecasting that uses the time series analysis technique was discussed in depth in Chapter 6. The decomposition method of time-series forecasting tries to identify four separate components of the basic underlying pattern: trend, seasonal, cyclical, and irregular. The mathematical form used to represent this decomposition, and eventually the model used to forecast, is

$$T = TSCI$$

The sales of saws for the Acme Tool Company (Table 8.1) will be forecasted using this approach. The data are run on a time-series computer program, and the results are shown in Tables 8.7 and 8.8. The seasonal pattern is presented in Table 8.7. Saw sales are high in the first and fourth quarters, and extremely low in the third quarter. Table 8.8 shows that the trend is increasing on an average of 10.565 saws per quarter. The cyclical pattern is also illustrated in Table 8.8. Sales are extremely high in 1971, extremely low in 1973, and above average in 1976. A large amount of irregular variation occurs for this variable, as indicated by the large fluctuations in the I column of Table 8.8. If we had more information about our variable, we could explain the nature of the irregularities.

Our forecast for 1977 is:

$$Y(1st) = TSCI$$

$$Y(1st) = (540.4)(1.341)(1.11)(1.00)$$

$$Y(1st) = 804.39$$

The trend is projected to be 540.4. We know first quarter sales are typically high so that our expected sales based on the trend are adjusted upward by multiplying by a seasonal index of 134.1. Next, we need a thorough analysis of the cyclical pattern of this variable. The state of the economy is important. Business indicators and any other variables that affect the sales of Acme saws must be considered. In order to complete this example, an index of 111 is chosen. Finally, an irregular index of 100 is used since these uncontrollable events are extremely difficult to anticipate. The forecasts for the second, third, and fourth quarters are shown below.

$$Y(2nd) = (550.96)(0.875)(1.10)(1.00)$$
$$= 530.3$$
$$Y(3rd) = (561.53)(0.643)(1.08)(1.00)$$
$$= 389.95$$
$$Y(4th) = (572.09)(1.141)(1.05)(1.00)$$
$$= 685.39$$

To determine the accuracy of this forecasting model, we can compute either the mean-squared error (*MSE*) or the mean absolute error (*MAD*). We could do so by using the six years of data that we used to identify the four basic factors. This would bias the results since we would be employing the same data to develop the forecasting technique as to evaluate it. It would be better to use only the first five years of data in determining a forecast for the sixth year. This was done, and the results are presented in Tables 8.9 and 8.10. The forecasts for 1976 are shown in Table 8.10, and the comparison of these results with the actual sales for 1976 are demonstrated in Table 8.11. The mean absolute deviation (*MAD*) is 31.43. This compares favorably with the *MAD* for the exponential smoothing model adjusted for trend and seasonal variation.

TABLE 8.9 *Sales of Saws for the Acme Tool Company: Seasonal Variation (1971–75).*

SALES OF SAWS FOR THE ACME TOOL COMPANY

SEASONAL VARIATION
(1971-75)

QUARTER	1971	1972	1973	1974	1975	MODIFIED QTR. MEAN	ADJUSTED SEASONAL INDEX MEAN * 1.020514
1		126.32	136.59	146.67	122.22	131.45	134.1
2		103.70	76.19	86.15	85.33	85.74	87.5
3	67.80	64.00	50.00	58.82		61.41	62.7
4	110.34	106.67	116.36	127.54		113.35	115.7
						391.95	400.0

Autoregressive Example

Linear models accounting for correlation between adjacent observations in a time series are called autoregressive models. This technique is demonstrated on the Carlson Dishwasher Sales example in Chapter 7. We use knowledge of the response at time period T to predict the response at time $(T + 1)$.

$$Y_{T+1} = b_0 + b_2 X_T \qquad \text{(8-13)}$$

where: $X_T = Y_T$

We refer to Eq. (8–13) as the first-order autoregressive model. For instance, the sales of saws for the Acme Tool Company (Table 8.1) indicate an obvious annual (four-quarter) cycle. Thus, a "good" autoregressive model for forecasting the future sales of Acme might be

$$Y_{T+1} = b_0 + b_2 Y_{T-3} \qquad \text{(8-14)}$$

266

TABLE 8.10 *Sales of Saws for the Acme Tool Company: Trend, Cyclical, and Irregular Variables (1971–75).*

SALES OF SAWS FOR THE ACME TOOL COMPANY
TREND, CYCLICAL, AND IRREGULAR
(1971-75)

		DATA	REGRESSION	SEAS. ADJ.			
PERIOD		Y	T	TCI	CI	C	I
1971	1	500.00	312.86	372.73	119.14		
	2	350.00	319.40	399.99	125.23	122.25	102.44
	3	250.00	325.94	398.91	122.39	117.21	104.42
	4	400.00	332.48	345.78	104.00	108.44	95.90
1972	1	450.00	339.02	335.45	98.95	106.23	93.14
	2	350.00	345.56	399.99	115.75	101.78	113.73
	3	200.00	352.10	319.12	90.63	92.90	97.56
	4	300.00	358.65	259.34	72.31	78.13	92.55
1973	1	350.00	365.19	260.91	71.45	68.41	104.43
	2	200.00	371.73	228.56	61.49	65.40	94.01
	3	150.00	378.27	239.34	63.27	71.54	88.45
	4	400.00	384.81	345.78	89.86	85.97	104.53
1974	1	550.00	391.35	410.00	04.76	98.38	106.49
	2	350.00	397.89	399.99	100.53	101.31	99.23
	3	250.00	404.44	398.91	98.63	104.95	93.98
	4	550.00	410.98	475.45	115.69	104.17	111.05
1975	1	550.00	417.52	410.00	98.20	107.23	91.58
	2	400.00	424.06	457.13	107.80	111.90	96.34
	3	350.00	430.60	558.47	129.69	118.71	109.25
	4	600.00	437.14	518.67	118.65		
1976	1		443.68				
	2		450.22				
	3		456.77				
	4		463.31				

REGRESSION FORECAST = 6.541 X PERIOD + 312.856

Y(1st) = TSCI

Y(1st) = (443.68)(1.34)(1.20)(1.00)

Y(1st) = 713.97

where: Y_{T-3} = the sales of saws lagged four quarters

Since we have already determined that a trend exists for this data, a better model might be:

TABLE 8.11   *Forecast Errors for Acme Tool Decomposition Forecast.*

Quarter	Actual Value Y_T	Forecast $\hat{F}_T$	Error $(\hat{F}_T - Y_T)$	Mean-Square Error $(\hat{F}_T - Y_T)^2$
1	750	713.97	−36.03	1298.16
2	500	480.61	−19.39	375.97
3	400	355.13	44.87	2013.32
4	650	675.42	25.42	646.18
				$\Sigma(\hat{F}_T - Y_T)^2 = 4333.63$

$$MSE = \frac{\Sigma(\hat{F}_T - Y_T)^2}{N} = \frac{4333.63}{4} = 1083.41$$

$$MAD = \frac{\Sigma|\hat{F}_T - X_T|}{N} = \frac{125.71}{4} = 31.43$$

$$Y_{T+1} = b_0 + b_2 Y_{T-3} + b_3 X_T \qquad\qquad \textbf{(8-15)}$$

where: X_T = time; $X = 0$ represents first quarter 1971

The data are shown in Table 8.12, and the results of the computer run are presented in Table 8.13. The forecast for first quarter 1977 is

TABLE 8.12   *Acme Tool Company Data Set-up to Be Run as an Autoregressive Model.*

T	Y_T	Y_{T-3}	X_T
1	450	500	0
2	350	350	1
3	200	250	2
4	300	400	3
5	350	450	4
6	200	350	5
7	150	200	6
8	400	300	7
9	550	350	8
10	350	200	9
11	250	150	10
12	550	400	11
13	550	550	12
14	400	350	13
15	350	250	14
16	600	550	15
17	750	550	16
18	500	400	17
19	400	350	18
20	650	600	19

TABLE 8.13 *Computer Output for the Acme Tool Company Autoregressive Model.*

COMPUTER OUTPUT FOR THE ACME TOOL COMPANY
AUTOREGRESSIVE MODEL

VARIABLE NO.	MEAN	STANDARD DEVIATION	CORRELATION X VS Y	REGRESSION COEFFICIENT	STD. ERROR OF REG.COEF.	COMPUTED T VALUE
2	375.	129.27	0.777	0.81	0.16	5.17
3	9.5	5.92	0.598	10.85	3.43	3.16

DEPENDENT

| 1 | 415. | 159.85 |

INTERCEPT	7.415	MULTIPLE CORRELATION	0.86626
STD. ERROR OF ESTIMATE	84.43	R SQUARED	0.75040
		CORRECTED R SQUARED	0.72103

ANALYSIS OF VARIANCE FOR THE REGRESSION

SOURCES OF VARIATION	DEGREES OF FREEDOM	SUM OF SQUARES	MEAN SQUARES	F VALUE
ATTRIBUTABLE TO REGRESSION	2	364318.75	182159.37	25.55
DEVIATION FROM REGRESSION	17	121180.81	7128.28	
TOTAL	19	485499.56		

TABLE OF RESIDUALS

CASE NO.	Y VALUE	Y ESTIMATE	RESIDUAL
1	450	413.37	36.63
2	350	302.44	47.56
3	200	232.10	-32.10
4	300	364.74	-64.74
5	350	416.19	-66.19
6	200	345.86	-145.86
7	150	234.92	-84.92
8	400	326.97	73.03
9	550	378.42	171.57
10	350	267.49	82.51
11	250	237.75	12.25
12	550	451.58	98.42
13	550	584.22	-34.22
14	400	432.69	-32.69
15	350	362.35	-12.35
16	600	616.78	-16.78
17	750	627.64	122.36
18	500	516.71	-16.71
19	400	486.96	-86.96
20	650	700.80	-50.80

$$Y_{T+1} = 7.415 + 0.81\, Y_{T-3} + 10.85\, X_T$$

$$Y_{20+1} = 7.415 + 0.81\, Y_{20-3} + 10.85\, X_{20}$$

$$Y_{21} = 7.415 + 0.81(750) + 10.85(20)$$

$$Y_{27} = 831.915$$

269

In order to determine the accuracy of this model we develop forecasts for 1976. Table 8.14 shows the computer results when the data for 1971–1975 are used. The regression equation is

$$Y_{T+1} = 13.3771 + 0.76\,Y_{T-3} + 12.71\,X_T$$

TABLE 8.14 *Computer Output for the Acme Tool Company Autoregressive Model Forecasts for 1976.*

COMPUTER OUTPUT FOR THE ACME TOOL COMPANY
AUTOREGRESSIVE MODEL FORECASTS FOR 1976

VARIABLE NO.	MEAN	STANDARD DEVIATION	CORRELATION X VS Y	REGRESSION COEFFICIENT	STD. ERROR OF REG.COEF.	COMPUTED T VALUE
2	350.0	122.47	0.69	0.76083	0.17939	4.24
3	7.5	4.76	0.46	12.71100	4.61480	2.75

DEPENDENT						
1	375.0	137.84039				

INTERCEPT	12.377	R-SQUARE	0.67
STD. ERR.	85.04	DURBIN-WATSON	1.01

ANALYSIS OF VARIANCE FOR THE REGRESSION

SOURCE OF VARIATION	DEGREES OF FREEDOM	SUM OF SQUARES	MEAN SQUARES	F VALUE
ATTRIBUTABLE TO REGRESSION	2	190980.18	95490.06	13.2
DEVIATION FROM REGRESSION	13	940i9.44	7232.26	
TOTAL	15	284999.62		

Table 8.15 indicates the forecasting errors when this model is applied to the data for 1976. The mean absolute error (MAD) equals 79.44. This is larger than the MAD for the previous two models.

Adaptive Filtering

Two techniques, moving averages and exponential smoothing, base forecasts on some type of weighted average of past measurements. The rationale is that past values contain information about what will occur in the future. Since past values include random fluctuations as well as information concerning the underlying pattern of a variable, an attempt is made to smooth these values. This approach assumes that extreme fluctuations represent randomness in a series of historical observations.

TABLE 8.15   *Forecast Errors for Acme Tool Autoregressive Model.*

	Quarter	Actual Value Y_T	Forecast $\hat{F}_T$	Error $(\hat{F}_T - Y_T)$	Square Error $(\hat{F}_T - Y_T)^2$
1976	1	750	634.74	−115.26	13284.87
	2	500	533.45	+33.45	1118.90
	3	400	508.16	+108.16	11698.59
	4	650	710.87	+60.87	3705.16
					29807.52

$$MSE = \frac{\Sigma(\hat{F}_T - Y_T)^2}{N} = \frac{29807.52}{4} = 7451.88$$

$$MAD = \frac{\Sigma|\hat{F}_T - Y_T|}{N} = \frac{317.74}{4} = 79.44$$

Moving averages are discussed in Chapter 6 and involve computing the mean of a certain number of values of a variable. This average now becomes the forecast for the next period; then the process is repeated until a forecast is made for the desired future period. This approach assigns an equal weight to each past value. However, a convincing argument can be made for emphasizing the most recent values. Exponential smoothing is utilized because decreasing weight is assigned the older observations. Both approaches involve a rule or set of rules that determine the weights.

Adaptive filtering is another technique for determining the appropriate weights. The iterative or trial and error method is used to determine the "best" weights. First, a given set of weights is used to compute a forecast. Then, the errors or differences between the forecasted values and actual values are determined. This information is used to adjust the weights so that the error will be reduced to a minimum level. The term adaptive filtering originated in telecommunication engineering to describe a process for filtering the noise of transmission out of a message. This is the same concept involved in our attempt to distinguish some underlying pattern in the values of a variable from the random fluctuations (noise).

The process of adapting or training the weights consists of eight steps:

1.   Specify the number of weights and their size.
2.   Specify the learning constant k.
3.   Prepare a forecast for the first period beyond the number of weights. (If four weights are being used, forecast period five.)
4.   Calculate the forecast error; that is, find the difference between the forecasted value for period five and the actual value.
5.   Use Eq. (8–16) to adjust the weights.

6. Normalize the adjusted weights.
7. Prepare a forecast for the next period (period six), and continue the process until a forecast has been made for the total series of values. This process can be referred to as a training iteration.
8. Use the weights that exist at this point as the initial set of weights, and repeat the whole process. The process is repeated until no change occurs in the weights during the training iteration and until the errors are close to zero.

Equation (8–16) is used for adjusting the weights once the error has been computed:

$$W' = W + 2ke_T X_T \qquad (8\text{-}16)$$

where: W' = the revised weight
W = the old weight
k = the learning constant
e = the forecast error
X = the observed values

Equation (8–16) indicates that the revised weight should equal the old weight plus some adjustment made for the forecast error. The adjustment is done for each weight and is based on the forecast error, the observed value, and the learning constant.

An example will help to illustrate adaptive filtering. Five observations are presented in Table 8.16. The set of observed values is normalized so that the maximum value equals 1.0. This approach has been found to make adaptive filtering more efficient. We now apply the eight-step process for training the weights.

TABLE 8.16   *Sample Values for Adaptive Filtering.*

Period T =	1	2	3	4	5
Observed Value	5	10	15	20	25
Normalized Value	0.2	0.4	0.6	0.8	1.0

1. Since the data presented in Table 8.16 are linear, two weights ($NW = 2$) should work well because two weights can uniquely determine a straight line. Seasonal patterns frequently dictate how many weights one should choose. Makridakis and Wheelwright describe a process that uses the highest autocorrelation to determine the appropriate number of weights.* Next, the size of the weights is set at $1/NW = \frac{1}{2} = 0.5$. (Note that the weights will always sum to 1 using $1/NW$).

---

*MAKRIDAKIS, S., AND WHEELWRIGHT, S. C., *Interactive Forecasting*, Palo Alto, Calif.: The Scientific Press, 1977, pp. 145–148.

Makridakis and Wheelwright advise the use of autocorrelations as initial values for the weights.**

2. The specification of the learning constant k determines how rapidly the best set of weights can be found. If too large a value of k is chosen, the adjustments in the weights will be too large and the optimal weights will never be determined. If only a few weights are chosen, then k can be larger. If a series includes considerable randomness, a smaller value of k is needed. Since our observations (Table 8.16) show no randomness and since only two weights will be used, $k = 0.8$ is chosen.

3. Since two weights were chosen, prepare a forecast for period 3.

$$\hat{X}_T = W_1 X_{T-2} + W_2 X_{T-1}$$
$$X_3 = W_1 X_1 + W_2 X_2$$
$$X_3 = .5(.2) + .5(.4)$$
$$X_3 = .3$$

4. Calculate the forecast error.

$$e_T = X_T - \hat{X}_T$$
$$e_T = .6 - .3$$
$$e_T = .3$$

5. Use Eq. (8–13) to adjust the weights.

$$W^1 = W + 2ke_T X_T$$
$$W_1' = 0.5 + 2(0.8)(0.3)(0.2) = 0.596$$
$$W_2' = 0.5 + 2(0.8)(0.3)(0.4) = 0.692$$
$$\overline{1.288}$$

6. Normalize the adjusted weights.

$$W_1 = \frac{0.596}{1.288} = 0.463 \qquad W_2 = \frac{0.692}{1.288} = 0.537$$

7. Prepare a forecast for the next period.

$$\hat{X}_T = W_1 X_{T-2} + W_2 W_{T-1}$$
$$\hat{X}_4 = W_1 X_2 + W_2 X_3$$
$$\hat{X}_4 = 0.463(0.4) + 0.537(0.6)$$

**MAKRIDAKIS, S., AND WHEELWRIGHT, S. C., *Interactive Forecasting*, Palo Alto, Calif.: The Scientific Press, 1977, pp. 149–152.

$$\hat{X}_4 = 0.507$$

$$e_T = X_T - \hat{X}_T$$

$$e_4 = 0.8 - 0.507$$

$$e_4 = 0.293$$

$$W_1^1 = 0.463 + 2(0.8)(0.293)(0.4) = 0.651$$

$$W_2^1 = 0.537 + 2(0.8)(0.293)(0.6) = \underline{0.818}$$

$$1.469$$

$$W_1 = \frac{0.651}{1.469} = 0.443 \qquad W_2 = \frac{0.818}{1.469} = 0.557$$

Prepare a forecast for the last period.

$$\hat{X}_5 = 0.443(0.6) + 0.557(0.8) = 0.711$$

$$e_5 = 1.0 - 0.711 = 0.289$$

$$W_1^1 = 0.443 + 2(0.8)(0.289)(0.6) = 0.720$$

$$W_2^1 = 0.557 + 2(0.8)(0.289)(0.8) = \underline{0.927}$$

$$1.647$$

$$W_1 = \frac{0.720}{1.647} = 0.437 \qquad W_2 = \frac{0.927}{1.647} = 0.563$$

8. Use the weights $W_1 = 0.437$ and $W_2 = 0.563$ as the initial set of weights, and repeat the process. Do this until the error is close to zero. The final weights will be $W_1 = -1$ and $W_2 = 2$. You can verify from the values given in Table 8.16 that the forecast error with these weights equals zero.

The use of adaptive filtering in the preparation of a forecast has two distinct phases. First, we apply the eight-step process for training the weights with historical data; and, second, we use these weights to forecast. In our example the forecast for period 6 is

$$\hat{X}_T = W_1 X_{T-2} + W_2 X_{T-1}$$

$$\hat{X}_6 = W_1 X_{6-2} + W_2 X_{6-1}$$

$$\hat{X}_6 = W_1 X_4 + W_2 X_5$$

$$\hat{X}_6 = -1(20) + 2(25)$$

$$\hat{X}_6 = 30$$

Adaptive Filtering Example

An illustration of how adaptive filtering can be applied as a forecasting technique is now in order. Consider the Cosmos Cosmetics Corporation, which desires to forecast demand for one of the company's products. Actual monthly demand in cases of Cosmos perfume is shown in Table 8.17 from January 1972 through December 1978.*

TABLE 8.17 *Demand in Cases for Cosmos Perfume.*

	1972	1973	1974	1975	1976	1977	1978
Jan.	147	210	466	503	490	423	491
Feb.	108	264	316	278	329	262	262
Mar.	165	354	423	402	383	407	353
Apr.	167	274	341	437	432	354	127
May	124	255	401	300	365	264	458
June	96	255	268	250	265	252	353
July	117	194	216	136	194	235	214
Aug.	282	444	629	592	521	545	528
Sept.	213	450	491	506	538	559	446
Oct.	162	350	355	433	358	405	391
Nov.	413	640	642	635	439	649	695
Dec.	401	592	705	693	603	655	593

As previously stated, the use of adaptive filtering to prepare a forecast requires two phases. First, we train a set of weights with historical data and then we use these weights to forecast. All 84 historical observations of Cosmos Perfume will be used in training the set of weights.

The first step in starting the training phase is to specify the number of weights and their size. Inspection of the data in Table 8.17 indicates that a seasonal pattern 12-months long appears to exist. Actually, an appropriate analysis would involve the use of autocorrelation coefficients in order to make this decision. The problem is worked using this approach in Chapter 9. Twelve weights seem appropriate. The forecast for a single month will be based only on the sales for the 12 preceding months. An arbitrary decision was made to let each weight have an initial value of $1/NW$ or 0.083.

The second step involves the specification of the learning constant k. Experience has shown that as the amount of randomness in a series increases and as the number of weights increases, the optimal value of k will decrease. For this problem a learning constant of .075 was selected. Different values of k give entirely different results. In our work with

---

*This data was originally taken from actual demand figures for a company. The data and computer output were provided by James L. Starr, Acting Manager of the Stanford Graduate School of Business Computer Facility.

275

this technique we have found that if a very small value is used for k, the error reduction on each iteration is small, which results in a large number of iterations. If a larger value of k is used, poor performance results from adapting the weights too quickly, and thus overreacting to random fluctuations.

The results of steps 3–8 are shown on the computer output in Table 8.18. The mean square error (MSE) after 30 iterations equals 7751.42. The mean percentage error (MPE), sometimes referred to as BIAS, equals -6.50936. The mean absolute percentages error ($MAPE$) equals 20.6608. The proportion of error reduction for the 30th iteration equals 0.00119281. This is calculated in the following manner:

$$\frac{7760.66 - 7751.42}{9.24} \qquad \frac{9.24}{7760.66} = 0.00119281$$

Table 8.18 also presents the optimal weights for each time lag. We are now ready to implement phase 2. The calculations for the forecast of January 1979 demand are shown below.

$$\hat{X}_T = W_1 X_{T-1} + W_2 X_{T-2} + W_3 X_{T-3} + W_4 X_{T-4} + W_5 X_{T-5}$$
$$+ W_6 X_{T-6} + W_7 X_{T-7} + W_8 X_{T-8} + W_9 X_{T-9}$$
$$+ W_{10} X_{T-10} + W_{11} X_{T-11} + W_{12} X_{T-12}$$

$$\hat{X}_{85} = .257(593) - .035(695) + .338(391) - .105(446) - .064(528)$$
$$- .153(214) - .013(353) + .064(458) + .316(127) - .181(353)$$
$$+ .107(262) + .485(491)$$

$$\hat{X}_{85} = 413.8$$

Notice that the demand for the 12 months of 1978 (see Table 8.17) is multiplied by the optimal weights in order to arrive at the forecast. Table 8.19 shows the forecast for 1979.

It is apparent that for adaptive filtering to be used as a practical forecasting tool it must be run on the computer. It is clearly a much more powerful technique than smoothing methods, but also somewhat more complicated. Adaptive filtering is both simple and effective, and should gain wider acceptance as more people become aware of its merits.

Summary

Naïve extrapolation is a technique used to make short-term forecasts. A forecast is obtained solely from historical values of the variable to be

TABLE 8.18   *Training the Weights for Cosmos Perfume.*

TRAINING THE WEIGHTS FOR COSMOS PERFUME

******** LEARNING PERFORMANCE ********

LEARNING CONSTANT = .075

ITERATION	MSE	MPE	MAPE	% ERROR REDUCTION
2	8859.78	-7.40170	21.7412	.0630133
3	8667.59	-7.38838	21.6105	.0221725
4	8525.76	-7.35329	21.5019	.0166357
5	8417.21	-7.30519	21.4002	.0128958
6	8331.40	-7.25014	21.3075	.0103006
7	8261.61	-7.19230	21.2203	.0084466
8	8203.53	-7.13436	21.1386	.0070798
9	8154.26	-7.07810	21.0601	.0060429
10	8111.77	-7.02455	20.9861	.0052373
11	8074.65	-6.97429	20.9243	.0045969
12	8041.86	-6.92758	20.8907	.0040774
13	8012.61	-6.88443	20.8620	.0036516
14	7986.28	-6.84473	20.8376	.0032963
15	7962.41	-6.80831	20.8180	.0029976
16	7940.61	-6.77494	20.8065	.0027449
17	7920.60	-6.74437	20.7951	.0025267
18	7902.11	-6.71634	20.7837	.0023393
19	7884.96	-6.69064	20.7724	.0021753
20	7868.97	-6.66703	20.7612	.0020325
21	7854.00	-6.64531	20.7502	.0019052
22	7839.95	-6.62529	20.7394	.0017921
23	7826.72	-6.60679	20.7287	.0016908
24	7814.22	-6.58968	20.7183	.0015993
25	7802.39	-6.57380	20.7081	.0015165
26	7791.16	-6.55906	20.6982	.0014410
27	7780.50	-6.54533	20.6885	.0013706
28	7770.35	-6.53253	20.6790	.0013065
29	7760.66	-6.52057	20.6698	.0012476
30	7751.42	-6.50936	20.6608	.0011928

OPTIMAL WEIGHTS

12	0.485
11	0.107
10	-0.181
9	0.316
8	0.064
7	-0.013
6	-0.153
5	-0.064
4	-0.105
3	0.338
2	-0.035
1	0.257

TABLE 8.19 *Cosmos Perfume Demand Forecast for 1979.*

COSMOS PERFUME DEMAND FORECAST FOR 1979

MEAN SQUARED ERROR (MSE) = 7751.42

MEAN ABSOLUTE PERCENTAGE ERROR (MAPE) = 20.6608

MEAN PERCENTAGE ERROR (MPE) OR BIAS = -6.50936

HOW MANY FORECASTS DO YOU WANT (0 IF NONE) 12

PERIOD	FORECAST
85	413.808
86	475.855
87	361.823
88	191.563
89	420.457
90	311.388
91	237.695
92	560.771
93	468.855
94	405.124
95	664.083
96	559.612

analyzed. No attempt is made to examine or recognize interrelationships with other variables. The naïve method is simple, and has been used successfully to forecast variables such as stock market prices and interest rates. Exponential smoothing is a popular technique for short-run forecasting. Its major advantages are low cost and simplicity. It is usually not as accurate as more sophisticated methods, such as autoregressive techniques. However, when forecasts are needed for inventory systems containing thousands of items, smoothing methods are often the only acceptable approach. Time-series analysis depends on the assumption that there are regular and repeating components interacting to produce a total series. The analyst's task is to examine and identify each of these components. Once the forecaster knows something about each of the parts, he/she is in a better position to say something about the expected value of the total series in some future period. Time-series techniques are appropriate for forecasting variables that fluctuate in some stable pattern over time. Autoregressive models are employed with economic variables in order to account for correlations between adjacent observations in a time series.

The adaptive filtering technique is both simple and economical. It provides the unique characteristic of automatically adjusting parameters. It is clearly more powerful than smoothing methods, but also more complicated. Adaptive filtering fills a gap in existing forecasting techniques because it can effectively handle any data pattern.

PROBLEMS

*1. Mr. Harvey, the inventory manager, wishes to compare forecasts using different forecasting approaches. Demand for a particular product had shifted downward last April because of a price increase. The following number of units were demanded in the past ten months.

Month	Units	Month	Units
Jan	891	Jun	798
Feb	899	Jul	775
Mar	909	Aug	782
Apr	867	Sep	769
May	829	Oct	765

  a. Use an appropriate naïve model, and forecast demand for November.
  b. Using a smoothing constant of 0.3, prepare an exponential smoothing of the data. Assume the initial value $F_T = 890$.
  c. Use a smoothing constant of 0.1 to prepare an exponential smoothing of the data. Assume the initial value $F_T = 890$.
  d. Compare the smoothed forecasts in parts (b) and (c). Does a decrease in the smoothing constant make the forecasting model less sensitive or more sensitive to a shift in demand? Explain why.
  e. If the random movements in monthly demand are relatively large, would it be better to set the smoothing constant relatively high or relatively low? Explain why.
  f. Forecast demand for November.

2. In order to evaluate the accuracy of an analyst's forecast, exponential smoothing is used to forecast company earnings. The accuracy of analyst's forecasts are determined by comparison with the smoothing forecast. The actual earnings per share of both Boeing and Exxon for the period 1962–76 are presented below.

	Actual Earnings Per Share for Boeing	Actual Earnings Per Share for Exxon
1962	$0.85	$1.94
1963	0.68	2.37
1964	1.41	2.44
1965	2.39	2.41
1966	2.07	2.53
1967	2.05	2.77
1968	1.92	2.97
1969	0.24	2.89
1970	0.51	2.96
1971	0.52	3.39
1972	0.70	3.42
1973	1.19	5.45
1974	1.71	7.02
1975	1.80	5.60
1976	2.43	5.90

a. Forecast earnings per share for 1977 for the Boeing Corporation. Choose a smoothing constant of either 0.1 or 0.4. Use an initial value of $F_T = 0.85$. Compare your forecasted value with actual earnings per share of $4.40.

b. Forecast earnings per share for 1977 for the Exxon Corporation. Choose a smoothing constant of either 0.1 or 0.4. Use an initial value of $F_T = 1.94$. Compare your forecasted value with actual earnings per share of $6.00.

c. Would you advise the use of a trend adjustment for either forecast? Explain.

3. The Davis Company is interested in using exponential smoothing for short-range forecasting purposes for inventory control. Monthly sales data are presented below for the past two years.

Davis Inventory

Month	1976	1977
Jan.	6.7	8.7
Feb.	7.1	9.4
Mar.	7.5	9.9
Apr.	7.8	10.3
May	8.1	10.5
Jun.	9.3	11.3
Jul.	8.5	11.5
Aug.	7.9	11.9
Sep.	7.7	11.3
Oct.	8.1	12.5
Nov.	7.7	12.9
Dec.	7.3	13.3

    a. Use an appropriate naïve model, and forecast inventory for January, 1978.

    b. Using a smoothing constant of 0.2, prepare an exponential smoothing of the data. Use the mean of the first four months as a starting value for F_T, and start the smoothing process in the fifth month.

    c. Using smoothing constants of $A = 0.2$ and $B = 0.4$, prepare an exponential smoothing adjusted for trend of the data. Use the mean and the slope of the first four months as initial values for F_T and T_T, respectively. Start the smoothing process in the fifth month.

    d. Use the MSE as a basis for evaluating the methods used in parts (b) and (c).

    e. Forecast inventory for January, 1978.

4. Boeing Company Sales in millions of dollars for 1975–78 are reported along with estimates for 1979 by Value Line Investment Survey.

	Quarter				Quarter	
1975	1	839.9	1977	1		755.9
	2	1039.8		2		1244.8
	3	794.6		3		891.3
	4	1044.6		4		1126.8
1976	1	742.0	1978	1		1020.0
	2	1165.7		2		1376.0
	3	798.7		3		1449.0
	4	1212.1		4		1655.0
			Estimates for 1979	1		1600
				2		2050
				3		2150
				4		2450

    a. Using smoothing constants of $A = 0.2$, $B = 0.5$, and $C = 0.3$; prepare an exponential smoothing forcast for 1978. Use three years 1975–77 and initial estimates $F_T = 930$, $T_T = 0$, $S1 = 0.9$, $S2 = 1.1$, $S3 = 0.9$, and $S4 = 1.1$ to forecast 1978. Evaluate the model using MAD. Use the model to forecast 1979.

    b. Use the decomposition method of time series to analyze the quarterly values 1975–78, and forecast for 1979.

    c. Use an autoregressive model to analyze the quarterly values for 1975–78, and forecast values for 1979.

    d. Make a final forecast for 1979, and then compare your forecast with actual Boeing Sales.

5. Given the values $X_1 = 1$, $X_2 = 3$, $X_3 = 6$, $X_4 = 8$, and $X_5 = 10$. Use the method of adaptive filtering to predict X_6. Use *two* weights and *one* training iteration. Let $k = 0.9$.

---

*Value Line Investment Survey, New York: Value Line, 1979, p. 105.

6. Apply the method of adaptive filtering to the Acme Tool data presented in Table 8.1.

BIBLIOGRAPHY

GILCHRIST, W., *Statistical Forecasting,* New York: John Wiley and Sons, 1976.

GROSS, C. W., AND PETERSON, R. T., *Business Forecasting.* Boston: Houghton Mifflin Company, 1976.

HARRISON, P. J., "Exponential Smoothing and Short-Term Sales Forecasting." *Management Science,* Vol. 13, No. 11, (1967), pp. 821–842.

HOLT, C. C., "Forecasting Seasonal and Trends by Exponentially Weighted Moving Averages." Office of Naval Research, Research Memorandum No. 52, (1957).

MAKRIDAKIS, S., AND WHEELWRIGHT, S. C., *Interactive Forecasting,* Palo Alto, Calif.: The Scientific Press, 1977.

———— *Forecasting Methods & Applications.* New York: John Wiley and Sons, 1978.

MONTGOMERY, D. C., AND JOHNSON, L. A., *Forecasting and Time Series Analysis,* New York: McGraw-Hill Book Company, 1976.

THIEL, H., AND WAGE, S., "Some Observations on Adaptive Filtering." *Management Science,* Vol. 10, No. 2, (1964), pp. 198–224.

WINTERS, P. R., "Forecasting Sales by Exponentially Weighted Moving Averages." *Management Science,* Vol. 6, (1960), pp. 324–342.

Box-Jenkins Methods*

9

Introduction

In Chapter 6 we learned how to decompose or break down a time series into several important components. Now we are going to identify these components using a different approach. The autocorrelation coefficients for different time lags of a variable will be used to identify the following about a data collection:

1. Are the data random?
2. Do the data have a trend (nonstationary)?
3. Are the data seasonal?
4. If seasonal, what is the seasonal pattern?

If a series is random, the correlation of Y_T and Y_{T-1} is close to zero. In Chapter 7 we learned that autocorrelation coefficients close to zero indicate that the successive values of a time series are not related to each other. The autocorrelation coefficient for the successive values of a time series—5, 10, 15, 20, 25, 30, 35, and 40—would be very high. A high degree of relationship exists between each successive value. By looking at autocorrelation coefficients for time lags of more than

---

*We are indebted to Yvonne Sloan, Assistant Professor of Decision Science at Eastern Washington University, for her significant contribution to the writing of this chapter.

one period, we can determine additional information on how values of a given time series are related.

In Chapter 8 we developed an autoregressive model for the Acme Tool Company data. A quarterly seasonal pattern appeared to exist in the data so we used the variable lagged four periods as a predictor. One way of testing the validity of this approach would be to determine the correlation between Y_T and Y_{T-4}. The autocorrelation coefficient for this example would be high. If it had been close to zero, the absence of a relationship between the same quarter of successive years would be indicated.

Sampling Distribution of Autocorrelations

Table 9.1 shows a time series of 30 values selected from two columns of a random number table. If we compute autocorrelation coefficients for this series of random numbers, they must theoretically equal zero. Of course, the 30 values in Table 9.1 are only one of a large number of possible samples of size 30. Each sample of size 30 that we choose will have different autocorelations. Some of the samples will have autocorrelations that are quite different from zero just by chance.

TABLE 9.1 *Time Series with 30 Selected Random Numbers.*

Period T	X_T	Period T	X_T	Period T	X_T
1	42	11	93	21	04
2	27	12	15	22	95
3	55	13	51	23	40
4	48	14	26	24	50
5	18	15	42	25	79
6	90	16	53	26	37
7	37	17	64	27	90
8	13	18	10	28	09
9	11	19	93	29	46
10	02	20	82	30	19

A sampling distribution of autocorrelations can be developed by taking an infinite number of samples of 30 random numbers. Quenouille* and others have demonstrated that the autocorrelation coefficients of random data have a sampling distribution that can be approximated by a normal curve with mean zero and standard deviation $1/\sqrt{n}$. We can now determine

---

*QUENOUILLE, M. H., "The Joint Distribution of Serial Correlation Coefficients." *Annals of Mathematical Statistics*, Vol. 20, (1949), pp. 561–71.

whether several sample autocorrelation coefficients come from a population whose mean is zero at various time lags.

For the data presented in Table 9.1, $n = 30$ and the standard error (standard deviation of the sampling distribution) is $1/\sqrt{30} = .18$. This means that 68% of all the sample autocorrelation coefficients should lie within a range specified by the 0, plus or minus .18 (if the time series data is truly random). Therefore, at the 95% confidence level this time series can be considered random if the calculated autocorrelation coefficients are within the interval

$$0 \pm Z \frac{1}{\sqrt{n}}$$

$$0 \pm 1.96 \, (0.18)$$

$$0 \pm 0.353$$

The autocorrelation coefficients for the data of Table 9.1 are graphed in Fig. 9–1. The two dotted lines parallel to the vertical axis are the 95% confidence limits ($-.353$ to $.353$). Twelve time lags are checked, and all their autocorrelation coefficients lie within these limits. We conclude what we already knew; namely, that the data are random.

Time Lags					Autocorrelations
12	•	*	•		0.00
11	•	*	•		0.00
10	•	*	•		0.00
9	•	*	•		0.00
8	•	I	•		0.00
7	•	I*	•		0.01
6	•	* I	•		−0.11
5	•	I	* •		0.25
4	•	* I	•		−0.18
3	•	I *	•		0.11
2	•	I *	•		0.11
1	*	I	•		−0.35

```
I I I I I I I I I I I I I I I I I I I I
-1                    0                    +1
```

FIGURE 9–1 *Autocorrelation Coefficients of a Random Series.*

285

We could test each time lag Y_T individually. The appropriate hypotheses are

$$H_0: \rho_T = 0$$

$$H_1: \rho_T \neq 0$$

However, the confidence level approach is easier and provides the same results. Using this approach, we are able to determine whether any time series can be considered random.

Do the Data Have a Trend?

A time series is referred to as *stationary* when it contains no growth or decline, and *nonstationary* when a trend is present. For nonstationary data the autocorrelations are typically significantly different from zero for the first several time lags, and only gradually drop to zero or show a spurious pattern as the number of time periods increases. Figure 9–2 illustrates the autocorrelations for a nonstationary series. The autocorrela-

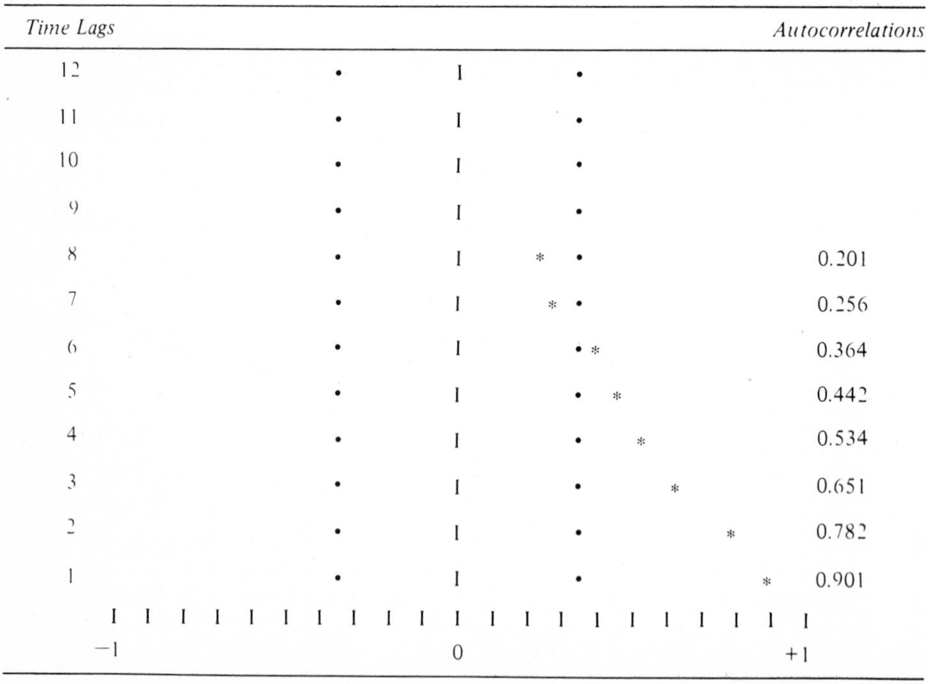

Time Lags							Autocorrelations
12	•	I	•				
11	•	I	•				
10	•	I	•				
9	•	I	•				
8	•	I	* •				0.201
7	•	I	* •				0.256
6	•	I	• *				0.364
5	•	I	•	*			0.442
4	•	I	•	*			0.534
3	•	I	•		*		0.651
2	•	I	•			*	0.782
1	•	I	•			*	0.901

```
   I I I I I I I I I I I I I I I I I I I I I
  -1                    0                    +1
```

FIGURE 9–2 *Autocorrelation Coefficients of a Series with a Trend (Nonstationary).*

286

tions for the first six time lags are significantly different from zero, and the pattern gradually drops to zero rather than dropping to zero exponentially. A straight line would fit the points extremely well.

When a trend exists in data, successive values are correlated with each other, and the autocorrelation coefficient for one time lag is quite large. The autocorrelation of two time lags will be large also. However, it will not be as large as for one time lag because one less term is used to calculate the numerator.

Figure 9–3 shows the autocorrelations for a stationary series that is not random. The autocorrelations are not significantly different from zero after two time lags; however, the significant autocorrelations for the first two time lags indicate the existence of some pattern other than trend.

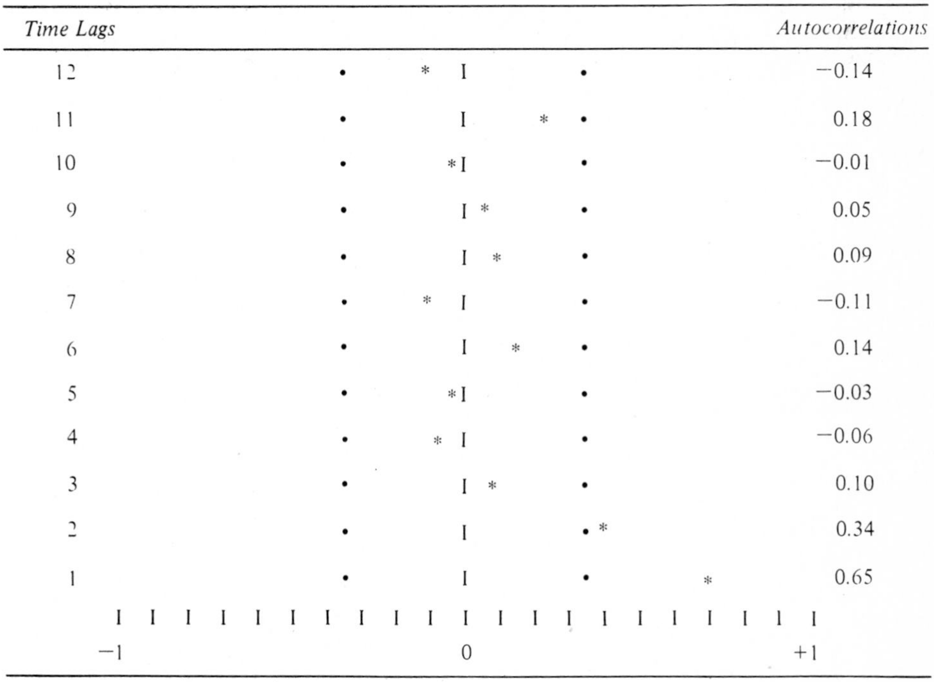

Time Lags					Autocorrelations
12	•	* I	•		−0.14
11	•	I	* •		0.18
10	•	*I	•		−0.01
9	•	I *	•		0.05
8	•	I *	•		0.09
7	•	* I	•		−0.11
6	•	I *	•		0.14
5	•	*I	•		−0.03
4	•	* I	•		−0.06
3	•	I *	•		0.10
2	•	I	• *		0.34
1	•	I	•	*	0.65

```
    I  I  I  I  I  I  I  I  I  I  I  I  I  I  I  I  I  I  I  I  I
   −1                           0                          +1
```

FIGURE 9–3 *Autocorrelation Coefficients of a Nonrandom Stationary Series.*

Removing the Trend (Nonstationary)

When a time series is nonstationary, as when a trend exists, spurious autocorrelations may dominate the pattern. For this reason, trends must be removed before further analysis can take place. Several methods for

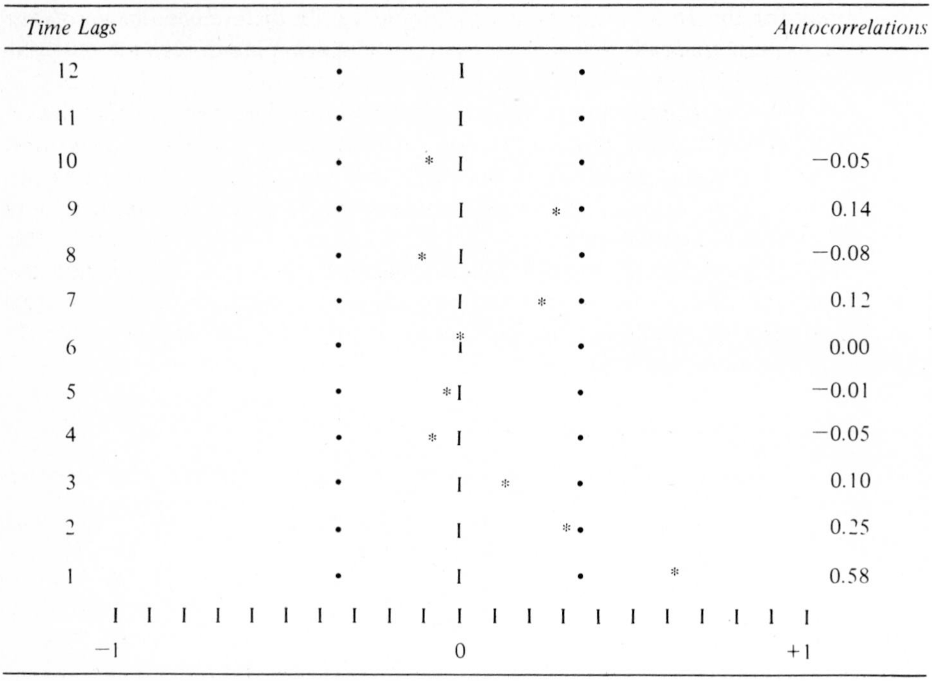

Time Lags					Autocorrelations
12	•	I	•		
11	•	I	•		
10	•	* I	•		−0.05
9	•	I	* •		0.14
8	•	* I	•		−0.08
7	•	I	* •		0.12
6	•	*I	•		0.00
5	•	* I	•		−0.01
4	•	* I	•		−0.05
3	•	I *	•		0.10
2	•	I	* •		0.25
1	•	I	•	*	0.58

```
I I I I I I I I I I I I I I I I I I I I I
-1                    0                   +1
```

FIGURE 9–4 *Autocorrelations of Nonstationary Data (Fig. 9–2) First Differenced.*

TABLE 9.2 *First and Second Differences.*

Period	X_T	First Difference $X'_T = X_T - X_{T-1}$	Second Difference $X''_T = X'_T - X'_{T-1}$
1	8		−
2	12	4 (1)	−
3	15	3	−1 (2)
4	19	4	1
5	25	6	2
6	30	5	−1
7	34	4	−1
8	40	6	2
9	50	10	4
10	57	7	−3

(1) $X'_2 = X_2 - X_{2-1} = 12 - 8 = 4$

(2) $X''_3 = X'_3 - X'_{3-1} = 3 - 4 = -1$

removing trends are discussed in Chapter 7. The most popular approach is the method of differencing. Figure 9–4 gives the autocorrelations for the first differences of the data that were shown to be nonstationary in Fig. 9–2. Notice that only the first autocorrelation coefficient is significantly different from zero. Evidently, the series of first differenced data have been transformed into stationary form.

If the autocorrelations of first differenced data still gradually trail to zero, a stationary state has not been reached. One solution to this problem is to take second differences. This is the same as first differencing the first differenced data. Table 9.2 illustrates the first and second differencing procedure.

Time Lags		Autocorrelations
24	. I . *	0.40795
23	. I * .	0.10304
22	. * I .	−0.09378
21	. I* .	0.07050
20	. *I .	−0.03335
19	* . I .	−0.27639
18	* . I .	−0.35800
17	* I .	−0.19261
16	. * .	−0.01105
15	. I * .	0.07554
14	. * .	−0.00335
13	. I .*	0.24965
12	. I . *	0.62506
11	. I . *	0.28117
10	. I * .	0.02974
9	. I *.	0.19808
8	. I * .	0.10315
7	.* I .	−0.13952
6	*. I .	−0.20162
5	. *I .	−0.07059
4	. I *.	0.18155
3	. I . *	0.32196
2	. I * .	0.18770
1	. I . *·	0.47991

```
I I I I I I I I I I I I I I I I I I I I I
−1                 0                 +1
```

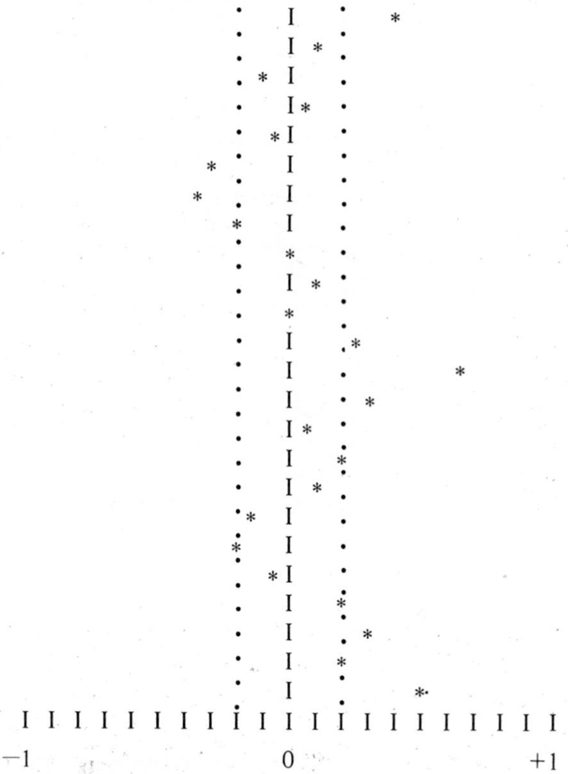

FIGURE 9–5 *Autocorrelation Coefficients Showing Seasonality for Cosmos Perfume Data.*

Are the Data Seasonal?

Seasonality exists when a pattern repeats itself regularly during a particular interval of time (usually a year). Using time series decomposition, we find a definite seasonal pattern for the registration of new passenger cars in Chapter 6. We could discover that a seasonal pattern exists through an analysis of the autocorrelations. The autocorrelation coefficient of 12-month lags would be a high positive value. If it were not significantly different from zero, we would conclude that months one year apart were unrelated or random.

For stationary data, seasonality is identified by finding autocorrelations of more than two or three time lags that are significantly different from zero. Figure 9–5 shows a graph of the autocorrelations for the Cosmos Perfume data presented in Chapter 8. Notice that the highest autocorrelation

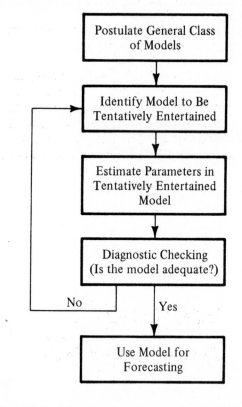

FIGURE 9–6   *Flow Diagram for Box-Jenkins Method.**

---

*From Box, G. P., and Jenkins, G. M., *Time Series Analysis Forecasting and Control*, San Francisco; Holden-Day, Inc., 1970, p. 19.

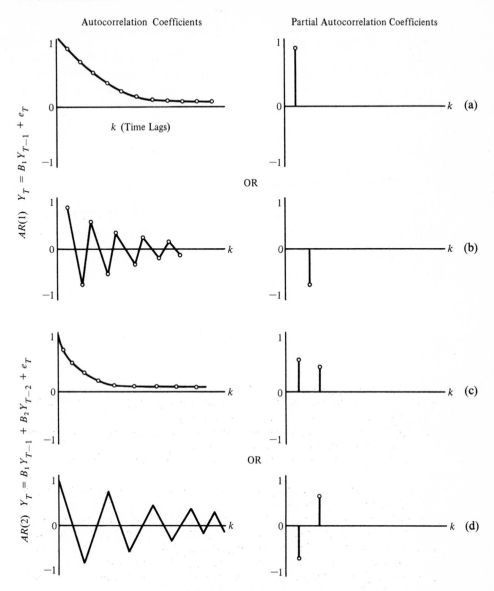

Autocorrelation Coefficients   Partial Autocorrelation Coefficients

FIGURE 9–7 *Autocorrelation and Partial Autocorrelation Coefficients of an AR (1) and an AR (2) Model.*

coefficient, $r_{12} = .625$, occurs at 12 time lags. This indicates seasonality
with a length of 12 months. The additional fact that $r_{24} = .408$ helps
confirm this observation. Seasonality is easily identified when the data
are stationary (have no trend), but is more difficult to identify when trend

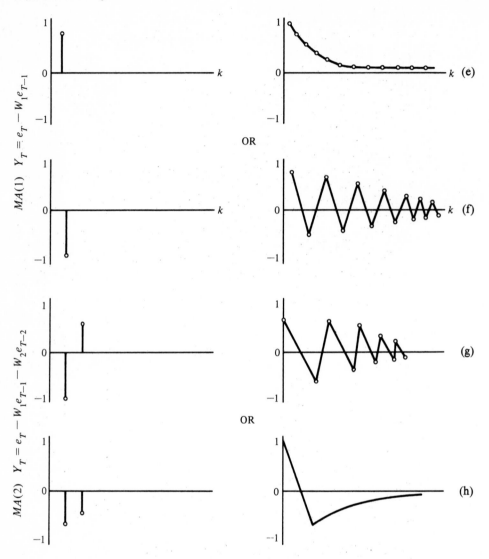

FIGURE 9–8 *Autocorrelation and Partial Autocorrelation Coefficients of an MA (1) and an MA (2) Model.*

is present. Therefore, when a trend is present the data should first be transformed into a stationary series, then checked for seasonality.

Box-Jenkins Technique

The Box-Jenkins method of forecasting is different from most methods we have discussed. This technique does *not* assume any particular pattern in the historical data of the series to be forecast. It uses an iterative approach of identifying a possible useful model from a general class of models. The chosen model is then checked against the historical data to see if it accurately describes the series. The model fits well if the residuals between the forecasting model and the historical data points are

$$ARMA(1,1) \quad Y_T = B_1 Y_{T-1} - W_1 e_{T-1} + e_T$$

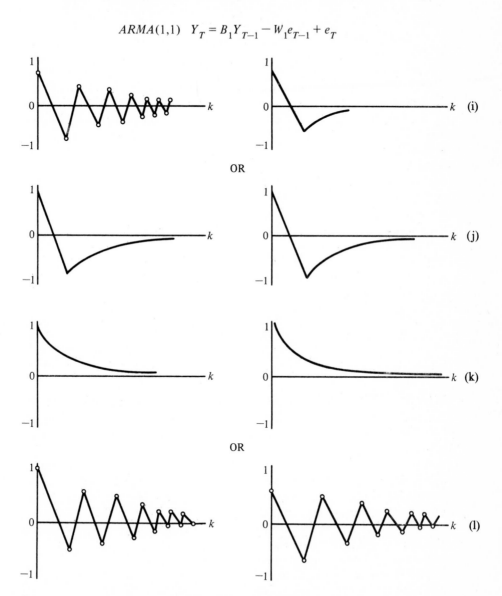

FIGURE 9–9 *Autocorrelation and Partial Autocorrelation Coefficients of a Mixed ARMA (1,1) Model.*

293

small, randomly distributed, and independent. If the specified model is *not* satisfactory, the process is repeated using another model designed to improve on the original one. This process is repeated until a satisfactory model is found. Figure 9–6 on page 290 illustrates the approach.

A general class of Box-Jenkins models for a stationary time series is the ARMA, or Auto Regression–Moving Average, models. (Remember that a stationary time series is one whose average value is not changing over time.) This group of models includes the AR models with only autoregressive terms, the MA models with only moving average terms, and the ARMA models with both autoregressive and moving average terms. The Box-Jenkins methodology allows the analyst to select the model that best fits the data.

Selection of an appropriate model can be made by comparing the distributions of autocorrelation coefficients of the time series being fitted to the theoretical distributions for the various models. Theoretical distributions for the autocorrelation coefficients for some of the more common ARMA models are shown in Figs. 9–7, 9–8, and 9–9 on pages 291, 292, and 293.

In selecting a model, it should be remembered that the distributions shown are theoretical distributions, and it is highly unlikely that the autocorrelations of actual data will be exactly identical to any of the theoretical distributions. However, the analyst should be able to match adequately most time series data through trial and error; and as one gains experience, the task becomes easier.

Partial Autocorrelations

Initially, we may not be aware of the appropriate order of autoregressive process to fit to a time series. This is the same type of problem we faced when deciding on the number of independent variables to include in a multiple regression model. Partial autocorrelations are used to help identify an appropriate ARMA model for forecasting. They allow the analyst to identify the degree of relationship between current values of a variable and earlier values of the same variable, while holding the effects of all other variables (time lags) constant.

A discussion of the derivation of partial autocorrelations is beyond the scope of this text.* Instead, we will concentrate on the fairly mechanical manner in which they are applied to each group of models.

---

*For a discussion of partial autocorrelations refer to Box, G., AND JENKINS, G., *Time Series Analysis: Forecasting and Control*, San Francisco: Holden-Day, Inc., 1976.

Autoregressive Model

An autoregressive model takes the form

$$Y_T = B_1 Y_{T-1} + B_2 Y_{T-2} + \cdots + B_p Y_{T-p} + e_T \qquad (9\text{-}1)$$

where

$$
\begin{aligned}
Y_T &= \text{dependent variable}\\
Y_{T-1}, Y_{T-2}, Y_{T-p} &= \text{independent variables that are the dependent variable lagged specific time periods}\\
B_1, B_2, B_p &= \text{regression coefficients}\\
e_T &= \text{residual term that represents random events not explained by the model}
\end{aligned}
$$

In Chapter 7, Eq. (7–1) introduces autoregressive models. However, Eq. (9–1) differs in several important ways. In Eq. (7–1) the regression coefficients are estimated using the linear least-squares method. In Eq. (9–1) the regression coefficients are found using a nonlinear least-squares method.

The nonlinear least-squares method generally uses an iterative solution technique to calculate the parameters, rather than using direct computation. Preliminary estimates are used as starting points, then these estimates are systematically improved until optimal values are found. Furthermore, the variance for Eq. (9–1) is calculated in a different manner that takes into account the fact that the independent variables are correlated with each other. Finally, Eq. (9–1) does not contain a constant term. This is done because the dependent variable values (Ys) are expressed as deviations from their mean ($Y' = Y - \bar{Y}$).

Figure 9–7 shows the equations of an AR model of order one, $AR(1)$ model, and an AR model of order two, $AR(2)$ model. Terms can be added to represent an $AR(p)$ model, where p is the number of past observations to be included in the forecast of the next period. Figure 9–7 illustrates the behavior of the theoretical autocorrelation and partial autocorrelation functions for an AR(1) model. Notice how differently the autocorrelation and partial autocorrelation functions behave. The autocorrelation coefficients trail off to zero gradually, while the partial autocorrelation coefficients drop to zero after the first time lag. Figure 9–7 also shows an AR(2) model. Again the autocorrelation coefficients trail off to zero while the partial autocorrelation coefficients drop to zero after the second time lag. This type of pattern will generally hold for any $AR(p)$ model; however, it must be remembered that sample autocorrelation functions are going to differ from these theoretical functions due to sampling variation.

An example of the usage of an $AR(2)$ model for forecasting is shown in Table 9.3. Assume that sales are shown for the last five periods of a series containing 100 observations. The $AR(2)$ model is chosen, and the Box-Jenkins computer program computes regression coefficients of $B_1 = .59$ and $B_2 = .40$. The forecast for period T will be

TABLE 9.3   *Forecasting Example with an Autoregressive Model.*

Period	Values	Forecasted Values	Residual e_T
$T-5$	240	238.3	1.7
$T-4$	230	240.1	-10.1
$T-3$	225	231.7	-6.7
$T-2$	240	224.8	$+15.2$
$T-1$	250	231.6	$+18.4$
T		243.5	

$$\hat{Y}_T = B_1\, Y_{T-1} + B_2\, Y_{T-2}$$
$$\hat{Y}_T = 0.59(250) + 0.40\,(240)$$
$$\hat{Y}_T = 243.5$$

Unfortunately, not all data series can be handled with autoregressive models. For this reason, the Box-Jenkins approach also considers the moving average (*MA*) model.

Moving Average Models

A moving average model takes the form

$$Y_T = e_T - W_1\, e_{T-1} - W_2\, e_{T-2} - \cdots - W_q\, e_{T-q} \tag{9-2}$$

where

$$Y_t = \text{dependent variable}$$
$$W_1, W_2, W_q = \text{weights}$$
$$e_T = \text{residual or error}$$
$$e_{T-1}, e_{T-2}, e_{T-q} = \text{previous values of the residuals}$$

Equation (9–2) is similar to (9–1) except that the dependent variable Y_T depends on previous values of the residuals, rather than the variable itself. Moving average models (*MA*) provide forecasts of Y_T based on a linear combination of past errors; whereas autoregressive models (*AR*) express Y_T as a linear function of some number of actual past values of Y_T. It is customary to show the weights with negative coefficients, even though the weights could be either positive or negative. The sum of $W_1 + W_2 + \cdots + W_q$ does not need to equal one, and the values of W_i are *not* "moving" with new observations as with the moving average computation in Chapter 6. The name moving average is misleading since the model is actually similar to exponential smoothing.

Figure 9–8 shows the equations of an *MA* model of order one, *MA* (1) model, and an *MA* (2) model. Terms can be added to represent an *MA* (*q*) model, where *q* is the number of past error terms to be included in the forecast of the next period. Figure 9–8 also illustrates the behavior of the theoretical autocorrelation coefficients for the MA (1) model. Note how fortunate it is that the autocorrelation and partial autocorrelation functions of AR and MA models behave very differently. The autocorrelation coefficients for the $MA(1)$ model drop to zero after the first time lag, while the partial autocorrelation coefficients trail off to zero gradually. Furthermore, the autocorrelation coefficients for the MA (2) model will drop to zero after the second time lag, while the partials trail off gradually. Again, it must be mentioned that sample autocorrelation functions are going to differ from these theoretical functions due to sampling variation.

An example of the usage of an $MA(2)$ model for forecasting is shown using the error terms presented in Table 9.3. If the Box-Jenkins program computes the values of W to be $W_1 = -14$, $W_2 = .35$, then

$$\hat{Y}_T = -W_1 e_{T-1} - W_2 e_{T-2}$$
$$\hat{Y}_T = -(-14)(18.4) - (0.35)(15.2)$$
$$\hat{Y}_T = 252.3$$

Autoregressive-Moving Average Models

In addition to AR and MA models, the two can be mixed providing a third class of general models called $ARMA$. Equations (9–1) and (9–2) are combined, forming

$$Y_T = B_1 Y_{T-1} + B_2 Y_{T-2} + \cdots + B_P Y_{T-P} + e_T$$
$$- W_1 e_{T-1} - W_2 e_{T-2} - \cdots - W_q e_{T-q} \qquad \text{(9–3)}$$

$ARMA$ models use combinations of past values and past errors, and offer a potential for fitting models that could not be adequately fitted using an AR or MA model separately.

Figure 9–9 shows the equation of an $ARMA$ (1,1) model, and the behavior of the theoretical autocorrelation and partial autocorrelation coefficients.

A significant difference between the Box-Jenkins methodology and previous methods is that Box-Jenkins does not make assumptions about the number of terms, nor the relative weights to be assigned to the terms. The analyst selects the appropriate model, including the number of terms, then the program calculates the coefficients using a nonlinear least-squares method. Forecasts for future periods can then be made, and confidence intervals can be constructed for these estimates.

Applying the Methodology

As shown in Fig. 9–6, the Box-Jenkins approach involves three separate stages. These stages are model identification, model estimation and testing, and applying the model.

Stage 1: Model Identification

a. The first step in model identification is to determine whether or not the series is stationary; that is, whether the mean value is changing over time. If the series is not stationary, it can generally be converted to a stationary series by the method of differencing. The analyst specifies the degree of differencing, and the Box-Jenkins algorithm converts the data into a stationary series, then performs subsequent computations using the converted data.

b. Once a stationary series has been obtained, the analyst must identify the form of the model to be used. This is accomplished by comparing the autocorrelation and partial autocorrelation coefficients of the data to be fitted with the corresponding distributions for the various $ARMA$ models. The theoretical distributions for some of the more common $ARMA$ models are shown in Figs. 9–7, 9–8, and 9–9 for help in selecting an appropriate model.

As can be seen, each model has a unique set of autocorrelations and partial autocorrelations, and the analyst should be able to match the corresponding coefficients of his/her data to one of the theoretical distributions.

Although it generally will not be possible to match data exactly with the theoretical distributions, tests can be done during Stage 2 to determine whether the model is adequate. Then an alternative model can be tried if the first model is unsatisafctory. After a little practice, the analyst should become more adept at identifying an adequate model.

In general, the analyst should identify the autocorrelations that drop off exponentially to zero. If the autocorrelations trail off exponentially to zero, an AR process is indicated; if the partial autocorrelations trail off, an MA process is indicated; and if both trail off, a mixed $ARMA$ process is indicated. By counting the number of autocorrelation and partial autocorrelation coefficients that are significantly different from zero, the order of the MA and/or AR processes can be determined.

Stage 2: Model Estimation and Testing of Model Adequacy

a. Once a tentative model has been selected, the parameters for that model must be estimated. For example, suppose an $ARMA$ (1,1) model has been selected. The mathematical form and forecast formula for the model are, respectively,

$$Y_T = B_1 Y_{T-1} - W_1 e_{T-1} + e_T$$

and

$$\hat{Y}_T = B_1 Y_{T-1} - W_1 e_{T-1}$$

In order to use the forecast equation, it is necessary to calculate values for B_1 and W_1. These calculations are done by the Box-Jenkins computer program using the minimum mean-squared error as the criteria for selecting the optimal values.

Assume that values for B_1 and W_1 have been computed to be .25 and .5. the tentative forecast model is now

$$\hat{Y}_T = .25 \, Y_{T-1} - .5 \, e_{T-1}$$

b. Before using the model for forecasting, it must be checked for adequacy. This is done by checking the error terms, $e_T = Y_T - \hat{Y}_T$, to be sure they are random. This can be done by checking the autocorrelations of the error terms to be sure they are not significantly different from zero. If only a very few error term autocorrelations are significantly different from zero, the model may be considered adequate. If several of these autocorrelations are large, the analyst should return to step 1(b) and select an alternative model, then continue the analysis.

The model can also be checked for adequacy by doing a Chi-Square (χ^2) test on the autocorrelations of the residuals. The test statistic is

$$Q = (N - d) \sum_{i=1}^{k} \hat{p}_i^2 \,(e)$$

which is approximately distributed as a Chi-Square with $k - p - q$ degrees of freedom. In this equation

where: N = length of time series
k = first k autocorrelations being checked
p = # AR terms
q = # MA terms
$\hat{p}_i\,(e)$ = sample autocorrelation function of the ith residual term
d = degree of differencing to obtain a stationary series

If the calculated value of Q is larger than the χ^2 for $k - p - q$ degrees of freedom, then the model should be considered inadequate; and the analyst should return to step 1(b), select an alternative model, and continue the analysis until a satisfactory model has been found.

Neither of these two tests for adequacy should be considered the final word, but they should generally be used together, along with considerable judgment on the analyst's part. If some large deviations can be adequately explained by unusual circumstances, for example, these deviations may be ignored if the rest of the model is deemed adequate.

It is possible that two or more models may be judged to be approximately equal, yet none of the models may be an exact fit for the data. In this case the principle of parsimony should prevail, and the simpler model should be chosen.

Stage 3: Forecasting with the Model

a. Once an adequate model has been found, forecasts for one period or several periods into the future can be made. Confidence intervals can also be constructed about these estimates. In general, the further into the future the forecast is, the larger the confidence interval will be. These forecasts and confidence intervals are computed by the Box-Jenkins program at the analyst's request.

b. As more data become available, the same model can be used to revise forecasts by choosing another time origin.

c. If the series appears to be changing over time, the model parameters may need to be recalculated, or an entirely new model may have to be developed. If small differences in forecast errors are noticed, this may indicate the parameters need to be recalculated, and the analyst should return to step 2(a). When large differences are noticed in the size of the forecast errors, this may indicate an entirely new model is needed, and the analyst should return to step 1(b) or even step 1(a) and repeat the process of fitting the time series to a new model.

Box-Jenkins Example

Table 9.4 represents 60 daily closing averages of the transportation index during the summer months of 1978. The first 55 observations are used for identifying, estimating, and diagnostically checking an appropriate model. The last 5 observations are held out so that forecasts from the selected model can be compared against the actual observations.

Stage 1: Identification

The first step in identifying a tentative model is to look at the autocorrelations and partial autocorrelations of the data. Plots of the autocorrelations and partial autocorrelations for the raw data are shown in Fig. 9–10.

The first 12 autocorrelations appear to be trailing off to zero, which indicates an AR process. Also, the partial autocorrelations drop to zero

TABLE 9.4   *Example of Forecasting the Transportation Index.*

Time Period	Closing Average	Time Period	Closing Average	Time Period	Closing Average
1	222.34	21	228.96	41	251.07
2	222.24	22	229.99	42	248.05
3	221.17	23	233.05	43	249.76
4	218.88	24	235.00	44	251.66
5	220.05	25	236.17	45	253.41
6	219.61	26	238.31	46	252.04
7	216.40	27	241.14	47	248.78
8	217.33	28	241.48	48	247.76
9	219.69	29	246.74	49	249.27
10	219.32	30	248.73	50	247.95
11	218.25	31	248.83	51	251.41
12	220.30	32	248.78	52	254.67
13	222.54	33	249.61	53	258.62
14	223.56	34	249.90	54	259.25
15	223.07	35	246.45	55	261.49
16	225.36	36	247.57	56	260.62
17	227.60	37	247.76	57	260.08
18	226.82	38	247.81	58	257.21
19	229.69	39	250.68	59	253.51
20	229.30	40	251.80	60	250.73

after the first lag. This indicates that a first order AR process is present. If an MA process is present, just the opposite is true; the autocorrelations drop to zero and the partial autocorrelations trail to zero.

Stage 2:   Estimation and Testing

Once a model has been tentatively chosen, an initial guess of the parameter value(s) must be supplied as a starting point for the program. Although formulas exist for calculating initial guesses for the parameters, it may be easier to simply use a trial and error approach.* The final value of the parameter may be significantly different from the intial guesses, but, generally, the program will converge on an optimal value for the parameters within a few iterations. If the program fails to converge after some specified number of iterations, a look at the trial values will indicate the direction of change needed, and new guesses can be made.

For the sample data, an AR (1) model is tentatively chosen, and

---

*The interested reader can find formulas for estimating model parameters in MAKRIDAKIS, S., AND WHEELWRIGHT, S., *Forecasting Methods & Applications,* New York: John Wiley and Sons, 1978.

Time Lags		Autocorrelations
12	. *	.38
11	. *	.44
10	. *	.50
9	. *	.56
8	. *	.61
7	. *	.66
6	. *	.71
5	. *	.75
4	. *	.79
3	. *	.85
2	. *	.90
1	. *	.95

```
    I  I  I  I  I  I  I  I  I  I  I  I  I  I  I  I  I  I  I  I  I
   -1                          0                          +1
```

FIGURE 9–10 (A) *Autocorrelations of Raw Data from Table 9.4.*

an initial guess of 0.9 used for the single parameter. The program converges on a value of 1.0019 after 5 iterations. The tentative model is now

$$\hat{Y}_T = 1.0019 \, Y_{T-1}$$

To check the adequacy of the model, we first look at a plot of the autocorrelations of the residuals to see whether or not any are significantly different from zero. Figure 9–11 is examined, and none of the autocorrelations are significantly different from zero, indicating that the model is adequate. The range of these autocorrelations is $-.19$ to $+.17$, and they show no particular pattern.

Another test of the adequacy of the model is the Chi-Square test of the autocorrelations. Using the first k autocorrelations for the test, the test statistic is

$$Q = (N - d) \sum_{i=1}^{k} \hat{p}_i^2(e) \qquad \text{with } k - p - q \text{ degrees of freedom}$$

Since no differencing is used in this model, the test statistic for the first 12 autocorrelations is $Q = N\Sigma_{i=1}^{12} \hat{p}_i^2 (e)$ with $12 - 1 = 11$ degrees of freedom. The calculated value of Q is 8.6, the tabled value for χ_{11}^2 is 17.28

Time Lags						Autocorrelations
12	•		*	•		−.01
11	•	*	I	•		−.13
10	•	*	I	•		−.10
9	•		*	•		−.01
8	•		*I	•		−.03
7	•	*	I	•		−.12
6	•		I *	•		.05
5	•		I*	•		.02
4	•		*I	•		−.03
3	•	*	I	•		−.05
2	•		*I	•		−.03
1	•		I	•	*	.95

```
    I I I I I I I I I I  I I I I I I I I I I I I
    −1                   0                    +1
```

FIGURE 9–10 (B) *Partial Autocorrelations.*

at the 10% level of significance and 19.68 at the 5% level of significance.

The Chi-Square test of the autocorrelations indicates that the model is adequate, and can be used for forecasting purposes. Also, an inspection of the actual residuals shows no particular pattern. The range of the residuals is from −3.496 to 5.215 with an average value of 0.6672. Both the analysis of the autocorrelations of the residuals and the Chi-Square test indicate that the model is adequate.

Even though the $AR(1)$ model was judged to be adequate, for comparison purposes, two additional models were tried. An $ARMA(1,1)$ was tried with no differencing, then with one degree of differencing. These models were checked using the same procedure as with the $AR(1)$ model, and were also accepted as being adequate.

It is now necessary to compare the three models and select one as a forecast model. Table 9.5 compares the results for the three models.

The Chi-Square statistic is approximately equal for the $AR(1)$ and $ARMA(1,1)$ model with no differencing, and slightly higher for the $ARMA(1,1)$ model with differencing. However, the $ARMA(1,1)$ models have lost an additional degree of freedom because the MA term was added. The $AR(1)$ model could, therefore, be considered slightly better than the

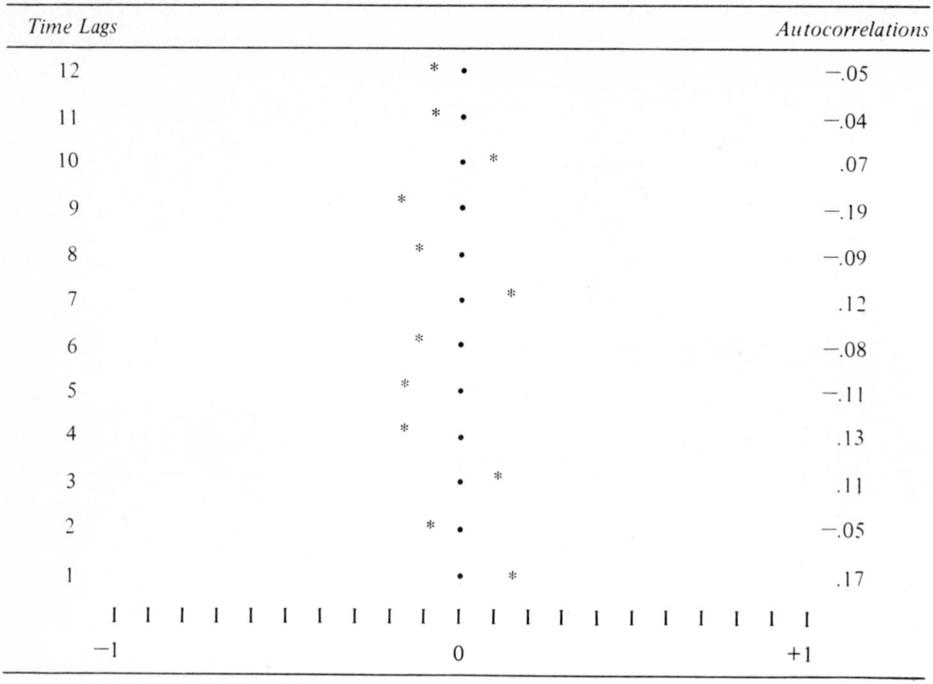

Time Lags		Autocorrelations
12	* ●	−.05
11	* ●	−.04
10	● *	.07
9	* ●	−.19
8	* ●	−.09
7	● *	.12
6	* ●	−.08
5	* ●	−.11
4	* ●	.13
3	● *	.11
2	* ●	−.05
1	● *	.17

ǀ ǀ

−1   0   +1

FIGURE 9–11   *Autocorrelations of Residuals.*

TABLE 9.5   *Comparison of AR (1) and ARMA (1,1) Models.*

	AR (1)	ARMA (1,1) No Differencing	ARMA (1,1) 1 Degree of Differencing
Chi-Square Q (12)	8.1	8.3	9.5
Degrees of Freedom	12 − 1 = 11	12 − 1 − 1 = 10	12 − 1 − 1 = 10
Forecast Errors:			
1 Period in Future	−1.37	−1.58	−1.97
2 Periods in Future	−2.40	−2.21	−3.54
3 Periods in Future	−5.77	−5.18	−7.36
4 Periods in future	−9.97	−8.97	−11.95
5 Periods in Future	−13.25	−11.85	−15.55
Range of Residuals	−3.496	−3.537	−4.155
	to	to	to
	5.215	5.272	4.261
Variance of Residuals	4.120	3.890	3.893
Autoregressive Parameter	1.0019	1.00036	0.9292
Moving Average Parameter	NA	−0.27399	0.7815

$ARMA(1,1)$ models as judged by the Chi-Square test. If the forecast errors for 1 to 5 periods into the future are checked, the $ARMA(1,1)$ model with no differencing has slightly closer estimates, although the estimates are almost identical. An analysis of the residuals for the three models shows that the range and variance of the residual terms are approximately equal for all three models. Other factors being about equal, the simpler model should be chosen. Therefore, the AR(1) model is accepted in this case.

Stage 3: Forecasting

Forecasts were made for 5 steps ahead using the model with observation number 55 as the starting value. The results of these forecasts and associated two standard error limits are shown in Table 9.6.

As shown in Table 9.6, the confidence intervals become larger as forecasts are made further into the future. The first 3 observations fell within the confidence interval predicted by the model, the last 2 observations did not.

TABLE 9.6   *Forecasts Using an AR (1) Model for the Transportation Index.*

Time Period	Lower Confidence Limit	Forecast	Upper Confidence Limit	Actual	Error
56	258.21	261.99	265.76	260.62	−1.33
57	257.14	262.48	267.83	260.08	−2.40
58	256.43	262.98	269.53	257.21	−5.77
59	255.91	263.48	271.05	253.51	−9.97
60	255.51	263.98	272.46	250.73	−13.25

The fact that forecasts for 4 and 5 periods into the future might not be very accurate at this particular point could have been anticipated by considering the original data. At period 55 the data appear to stop a steady climb and suddenly seem to start decreasing. If the parameters have been estimated using only data that have shown a climbing trend, the model probably will not be able to predict decreases very well, especially more than a few periods into the future. Of course, the transportation index is seasonal, but the seasonal nature of the data was purposely voided for illustration purposes by selecting the data over a short time span. In an actual application, if seasonality is suspected, much more data should be used in developing the model.

Summary

The Box-Jenkins approach to time series analysis is a very powerful tool for providing more accurate short-range forecasts. It combines the strengths of both the autoregressive and moving average methods without making assumptions about the number of terms in the forecast equation or the interrelationships between their coefficients. Also, we are provided with a statistical test for determining the adequacy of the fitted model, as well as a means of constructing confidence intervals about the forecasts.

However, the Box-Jenkins approach is not without some disadvantages.* Some of these disadvantages are:

1. A relatively large amount of data is required. It should be recognized that if the data are seasonal, such as yearly seasonal data, then monthly observations for one year generally consitute one data point and not twelve. Makridakis et al. estimates minimum data requirements for reliable use of the Box-Jenkins method to be 72 data points, assuming a seasonal pattern of 12 months' duration. In many cases of this type sufficient historical data for reliable use of the Box-Jenkins method are simply not available, and some other time series method should be used.

   The Box-Jenkins method is generally considered to be more applicable when the data occur over a relatively short period of time. Some of the applications appropriate for this method would be: (1) analysis of stock prices on a daily or weekly basis and (2) data from a chemical or manufacturing process where samples can be taken often.

2. There are no easy ways to update the parameters of the model as new data become available, as in direct smoothing models. The model has to be periodically completely refitted, or worse, a new model must be developed.

3. To build a satisfactory model requires a high investment in the analyst's time and other resources. The costs of model development, computer run-time, and storage requirements are substantially higher for Box-Jenkins models than for the more traditional techniques such as smoothing,

---

*For a summary of the relative computer and analyst time requirements, minimum data requirements, applications, etc., for various forecasting methods, refer to Makridakis, S., et al., "An Interactive Forecasting System," American Statistician **28,** p. 157.

*For a summary of some disadvantages of the Box-Jenkins methodology, refer to Montgomery, D. C., and Johnson, L. A., *Forecasting and Time Series Analysis*, New York: McGraw-Hill Book Company, 1976.

*Usage levels for various demand forecasting techniques in the process industries is shown in Taylor, Samuel G., "The APICS Process Industry Survey: Implications for Education and Research," *Proceedings and Abstracts of the American Institute for Decision Sciences Eighth Annual Meeting*, Western Regional Conference, 1979, pp. 202–204.

decomposition, and regression analysis. If only a few time series are involved, this may not be important. However, if many different time series are involved, such as is typically found in an application in production–inventory control systems, the improvement in accuracy from using the Box-Jenkins methodology may not justify the additional cost.

4. Generally, many statisticians lack knowledge about the methodology. Many potential users consider the Box-Jenkins methodology more difficult to understand than smoothing or decomposition models, and the results are considered more difficult to interpret.

   However, the methodology does offer a potential for more accurate short-term forecasting when the extra time and effort involved in its use can be justified.

PROBLEMS

*1. a. For a sample of 100 observations of random data, calculate a 95% confidence interval for the autocorrelation coefficients.
   b. If all the autocorrelation coefficients are within the interval and show no particular pattern, what conclusion can be drawn?
   c. If the first five autocorrelation coefficients are significantly different from zero and the pattern gradually trails to zero, what conclusion can be drawn?
   d. If r_4, r_8, and r_{12} are significantly different from zero, what conclusion can be drawn?

2. Suppose the following time series model has been fitted to historical data, and has been checked and found to be an adequate model.

$$Y_T = 35^* + e_T + .25 e_{T-1} - .3 e_{T-2}$$

If the first four observations are $Y_1 = 32.5$, $Y_2 = 36.6$, $Y_3 = 33.2$, and $Y_4 = 31.9$, compute forecasts for periods 5, 6, and 7 from origin 4. Let e_{T-1} and e_{T-2} equal 0 for period 1.

*3. A time series model has been fitted to historical data, yielding

$$Y_T = 50^* + .45\, Y_{T-1} + e_T$$

Suppose at time $t = 50$ the observation is $Y_{50} = 100$.
   a. Determine forecasts for periods 51, 52, and 53 from origin 50.
   b. Suppose the observed value of $Y_{51} = 90$. Revise the forecasts for periods 52 and 53.
   c. Suppose the estimate of the variance of the error term $(\hat{\sigma}^2)$ is 1.2. Compute a 95% confidence interval about the estimate for period 51.

---

*Refer to page 295 for a discussion of the constant.

4. Fill in the missing information in the table, indicating whether the theoretical distributions of autocorrelations and partial autocorrelations trail off or drop off for these models.

Behavior of Theoretical Distributions.

Model	Autocorrelations	Partial Autocorrelations
AR		
MA		
ARMA		

*5. Given the following graphs of the autocorrelations and partial autocorrelations of the original data for some time series, identify a potential model for each:

Autocorrelations	*Partial Autocorrelations*
Time Lags	*Time Lags*

a.
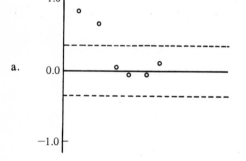
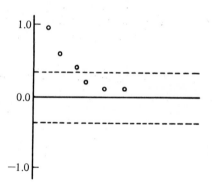

b.
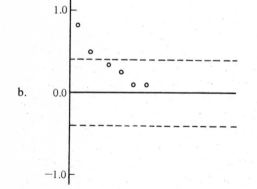
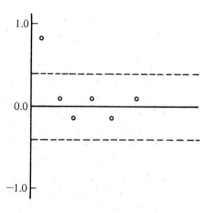

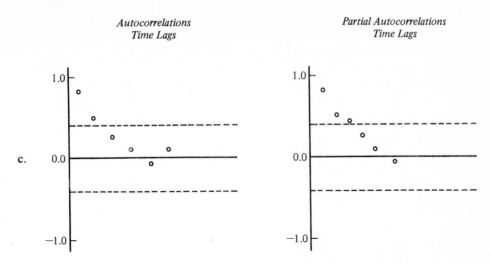

Autocorrelations
Time Lags

Partial Autocorrelations
Time Lags

c.

*6. After fitting an $MA(1)$ model to the first differences for 24 observations of a time series, the autocorrelations of the first 10 residuals were as shown.

    a. What does inspection of the autocorrelations of the residuals tell you about the adequacy of the model?

    b. Calculate the Chi-Square statistic for this data, and test to see whether the model is adequate based on the Chi-Square test.

Time Lags		Autocorrelations
10		.10
9		.03
8		−.01
7		.05
6		.12
5		−.10
4		−.19
3		−.09
2		.08
1		−.02
	−.3 −.2 −.1 0 .1 .2 .3	

7. The Chips Bakery has been having trouble forecasting the demand for their special high fiber bread, and would like your assistance. Data for the weekly demand, and the autocorrelations of the raw data and the various differences, are shown.

a. Inspect the plots and suggest an appropriate model for forecasting weekly sales demand. How did you decide on this model?

b. Make initial estimates for the parameters, and run the parameter estimation phase of the Box-Jenkins program. What is the equation for forecasting weekly sales demand for the high fiber bread?

c. Perform the necessary diagnostic tests to determine whether the chosen model is adequate or not.

d. Using the Box-Jenkins program, forecast the demand for the next 4 weeks starting with week 53, and construct 95% confidence intervals about these forecasts.

Weekly Sales Demand for High Fiber Bread.

			(thousands of loaves)				
Week	Demand	Week	Demand	Week	Demand	Week	Demand
1	22.46	14	30.21	27	39.29	40	47.31
2	20.27	15	30.09	28	39.61	41	50.08
3	20.97	16	33.04	29	41.02	42	50.25
4	23.68	17	31.21	30	42.52	43	49.00
5	23.25	18	32.44	31	40.83	44	49.97
6	23.48	19	34.73	32	42.15	45	52.52
7	24.81	20	34.92	33	43.91	46	53.39
8	25.44	21	33.37	34	45.67	47	52.37
9	24.88	22	36.91	35	44.53	48	54.06
10	27.38	23	37.75	36	45.23	49	54.88
11	27.74	24	35.46	37	46.35	50	54.82
12	28.96	25	38.48	38	46.28	51	56.23
13	28.48	26	37.72	39	46.70	52	57.54

Autocorrelation Function of the Raw Data.

Time Lag	Autocorrelation
1	.94
2	.88
3	.82
4	.77
5	.71
6	.65
7	.59
8	.53
9	.48
10	.43
11	.38
12	.32

Autocorrelation Function of the First Differenced Series.

Time Lag	Autocorrelation
1	$-.40$
2	$-.29$
3	$.17$
4	$.21$
5	$-.22$
6	$-.05$
7	$.20$
8	$-.03$
9	$-.03$
10	$-.23$
11	$.21$
12	$.14$

Autocorrelation Function of the Second Differenced Series.

Time Lag	Autocorrelation
1	$-.53$
2	$-.10$
3	$.11$
4	$.18$
5	$-.20$
6	$-.04$
7	$.16$
8	$-.05$
9	$.06$
10	$-.23$
11	$.16$
12	$.13$

8. The following are weekly stock quotations for IBM stock for 1978.
   a. Obtain plots of the data, autocorrelations, and partial autocorrelations using the Box-Jenkins program; then use this information to suggest an appropriate forecast model(s).
   b. Is the series stationary? What correction would you recommend if the data is nonstationary?
   c. Make initial estimates for the model parameters; then use the Box-Jenkins program to calculate improved parameter values.
   d. Perform diagnostic tests to determine whether the model is adequate or not.
   e. After a satisfactory model has been found, make forecasts for January, 1979.

Weekly Stock Quotations for IBM Stock for 1978.

JAN.	6	267	JUL.	7	258
	13	267		14	259
	20	268		21	268
	27	264		28	276
FEB.	3	263	AUG.	4	285
	10	260		11	288
	17	256		18	295
	24	256		25	297
MAR.	2	252	SEP.	1	292
	10	245		8	299
	17	243		15	294
	24	240		22	284
	31	238		29	277
APR.	7	241	OCT.	6	279
	14	244		13	287
	21	254		20	276
	28	262		27	273
MAY	5	261	NOV	3	270
	12	265		10	264
	19	261		17	261
	26	261		24	268
JUN.	2	257	DEC.	1	270
	9	268		8	276
	16	270		15	274
	23	266		22	284
	30	259		29	304

BIBLIOGRAPHY

Box, G. E., AND Jenkins, G. M., *Time Series Analysis: Forecasting and Control*, San Francisco: Holden-Day, 1976.

Chambers, J., et al., "How to Choose the Right Forecasting Technique," Harvard Business Review, July-Aug, 1971, pp. 45–74.

Ferratt, T. W., AND Mabert, V. A., "A Description and Application of the Box-Jenkins Methodology," *Decision Sciences*, Vol. 3, 1972, pp.83–107.

Makridakis, S., AND Wheelwright, S. C., *Forecasting Methods for Management*, New York: John Wiley and Sons, 1973.

——— *Interactive Forecasting*, Palo Alto, Calif.: The Scientific Press, 1977.

——— *Forecasting Methods & Applications*, New York: John Wiley and Sons, 1978.

Makridakis, S., et al., "An Interactive Forecasting System," *The American Statistician* **28**, pp. 153–158.

MONTGOMERY, D. C., AND JOHNSON, L. A., *Forecasting and Time Series Analysis*, New York: McGraw-Hill Book Company, 1976.

QUENOUILLE, M. H., "The Joint Distribution of Serial Correlation Coefficients," *Annals of Mathematical Statistics*, Vol. 20, 1949, pp. 561–71.

REILLY, DAVID P., "Box-Jenkins for the Layman." Celanese Corporation, October 16, 1975.

Simulation as a Forecasting Tool*

10 At this point you have been introduced to a variety of business forecasting techniques, whose principal purposes have been to explain the behavior of certain variables in the past and to predict their behavior in the future. As you are aware, these techniques are applicable in many different situations. However, standard forecasting packages make two assumptions that sometimes are not valid. The first assumption is that the relationship between the dependent variables and the independent variables is linear or can be transformed in such a way that it may be treated as linear. The second assumption is that the variables are normally distributed with approximately equal variances. While standard forecasting models are not particularly sensitive to modest departures from these assumptions, there are cases in which the use of general linear forecasting techniques will produce grossly inaccurate results. In these cases it is possible to construct a computer-based model tailored to the particular situation. Since customized models are much more expensive to produce, the analyst should always consider first if the benefits of improved accuracy

---

*This discussion is by courtesy of Susan L. Solomon, a Professor of Decision Science at Eastern Washington University. She has contributed to numerous simulation conferences and is a past Chairman, Vice-Chairman, and Treasurer of the Special Interest Group on Simulation (SIGSIM) of the Association for Computing Machinery (ACM).

of a customized model are worth the costs of preparing it. When the answer to this question is affirmative, the analyst develops a simulation model.

Types of Simulation Models

Simulation models can be physical models, either exact replicas or scaled-down versions. The aerospace industry often creates and experiments with such models to forecast the performance of contemplated new aircraft and spacecraft. Mathematicians and engineers draft differential equation models to predict the reaction of a dam to various water flow patterns and stresses. Econometricians develop difference equation models to anticipate the effect on GNP when the Federal Reserve changes its monetary policy. Financial planners attempt to evaluate alternative capital investment strategies on paper through modeling before committing real dollars. Prospective managers are given artificial experience in decision making with gaming models, which permit them to observe the consequences of their decisions prior to actual implementation of those decisions. Perhaps the most common use of simulation modeling in business is for the evaluation of service facilities. In every one of the examples just cited, it is possible to predict the consequences of certain actions and test alternatives if the outcome seems undesirable, at lower cost and with less disruption than if the experiment were conducted in the real world.

1. **Physical scale models**—planning layout of facilities and testing new products.
2. **Simple mathematical models**—product mix determination, delivery routing, and capital budgeting using linear programming; inventory analysis for determining economic order quantity and reorder point; project scheduling and isolation of bottlenecks and slack using critical path scheduling.
3. **Linear statistical models**—standard regression using cross-section and time series data to predict levels of economic variables.
4. **Complex mathematical models and nonlinear statistical models**—simulation of physical processes such as waste disposal and simulation of waiting-line systems.

FIGURE 10-1 *Types of Models Used in Business Forecasting and Their Principal Purposes.*

315

Steps in Constructing a Simulation Model

Most quantitative techniques in business are analytical in nature. That is, the logic flow proceeds from a generally applicable model formulation to a specific model for a given situation by collecting data about the situation for input to the general model. This is what occurs, for example, in constructing a simple regression equation. The analyst knows that the general form of the model will be $Y_R = b_0 + bX$; only the values of b_0 and b will be particularized to the situation.

Simulation is said to be a synthetic, as opposed to an analytical, technique. Instead of proceeding from the general case to the specific case, the analyst begins with the specific case and constructs a model from which to generalize.

1. IDENTIFY THE PROBLEM.
2. GATHER THE INPUT DATA AND TEST IT FOR STATISTICAL DISTRIBUTION.
3. CODE THE SIMULATION PROGRAM.
4. VERIFY AND VALIDATE THE COMPUTER MODEL.
5. EXPERIMENT WITH THE MODEL TO TEST ALTERNATIVE SYSTEM CONFIGURATIONS.

FIGURE 10–2 *Steps in Performing a Simulation.*

Problem Recognition and Data Collection

The first step in the construction of a simulation model is the recognition of a present or anticipated problem. At this stage the analyst endeavors to learn as much as possible about the system in question. If it currently exists, the analyst observes it and interviews those who deal with it. If it does not yet exist, the analyst gathers as much information as possible about the planned or possible inputs, processing, and outputs of the system. When possible, this information is reduced to very compact form. For example, when inputs are found to conform closely to a known statistical distribution, the properties of that distribution can be used to summarize the characteristics of the input.

Model Construction

Next, the analyst begins construction of the model. Just as an architect or artist must select the medium most appropriate to a particular structure, the analyst must determine whether a physical, mathematical, or other computer model is best. If he/she chooses a computer model, the analyst must select a programming language in which to convey model parameters to the computer. The choice depends on whether a continuous or discrete-event system is to be described; whether special-purpose simulation languages, packages, or programs already exist for similar situations; the background and expertise of the analyst; the complexity of the situation to be modeled; and the nature of the available computer facilities.

Validation and Verification

Programming a simulation model is fraught with all the exigencies of computer programming in general. Compilation of grammatical errors and execution of logical errors must be corrected. When this is accomplished, the model is said to have been *verified;* that is, it seems to behave as the experimenter intended. A simulation model faces another important test as well. It must be *validated;* that is, it must correspond closely with the real system in all important respects. The model will usually be simpler than the real system. Any characteristics of the real system that are of no or only slight importance to its operation will have been omitted from the model for the sake of economy and ease of manipulation. Nevertheless, the analyst must take care that all relevant properties of the real system are present in the model. This task is especially difficult when the system being modeled does not yet exist; indeed, based on the results of the simulation, the specifications for the real system may be altered drastically. Validation often is based on subjective considerations when there is a dearth of facts about the real system. If the real system already exists, the observed inputs to the real system are used as inputs to the simulation; the outputs or performance of the model should match the output or performance of the real system, given identical input. If a discrepancy is found, the analyst must modify the model until it is accurate in this sense.

Design of Experiments

Once the model has been validated and verified, three kinds of experiments become possible. First, the magnitude and/or the distribution of the inputs can be changed and the effect on system output observed. Second, the magnitude and/or the distribution of system processing characteristics can be changed and the effect on system output observed. Finally, the structure of the model itself can be changed and the effect on system output observed.

Ordinarily, simple observation of the output in each of these three types of experiments is not sufficient. The analyst wishes to contrast the various outputs with each other to establish formally if the differences among them are statistically significant. Classical hypothesis testing, analysis of variance, and Chi-Square contingency tests are commonly used to detect whether or not differences in certain means or proportions are significant when input or processing characteristics are varied. Confidence intervals estimate likely system performance bounds. Before these statistical methods can be used, the analyst must ensure that the conditions on their correct usage are met.

The principal obstacle to be overcome is the detection and remedy of autocorrelation in the time series output of the simulation. Another consideration is that the output reflect the performance of the system at steady state; that is, under conditions that are typical of its operation, rather than at peak or slack periods.

Once the output data stream meets these restrictions, the analyst must decide what sample size or simulation run length will be adequate. As with real-world sampling, considerations are the variance of the observed data, the level of confidence or significance desired, and the maximum width of confidence intervals that is tolerable. The sample is then selected, the statistical experiments performed, and the conclusions reported to management. Decision makers should then be in an excellent position to make decisions based on the performance predictions generated by the simulation model.

An Illustration

The First National Bank of Cheney has one drive-up window staffed by a teller during regular banking hours. The bank has experienced a number of customer complaints about delays at the drive-up window, and fears the loss of business as a result. An observer has noted the arrival and service rate patterns at randomly selected times of non-peak demand. The results are shown in Table 10.1.

TABLE 10.1   *Observed Data For Cheney National Bank.*

Arrival Rate per Minute	Observed Frequency	Service Rate per Minute	Observed Frequency
1	35	0	30
2	40	1	40
3	25	2	15
	$n = 100$	3	10
		4	5
			$n = 100$

318

Establishing the Arrival and Service Patterns

Inspection of the data suggests that arrival rate may be uniformly distributed and that service rate may be Poisson distributed. Thus, analytical waiting-line formulae, which are commonly used to assess performance characteristics (e.g., average waiting time and average number in the waiting line), would not apply because the statistical distributions that they assume (Poisson arrival *and* service rates) are not true of this situation.

First, the hypotheses about arrival and service distributions should be formally tested using a Chi-Square or Kolmogorov-Smirnov goodness-of-fit test. Since Chi-Square is the more readily available statistic, it is utilized in the hypothesis tests shown below.

Null Hypothesis 1. Arrival rate is uniformly distributed over the range 1 to 3 per minute.

Alternate Hypothesis 1. Null hypothesis 1 is incorrect. Some other pattern characterizes arrival rate.

TABLE 10.2 *Test of Uniform Distribution of Arrivals.*

Arrival Rate per Minute	Observed Frequency f_0	Expected* Frequency $f_e = np$	Computed $\chi^2 = \Sigma \dfrac{(f_0 - f_e)^2}{f_e}$
1	35	$100 \times 1/3 = 33.3$	$(35 - 33.3)^2/33.3$
2	40	$100 \times 1/3 = 33.3$	$(40 - 33.3)^2/33.3$
3	25	$100 \times 1/3 = 33.3$	$(25 - 33.3)^2/33.3$
	$n = 100$	$n = 100$	3.5

*See Table of values of Chi Square in the Appendix.

The Chi-Square statistic compares observed data with what would be expected if the null hypothesis were true. Degrees of freedom for a Chi-Square goodness-of-fit test are computed as the number of classes with expected frequencies of 5 or more, minus the number of sample statistics (n, $\bar{x}$, and/or s) used to compute the expected frequencies. In this example are 3 classes with expected frequencies of 5 or more, and only one sample statistic (n) is necessary to compute the expected frequencies. Hence, degrees of freedom $= 3 - 1 = 2$. The critical level of χ^2 with 2 D.F. and a significance level of 0.05 is 5.991. Since computed χ^2 is less than critical χ^2, it appears that the null hypothesis of uniformly distributed arrival rate cannot be rejected at the 0.05 level of significance.

Null Hypothesis 2. Service rate is Poisson distributed with a mean of

$$\left[\frac{(0 \times 30) + (1 \times 40) + (2 \times 15) + (3 \times 10) + (4 \times 5)}{100} \right]$$

$$= \left[\frac{0 + 40 + 30 + 30 + 20}{100} \right] = \frac{120}{100} = 1.2 \text{ customers per minute.}$$

Alternate Hypothesis 2. Null Hypothesis 2 is incorrect. Some other pattern characterizes service rate.

TABLE 10.3 *Test of Poisson Distribution of Service.*

Service Rate per Minute	Observed Frequency f_0	Expected* Frequency $f_e = np$	Computed $\chi^2 = \Sigma \dfrac{(f_0 - f_e)^2}{f_e}$
0	30	$100 \times 0.301 = 30.1$	$(30 - 30.1)^2/30.1$
1	40	$100 \times 0.361 = 36.1$	$(40 - 36.1)^2/36.1$
2	15	$100 \times 0.216 = 21.6$	$(15 - 21.6)^2/21.6$
3	10⎫ 15	$100 \times 0.087 = 8.7$⎫ 12.1	$(15 - 12.1)^2/12.1$
4 or more	5⎭	$100 \times 0.034 = 3.4$⎭	
	$n = 100$	$n = 100$	3.1

*Values of p are drawn from a table of the Poisson Distribution with $\mu = 1.2$ found in the Appendix.

The last class has been relabeled "4 or more" even though the observed data did not contain values greater than 4 so that the frequency distribution would reflect a mutually exclusive, collectively exhaustive list of all possible values of the Poisson distribution with $\mu = 1.2$. Such an adjustment is not needed in the case of the uniform distribution postulated for arrival rate, since the uniform distribution may be restricted to any desired range.

Since the expected frequency of the last class is less than 5, that class is merged with the preceding class before computing χ^2. Effectively, four classes remain in the Chi-Square calculation. Since two sample statistics ($\bar{x}$ and n) are needed, respectively, to select the appropriate Poisson table of probabilities and to compute the expected number in each class, degrees of freedom $= 4 - 2 = 2$. The critical level of χ^2 is less than critical χ^2; it appears that the null hypothesis of Poisson distributed service rate cannot be rejected at the 0.05 level of significance.

The nature of the arrival and service patterns has been corroborated statistically. The only issue remaining in the system description is the queue discipline, the order in which customers are served. By the very nature of this service facility, service must be rendered to customers in first-come, first-served order. Alternatives that often are possible in other situations include priority, random, or last-in-first-out queue disciplines.

Programming the Simulation Model

Before the simulation model can be programmed, a suitable language must be selected from about 40 alternatives. The most popular, easiest to learn, and most appropriate for evaluation of service facilities is GPSS, the General Purpose System Simulator. GPSS requires the analyst to describe the model in terms of time rather than rates. For example, if service rate is Poisson distributed with a mean rate of 1.2 customers per minute, an equivalent statement would be that service time is negative exponentially distributed with a mean time of $1/1.2 = 0.83$ minutes, or 50 seconds per customer. Likewise, if arrival rate is uniform between 1 and 3 customers per minute, that implies the time between arrivals is uniformly distributed between 20 and 60 seconds.

TABLE 10.4   *GPSS Program for Cheney National Bank.*

GPSS PROGRAM FOR CHENEY NATIONAL BANK

```
        JOB
  1     FUNCTION            RN1, C24

        0,0/.1,.104/.2,.222/.3,.355/.4,.509/.5,.69/.6,.915/.7,1.2/.75,
        1.38/.8,1.6/.84,1.83/.88,2.12/.9,2.31/.92,2.52/.94,2.81/.95,
        2.99/.96,3.2/.97,3.5/.98,3.9/.99,4.6/.995,5.3/.998,6.2/.999,
        7/.9998,8
```

GENERATE	40, 20	Create customers
QUEUE	1	Join waiting line, if necessary
SEIZE	1	Acquire use of server
DEPART	1	Relinquish position in waiting line, if any
ADVANCE	50, FN1	Use server
RELEASE	1	Relinquish use of server
TABULATE TRANSIT		Accumulate transit time statistics
TERMINATE	1	Remove customer from model
START	100	Run the model until 100 customers
TRANSIT TABLE	M1, 50, 50, 20.	have been simulated
END		

All time specifications in the model must be in like time units and expressed as integers; in this case the most convenient time unit is seconds. Function 1 gives the percentage points of the negative exponential cumulative distribution function with a mean of 1.0. The transit time table gathers information on the time a customer takes in the queue and in service.

Even before running the simulation, it is possible to conjecture about the result, since the simulation output should closely match the performance of the real system if the model is valid. Comparing the mean inter-arrival time (40 seconds) with the mean service time (50 seconds), one might anticipate an ever-lengthening queue, which would justifiably engender customer displeasure.

The simulation output supports this suspicion. At the end of the simulation run the queue in the model is 31 units long, the longest since the beginning of the run. In actuality this would never occur. First, the

TABLE 10.5   *Simulation of Original System.*

```
                    SIMULATION OF ORIGINAL SYSTEM

                         SIMULATOR SOURCE PROGRAM

BLOCK
NUMBER
         JOB
        1 FUNCTION RN1,C24
        0,0/.1,.104/.2,.222/.3,.355/.4,.509/.5,.69/.6,.915/.7,1.2/.75,1.38/
        .8,1,6/.84,1.83/.88,2.12/.9,2.31/.92,2.52/.94,2.81/.95,2.99/.96,3.2/
        .97,3.5/.98,3.9/.99,4.6/.995,5.3/.998,6.2/.999,7/.9998,8
00001   GENERATE 40,20
00002   QUEUE 1
00003   SEIZE 1
00004   DEPART 1
00005   ADVANCE 50,FN1
00006   RELEASE 1
00007   TABULATE TRANSIT
00008   TERMINATE 1
        TRANSIT TABLE M1,50,50,20
        START 100
        END
```

TABLE 10.5 (CONT.)   *Summary Statistics for Facility 1.*

Average Utilization: 96.8 percent of the time
Total Number of Users During the Run: 100
Average Service Time per User: 49.38 seconds
Maximum Length of Queue During the Run: 31 people
Average Length of the Queue: 12.041 people
Total Number of Users Who Passed Through the Waiting Area: 129
Number of Users Who Did Not Have to Wait at All (Zero Entries): 6
Percent of Users Who Did Not Have to Wait at All (Zero Entries): 4.65
Average Waiting Time for All Users: 475.946 seconds
Average Waiting Time for Those Users Who Had to Wait a Nonzero Amount
  of Time: 499.163 seconds

TABLE 10.5 (CONT.) *Frequency Distribution of System Transit Time—*
Waiting Plus Service
$$(n = 100, \bar{X} = 503.98 \text{ seconds}, s = 409.866 \text{ seconds})$$

Transit Time, (in seconds)	Observed Frequency	Percent	Cumulative ≦ Percent
0–50	6	6	6
50–100	4	4	10
100–150	9	9	19
150–200	10	10	29
200–250	8	8	37
250–300	8	8	45
300–350	15	15	60
350–400	2	2	62
400–450	0	0	62
450–500	2	2	64
500–550	3	3	67
550–600	0	0	67
600–650	0	0	67
650–700	0	0	67
700–750	1	1	68
750–800	0	0	68
800–850	4	4	72
850–900	1	1	73
900–950	0	0	73
950–1000	2	2	75

Number of Users Whose Transit Time Exceeded 1000 Seconds: 25
Average Transit Time for Those Users Whose Transit Time Exceeded
  1000 Seconds: 1123.68 seconds

waiting line area probably does not have this capacity; and second, a customer arriving only to observe, say, fifteen cars preceding him would undoubtedly decline to join the queue and go elsewhere instead.

Testing Alternative Systems

Now that the model has been formulated, programmed, and validated, the analyst can consider experimenting with it to forecast the effects of alternative system designs on performance. Two alternatives that seem rather obvious are: a more efficient teller or a second lane with its own drive-up window. Certainly, the first alternative would be less expensive than the second because it requires no capital outlay, but the speed with which any teller can work has distinct limits.

1. Original system with one slow teller:

   FIFO Queue

   Customers ⟶ Drive-up Window

2. Original system with one fast teller:

   FIFO Queue

   Customers ⟶ Drive-up Window

3. System with two queues and two slow tellers:

FIGURE 10–3 *The First National Bank of Cheney Alternative System Configurations.*

The model using the faster teller merely replaces the old ADVANCE block with a new one having, say, an average service time of 40 seconds, negative exponentially distributed, instead of 50 seconds.

The model using the second lane is more complex. Customers join the shortest queue when arriving at the drive-up teller area. It will be assumed that the efficiency of the second teller is the same as the first.

Examination of Output

A summary of 4 performance measures for each system (run for 100 simulated customers) is shown in Table 10.8.

TABLE 10.6 *Summary Statistics for Facility 1.*

Average Utilization: 89.5 percent of the time
Total Number of Users During the Run: 100
Average Service Time per User: 39.51 seconds
Maximum Length of Queue During the Run: 15 people
Average Length of the Queue: 4.953 people
Total Number of Users Who Passed Through the Waiting Area: 112
Number of Users Who Did Not Have to Wait at All (zero Entries): 17
Percent of Users Who Did Not Have to Wait at All (zero Entries): 15.17
Average Waiting Time for All Users: 195.304 seconds
Average Waiting Time for Those Users Who Had to Wait a Nonzero Amount of Time: 230.253 seconds

TABLE 10.6 (CONT.) *Frequency Distribution of System Transit Time—*
Waiting Plus Service
($n = 100$, $\bar{X} = 234.32$ seconds, $s = 211.347$ seconds).

Transit Time (in seconds)	Observed Frequency	Percent	Cumulative $\leq$ Percent
0–50	23	23	23
50–100	17	17	40
100–150	14	14	54
150–200	8	8	62
200–250	4	4	66
250–300	1	1	67
300–350	0	0	67
350–400	1	1	68
400–450	5	5	73
450–500	8	8	81
500–550	6	6	87
550–600	10	10	97
600–650	2	2	99
650–700	1	1	100

TABLE 10.7 *Simulation of Two-Teller System.*

SIMULATION OF TWO-TELLER SYSTEM

SIMULATOR SOURCE PROGRAM

```
BLOCK
NUMBER
          JOB
          1 FUNCTION RN1,C24
          0,0/.1,.104/.2,.222/.3,.355/.4,.509/.5,.69/.6,.915/.7,1.2/.75,1.38/
          .8,1.6/.84,1.83/.88,2.12/.9,2.31/.92,2.52/.94,2.81/.95,2.99/.96,3.2/
          .97,3.5/.98,3.9/.99,4.6/.995,5.3/.998,6.2/.999,7/.9998,8
00001     GENERATE 40,20
00002     TEST L Q1,Q2,TEST2
00003     LINE1 QUEUE 1
00004     SEIZE 1
00005     DEPART 1
00006     ADVANCE 50,FN1
00007     RELEASE 1
00008     TABULATE TRANSIT
00009     TERMINATE 1
00010     TEST2 TEST L Q2,Q1,EQUAL
```

Table 10.7   *Continued*

00011	LINE2 QUEUE 2
00012	SEIZE 2
00013	DEPART 2
00014	ADVANCE 50,FN1
00015	RELEASE 2
00016	TABULATE TRANSIT
00017	TERMINATE 1
00018	EQUAL TRANSFER .500,LINE1,LINE2
	TRANSIT TABLE M1,50,50,20
	START 100
	END

Table 10.7   *Simulation of Two-Teller System. (Cont.)*
Summary Statistics for Facility 1

Average Utilization: 73.5 percent of the time
Total Number of Users During the Run: 53
Average Service Time per User: 57.755 seconds
Maximum Length of Queue During the Run: 2 people
Average Length of Queue: 0.346 people
Total Number of Users Who Passed Through the Waiting Area: 55
Number of Users Who Did Not Have to Wait at All (Zero Entries): 26
Percent of Users Who Did Not Have to Wait at All (Zero Entries): 47.27
Average Waiting Time for All Users: 26.182 seconds
Average Waiting Time for Those Users Who Had to Wait a Nonzero Amount of Time: 49.655 seconds

Summary Statistics for Facility 2

Average Utilization: 70.8 percent of the time
Total Number of Users During the Run: 48
Average Service Time per User: 61.396 seconds
Maximum Length of Queue During the Run: 2 people
Average Length of Queue: 0.389 people
Total Number of Users Who Passed Through the Waiting Area: 49
Number of Users Who Did Not Have to Wait at All (Zero Entries): 23
Percent of Users Who Did Not Have to Wait at All (Zero Entries): 46.96
Average Waiting Time for All Users: 33.020 seconds
Average Waiting Time for Those Users Who Had to Wait a Nonzero Amount of Time: 62.231 seconds

TABLE 10.7 (CONT.) *Frequency Distribution of System Transit Time—*
Waiting Plus Service
$(n = 100, \bar{X} = 87.15$ seconds, $s = 66.473$ seconds$)$.

Transit Time (in seconds)	Observed Frequency	Percent	Cumulative Percent
0–50	31	31	31
50–100	37	37	68
100–150	17	17	85
150–200	9	9	94
200–250	2	2	96
250–300	4	4	100

For each performance measure the fast-teller system appears to be better than the slow-teller system, but seems not as good as the two-teller system. It remains to evaluate whether the differences between the systems are statistically significant.

Testing the Significance of Differences in Alternative System Configurations

Since the output of the simulations displays the proportion of customers who experienced no delay (queue zero entries) and the proportion of time that servers were busy (facility average utilization), several tests of hypotheses can be performed. Tables 10.9 and 10.10 illustrate these hypothesis tests.

$$\text{Computed } \chi^2 = \frac{(123 - 102.1)^2}{102.1} + \frac{(95 - 88.6)^2}{88.6} + \dots$$

$$+ \frac{(17 - 23.4)^2}{23.4} + \frac{(49 - 21.7)^2}{21.7} = 40.84$$

TABLE 10.8 *Performance Characteristics of Alternative Systems.*

Performance Measure	SYSTEM		
	One Slow Teller	One Fast Teller	Two Slow Tellers (averages of both)
Proportion of Time Teller is Busy	0.968	0.895	0.722
Average Queue Length	12	5	0.4
Maximum Queue Length	31	15	2
Proportion of Customers Who Do Not Have to Wait	0.0465	0.1517	0.4710

TABLE 10.9   *Test of Equality of Proportions of Customers Not Delayed*

H_0:   The proportion of customers experiencing no delays is the same for all three alternate system designs.

H_1:   The proportion is different.

   $\alpha = .05$

SIMULATED OBSERVATIONS AND EXPECTATIONS*

		SYSTEM		
	One Slow Server	One Fast Server	Two Slow Servers (combined)	
Number of Customers Who Had to Wait	123(102.1)	95(88.6)	55(82.3)	$n = 273$
Number of Customers Who Did Not Have to Wait	6 (26.9)	17(23.4)	49(21.7)	$n = 72$
	$n = 129$	$n = 112$	$n = 104$	345

*Expected frequencies are in parentheses.

Critical χ^2 with 2 degrees of freedom at $\alpha = .05$ is 5.991. Therefore, the null hypothesis may be rejected.

   The statistic shows significant difference in the proportion of customers who do not have to wait when the three alternative system designs are compared.

Computed χ^2 is clearly a value far in excess of critical χ^2 with 2 degrees of freedom at $\alpha = .05$. The difference in the proportions of busy time

TABLE 10.10   *Test of Equality of Proportions of Time Busy.*

H_0:   The proportion of time that the servers are busy (or idle) is the same for all three alternate system designs.

H_1:   The proportion is different.

   $\alpha = .05$

SIMULATED OBSERVATIONS AND EXPECTATIONS*

	One Slow Server	One Fast Server	Two Slow Servers	(combined)
Number of Time Units Busy	4938 (4261.4)	3951 (3688.3)	6017 (6956.4)	$n = 14906$
Number of Time Units Idle	163 (839.6)	464 (726.7)	2310 (1370.6)	$n = 2937$
	$n = 5101$	$n = 4415$	$n = 8327$	$n = 17843$

*Expected frequencies are in parentheses.

for servers is very significant when the three alternate system designs are contrasted.

Other measures of system performance might include average transit time per customer (the time a customer spends in the waiting line and in service), average queue length, and maximum queue length. Unfortunately, the simulation output does not give the stream of individual observations of these variables necessary to test a hypothesis of the equality of three or more means using analysis of variance.

Confidence Interval Estimates of System Performance

It is possible that management may be interested in estimating system performance parameters rather than testing hypotheses about the difference in alternate system designs.

Suppose, for example, that it is desired to estimate the proportion of customers who will experience no delays in each of the three alternative systems. A 95 percent confidence interval for the true proportion of customers who will not have to wait at all is:

- For the original system,

$$0.0465 \pm 1.96 \sqrt{\frac{(0.0465)(0.9535)}{129}}$$

or

$$0.0102 \text{ to } 0.0828$$

- For the system with one fast teller,

$$0.1518 \pm 1.96 \sqrt{\frac{(0.1518)(0.8483)}{112}}$$

or

$$0.0854 \text{ to } 0.2182$$

- For the system with two slow tellers,

$$0.4712 \pm 1.96 \sqrt{\frac{(0.4712)(0.5288)}{104}}$$

or

$$0.3752 \text{ to } 0.5672$$

Sources of Bias in Inference from Data

Several aspects of simulation output aggregation can cause distortion of subsequent statistical analysis, and in fact, violate the assumptions underlying the use of classical statistical methods. First, in preparing aggregative descriptive statistics, GPSS accumulates information about every customer or about potentially every time unit, depending on which is appropriate to the performance measure being summarized. For example, the proportion of entries in the queue who waited only zero time units (i.e., who were served immediately upon arrival) is accumulated by observing each simulated customer as the entry leaves the QUEUE block to ascertain whether it spent a nonzero number of time units there. Clearly, by observing each successive customer the probability that the observations will be time-dependent or autocorrelated is substantial. If this is so, variance estimates computed from such data are biased, and their use for hypothesis testing or confidence interval estimation is inappropriate.

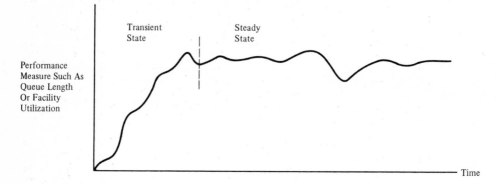

FIGURE 10–4   *The Initial Condition of the Model.*

A second source of possible bias in the collection and use of aggregate simulation performance measures is the potential inclusion of observations processed during the transient state or a typical initial condition of the model. Thus, when the drive-up teller window opens for business in the morning, the server is, by definition, idle. Only after the system has been in operation for a while does the length of the waiting line and customer transit time tend to stabilize.

Procedures to Eliminate or Compensate for Bias

Simulation-generated time series are treated similarly to real-world time series in terms of approaches to potential bias. The detection of bias requires printing of the individual members of the time series, not just the mean and standard deviation of the series. To detect autocorrelation, the time series is tested for correlation with its own members lagged 1, 2, ..., or n time periods. If consecutive observations are found to be autocorrelated, they may be replaced by their arithmetic mean or one may be deleted; and the test for autocorrelation performed on the modified series, until no statistically significant autocorrelation remains. Averaging or deletion lowers the effective sample size, however, and frequently necessitates extending the simulation run so that the sample size is restored to the level previously established for hypothesis testing or confidence interval estimation.

Determining the point at which the transient state of the system stabilizes and steady state begins is dealt with less scientifically. A plot of observations of queue length or transit time often yields a graph with steadily increasing values that are followed by minor fluctuations around a horizontal line. [Nevertheless, some systems never achieve steady state, such as when arrival rate exceeds service rate (as in the slow teller system first described). Then the analyst is forced to focus on transient state system behavior.] Nonparametric statistics such as the median test, the number-of-runs test, or the sign test are sometimes used to verify the stability of a pattern of observations around a central point. Some simulation analysts simply extend the length of the simulation run to average in transient data, while others truncate transient output before gathering sample data that are to be used for hypothesis testing or interval estimation concerning steady state performance.

Conclusion

On the one hand, simulation is a convenient and effective forecasting technique that can be utilized in the presence of nonlinear inputs and outputs. On the other hand, simulation methodology incorporates a number of statistical tools, such as correlation analysis and hypothesis testing, which are common to more standard forecasting methods as well.

Unless the system whose performance is to be predicted is decidedly nonlinear, conventional forecasting techniques should always be considered first for reasons of economy. Nevertheless, it is reassuring to be aware that a method exists for forecasting the behavior of a system, no matter how complex or unusual, if it is necessary or desirable to do so.

PROBLEMS

1. Under what circumstances is simulation a desirable forecasting method?
2. Define the steps in designing and executing a simulation for forecasting purposes.

3. Select a simple waiting-line situation with which you are familiar, and describe how you would repeat the procedures in this chapter for data collected from that system. Suggest a simple modification to the structure of the system. State how you would perform a statistical experiment to test if it would make a significant difference in system performance.

4. Explain the general nature and purpose of each statistical technique discussed in this chapter (e.g., goodness-of-fit tests, sample size determination, testing for autocorrelation, testing for steady state, and testing the difference in means).

BIBLIOGRAPHY

BOBILLIER, P. A., KAHAN, B. C., AND PROBST, A. R., *Simulation With GPSS and GPSS V,* Englewood Cliffs, N.J.: Prentice-Hall, 1970.

EMSHOFF, J. R., AND SISSON, R. L., *Design and Use of Computer Simulation Models,* New York: MacMillan, 1970.

FISHMAN, G. S., *Concepts and Methods in Discrete Event Digital Simulation,* New York: John Wiley and Sons, 1973.

GORDON, G., *System Simulation,* Second Edition. Englewood Cliffs, N.J.: Prentice-Hall, 1978.

GROSS, C. W., AND PETERSON, R. T., *Business Forecasting,* Boston: Houghton-Mifflin, 1976.

MAISEL, H., AND GNUGNOLI, G., *Simulation of Discrete Stochastic Systems,* Chicago: Science Research Associates, 1972.

MCMILLAN, C., AND GONZALEZ, R. F., *Systems Analysis: A Computer Approach to Decision Models,* Third Edition, Homewood, Ill.: Richard D. Irwin, Inc., 1973.

MEIER, R. C., NEWELL, W. T., AND PAZER, H. L., *Simulation in Business and Economics,* Englewood Cliffs, N.J.: Prentice-Hall, 1969.

MONTGOMERY, D. C., AND JOHNSON, L. A., *Forecasting and Time Series Analysis,* New York: McGraw-Hill, 1976.

NAYLOR, T. H., BALINTFY, J. L., BURDICK, D. S., AND CHU, K., *Computer Simulation Techniques,* New York: John Wiley and Sons, 1966.

PINDYCK, R. S., AND RUBINFELD, D. L., *Econometric Models and Economic Forecasts,* New York: McGraw-Hill, 1976.

SCHMIDT, J. W., AND TAYLOR, R. E., *Simulation and Analysis of Industrial Systems,* Homewood, Ill.: Richard D. Irwin, Inc., 1970.

SCHRIEBER, A. N. (ED.), *Corporate Simulation Models,* Seattle: University of Washington, 1970.

SHANNON, R. E., *Systems Simulation: The Art and Science,* Englewood Cliffs, N.J.: Prentice-Hall, 1975.

332

APPENDICES

Formulas

CORRELATION DERIVATION

$$r = \frac{\Sigma Z_x Z_Y}{N} = \Sigma \frac{\left(\dfrac{X - \mu_x}{\sigma_x}\right)\left(\dfrac{Y - \mu_x}{\sigma_Y}\right)}{N}$$

$$= \frac{\dfrac{\Sigma(X - \mu_x)(Y - \mu_Y)}{\sqrt{\dfrac{\Sigma X^2}{N} - \left(\dfrac{\Sigma X}{N}\right)^2} \sqrt{\dfrac{\Sigma Y^2}{N} - \left(\dfrac{\Sigma Y}{N}\right)^2}}}{N}$$

$$r = \frac{\dfrac{\Sigma(X - \mu_x)(Y - \mu_Y)}{\sqrt{\dfrac{N\Sigma X^2 - (\Sigma X)^2}{N^2}} \sqrt{\dfrac{N\Sigma Y^2 - (\Sigma Y)^2}{N^2}}}}{N}$$

$$\frac{N\,\Sigma(X - \mu_x)(Y - \mu_Y)}{\sqrt{N\Sigma X^2 - (\Sigma X)^2} \sqrt{N\Sigma Y^2 - (\Sigma Y)^2}}$$

$$r = \frac{N\,\Sigma(XY - Y\mu_x - X\mu_Y + \mu_x\mu_Y)}{\sqrt{N\Sigma X^2 - (\Sigma X)^2} \sqrt{N\Sigma Y^2 - (\Sigma Y)^2}}$$

$$r = \frac{N\left[\Sigma XY - \dfrac{\Sigma X \Sigma Y}{N} - \dfrac{\Sigma X \Sigma Y}{N} + N\left(\dfrac{\Sigma X}{N}\dfrac{\Sigma Y}{N}\right)\right]}{\sqrt{N\Sigma X^2 - (\Sigma X)^2}\ \sqrt{N\Sigma Y^2 - (\Sigma Y)^2}}$$

$$r = \frac{N\left(\Sigma XY - \dfrac{\Sigma X \Sigma Y}{N} - \dfrac{\Sigma X \Sigma Y}{N} + \dfrac{\Sigma X \Sigma Y}{N}\right)}{\sqrt{N\Sigma X^2 - (\Sigma X)^2}\ \sqrt{N\Sigma Y^2 - (\Sigma Y)^2}}$$

$$r = \frac{N\left(\Sigma XY - \dfrac{\Sigma X \Sigma Y}{N}\right)}{\sqrt{N\Sigma X^2 - (\Sigma X)^2}\ \sqrt{N\Sigma Y^2 - (\Sigma Y)^2}}$$

$$r = \frac{N\Sigma XY - \Sigma X \Sigma Y}{\sqrt{N\Sigma X^2 - (\Sigma X)^2}\ \sqrt{N\Sigma Y^2 - (\Sigma Y)^2}}$$

LEAST-SQUARES DERIVATION

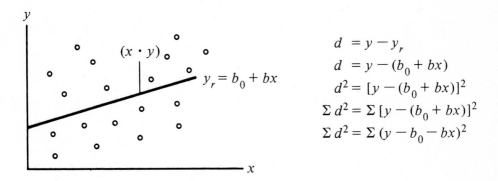

$$d = y - y_r$$
$$d = y - (b_0 + bx)$$
$$d^2 = [y - (b_0 + bx)]^2$$
$$\Sigma d^2 = \Sigma [y - (b_0 + bx)]^2$$
$$\Sigma d^2 = \Sigma (y - b_0 - bx)^2$$

PARTIAL DERIVATIVES

$$\frac{\delta \Sigma}{\delta b} = 2\Sigma(y - bx - b_0)(-x)$$

$$= 2\Sigma(-xy + bx^2 + b_0 x)$$

$$\frac{\delta \Sigma}{\delta b_0} = 2\Sigma(y - bx - b_0)(-1)$$

$$= 2\Sigma(-y + bx + b_0)$$

TO OBTAIN MINIMUMS SET PARTIALS = 0

$$\frac{\delta \Sigma}{\delta b} = 0: \quad 2\Sigma(-xy + bx^2 + b_0 x) = 0 \qquad \frac{\delta \Sigma}{\delta b_0} = 0: \quad 2\Sigma(-y + bx + b_0) = 0$$

$$\Sigma(-xy + bx^2 + b_0 x) = 0 \qquad\qquad \Sigma(-y + bx + b_0) = 0$$

$$-\Sigma xy + b_0 \Sigma x + bx^2 = 0 \qquad\qquad -\Sigma y + Nb_0 + b\Sigma x = 0$$

FIND A b_0 AND b SUCH THAT Σd^2 IS A MINIMUM

$$b_0 \Sigma x + b\Sigma x^2 = \Sigma xy \quad *(N)$$

$$\underline{Nb_0 + b\Sigma x = \Sigma y \quad *(\Sigma x)}$$

$$Nb_0 \Sigma x + Nb\Sigma x^2 = N\Sigma xy$$

$$\underline{Nb_0 \Sigma x + b(\Sigma x)^2 = \Sigma x \Sigma y}$$

$$Nb\Sigma x2 - b(\Sigma x)^2 = N\Sigma xy - \Sigma x \Sigma y$$

$$b(N\Sigma x^2 - (\Sigma x)^2) = N\Sigma xy - \Sigma x \Sigma y \qquad\qquad \text{SLOPE FORMULA}$$

$$b = \frac{N\Sigma xy - \Sigma x \Sigma y}{N\Sigma x^2 - (\Sigma x)^2}$$

$$Nb_0 + b\Sigma x = \Sigma y$$

$$Nb_0 = \Sigma y - b\Sigma x$$

$$b_0 = \frac{\Sigma y}{N}\; \frac{b\Sigma x}{N} \qquad\qquad \text{Y-INTERCEPT FORMULA}$$

$$b_0 = \bar{y} - b\bar{x}$$

Tables

B

TABLE B.1   *Table of Random Digits.**

43732	52254	51717	24199	14995	28638	94266	95896	97286	93363
29127	93840	32774	55120	65026	42329	24853	20025	76811	81401
24907	74544	66673	00700	66710	66969	74990	20032	21995	06036
27618	67022	10133	91336	55075	03262	96546	49329	25175	18575
76254	64180	39786	34653	87041	62316	40460	13053	81241	04385
62416	36939	55843	27845	49480	77704	47938	49743	45798	81296
31941	66753	21574	01290	78304	10121	25145	44925	96389	02748
48769	40172	91480	49345	40787	26343	44517	27111	69002	07130
19841	14663	09283	61166	78039	33309	94009	13456	49850	07814
95278	45022	96058	47206	45136	06897	13029	98610	47895	29255
11681	17274	17775	70451	22664	67014	88052	07139	86031	41752
19662	09277	24043	30468	25419	44660	52122	77683	89932	61867
38220	45565	14942	08320	43174	92076	52890	98982	51549	24199
74342	90018	21144	33405	63152	95923	77259	09132	55290	49080
36330	30763	76197	40481	45306	40321	67829	49329	59366	84654
55667	24316	35987	50597	08340	19788	50319	57122	43216	85841
97044	03505	01390	48719	77194	08143	85905	95243	18460	81857
10801	41372	68587	75813	97859	89824	00856	68893	89724	13555
62086	15756	82269	62301	54394	88005	69419	92167	81404	27619
82969	15207	17095	99636	32773	53706	01064	71431	60025	76456

TABLE B.1 *Table of Random Digits. (cont.)*

```
92689 66288 41679 28175 43057 31307 79854 99889 65340 67466
82257 95475 34860 82583 88431 28935 87509 20727 37989 73978
03500 89229 23013 34269 86323 82028 09026 03845 47049 09033
49935 10627 06590 00319 21022 67060 97351 83563 49386 68421
90394 48453 98568 59114 67484 92490 15912 17007 06152 46270

46528 28504 62341 69676 36687 62032 57678 78816 59456 60820
61139 84737 07313 96815 80079 28473 00893 54263 84568 89126
72052 17047 82703 98378 61551 52642 01676 82279 78996 97089
96412 05437 41920 79190 96446 75572 86149 04486 64642 99840
38542 80332 61559 51540 27508 77623 52532 76913 03934 25756

13240 10094 36445 78755 02259 79075 86304 44848 05617 19112
73520 51141 98860 57952 91325 24661 21656 40584 88869 66593
80523 22661 47316 22278 41056 46455 72563 09140 32256 48198
46746 30636 21103 65113 40794 62196 72234 26648 48913 34334
93786 00483 52986 55922 30830 40750 63223 63371 65047 20933

16286 09146 89517 87223 79385 41937 91686 50357 70316 09026
46721 17036 59388 17337 96097 60336 81050 02307 69823 10816
52053 30051 42444 54844 77985 70091 60464 79822 63536 15688
67526 93477 21244 58252 75052 19270 62520 47603 61395 25861
77360 06067 93429 68336 45621 75564 73052 00972 10065 97831

46689 76298 22771 73816 08640 77702 13451 51694 53359 83400
01401 68433 58746 01648 68134 22848 67255 66420 70730 78826
53605 54676 09068 58018 61071 32171 47150 68624 56213 75608
01524 52265 96518 45107 36343 93236 84759 25889 43255 98284
12742 23345 74617 19338 29434 91944 62796 37134 18666 31430
```

338

TABLE B.2 *Table of Areas for Standard Normal Probability Distribution.**

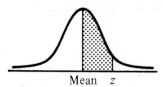

Mean   *z*

z	.00	.01	.02	.03	.04	.05	.06	.07	.08	.09
0.0	.0000	.0040	.0080	.0120	.0160	.0199	.0239	.0279	.0319	.0359
0.1	.0398	.0438	.0478	.0517	.0557	.0596	.0636	.0675	.0714	.0753
0.2	.0793	.0832	.0871	.0910	.0948	.0987	.1026	.1064	.1103	.1141
0.3	.1179	.1217	.1255	.1293	.1331	.1368	.1406	.1443	.1480	.1517
0.4	.1554	.1591	.1628	.1664	.1700	.1736	.1772	.1808	.1844	.1879
0.5	.1915	.1950	.1985	.2019	.2054	.2088	.2123	.2157	.2190	.2224
0.6	.2257	.2291	.2324	.2357	.2389	.2422	.2454	.2486	.2518	.2549
0.7	.2580	.2612	.2642	.2673	.2704	.2734	.2764	.2794	.2823	.2852
0.8	.2881	.2910	.2939	.2967	.2995	.3023	.3051	.3078	.3106	.3133
0.9	.3159	.3186	.3212	.3238	.3264	.3289	.3315	.3340	.3365	.3389
1.0	.3413	.3438	.3461	.3485	.3508	.3531	.3554	.3577	.3599	.3621
1.1	.3643	.3665	.3686	.3708	.3729	.3749	.3770	.3790	.3810	.3830
1.2	.3849	.3869	.3888	.3907	3925	.3944	.3962	.3980	.3997	.4015
1.3	.4032	.4049	.4066	.4082	.4099	.4115	.4131	.4147	.4162	.4177
1.4	.4192	.4207	.4222	.4236	.4251	.4265	.4279	.4292	.4306	.4319
1.5	.4332	.4345	.4357	.4370	.4382	.4394	.4406	.4418	.4429	.4441
1.6	.4452	.4463	.4474	.4484	.4495	.4505	.4515	.4525	.4535	.4545
1.7	.4554	.4564	.4573	.4582	.4591	.4599	.4608	.4616	.4625	.4633
1.8	.4641	.4649	.4656	.4664	.4671	.4678	.4686	.4693	.4699	.4706
1.9	.4713	.4719	.4726	.4732	.4738	.4744	.4750	.4756	.4761	.4767
2.0	.4772	.4778	.4783	.4788	.4793	.4798	.4803	.4808	.4812	.4817
2.1	.4821	.4826	.4830	.4834	.4838	.4842	.4846	.4850	.4854	.4857
2.2	.4861	.4864	.4868	.4871	.4875	.4878	.4881	.4884	.4887	.4890
2.3	.4893	.4896	.4898	.4901	.4904	.4906	.4909	.4911	.4913	.4916
2.4	.4918	.4920	.4922	.4925	.4927	.4929	.4931	.4932	.4934	.4936
2.5	.4938	.4940	.4941	.4943	.4945	.4946	.4948	.4949	.4951	.4952
2.6	.4953	.4955	.4956	.4957	.4959	.4960	.4961	.4962	.4963	.4964
2.7	.4965	.4966	.4967	.4968	.4969	.4970	.4971	.4972	.4973	.4974
2.8	.4974	.4975	.4976	.4977	.4977	.4978	.4979	.4979	.4980	.4981
2.9	.4981	.4982	.4982	.4983	.4984	.4984	.4985	.4985	.4986	.4986
3.0	.49865	.4987	.4987	.4988	.4988	.4989	.4989	.4989	.4990	.4990
4.0	.4999683									

Illustration: For *z* = 1.93, shaded area is .4732 out of total area of 1.

TABLE B.3　*Poisson Probabilities.*

					μx					
X	0.1	0.2	0.3	0.4	0.5	0.6	0.7	0.8	0.9	1.0
0	.9048	.8187	.7408	.6703	.6065	.5488	.4966	.4493	.4066	.3679
1	.0905	.1637	.2222	.2681	.3033	.3293	.3476	.3595	.3659	.3679
2	.0045	.0164	.0333	.0536	.0758	.0988	.1217	.1438	.1647	.1839
3	.0002	.0011	.0033	.0072	.0126	.0198	.0284	.0383	.0494	.0613
4		.0001	.0002	.0007	.0016	.0030	.0050	.0077	.0111	.0153
5				.0001	.0002	.0004	.0007	.0012	.0020	.0031
6							.0001	.0002	.0003	.0005
7										.0001

					μx					
X	1.5	2.0	2.5	3.0	3.5	4.0	4.5	5.0	6.0	7.0
0	.2231	.1353	.0821	.0498	.0302	.0183	.0111	.0067	.0025	.0009
1	.3347	.2707	.2052	.1494	.1057	.0733	.0500	.0337	.0149	.0064
2	.2510	.2707	.2565	.2240	.1850	.1465	.1125	.0842	.0446	.0223
3	.1255	.1804	.2138	.2240	.2158	.1954	.1687	.1404	.0892	.0521
4	.0471	.0902	.1336	.1680	.1888	.1954	.1898	.1755	.1339	.0912
5	.0141	.0361	.0668	.1008	.1322	.1563	.1708	.1755	.1606	.1277
6	.0035	.0120	.0278	.0504	.0771	.1042	.1281	.1462	.1606	.1490
7	.0008	.0034	.0099	.0216	.0385	.0595	.0824	.1044	.1377	.1490
8	.0001	.0009	.0031	.0081	.0169	.0298	.0463	.0653	.1033	.1304
9		.0002	.0009	.0027	.0066	.0132	.0232	.0363	.0688	.1014
10			.0002	.0008	.0023	.0053	.0104	.0181	.0413	.0710
11				.0002	.0007	.0019	.0043	.0082	.0225	.0452
12				.0001	.0002	.0006	.0016	.0034	.0113	.0264
13					.0001	.0002	.0006	.0013	.0052	.0142
14						.0001	.0002	.0005	.0022	.0071
15							.0001	.0002	.0009	.0033
16									.0003	.0014
17									.0001	.0006
18										.0002
19										.0001

Example:　If $\mu_x = 1$, $P(X = 2) = .1839$.
Source:　Abridged from E. C. Molina, *Poisson's Exponential Binominal Limit*. New Jersey: Bell Telephone Laboratories, reprinted by permission.

TABLE B.4   *Critical Values of t.*

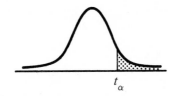

t_α

d.f.	$t_{.100}$	$t_{.050}$	$t_{.025}$	$t_{.010}$	$t_{.005}$
1	3.078	6.314	12.706	31.821	63.657
2	1.886	2.920	4.303	6.965	9.925
3	1.638	2.353	3.182	4.541	5.841
4	1.533	2.132	2.776	3.747	4.604
5	1.476	2.015	2.571	3.365	4.032
6	1.440	1.943	2.447	3.143	3.707
7	1.415	1.895	2.365	2.998	3.499
8	1.397	1.860	2.306	2.896	3.355
9	1.383	1.833	2.262	2.821	3.250
10	1.372	1.812	2.228	2.764	3.169
11	1.363	1.796	2.201	2.718	3.106
12	1.356	1.782	2.179	2.681	3.055
13	1.350	1.771	2.160	2.650	3.012
14	1.345	1.761	2.145	2.624	2.977
15	1.341	1.753	2.131	2.602	2.947
16	1.337	1.746	2.120	2.583	2.921
17	1.333	1.740	2.110	2.567	2.898
18	1.330	1.734	2.101	2.552	2.878
19	1.328	1.729	2.093	2.539	2.861
20	1.325	1.725	2.086	2.528	2.845
21	1.323	1.721	2.080	2.518	2.831
22	1.321	1.717	2.074	2.508	2.819
23	1.319	1.714	2.069	2.500	2.807
24	1.318	1.711	2.064	2.492	2.797
25	1.316	1.708	2.060	2.485	2.787
26	1.315	1.706	2.056	2.479	2.779
27	1.314	1.703	2.052	2.473	2.771
28	1.313	1.701	2.048	2.467	2.763
29	1.311	1.699	2.045	2.462	2.756
inf.	1.282	1.645	1.960	2.326	2.576

From "Table of Percentage Points of the *t*-Distribution." Computed by Maxine Merrington, *Biometrika*, Vol. 32 (1941), p. 300. Reproduced by permission of Professor D. V. Lindley.

TABLE B.5 *Critical Values of Chi Squares.*

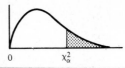

d.f.	$\chi^2 0.995$	$\chi^2 0.990$	$\chi^2 0.975$	$\chi^2 0.950$	$\chi^2 0.900$
1	0.0000393	0.0001571	0.0009821	0.0039321	0.0157908
2	0.0100251	0.0201007	0.0506356	0.102587	0.210720
3	0.0717212	0.114832	0.215795	0.351846	0.584375
4	0.206990	0.297110	0.484419	0.710721	1.063623
5	0.411740	0.554300	0.831211	1.145476	1.61031
6	0.675727	0.872085	1.237347	1.63539	2.20413
7	0.989265	1.239043	1.68987	2.16735	2.83311
8	1.344419	1.646482	2.17973	2.73264	3.48954
9	1.734926	2.087912	2.70039	3.32511	4.168216
10	2.15585	2.55821	3.24697	3.94030	4.86518
11	2.60321	3.05347	3.81575	4.57481	5.57779
12	3.07382	3.57056	4.40379	5.22603	6.30380
13	3.56503	4.10691	5.00874	5.89186	7.04150
14	4.07468	4.66043	5.62872	6.57063	7.78953
15	4.60094	5.22935	6.26214	7.26094	8.54675
16	5.14224	5.81221	6.90766	7.96164	9.31223
17	5.69724	6.40776	7.56418	8.67176	10.0852
18	6.26481	7.01491	8.23075	9.39046	10.8649
19	6.84398	7.63273	8.90655	10.1170	11.6509
20	7.43386	8.26040	9.59083	10.8508	12.4426
21	8.03366	8.89720	10.28293	11.5913	13.2396
22	8.64272	9.54249	10.9823	12.3380	14.0415
23	9.26042	10.19567	11.6885	13.0905	14.8479
24	9.88623	10.8564	12.4011	13.8484	15.6587
25	10.5197	11.5240	13.1197	14.6114	16.4734
26	11.1603	12.1981	13.8439	15.3791	17.2919
27	11.8076	12.8786	14.5733	16.1513	18.1138
28	12.4613	13.5648	15.3079	16.9279	18.9302
29	13.1211	14.2565	16.0471	17.7083	19.7677
30	13.7867	14.9535	16.7908	18.4926	20.5992
40	20.7065	22.1643	24.4331	26.5093	29.0505
50	27.9907	29.7067	32.3574	34.7642	37.6886
60	35.5347	37.4848	40.4817	43.1879	46.4589
70	43.2752	45.4418	48.7576	51.7393	55.3290
80	51.1720	53.5400	57.1532	60.3915	64.2778
90	59.1963	61.7541	65.6466	69.1260	73.2912
100	67.3276	70.0648	74.2219	77.9295	82.3581

TABLE B.5   *Critical Values of Chi Square. (cont.)*

$\chi^2 0.100$	$\chi^2 0.050$	$\chi^2 0.025$	$\chi^2 0.010$	$\chi^2 0.005$	*d.f.*
2.70554	3.84146	5.02389	6.63490	7.87944	1
4.60517	5.99147	7.37776	9.21034	10.5966	2
6.25139	7.81473	9.34840	11.3449	12.8381	3
7.77944	9.48773	11.1433	13.2767	14.8602	4
9.23635	11.0705	12.8325	15.0863	16.7496	5
10.6446	12.5916	14.4494	16.8119	18.5476	6
12.0170	14.0671	16.0128	18.4753	20.2777	7
13.3616	15.5073	17.5346	20.0902	21.9550	8
14.6837	16.9190	19.0228	21.6660	23.5893	9
15.9871	18.3070	20.4831	23.2093	25.1882	10
17.2750	19.6751	21.9200	24.7250	26.7569	11
18.5494	21.0261	23.3367	26.2170	28.2995	12
19.8119	22.3621	24.7356	27.6883	29.8194	13
21.0642	23.6848	26.1190	29.1413	31.3193	14
22.3072	24.9958	27.4884	30.5779	32.8013	15
23.5418	26.2962	28.8454	31.9999	34.2672	16
24.7690	27.5871	30.1910	33.4087	35.7185	17
25.9894	28.8693	31.5264	34.8053	37.1564	18
27.2036	30.1435	32.8523	36.1908	38.5822	19
28.4120	31.4104	34.1696	37.5662	39.9968	20
29.6151	32.6705	35.4789	38.9321	41.4010	21
30.8133	33.9244	36.7807	40.2894	42.7956	22
32.0069	35.1725	38.0757	41.6384	44.1813	23
33.1963	36.4151	39.3641	42.9798	45.5585	24
34.3816	37.6525	40.6465	44.3141	46.9278	25
35.5631	38.8852	41.9232	45.6417	48.2899	26
36.7412	40.1133	43.1944	46.9630	49.6449	27
37.9159	41.3372	44.4607	48.2782	50.9933	28
39.0875	42.5569	45.7222	49.5879	52.3356	29
40.2560	43.7729	46.9792	50.8922	53.6720	30
51.8050	55.7585	59.3417	63.6907	66.7659	40
63.1671	67.5048	71.4202	76.1539	79.4900	50
74.3970	79.0819	83.2976	88.3794	91.9517	60
85.5271	90.5312	95.0231	100.425	104.215	70
96.5782	101.879	106.629	112.329	116.321	80
107.565	113.145	118.136	124.116	128.299	90
118.498	124.342	129.561	135.807	140.169	100

From "Tables of the Percentage Points of the χ^2-Distribution," *Biometrika*, Vol. 32 (1941), pp. 188–189, by Catherine M. Thompson. Reproduced by permission of Professor D. V. Lindley.

TABLE B.6   *Binomial Probabilities.*

						p					
n	$\bar{p}$	.05	.10	.15	.20	.25	.30	.35	.40	.45	.50
2	0	.9025	.8100	.7225	.6400	.5625	.4900	.4225	.3600	.3025	.2500
	$\frac{1}{2}$	.0950	.1800	.2550	.3200	.3750	.4200	.4550	.4800	.4950	.5000
	1	.0025	.0100	.0225	.0400	.0625	.0900	.1225	.1600	.2025	.2500
3	0	.8574	.7290	.6141	.5120	.4219	.3430	.2746	.2160	.1664	.1250
	$\frac{1}{3}$	.1354	.2430	.3251	.3840	.4219	.4410	.4436	.4320	.4084	.3750
	$\frac{2}{3}$	.0071	.0270	.0574	.0960	.1406	.1890	.2389	.2880	.3341	.3750
	1	.0001	.0010	.0034	.0080	.0156	.0270	.0429	.0640	.0911	.1250
4	0	.8145	.6561	.5220	.4096	.3164	.2401	.1785	.1296	.0915	.0625
	$\frac{1}{4}$	.1715	.2916	.3685	.4096	.4219	.4116	.3845	.3456	.2995	.2500
	$\frac{2}{4}$	.0135	.0486	.0975	.1536	.2109	.2646	.3105	.3456	.3675	.3750
	$\frac{3}{4}$	.0005	.0036	.0115	.0256	.0469	.0756	.1115	.1536	.2005	.2500
	1		.0001	.0005	.0016	.0039	.0081	.0150	.0256	.0410	.0625
5	0	.7738	.5905	.4437	.3277	.2373	.1681	.1160	.0778	.0503	.0312
	$\frac{1}{5}$	.2036	.3280	.3915	.4096	.3955	.3602	.3124	.2592	.2059	.1562
	$\frac{2}{5}$	.0214	.0729	.1382	.2048	.2637	.3087	.3364	.3456	.3369	.3125
	$\frac{3}{5}$	.0011	.0081	.0244	.0512	.0879	.1323	.1811	.2304	.2757	.3125
	$\frac{4}{5}$		.0004	.0022	.0064	.0146	.0284	.0488	.0768	.1128	.1562
	1			.0001	.0003	.0010	.0024	.0053	.0102	.0185	.0312
6	0	.7351	.5314	.3771	.2621	.1780	.1176	.0754	.0467	.0277	.0156
	$\frac{1}{6}$	.2321	.3543	.3993	.3932	.3560	.3025	.2437	.1866	.1359	.0938
	$\frac{2}{6}$	.0305	.0984	.1762	.2458	.2966	.3241	.3280	.3110	.2780	.2344
	$\frac{3}{6}$	.0021	.0146	.0415	.0819	.1318	.1852	.2355	.2765	.3032	.3125
	$\frac{4}{6}$	.0001	.0012	.0055	.0154	.0330	.0595	.0951	.1382	.1861	.2344
	$\frac{5}{6}$		.0001	.0004	.0015	.0044	.0102	.0205	.0369	.0609	.0938
	1				.0001	.0002	.0007	.0018	.0041	.0083	.0156
7	0	.6983	.4783	.3206	.2097	.1335	.0824	.0490	.0280	.0152	.0078
	$\frac{1}{7}$	.2573	.3720	.3960	.3670	.3115	.2471	.1848	.1306	.0872	.0547
	$\frac{2}{7}$	.0406	.1240	.2097	.2753	.3115	.3177	.2985	.2613	.2140	.1641
	$\frac{3}{7}$	.0036	.0230	.0617	.1147	.1730	.2269	.2679	.2903	.2918	.2734
	$\frac{4}{7}$	.0002	.0026	.0109	.0287	.0577	.0972	.1442	.1935	.2388	.2734
	$\frac{5}{7}$		.0002	.0012	.0043	.0115	.0250	.0466	.0774	.1172	.1641
	$\frac{6}{7}$			.0001	.0004	.0013	.0036	.0084	.0172	.0320	.0547
	1					.0001	.0002	.0006	.0016	.0037	.0078
8	0	.6634	.4305	.2725	.1678	.1001	.0576	.0319	.0168	.0084	.0039
	$\frac{1}{8}$	.2793	.3826	.3847	.3355	.2670	.1977	.1373	.0896	.0548	.0312
	$\frac{2}{8}$	.0515	.1488	.2376	.2936	.3115	.2965	.2587	.2090	.1569	.1094
	$\frac{3}{8}$	.0054	.0331	.0839	.1468	.2076	.2541	.2786	.2787	.2568	.2188
	$\frac{4}{8}$	.0004	.0046	.0185	.0459	.0865	.1361	.1875	.2322	.2627	.2734
	$\frac{5}{8}$		.0004	.0026	.0092	.0231	.0467	.0808	.1239	.1719	.2188
	$\frac{6}{8}$			.0002	.0011	.0038	.0100	.0217	.0413	.0703	.1094
	$\frac{7}{8}$				.0001	.0004	.0012	.0033	.0079	.0164	.0312
	1						.0001	.0002	.0007	.0017	.0039

Example: If $p = .25$, $n = 5$, $P(\bar{p} = 3/5) = .0879$.

TABLE B.7   *Table of F Distribution.*

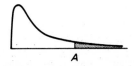

A

F scale value corresponding to area .05 in right tail in light-face type

F scale value corresponding to area .01 in right tail in bold-face type

δ_1	δ_2									
	1	2	3	4	5	6	7	8	9	10
1	161	200	216	225	230	234	237	239	241	242
	4,052	**4,999**	**5,403**	**5,625**	**5,764**	**5,859**	**5,928**	**5,981**	**6,022**	**6,056**
2	18.51	19.00	19.16	19.25	19.30	19.33	19.36	19.37	19.38	19.39
	98.49	**99.00**	**99.17**	**99.25**	**99.30**	**99.33**	**99.36**	**99.37**	**99.39**	**99.40**
3	10.13	9.55	9.28	9.12	9.01	8.94	8.88	8.84	8.81	8.78
	34.12	**30.82**	**29.46**	**28.71**	**28.24**	**27.91**	**27.67**	**27.49**	**27.34**	**27.23**
4	7.71	6.94	6.59	6.39	6.26	6.16	6.09	6.04	6.00	5.96
	21.20	**18.00**	**16.69**	**15.98**	**15.52**	**15.21**	**14.98**	**14.80**	**14.66**	**14.54**
5	6.61	5.79	5.41	5.19	5.05	4.95	4.88	4.82	4.78	4.74
	16.26	**13.27**	**12.06**	**11.39**	**10.97**	**10.67**	**10.45**	**10.29**	**10.15**	**10.05**
6	5.99	5.14	4.76	4.53	4.39	4.28	4.21	4.15	4.10	4.06
	13.74	**10.92**	**9.78**	**9.15**	**8.75**	**8.47**	**8.26**	**8.10**	**7.98**	**7.87**
7	5.59	4.74	4.35	4.12	3.97	3.87	3.79	3.73	3.68	3.63
	12.25	**9.55**	**8.45**	**7.85**	**7.46**	**7.19**	**7.00**	**6.84**	**6.71**	**6.62**
8	5.32	4.46	4.07	3.84	3.69	3.58	3.50	3.44	3.39	3.34
	11.26	**8.65**	**7.59**	**7.01**	**6.63**	**6.37**	**6.19**	**6.03**	**5.91**	**5.82**
9	5.12	4.26	3.86	3.63	3.48	3.37	3.29	3.23	3.18	3.13
	10.56	**8.02**	**6.99**	**6.42**	**6.06**	**5.80**	**5.62**	**5.47**	**5.35**	**5.26**
10	4.96	4.10	3.71	3.48	3.33	3.22	3.14	3.07	3.02	2.97
	10.04	**7.56**	**6.55**	**5.99**	**5.64**	**5.39**	**5.21**	**5.06**	**4.95**	**4.85**
11	4.84	3.98	3.59	3.36	3.20	3.09	3.01	2.95	2.90	2.86
	9.65	**7.20**	**6.22**	**5.67**	**5.32**	**5.07**	**4.88**	**4.74**	**4.63**	**4.54**

(Continued)

TABLE B.7   *Table of F Distribution (Cont.).*

δ_1	δ_2									
	1	2	3	4	5	6	7	8	9	10
12	4.75	3.88	3.49	3.26	3.11	3.00	2.92	2.85	2.80	2.76
	9.33	6.93	5.95	5.41	5.06	4.82	4.65	4.50	4.39	4.30
13	4.67	3.80	3.41	3.18	3.02	2.92	2.84	2.77	2.72	2.67
	9.07	6.70	5.74	5.20	4.86	4.62	4.44	4.30	4.19	4.10
14	4.60	3.74	3.34	3.11	2.96	2.85	2.77	2.70	2.65	2.60
	8.86	6.51	5.56	5.03	4.69	4.46	4.28	4.14	4.03	3.94
15	4.54	3.68	3.29	3.06	2.90	2.79	2.70	2.64	2.59	2.55
	8.68	6.36	5.42	4.89	4.56	4.32	4.14	4.00	3.89	3.80
16	4.49	3.63	3.24	3.01	2.85	2.74	2.66	2.59	2.54	2.49
	8.53	6.23	5.29	4.77	4.44	4.20	4.03	3.89	3.78	3.69
17	4.45	3.59	3.20	2.96	2.81	2.70	2.62	2.55	2.50	2.45
	8.40	6.11	5.18	4.67	4.34	4.10	3.93	3.79	3.68	3.59
18	4.41	3.55	3.16	2.93	2.77	2.66	2.58	2.51	2.46	2.41
	8.28	6.01	5.09	4.58	4.25	4.01	3.85	3.71	3.60	3.51
19	4.38	3.52	3.13	2.90	2.74	2.63	2.55	2.48	2.43	2.38
	8.18	5.93	5.01	4.50	4.17	3.94	3.77	3.63	3.52	3.43
20	4.35	3.49	3.10	2.87	2.71	2.60	2.52	2.45	2.40	2.35
	8.10	5.85	4.94	4.43	4.10	3.87	3.71	3.56	3.45	3.37
21	4.32	3.47	3.07	2.84	2.68	2.57	2.49	2.42	2.37	2.32
	8.02	5.78	4.87	4.37	4.04	3.81	3.65	3.51	3.40	3.31
22	4.30	3.44	3.05	2.82	2.66	2.55	2.47	2.40	2.35	2.30
	7.94	5.72	4.82	4.31	3.99	3.76	3.59	3.45	3.35	3.26
23	4.28	3.42	3.03	2.80	2.64	2.53	2.45	2.38	2.32	2.28
	7.88	5.66	4.76	4.26	3.94	3.71	3.54	3.41	3.30	3.21
24	4.26	3.40	3.01	2.78	2.62	2.51	2.43	2.36	2.30	2.26
	7.82	5.61	4.72	4.22	3.90	3.67	3.50	3.36	3.25	3.17
25	4.24	3.38	2.99	2.76	2.60	2.49	2.41	2.34	2.28	2.24
	7.77	5.57	4.68	4.18	3.86	3.63	3.46	3.32	3.21	3.13

Illustration: The F scale value for $\delta_2 = 3$, $\delta_1 = 10$ corresponding to area .01 in right tail is 6.55.

Source: Abridged by permission from *Statistical Methods*, 6th ed., by George W. Snedecor and William C. Cochran. © 1967 by the Iowa State University Press, Ames, Iowa.

TABLE B.8   *Five-Place Logarithms.*

N	0	1	2	3	4	5	6	7	8	9
0	− ∞	00000	30103	47712	60206	69897	77815	84510	90309	95424
10	00000	00432	00860	01284	01703	02119	02531	02938	03342	03743
11	04139	04532	04922	05308	05690	06070	06446	06819	07188	07555
12	07918	08279	08636	08991	09342	09691	10037	10380	10721	11059
13	11394	11727	12057	12385	12710	13033	13354	13672	13988	14301
14	14613	14922	15229	15534	15836	16137	16435	16732	17026	17319
15	17609	17898	18184	18469	18752	19033	19312	19590	19866	20140
16	20412	20683	20952	21219	21484	21748	22011	22272	22531	22789
17	23045	23300	23533	23805	24055	24304	24551	24797	25042	25285
18	25527	25768	26007	26245	26482	26717	26951	27184	27416	27646
19	27875	28103	28330	28556	28780	29003	29226	29447	29667	29885
20	30103	30320	30535	30750	30963	31175	31387	31597	31806	32015
21	32222	32428	32634	32838	33041	33244	33445	33646	33846	34044
22	34242	34439	34635	34830	35025	35218	35411	35603	35793	35984
23	36173	36361	36549	36736	36922	37107	37291	37475	37658	37840
24	38021	38202	38382	38561	38739	38917	39094	39270	39445	39620
25	39794	39967	40140	40312	40483	40654	40824	40993	41162	41330
26	41497	41664	41830	41996	42160	42325	42488	42651	42813	42975
27	43136	43297	43457	43616	43775	43933	44091	44248	44404	44560
28	44716	44871	45025	45179	45332	45484	45637	45788	45939	46090
29	46240	46389	46538	46687	46835	46982	47129	47276	47422	47567
30	47712	47857	48001	48144	48287	48430	48572	48714	48855	48996
31	49136	49276	49415	49554	49693	49831	49969	50106	50243	50379
32	50515	50651	50786	50920	51055	51188	51322	51455	51587	51720
33	51851	51983	52114	52244	52375	52504	52634	52763	52892	53020
34	53148	53275	53403	53529	53656	53782	53908	54033	54158	54283
35	54407	54531	54654	54777	54900	55023	55145	55267	55388	55509
36	55630	55751	55871	55991	56110	56229	56348	56467	56585	56703
37	56820	56937	57054	57171	57287	57403	57519	57634	57749	57864
38	57978	58092	58206	58320	58433	58546	58659	58771	58883	58995
39	59106	59218	59329	59439	59550	59660	59770	59879	59988	60097
40	60206	60314	60423	60531	60638	60746	60853	60959	61066	61172
41	61278	61384	61490	61595	61700	61805	61909	62014	62118	62221
42	62325	62428	62531	62634	62737	62839	62941	63043	63144	63246
43	63347	63448	63548	63649	63749	63849	63949	64048	64147	64246
44	64345	64444	64542	64640	64738	64836	64933	65031	65128	65225
45	65321	65418	65514	65610	65706	65801	65896	65992	66087	66181
46	66276	66370	66464	66558	66652	66745	66839	66932	67025	67117
47	67210	67302	67394	67486	67578	67669	67761	67852	67943	68034
48	68124	68215	68305	68395	68485	68574	68664	68753	68842	68931
49	69020	69108	69197	69285	69373	69461	69548	69636	69723	69810

Table B.8 *Five-Place Logarithms (Cont.).*

N	0	1	2	3	4	5	6	7	8	9
50	69897	69984	70070	70157	70243	70329	70415	70501	70586	70672
51	70757	70842	70927	71012	71096	71181	71265	71349	71433	71517
52	71600	71684	71767	71850	71933	72016	72099	72181	72263	72346
53	72428	72509	72591	72673	72754	72835	72916	72997	73078	73159
54	73239	73320	73400	73480	73560	73640	73719	73799	73878	73957
55	74036	74115	74194	74273	74351	74429	74507	74586	74663	74741
56	74819	74896	74974	75051	75128	75205	75282	75358	75435	75511
57	75587	75664	75740	75815	75891	75967	76042	76118	76193	76268
58	76343	76418	76492	76567	76641	76716	76790	76864	76938	77012
59	77085	77159	77232	77305	77379	77452	77525	77597	77670	77743
60	77815	77887	77960	78032	78104	78176	78247	78319	78390	78462
61	78533	78604	78675	78746	78817	78888	78958	79029	79099	79169
62	79239	79309	79379	79449	79518	79588	79657	79727	79796	79865
63	79934	80003	80072	80140	80209	80277	80346	80414	80482	80550
64	80618	80686	80754	80821	80889	80956	81023	81090	81158	81224
65	81291	81358	81425	81491	81558	81624	81690	81757	81823	81889
66	81954	82020	82086	82151	82217	82282	82347	82413	82478	82543
67	82607	82672	82737	82802	82866	82930	82995	83059	83123	83187
68	83251	83315	83378	83442	83506	83569	83632	83696	83759	83822
69	83885	83948	84011	84073	84136	84198	84261	84323	84386	84448
70	84510	84572	84634	84696	84757	84819	84880	84942	85003	85065
71	85126	85187	85248	85309	85370	85431	85491	85552	85612	85673
72	85733	85794	85854	85914	85974	86034	86094	86153	86213	86273
73	86332	86392	86451	86510	86570	86629	86688	86747	86806	86864
74	86923	86982	87040	87099	87157	87216	87274	87332	87390	87448
75	87506	87564	87622	87679	87737	87795	87852	87910	87967	88024
76	88081	88138	88195	88252	88309	88366	88423	88480	88536	88593
77	88649	88705	88762	88818	88874	88930	88986	89042	89098	89154
78	89209	89265	89321	89376	89432	89487	89542	89597	89653	89708
79	89763	89818	89873	89927	89982	90037	90091	90146	90200	90255
80	90309	90363	90417	90472	90526	90580	90634	90687	90741	90795
81	90849	90902	90956	91009	91062	91116	91169	91222	91275	91328
82	91381	91434	91487	91540	91593	91645	91698	91751	91803	91855
83	91908	91960	92012	92065	92117	92169	92221	92273	92324	92376
84	92428	92480	92531	92583	92634	92686	92737	92788	92840	92891
85	92942	92993	93044	93095	93146	93197	93247	93298	93349	93399
86	93450	93500	93551	93601	93651	93702	93752	93802	93852	93902
87	93952	94002	94052	94101	94151	94201	94250	94300	94349	94399
88	94448	94498	94547	94596	94645	94694	94743	94792	94841	94890
89	94939	94988	95036	95085	95134	95182	95231	95279	95328	95376
90	95424	95472	95521	95569	95617	95665	95713	95761	95809	95856
91	95904	95952	95999	96047	96095	96142	96190	96237	96284	96332
92	96379	96426	96473	96520	96567	96614	96661	96708	96755	96802
93	96848	96895	96942	96988	97035	97081	97128	97174	97220	97267
94	97313	97359	97405	97451	97497	97543	97589	97635	97681	97727
95	97772	97818	97864	97909	97955	98000	98046	98091	98137	98182
96	98227	98272	98318	98363	98408	98453	98498	98543	98588	98632
97	98677	98722	98767	98811	98856	98900	98945	98989	99034	99078
98	99123	99167	99211	99255	99300	99344	99388	99432	99476	99520
99	99564	99607	99651	99695	99739	99782	99826	99870	99913	99957

Source: From *Self-Correcting Problems in Statistics,* by John Neter, William Wasserman, and G. A. Whitmore. © 1979, published by Allyn and Bacon, Inc., by permission of the authors and publisher.

TABLE B.9 *Durbin-Watson Test Bounds.*

Level of Significance $\alpha = .05$

n	$p-1=1$		$p-1=2$		$p-1=3$		$p-1=4$		$p-1=5$	
	d_L	d_U	d_L	d_U	d_L	d_U	d_L	d_U	d_L	d_U
15	1.08	1.36	0.95	1.54	0.82	1.75	0.69	1.97	0.56	2.21
16	1.10	1.37	0.98	1.54	0.86	1.73	0.74	1.93	0.62	2.15
17	1.13	1.38	1.02	1.54	0.90	1.71	0.78	1.90	0.67	2.10
18	1.16	1.39	1.05	1.53	0.93	1.69	0.82	1.87	0.71	2.06
19	1.18	1.40	1.08	1.53	0.97	1.68	0.86	1.85	0.75	2.02
20	1.20	1.41	1.10	1.54	1.00	1.68	0.90	1.83	0.79	1.99
21	1.22	1.42	1.13	1.54	1.03	1.67	0.93	1.81	0.83	1.96
22	1.24	1.43	1.15	1.54	1.05	1.66	0.96	1.80	0.86	1.94
23	1.26	1.44	1.17	1.54	1.08	1.66	0.99	1.79	0.90	1.92
24	1.27	1.45	1.19	1.55	1.10	1.66	1.01	1.78	0.93	1.90
25	1.29	1.45	1.21	1.55	1.12	1.66	1.04	1.77	0.95	1.89
26	1.30	1.46	1.22	1.55	1.14	1.65	1.06	1.76	0.98	1.88
27	1.32	1.47	1.24	1.56	1.16	1.65	1.08	1.76	1.01	1.86
28	1.33	1.48	1.26	1.56	1.18	1.65	1.10	1.75	1.03	1.85
29	1.34	1.48	1.27	1.56	1.20	1.65	1.12	1.74	1.05	1.84
30	1.35	1.49	1.28	1.57	1.21	1.65	1.14	1.74	1.07	1.83
31	1.36	1.50	1.30	1.57	1.23	1.65	1.16	1.74	1.09	1.83
32	1.37	1.50	1.31	1.57	1.24	1.65	1.18	1.73	1.11	1.82
33	1.38	1.51	1.32	1.58	1.26	1.65	1.19	1.73	1.13	1.81
34	1.39	1.51	1.33	1.58	1.27	1.65	1.21	1.73	1.15	1.81
35	1.40	1.52	1.34	1.58	1.28	1.65	1.22	1.73	1.16	1.80
36	1.41	1.52	1.35	1.59	1.29	1.65	1.24	1.73	1.18	1.80
37	1.42	1.53	1.36	1.59	1.31	1.66	1.25	1.72	1.19	1.80
38	1.43	1.54	1.37	1.59	1.32	1.66	1.26	1.72	1.21	1.79
39	1.43	1.54	1.38	1.60	1.33	1.66	1.27	1.72	1.22	1.79
40	1.44	1.54	1.39	1.60	1.34	1.66	1.29	1.72	1.23	1.79
45	1.48	1.57	1.43	1.62	1.38	1.67	1.34	1.72	1.29	1.78
50	1.50	1.59	1.46	1.63	1.42	1.67	1.38	1.72	1.34	1.77
55	1.53	1.60	1.49	1.64	1.45	1.68	1.41	1.72	1.38	1.77
60	1.55	1.62	1.51	1.65	1.48	1.69	1.44	1.73	1.41	1.77
65	1.57	1.63	1.54	1.66	1.50	1.70	1.47	1.73	1.44	1.77
70	1.58	1.64	1.55	1.67	1.52	1.70	1.49	1.74	1.46	1.77
75	1.60	1.65	1.57	1.68	1.54	1.71	1.51	1.74	1.49	1.77
80	1.61	1.66	1.59	1.69	1.56	1.72	1.53	1.74	1.51	1.77
85	1.62	1.67	1.60	1.70	1.57	1.72	1.55	1.75	1.52	1.77
90	1.63	1.68	1.61	1.70	1.59	1.73	1.57	1.75	1.54	1.78
95	1.64	1.69	1.62	1.71	1.60	1.73	1.58	1.75	1.56	1.78
100	1.65	1.69	1.63	1.72	1.61	1.74	1.59	1.76	1.57	1.78

TABLE B.9   *Durbin-Watson Test Bounds (Cont.).*

Level of Significance $\alpha = .01$

n	$p - 1 = 1$		$p - 1 = 2$		$p - 1 = 3$		$p - 1 = 4$		$p - 1 = 5$	
	d_L	d_U	d_L	d_U	d_L	d_U	d_L	d_U	d_L	d_U
15	0.81	1.07	0.70	1.25	0.59	1.46	0.49	1.70	0.39	1.96
16	0.84	1.09	0.74	1.25	0.63	1.44	0.53	1.66	0.44	1.90
17	0.87	1.10	0.77	1.25	0.67	1.43	0.57	1.63	0.48	1.85
18	0.90	1.12	0.80	1.26	0.71	1.42	0.61	1.60	0.52	1.80
19	0.93	1.13	0.83	1.26	0.74	1.41	0.65	1.58	0.56	1.77
20	0.95	1.15	0.86	1.27	0.77	1.41	0.68	1.57	0.60	1.74
21	0.97	1.16	0.89	1.27	0.80	1.41	0.72	1.55	0.63	1.71
22	1.00	1.17	0.91	1.28	0.83	1.40	0.75	1.54	0.66	1.69
23	1.02	1.19	0.94	1.29	0.86	1.40	0.77	1.53	0.70	1.67
24	1.04	1.20	0.96	1.30	0.88	1.41	0.80	1.53	0.72	1.66
25	1.05	1.21	0.98	1.30	0.90	1.41	0.83	1.52	0.75	1.65
26	1.07	1.22	1.00	1.31	0.93	1.41	0.85	1.52	0.78	1.64
27	1.09	1.23	1.02	1.32	0.95	1.41	0.88	1.51	0.81	1.63
28	1.10	1.24	1.04	1.32	0.97	1.41	0.90	1.51	0.83	1.62
29	1.12	1.25	1.05	1.33	0.99	1.42	0.92	1.51	0.85	1.61
30	1.13	1.26	1.07	1.34	1.01	1.42	0.94	1.51	0.88	1.61
31	1.15	1.27	1.08	1.34	1.02	1.42	0.96	1.51	0.90	1.60
32	1.16	1.28	1.10	1.35	1.04	1.43	0.98	1.51	0.92	1.60
33	1.17	1.29	1.11	1.36	1.05	1.43	1.00	1.51	0.94	1.59
34	1.18	1.30	1.13	1.36	1.07	1.43	1.01	1.51	0.95	1.59
35	1.19	1.31	1.14	1.37	1.08	1.44	1.03	1.51	0.97	1.59
36	1.21	1.32	1.15	1.38	1.10	1.44	1.04	1.51	0.99	1.59
37	1.22	1.32	1.16	1.38	1.11	1.45	1.06	1.51	1.00	1.59
38	1.23	1.33	1.18	1.39	1.12	1.45	1.07	1.52	1.02	1.58
39	1.24	1.34	1.19	1.39	1.14	1.45	1.09	1.52	1.03	1.58
40	1.25	1.34	1.20	1.40	1.15	1.46	1.10	1.52	1.05	1.58
45	1.29	1.38	1.24	1.42	1.20	1.48	1.16	1.53	1.11	1.58
50	1.32	1.40	1.28	1.45	1.24	1.49	1.20	1.54	1.16	1.59
55	1.36	1.43	1.32	1.47	1.28	1.51	1.25	1.55	1.21	1.59
60	1.38	1.45	1.35	1.48	1.32	1.52	1.28	1.56	1.25	1.60
65	1.41	1.47	1.38	1.50	1.35	1.53	1.31	1.57	1.28	1.61
70	1.43	1.49	1.40	1.52	1.37	1.55	1.34	1.58	1.31	1.61
75	1.45	1.50	1.42	1.53	1.39	1.56	1.37	1.59	1.34	1.62
80	1.47	1.52	1.44	1.54	1.42	1.57	1.39	1.60	1.36	1.62
85	1.48	1.53	1.46	1.55	1.43	1.58	1.41	1.60	1.39	1.63
90	1.50	1.54	1.47	1.56	1.45	1.59	1.43	1.61	1.41	1.64
95	1.51	1.55	1.49	1.57	1.47	1.60	1.45	1.62	1.42	1.64
100	1.52	1.56	1.50	1.58	1.48	1.60	1.46	1.63	1.44	1.65

Source: Reprinted, with permission, from J. Durbin and G. S. Watson. "Testing for Serial Correlation in Least Squares Regression. II," *Biometrika*, Vol. 38 (1951), pp. 159–178.

Ratio or Semilogarithmic Graphs

C Many types of problems are encountered, however, where a graph with an arithmetic vertical scale does not prove useful.

As a typical example of such a situation, consider the case of the Alexander Furniture Company. This concern has been manufacturing a line of furniture that we shall call product line A. In 1968 it began producing an additional line of furniture—product line B—which differed from the old line in both style and price range. Sales of both lines had been increasing during the period 1978–1982, as may be seen from Figure C-1. This graph, which utilizes an arithmetic vertical scale, conveys the distinct impression that product line A performed much better during this period than product line B. Such an impression arises because the *absolute* increase in sales of product line A was much greater than that of product line B, and therefore the curve for line A climbs more steeply on the chart.

The company's management had no expectations that the sales volume of the new line would match that of the established one as yet, nor that the increases in sales of the new line would equal or surpass those of the established line. Hence, interest did not center on a comparison of the *absolute* sales or of the *absolute* increases as much as on a comparison of the *relative* increases in the sales of both lines. Specifically, the

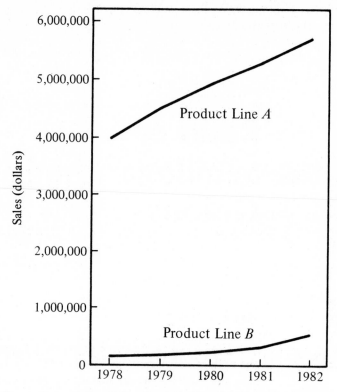

FIGURE C–1   *Sales of Two Product Lines by Alexander Furniture Company, 1978–1982, Arithmetic Line Graph.*

question was asked whether sales of line B were increasing more rapidly than those of line A. This question can be answered by calculating link relatives of sales for each product line and plotting these on arithmetic graph paper. A graph with a ratio or logarithmic scale also will answer the question, and without any intermediate calculations.

Before continuing the discussion relating to the Alexander Furniture Company, we shall discuss the characteristics of a ratio or logarithmic scale.

Ratio or Logarithmic Scale

Figure C-2 shows a graph in which the horizontal, or time, scale is a conventional arithmetic scale. The vertical scale, however, is a *ratio* or *logarithmic scale*—i.e., a scale in which equal intervals represent equal differences in the logarithms of numbers. Such a graph is called a *ratio* or *semilogarithmic graph*.

Note the graduated spacing of the tick marks on the vertical scale. Two sets of numbers are shown in the vertical scale. The inner numbers, consisting of 1, 2, etc., are not part of the scale proper, but are guide numbers found on semilogarithmic graph paper. Ordinarily these guide numbers are not reproduced with the graph, but we include them here to show how a ratio scale is set up.

The bottom guide number is 1 and serves as the starting point of the scale. Any positive scale number other than zero may be placed here. In the case of the Alexander Furniture Company, the smallest sales volume was $135,000; hence it is most convenient to begin the base line of the scale with $100,000. While we may begin with any positive value at the base line other than zero, it usually is easiest to start with 1, 10, or some multiple of 10 since the major horizontal divisions marked by ticks will then represent round numbers. Opposite guide number 2, we place the value that is twice that of the base line, or $200,000. Similarly, we write $300,000 corresponding to guide number 3, and so on. The guide number

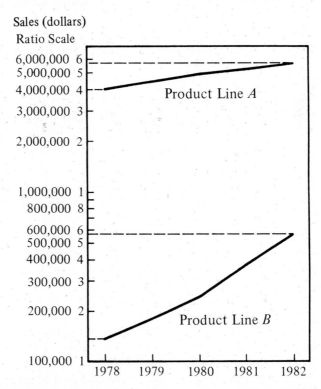

Figure C–2 *Sales of Two Product Lines by Alexander Furniture Company, 1978–1982, Ratio or Semilogarithmic Line Graph.*

353

1 that follows number 9 is assigned a value ten times that of the base line; in the present case it is given a value of $1,000,000. Note that the vertical distances between the guide numbers, which have been getting smaller up to this point, now become larger. In fact, the same sequence of graduations is starting all over again. Each full sequence of graduations is called a *cycle*. In labeling the next cycle we proceed as before. We must write $2,000,000 corresponding to the guide number 2 in the second cycle, since this is twice the value of the base of the second cycle. Note that the top of the first cycle has now become the base of the second one. Proceeding in this manner, we fill in the vertical scale in Fig. C-2. Note that the second cycle is not complete, since there is no need to carry the scale to $10,000,000.

Ratio or semilogarithmic graph paper is available in one, two, three, or even more, cycles. The number of cycles needed depends, of course, on the range of the data. Should a series be plotted in which the largest value is eight times the smallest, one-cycle paper would usually be used, since we know that the top of a cycle has a value ten times as great as that of the base line. On the other hand, a series whose largest value is, say, twelve times the smallest would require semilogarithmic graph paper with at least two cycles.

Once the vertical scale has been labeled, the plotting of the series proceeds in the usual manner. Semilogarithmic graph paper generally shows grid lines between the guide numbers on the vertical scale to aid in the plotting. If, say, there are 20 spaces between guide numbers 1 and 2 on the graph paper used to plot Fig. C-2, each of the spaces would represent $5,000 in the first cycle and $50,000 in the second cycle. These additional grid lines on the vertical scale enable one to plot the data quite accurately.

Interpretation of Ratio or Logarithmic Scale

Having considered the mechanics of labeling the vertical scale and plotting points, we now discuss ways of interpreting a semilogarithmic graph. First, compare the distance on the vertical scale of Fig. C-2 between $100,000 and $300,000, and between $300,000 and $900,000. Note that in each instance the same distance has been covered on the vertical scale, despite the fact that the first case represents an increase of $200,000 while the second represents an increase of $600,000. Note also that the *relative* increase in each case is the same, namely 200 per cent. If the vertical distance for any other case in which there is a 200 per cent increase is measured, it will be found that the distance required for a 200 per cent increase on the vertical scale of Fig. C-2 is always the same.

In general, the ratio scale has the following important characteristics:

Equal percent changes require equal vertical distances on the ratio scale; the greater the relative change, the larger the vertical distance required.

We now return to our discussion of the sales of product lines A and B of the Alexander Furniture Company. In Fig. C-2, horizontal dashed lines have been superimposed on the graph to aid in comparing the vertical distances required to portray the increase in sales between 1978 and 1982 for each of the two product lines. Since the vertical distance is greater for product line B than for product line A, we conclude that the newer product line experienced a greater *relative* increase in sales between these two years.

The measurement of vertical distance in this way is not necessary in order to interpret the ratio graph. Note from Fig. C-2 that the curve for product line B is steeper than that for product line A, since the curve for B has to cover a larger vertical distance during the same time period. Hence we simply say that:

The steeper the curve on a ratio chart, the larger the percent change.

This means that one need only compare the slopes of the curves to draw conclusions about relative changes. If the two lines in Fig. C-2 had been parallel, equal rates of change would have been indicated, of course, because two parallel straight lines have the same slope.

In addition to comparing relative changes between two periods in several series on a ratio graph, one also can study relative changes from period to period in any given series. For instance, Fig. C-3(a) presents a ratio graph in which the series is represented by a straight line. It is at once evident that the percent increase from period to period in this series is a constant one, because a straight line has a constant slope. While a straight line on an arithmetic chart indicates a constant *amount* of change, a straight line on a ratio chart indicates a constant *rate* of change.

Figure C-3(b) presents on a ratio graph a series whose rate of increase is becoming greater and greater as each successive point is plotted. This is known because the curve becomes steeper and steeper. In short, one states that this series is increasing at an increasing rate.

Similarly, one can readily see that the series in Fig. C-3(c) is increasing at a decreasing rate because the curve is becoming less and less steep. Figure C-3(d) presents a series that is decreasing at a constant rate, while Figs. C-3(e) and C-3(f) present two series that are decreasing at increasing and decreasing rates respectively.

Let us now interpret Fig. C-2 more fully. While the sales of both product lines have been increasing, sales of the new product line have been increasing more rapidly. Indeed, sales of product line B have been increasing at an increasing rate while sales of product line A have been

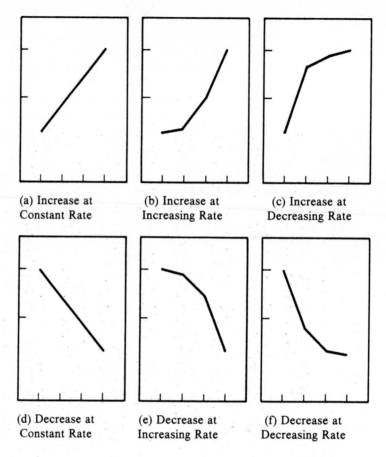

FIGURE C–3   *Examples of Different Patterns on Ratio Paper.*

increasing at a decreasing rate. Thus, while sales of the new product line are still far less than those of the established line, and while the *absolute* increases in sales of the new line are far less than those of the established one, the ratio graph shows that the new product line has been catching on. Thus, the ratio graph provides ready answers to management's questions about the *relative* increases in sales of the two product lines.

Answers to Selected Problems *

Chapter 2

1. H_0: $\pi_1 = \pi_2$ *Sample Statistic:* $p_1 - p_2 = -.03$
    H_1: $\pi_1 \neq \pi_2$
Sampling Distribution: normal with mean = 0, standard deviation =

$$\sqrt{\pi(1 - \pi)\left(\frac{1}{n_1} + \frac{1}{n_2}\right)} = 0.059$$

$$\text{where est. } \pi = \frac{100\,(0.25) + 125\,(0.28)}{225} = 0.267$$

For $\alpha = 0.05$, $Z = 1.96$
Decision Rule Points: $0 \pm 1.96\,(0.059) = -0.116$ to 0.116
Since $p_1 - p_2 = -0.03$, do not reject H_0.

2. H_0: $\pi = .05$ *Sample Statistic:* $p = .07$
    H_1: $\pi > .05$
Sampling Distribution: normal with mean = .05,

$$\textit{Standard deviation} = \sqrt{\frac{(0.05)(0.95)}{100}} = 0.022$$

For $\alpha = 0.02$, $Z = 2.05$
Decision Rule Point: $0.05 + 2.05\,(0.022) = 0.095$
Since $p = 0.07$, do not reject H_0.

3. H_0: $\mu = 75$

---

* Those problems marked in text with an asterisk.

H_1: $\mu > 75$

Sampling Distribution: *Normal with mean* $= 75$,

$$\text{Standard deviation} = \frac{\sigma}{\sqrt{n}} = \frac{10}{\sqrt{30}} = 1.83$$

For $\alpha = 0.05$, $Z = 1.65$ $75 + 1.65(1.83) = 78.02$

Decision Rule: If $\bar{X} > 78.02$, reject H_0.

4. H_0: $\sigma^2 = 4$ *Sample Statistic:* $\dfrac{(n-1)(S^2)}{\sigma^2} = \dfrac{(29)(6.76)}{4} = 49.01$

   H_1: $\sigma^2 > 4$

Sampling Distribution: Chi-Square with $df = n - 1 = 29$

For $\alpha = 0.05$ χ^2 *table* $= 42.56$

Since $\dfrac{(n-1)(S^2)}{\sigma^2} > 42.56$, reject H_0.

6. H_0: $\sigma_1^2 = \sigma_2^2$ *Sample Statistic* $= \dfrac{8}{4} = 2$

   H_1: $\sigma_1^2 \neq \sigma_2^2$

Sampling Distribution: F with $df_n = 21$, $df_d = 11$

F table for $\alpha = 0.01$ approximately 2.65

Since $\dfrac{S_1^2}{S_2^2} = 2$, which is less than 2.65, do not reject H_0.

7. H_0: $\mu_1 = \mu$ Sample Statistic: $\bar{X}_1 - \bar{X}_2 = -10$

   H_1: $\mu_1 \neq \mu_2$

Sampling Distribution: *normal with mean* $= 0$,

$$\text{Standard deviation} = \sqrt{\frac{20^2}{35} + \frac{15^2}{18}} = 4.89$$

For $\alpha = .01$, $Z = 2.58$

Decision Rule Points: $0 \pm 2.58(4.89) = -12.62$ to 12.62

Since $\bar{X}_1 - \bar{X}_2$ is between -12.62 and 12.62, do not reject H_0.

9.

	<500	500+	
C	(45) 30	(45) 60	90
no C	(45) 60	(45) 30	90
	90	90	180

$$\chi^2 = \frac{(30-45)^2}{45} + \frac{(60-45)^2}{45} + \frac{(60-45)^2}{45} + \frac{(30-45)^2}{45} = 20$$

$df = (r-1)(c-1) = 1$ χ^2 *table for* $\alpha = 0.05$ is 3.84

Since $20 > 3.84$, reject the hypothesis that sales volume and graduate status are independent.

12.

A	B	C	D	E	
74	53	81	70	82	*Observed*
72	72	72	72	72	*Expected*

$$\chi^2 = \frac{(74-72)^2}{72} + \frac{(53-72)^2}{72} + \frac{(81-72)^2}{72} + \frac{(70-72)^2}{72} + \frac{(82-72)^2}{72} = 7.64$$

For $\alpha = 0.05$ and $df = k - 1 = 4$, χ^2 table $= 9.49$
Since $7.64 < 9.49$, do not reject the null hypothesis that people in the population prefer the five brands equally.

Chapter 3

3. b. Appears to be a positive correlation.

c. $r = .82$

d. H_0: $\rho = 0$ for $\alpha = 0.05$, $df = n - 2 = 6$

H_1: $\rho \neq 0$ $t = 2.447$

$S_r = 0.234$ $t = \dfrac{0.82}{0.234} = 3.50$

Since $3.50 > 2.447$, reject the hypothesis that the population correlation coefficient is zero.

8. a. $r = .84$

b. Yes, since

H_0: $\rho = 0$ $\alpha = 0.05$ and $df = n - 2 = 8$

H_1: $\rho \neq 0$ $t = 2.306$

$S_r = 0.192$ $t = \dfrac{0.84}{0.192} = 4.375$

Since $4.375 > 2.306$, reject the null hypothesis that the population correlation coefficient is zero.

10. a. $r = .60$

b. No, since

H_0: $\rho = 0$ $\alpha = .05$ and $df = n - 2 = 3$
H_1: $\rho \neq 0$ $t = 3.182$

$Sr = .4619$ $t = \dfrac{0.60}{0.4619} = 1.30$

Since $1.30 < 3.182$, fail to reject the null hypothesis that the population correlation coefficient is zero.

Chapter 4

3. a. H_0: $\rho = 0$
   H_1: $\rho \neq 0$
   Decision Rule: reject H_0 if $t > 2.3$ ($\alpha = 0.05$)
   reject H_0 if $t > 3.36$ ($\alpha = 0.01$)

   Computed $t = \dfrac{r}{Sr} = \dfrac{0.848}{0.1874} = 4.52$

   Since $4.52 > 2.3$ and 3.36, reject H_0 and conclude that the population has a non-zero correlation coefficient.

b. $Y_R = 828.13 + 10.79\,X$

c. $1367.46

d. 71.9%

e. $\dfrac{\Sigma(Y - Y_R)^2}{n - 2} = \dfrac{36120.75}{8} = 4515.09$

f. $\dfrac{\Sigma(Y - \bar{Y})^2}{n - 1} = \dfrac{128552.5}{10 - 1} = 14{,}283.61$

   Computed $t = 16.29391$, rejecting the hypothesis that $\rho = 0$.
   $Y_R = -3.25725 + 1.03435\,X$

5. a. H_0: $\rho = 0$
   H_1: $\rho \neq 0$
   Decision Rule: reject H_0 if $t > 1.83$ ($\alpha = 0.05$)
   reject H_0 if $t > 2.82$ ($\alpha = 0.01$)

   $t = \dfrac{r}{Sr} = \dfrac{0.96220}{0.09078669} = 10.59836$

   Since $10.59836 > 2.26$ or 3.25, reject H_0 and conclude that the population has a non-zero correlation coefficient.

b. $Y_R = -9.49153 + 2.76520\,X$

c. $r^2 = .92582$. Knowledge of years of education explains 92.58% of the variability in annual income.

8. a. H_0: $\rho = 0$ *Decision Rule:* reject H_0 if $t < -2.31$ ($\alpha = 0.05$)
   H_1: $\alpha \neq 0$ reject H_0 if $t < -3.36$ ($\alpha = 0.01$)
   Computed $t = -2.77394$
   The null hypothesis may be rejected at the 5% significance level but not at the 1% significance level.

b. Yes, as long as a great deal of accuracy is not necessary.
   $Y_R = 3538.1223 - 418.2632$

c. Yes. When $X = 4.0$, $Y_R = 1865$

d. $r^2 = .49028$. Less than half the variability in investment can be explained through knowledge of interest rate. As in all regression problems, no cause and effect relationship between variables is established.

11. a. To a very close extent. $r = .95931$, indicating a high correlation between the variables.

b. $Y_R = 101.2$

$$Y_R \pm Z S_{y \cdot x}$$
101.2 $\pm$ 1.96 (0.743)
99.74 to 102.66

c. $Z = \dfrac{101 - 101.2}{0.743} = -0.27$ Probability = .6064

d. The t distribution would be appropriate. The standard error of the forecast would be used in place of the standard error of the estimate.
$$Y_R \pm t S_F$$
101.2 $\pm$ 2.069 (0.78)
99.6 to 102.8

Chapter 5

2. a. Both high temperature and traffic count are positively related to number of six-packs, and have potential as good predictor variables. Some collinearity exists between the predictors, but not enough to limit their value.

   b. Reject $T > 2.9$ or $T < -2.9$.
   $$T = \frac{b_2}{S_{b_2}} = \frac{0.78207}{0.22694} = 3.45$$
   Reject and conclude that the regression coefficient for the high temperature variable is significantly different from zero in the population.
   $$T = \frac{b_3}{S_{b_3}} = \frac{0.06795}{0.02026} = 3.35$$
   Reject and conclude that the regression coefficient for the traffic count variable is significantly different from zero in the population.

   c. $Y_R = -26.70621 + 0.78207(60) + 0.06795(500)$
   $Y_R = 54$ six-packs

   d. $R^2 = 1 - 2727.9/14316.9 = 0.809$

   We can explain 80.9% of the number of six-packs sold variance using high temperature and traffic count as predictor variables.

   e. $S_{y \cdot 1x} = \sqrt{\dfrac{\Sigma(Y - Y_R)^2}{n - 3}} = \sqrt{\dfrac{2727.914}{20 - 3}} = \sqrt{160.46} = 12.67$

   f. Beer sales increase by .78 for every increase in high temperature of one degree, when the traffic count remains constant.

   g. The equation explains 80.9% of what we need to know for perfect prediction. Both predictor variables are making a significant contribution to the prediction of beer sold.

4. a. Number of retail outlets is positively, $r = .74$, related to annual sales, and should be a good predictor variable. Number of automobiles registered is moderately, $r = .55$, related to annual sales; and because of collinearity, $r = .67$, it should not be a good predictor when used in conjunction with number of retail outlets.

b. There were 2011 retail outlets, 24.6 million automobiles registered, and annual sales of 52.3 million dollars.

$$Y_R = 10.11 + 0.011X_2 + 0.195X_3$$
$$Y_R = 36.997$$
$$e = Y - Y_R = 15.303$$

c. $Y_R = 10.11 + 0.011 (2500) + 0.195 (20.2)$
$$Y_R = 41.549$$

d. The standard error of the estimate is 10.3 or quite large. We can only explain 55% of sales variable variance using this equation. Due to collinearity our regression coefficients are not stable. The prediction is probably not very accurate.

e.
$$Sy \cdot x_2 x_3 = \sqrt{\frac{\Sigma(Y - Y_R)^2}{n - 3}}$$

$$= \sqrt{\frac{849.56494}{11 - 3}}$$

$$= \sqrt{106.195}$$

$$= 10.3$$

f. If we add one retail outlet, and the number of automobiles registered remains constant, then sales increase by .011 million or $11,000 dollars. If we add one million automobile registrations, and the number of retail outlets remains constant, then sales increase by .195 million or 195,000 dollars. These regression coefficients are probably not valid due to collinearity.

g. Yes! Try some new predictors variables.

6. a. Reject $T > 3.1$ or $T < -3.1$
$$T = .65/.05 = 13$$
Reject and conclude that the regression coefficient for the aptitude test variable is significantly different from zero in the population.
$$T = 20.6/1.69 = 12.2$$
Reject and conclude that the regression coefficient for the effort index variable is significantly different from zero in the population.

b. If the effort index increases one point and aptitude test score remains constant, sales performance increases by 20,600.

c. $R^2 = 1 - (3.56)^2/(16.57)^2 = 1 - 12.67/274.56 = 1 - 0.046 = 0.954$

d. $Y_R = 16.57 + .65(75) + 20.6(.5)$
$$Y_R = 75.62$$

e. 139.63

f. 3571.43

g. 3431.8

h. $R^2 = 1 - 139.63/3571.43 = .961$
We can explain 96.1% of the sales performance variable variance through our knowledge of the relationships between sales, aptitude, and effort index.

8. a. Advertising expenditures, number of inventory lines, and number of salesmen are all well related to sales. Multicollinearity is potentially present between the independent variables mentioned above.

b. The advertising expenditure variable explains 90% of the sales variable variance when used alone. Both number of salesmen and number of inventory lines can be included in the model, resulting in significant T values and an R^2 of 92.6%. The average monthly temperature does not contribute to the prediction of sales.

c. Critical $T = 2.75$
$$Y_R = 9.78 + 2.63X_2 + 0.066X_5$$

d. $Y_R = 20.46 + .07859X_5$
It is very simple and yet explains 90% of the sales variable variance. This model has no collinearity problem.

e. Yes! The net regression coefficients might not be reliable.

f. $Y_R = 20.46 + 0.07859X_5$
$Y_R = 20.46 + 0.07859 (750)$
$Y_R = 79.4$ thousand

g. About 68% of the actual sales quantities for samples of size 40 fall within 9642 units of the quantity estimated from my model.

12. a. Floor, Bath, Fire, and Shower are all fairly highly related to Price. Cars and Bed are moderately related to Price and Base is not related at all. Possible multicollinearity exists between
  • Shower and Bath
  • Fire and Bath
  • Shower and Fire
  • Floor and Bed
  • Floor and Bath

b. Floor and Fire

c. .90

d. 81%

e. $5619.17

f. $F\dfrac{(0.81 - 0)/(3 - 1)}{(1 - 0.81)/(70 - 3)} = 150$

g. The regression equation containing both Floor and Fire is explaining a significant amount of the Price variable variance.

h. $Y_R = -1993.21 + 4003.02\ X_5 + 17.71X_8$

i. If floor space is increased by one square foot with the number of fireplaces remaining constant, the price will increase by $17.71.

j. 1.62

k. $F = \dfrac{(0.81 - 0.76)/(3 - 2)}{(1 - 0.81)/(70 - 3)} = 17.6$

l. The Fire variable is making a unique contribution to the prediction of Price.

m. Shower

n. 66%

o. $S_y.x_5x_8 = \sqrt{\dfrac{\Sigma(Y - Y_R)^2}{N - K}} = \sqrt{\dfrac{2115530626.57}{70 - 3}} = 5619.17$

p. $R_c^{\,2} = 1 - \dfrac{\dfrac{\Sigma(Y - Y_R)^2}{N - K}}{\dfrac{\Sigma(Y - \bar{Y})^2}{N - 1}} = 1 - \dfrac{\dfrac{2115530626.57}{70 - 3}}{\dfrac{11587918214.27}{70 - 1}} = 0.81$

q. $Y_R = -1993.21 + 4003.02 X_5 + 17.71 X_8$

r. Yes! He would add the Shower variable, and the model would be

$$Y_R = -2577.12 + 2753.47\, X_4 + 2591.39\, X_5 + 16.75\, X_8$$

s. $Y_R = -1993.21 + 4003.02(1) + 17.71(1800)$
   $Y_R = 33887.81$

Chapter 6

1. a. 15 Years   1968 is the $X = 0$ year
   b. 535 Units $Yr = 400 + 15(9)$
   c. The average increase in sales is 15 units for a one year change in X.
   d. $Y_R = 400 + 15(-3) = 355$ Units

4. a. $Y_R = 89.8(1.08)^x = 166.2$ $x = 8$
   b. $Y_R = 89.8(1.08)^x = 122.2$ $x = 4$
   c. 8%

7. b. $\Sigma Y = 154$ $\Sigma X^2 = 330$ $\Sigma Y^2 = 2483.52$ $\Sigma XY = 143$
      $Y_R = 15.4 + .433 X$
   c. $Y_R = 15.4 + .433(11) = 20.163$
   d. $S_{y \cdot x} = 2.5$
   e. Change in Population

9. b. $\Sigma Y = 49.8$ $\Sigma X^2 = 28$ $\Sigma X^4 = 196$ $\Sigma XY = 1.9$ $\Sigma X^2 Y = 183.9$
      $\Sigma Y^2 = 357.42$
      $Y_R = 7.84 + 0.0679 X - 0.182 X^2$
   c. $Y_R = 7.84 + 0.0679(5) - 0.182(5)^2 = 3.6295$
   d. $S_{y \cdot x} = 0.27$
   e. (0.19, 7.846)

10. b. $\Sigma \text{Log } Y = 11.4402$ $\Sigma X^2 = 168$ $\Sigma X \text{Log } Y = 10.1968$
       $\text{Log } Y_R = 1.43 + X(0.0607)$
       $Y_R = 26.9(1.15)^x$
    c. $\text{Log } Y_R = 1.43 + (9)(0.0607) = 1.973$ Antilog $= 94.7$
    d. 30%

13. b. $\Sigma Y = 274$ $\Sigma X^2 = 168$ $\Sigma XY = -886$
       $Y_R = 34.25 - 5.2738 X$
    c. $\Sigma Y = 274$ $\Sigma X^2 = 168$ $\Sigma \text{Log } Y = 11.2366$ $\Sigma X \text{Log } Y = -12.0346$
       $\text{Log } Y_R = 1.4046 - 0.0716 X$
       $Y_R = 25.4\,(1/1.18^x)$ or $25.4\,(.85)^x$

d. $\Sigma X = 274$ $\Sigma X^2 = 168$ $\Sigma X^4 = 6216$ $\Sigma XY = -886$
$\Sigma X^2 Y = 7026$
$Y_R = 24.3128 - 5.2738 X + .4732 X^2$
Minimum point: (5.57, 9.6)

e. *Least-Squares Method:* $Y_R = 34.25 - 5.2738(15) = -44.857$
Logarithmic Straight Line Method: $\text{Log } Y_R = 1.4046 - 0.0716(15)$
$= 0.3306$
$Y_R = 2.14$
Parabola Method: $Y_R = 24.3128 - 5.2738(15) + 0.4732(15)^2 = 51.6758$

16. **a.** $CI = \dfrac{12.3}{11.5}(100) = 106.95$

 b. $CI = \dfrac{17.6}{19.29}(100) = 91.19$

 c. $Y_R = 15.4 + 0.433(11) = 20.166$
$Y_R(1975) = 20.166(0.9119) = 18.4$

20. **a.** $Y_R = 0.172 + 0.0027 X$ (using 1969 as 0 year)
$Y_R = 0.183 + 0.0027 X$ (using 1973 as 0 year)
 b. $Y_R = 0.172 + 0.0027(9) = 0.196$
 c.   9,000,000 (0.00196) = 17,640 or 17.64
 d. $Y_R = -5.53237 + 2.53660 X$
 e. $Y_R = -5.53237 + 2.53660(9) = 17.297$
 f. $Y_R = 11.8 + 0.655 X$ (using 1969 as 0 year)
$Y_R = 14.42 + 0.655 X$ (using 1973 as 0 year)
 g. $Y_R = 11.8 + 0.655(9) = 17.7$
 h.   Three different models give same estimate. Mills's sales are increasing at a constant amount.

23. **a.** $\text{Jan} = \dfrac{500}{1.15} = 435$:   435(1.42) = 617 people

 b. $Y_R = 255 + 3 X$ X for Jan. 15, 1971 = 0
$Y_R = 255 + 3(72)$ X for Jan. 1977 = 72
$Y_R = 471$
471(115%) = 541
 c.   3 since the b or slope is 3.
 d.   Rounded down
Jan. $Y_R = 255 + 3(60) = 435(115\%) = 500$
Feb. $Y_R = 255 + 3(61) = 438(142\%) = 621$
Mar. $Y_R = 255 + 3(62) = 441(95\%) = 418$
Apr. $Y_R = 255 + 3(63) = 444(38\%) = 168$
May $Y_R = 255 + 3(64) = 446(47\%) = 210$
Jun. $Y_R = 255 + 3(65) = 450(125\%) = 562$
Jul. $Y_R = 255 + 3(66) = 453(150\%) = 679$
Aug. $Y_R = 255 + 3(67) = 456(154\%) = 702$
Sep. $Y_R = 255 + 3(68) = 459(90\%) = 413$
Oct. $Y_R = 255 + 3(69) = 462(65\%) = 300$
Nov. $Y_R = 255 + 3(70) = 465(80\%) = 372$
Dec. $Y_R = 255 + 3(71) = 468(99\%) = 463$

24.

a.

Quarter	1971	1972	1973	1974	1975	Modified Quarter Mean	0.997321 Adjusted Mean
I		114.38	101.97	106.20	116.24	110.29	110.0
II		102.89	106.16	102.70	96.72	102.79	102.5
III	76.62	86.03	94.08	91.25		88.64	88.4
IV	84.98	102.07	99.59	99.13		99.36	99.1
						401.07	400.0

b. They are identical.

c. The first two quarters are when most of the steel mill products are transported; they are shipped early so the automobile industry can have their new cars out on time.

25. a. $\Sigma X = 21 \qquad \Sigma Y = 860 \qquad \Sigma X^2 = 91 \qquad \Sigma XY = 3444$
$Y_R = 30.286 + 30.857 X$

b. $X = 0$ July 1, 1970 to Feb. 15, 1973 $= 10.5$ quarters
$$Y_R = 7.57 + 1.928 X$$
$$= 7.57 + 1.928(X + 10.5)$$
$$= 27.8 + 1.928 X$$

c.

Quarter	1973	1974	1975	1976	Modified Mean	0.990274 Adj Mean
I		85.41	96.97	82.63	85.41	84.6
II		115.11	105.82	99.31	105.82	104.8
III	101.69	100.00	107.32		101.69	100.7
IV	116.48	80.00	111.00		111.00	109.9
					403.93	400.0

d. I $= 49.6$
II $= 63.5$
III $= 62.9$
IV $= 70.8$

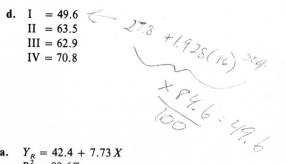

Chapter 7

3. a. $Y_R = 42.4 + 7.73 X$
$R^2 = 89.6\%$

b. D.W. $= 1.29$ Inconclusive

c. $Y_R = 29.67 + 6.61 X_2 + 82.04 X_3$
$R^2 = 93.7\%$

d. Critical T for 13 D.F. $= 2.16$

The computed Ts for the multiple regression run are 9.6 and 2.9. Use multiple regression run.

e. The test is inconclusive.

f.

1978	1st qtr.	142.0
	2nd qtr.	95.8
	3rd qtr.	574.4
	4th qtr.	409.1

5. **a.** (1) Critical T for 17 D.F. = 2.878
The computed $T = 2.18$; therefore, the regression coefficient is not significantly different from zero.
(2) Critical $F = 10.04$
Computed $F = 4.75$; therefore, fail to reject that income makes a contribution.
(3) Critical D.W. $L = 1.20$ $\mu = 1.41$
Computed D.W. = .41; therefore, autocorrelation is present.

b. (1) Critical $T = 2.898$
Computed $T = 8.81$; therefore, war years item makes a contribution.
(2) Critical D.W. $L = 1.20$ $\mu = 1.41$
Computed D.W. = 2.05; therefore, no autocorrelation is present.

Chapter 8

1. **b.** 789.5
   c. 840.1
   d. Less sensitive
   e. Low

4. **a.** $MAD = 330$

1979	1st qtr.	1030
	2nd qtr.	1473
	3rd qtr.	1507
	4th qtr.	1901

b.

1979	1st qtr.	$Y = 1396.3(.792)(1.10)(1.00)$
		$Y = 1216.5$
	2nd qtr.	$Y = 1434.4(1.216)(1.12)(1.00)$
		$Y = 1953.5$
	3rd qtr.	$Y = 1472.6(.859)(1.13)(1.00)$
		$Y = 1429.4$
	4th qtr.	$Y = 1510.7(1.134)(1.15)(1.00)$
		$Y = 1970.1$

c.	1979	1st qtr.	1446.8
		2nd qtr.	1776.3
		3rd qtr.	1879.3
		4th qtr.	2088.7

Chapter 9

1. a. $0 \pm .196$
   b. Series is random.
   c. Series is not stationary.
   d. Seasonal series with period of 4.

3. a. $\hat{Y}_{51} = 95$
      $\hat{Y}_{52} = 92.75$
      $\hat{Y}_{53} = 91.74$
   b. $\hat{Y}_{52} = 90.5$
      $\hat{Y}_{53} = 90.72$
   c. 92.84 to 97.16

5. a. MA
   b. AR
   c. $ARMA$

6. a. Implies model is adequate.
   b. $Q = 2.0447 \quad df = 9$
      Implies model is adequate.